THE WORLD ENCYCLOPEDIA OF
CHEESE

THE WORLD ENCYCLOPEDIA OF
CHEESE

JULIET HARBUTT
WITH RECIPES BY
ROZ DENNY

LORENZ BOOKS

Paperback edition published by Lorenz Books
27 West 20th Street, New York, NY 10011

LORENZ BOOKS are available for bulk purchase for sales promotion
and for premium use. For details, write or call the sales director,
Lorenz Books, 27 West 20th Street, New York, NY 10011;
(800) 354-9657

Lorenz Books is an imprint of
Anness Publishing Inc.

ISBN 0 7548 0204 3

Publisher: Joanna Lorenz
Senior Editor: Linda Fraser
Copy Editor: Jenni Fleetwood
Designer: Nigel Partridge
Photography: John Heseltine and William Lingwood
Home Economists: Carole Handslip (recipes) and Carol Tennant (cheeses)

Printed and bound in Indonesia

© Anness Publishing Limited 1998
Updated © 1999
1 3 5 7 9 10 8 6 4 2

CONTENTS

INTRODUCTION

In shops and markets around the world, thousands of cheeses tempt our eyes and challenge our tastebuds. Wrinkled and mouldy, smooth and sunshine yellow, orange and smelly or brilliant white, they are all labelled cheese, and their shapes and sizes, flavours and textures range from the sublime to the truly extraordinary. Yet they are all made from the same basic raw material – milk. What changes this simple product into something so complex and diverse?

DIFFERENT KINDS OF MILK

First, the type of animal yielding milk makes a difference. The cow's milk we drink is slightly sweet, mild and subtle in flavour. Most of it comes from Friesian cows, yet there are more than 50 different breeds whose milk is suitable for cheesemaking. Milk from Guernsey cows, for instance, is rich and pale yellow with larger fat globules than most other types, so this milk tastes smoother and fuller. Water buffalo's milk – used in Italy for making mozzarella – is ivory white, earthy and slightly nutty.

Sheep's milk is also mild but has undertones of roast lamb and lanolin. It is slightly sweeter than cow's milk. As sheep's milk cheese matures, these characteristics are intensified, as exemplified in the hard mature sheep's milk cheeses like the famous Pecorinos of Italy or the Basque and Pyrenees cheeses of France and Spain. Typically they are very nutty – as if fresh milk has been infused with crushed walnuts or brazil nuts – and the sweetness comes through to suggest burnt caramel, sweet fudge or caramelized onions. The aroma of lanolin, like the smell of wet wool, also adds its own distinct personality to the final cheese.

The most misunderstood of all cheeses are those made from goat's milk. There's an explanation for the negative way it is often perceived: if the milk, which is mild with a slightly aromatic background, is handled badly, the microscopic globules of fat suspended in the milk burst and release their contents. These impart a

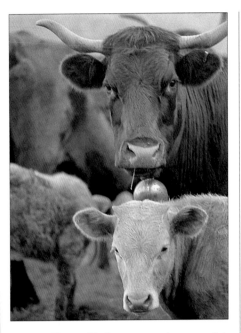

ABOVE: The milk from cows has a mild, subtle, slightly sweet flavour

bitter, nasty, "billy goat" flavour to the milk. If you have ever been close to a billy or male goat, it is a smell you are unlikely to forget. However, if the milk is handled with care, those same fat globules will gradually break down and will contribute to the delicious, herbaceous taste of the cheese. A good goat's milk cheese tastes as though the milk has absorbed the oils and aromas of tarragon, thyme or marjoram, set against a background of dry, crisp white wine.

There are as many different breeds of goat and sheep as there are cows. In some countries, cheese is made from the milk of llamas, camels or even reindeer, adding yet another dimension to the cheese.

Milk is not produced all year round but only after the animal has given birth. Unlike humans, animals come into season only once a year. Although farmers can control and manipulate their animals' natural urges, sheep and goats are more difficult to persuade to mate out of season than cows. Added to this, they have a shorter lactation period than cows, so there are times when their milk is not available. Some producers freeze goat's or sheep's milk for these times and continue to make excellent cheeses. Others believe

in the old ways and simply stop milking their animals. Their cheeses are therefore seasonal. But the type of animal is only one factor that affects the flavour.

THE GRAZING, THE SOIL AND THE SEASONS

Of equal significance is what the animals eat. Even the most unobservant amongst us cannot fail to see and smell the difference between fresh grass, wild clover and unspoilt meadows compared with compacted feed, silage, turnips and straw.

You only have to taste the great mountain cheeses of Europe (where, by law, the herds can only graze on natural pastures or sweet hay cut from Alpine meadows), to appreciate the difference. The amount of milk these cows give may be lower than that yielded by animals fed on lush green pastures or carefully prepared balanced diets of dried food supplement and vitamins, but the milk is rich and thick and the flavour is concentrated.

The seasons will also affect the taste and even the texture of cheeses from animals that seek their own grazing and do not rely on their keepers. In spring, the herbage is sweet, moist and green as the young shoots come through; in early summer the grazing is bountiful and varied compared with mid- to late summer when the earth becomes parched and dry and only hardy grasses survive. With the autumn rains comes another burst of new growth before the winter forces many animals inside to become reliant during the winter months on the hay the farmer has cut. The flavour of the milk reflects these differences and changes with the seasons.

The soil and geology of an area will also affect the flavour of the milk and may even govern the type of cheese that can be made. Clay and limestone will support different grasses to volcanic soils and granite. The grasses that grow will absorb different minerals, each making a minute but significant impact on the flavour of the milk. Rainfall, humidity and temperature also affect what will grow and which animals will thrive where.

MAKING CHEESE

Once the milk has been obtained, the skill of the cheesemaker is needed to convert it into a form that will last for days or even years. To achieve this, the cheesemaker must first separate the milk into the solids, protein and fats (known collectively as curds) and the liquid or whey (that consists mainly of water). This process is known as coagulation.

THE STARTER

If left in a warm place, milk will sour and coagulate or curdle by itself. This souring process is due to the action of millions of tiny bacteria who "eat" lactose (milk sugars), turning them into lactic acid or sour milk. To speed up the process and to stop the milk becoming bitter and unpleasantly sour, a little warm "matured" or slightly sour milk, taken from the previous evening's milk, is added to the new, fresh batch of unpasteurized milk. This speeds up or starts the process of coagulating the milk and is known as a starter or starter culture. It is not unlike adding the culture to yogurt – and in fact some cheesemakers use home-made yogurt as their starter.

If the milk is pasteurized, all these bacteria will have been lost and must be

BELOW: The cheesemaker stirring a vat of coagulating milk for Parmesan

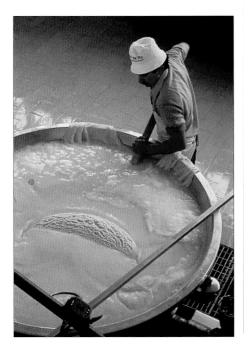

replaced in order for the milk to sour and curdle. The replacements consist of a combination of cultures grown in laboratories. Some the cheesemaker can just tip into the vat of milk; others are a blend specifically requested by the cheesemaker and must be grown in an incubator before they can be added to the milk. These cultures are valuable, but they will never replace the myriad different bacteria naturally present in unpasteurized milk.

Certain types of cheese must use specific cultures if the desired result is to be obtained. Invisible to the naked eye, these cultures work alongside the numerous enzymes on the lactose, protein and fat through all the stages of cheesemaking. Each thrives at a specific range of temperatures and degree of acidity and contributes to the final flavour and texture of the cheese. As the level of acidity changes in the milk (and later in the young curd), some die off or become dormant, while others, preferring the new climate, will spring into action. Their unique characteristics combine to create a kaleidoscope of flavours that no amount of copying can emulate.

THE RENNET

Although the starter culture speeds up the process of souring the milk and would eventually cause it to curdle, it produces quite a sharp, acidic cheese, so it is only suitable when making a cheese that will be eaten young. The use of rennet significantly improves cheesemaking techniques, and it was its discovery centuries ago that allowed shepherds to make harder cheeses that lasted through the winter months when their animals and the land were barren.

All milk-fed animals are born with an enzyme in their stomachs that attacks the milk and converts it into solids (which they can digest) and liquid (which is mainly waste). The travelling herdsman probably discovered the effects of the enzyme – rennet – when they stored their milk in sacks made from the stomach of a young kid or lamb and found the warm

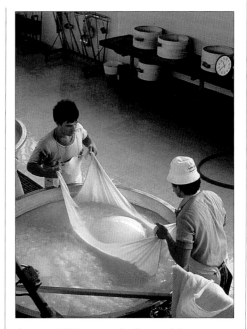

ABOVE: Lifting newly formed Parmesan out of the whey using cheesecloth

milk had soured slightly and separated into curds and whey.

If too much rennet is used, there is a risk that the finished cheese will be hard, dry and friable, and have a pronounced bitter taste, especially if acidification is insufficient. When preparing cheese with a rapid coagulation rate, the dosage of the rennet is higher than for cheeses that coagulate slowly.

Rennet also helps to break down the curd into a smooth, even consistency, contributing to the texture and flavour.

The use of this animal product means that many vegetarians are reluctant to eat cheese. Fortunately, manufacturers and chemists recognized that vegetarianism was not a passing fad but represented an increasingly significant proportion of the population and have created non-animal alternatives. Over 85 per cent of cheeses made in Britain and 60 per cent in New Zealand use a rennet substitute suitable for vegetarians. Some traditional cheeses dating back thousands of years use vegetable or fungal alternatives to trigger coagulation. These include the juices or tissues of certain plants, such as thistle and Lady's Bed Straw. Fig juice has also been used to start coagulation.

THE TYPES OF CHEESE AND HOW THEY ARE MADE

The type of cheese that is produced by the cheesemaker is determined by the amount of moisture he eliminates from the curd and the size of cheese that he wants to make. The amount of moisture in the curd will also determine what sort of rind or mould will grow on the cheese. The presence of rind is a huge advantage for the consumer. You may not be able to judge a wine by its bottle or a book by its cover, but the essential characteristics of a cheese can certainly be judged by a glance at the rind.

From just a brief glance at the rind and texture of a hitherto unknown cheese you can tell roughly what sort of texture, taste and strength of flavour you can expect. With practice – and the occasional squeeze and sniff – you can even learn to determine the condition and maturity of a cheese. Using the "rind" as a guide gives you an insight into the character, background and probable traits and foibles of virtually any cheese you encounter and enables you to dazzle your friends and family with your expertise.

LOW-FAT CHEESES

Traditional cheeses, such as Parmesan and Single Gloucester, were made with skimmed milk. The cream was skimmed off to use for cooking or to make butter. Today, with the growing obsession with low-fat foods, increasing numbers of cheeses are being made in low-fat versions. The fat, however, is what gives the cheese its texture and depth of the flavour. Consequently low-fat versions of traditional cheeses tend to lack both body and texture. It is far better to use a smaller amount of a traditional cheese than a large quantity of a bland, low-fat substitute.

Try using a soft cheese as they have a higher moisture content and therefore a lower percentage of fat than a harder cheese. Or, simply use less of a more mature, stronger-tasting hard cheese.

FRESH CHEESES
(NO VISIBLE RIND OR GROWTH OF MOULD)

EXAMPLES: *ricotta, feta, Myzlthra, mozzarella, cream cheese, fresh chèvre*

The milk is warmed, the starter culture is added and the acidity starts to increase. For some cheeses, like fromage frais, the starter is sufficient. These are called LACTIC CHEESES. Most cheeses, however, require the addition of rennet. This is stirred into the milk, then left for a few hours until it coagulates and resembles a very floppy milk jelly. The amount of moisture remaining with the whey will determine how soft or hard the final cheese will be.

Fresh cheeses are high in moisture. The young curd is carefully placed in sacks or small perforated containers and drained slowly without pressure for a few hours so that the curd retains much of the whey. Once sufficient whey has been drained off, the curds are either mixed or sprinkled with salt. They are now ready to be eaten. Some fresh cheeses are allowed to mature and grow either a white or bluish-grey mould, which places them in a different category.

Milk was a precious commodity to the herdsmen and their families. It was vital that none should be wasted, so some cheesemakers made cheeses from the whey, which contains small amounts of fat, vitamins and proteins. The most famous of these WHEY CHEESES is ricotta. This is made by boiling the whey, thus causing the small solid particles to float to the top. These are then scooped off, put in basket moulds to drain and sold within a few days. Whey cheeses tend to be used for cooking rather than eating fresh, as are most of these fresh cheeses. Scandinavian cheesemakers boil the whey slowly for hours, reducing it to a sticky toffee-like substance known as Gjetost or Mesost.

The other style of fresh cheeses are STRETCHED CURD CHEESES, with their irresistible stringy, impossible-to-control texture. These came originally from the Middle East, but the best known example today is mozzarella. The young curd is heated in the whey before being stretched or kneaded until the strings do not break when stretched. The pliant curd is then "spun" into balls or plaited and tossed in hot water to seal the cheese.

COMMON CHARACTERISTICS: Fresh cheeses are always mild and high in moisture and therefore low in fat. They have a slightly acidic or lactic taste. Most are used for cooking but some may be wrapped in leaves or dusted with paprika, charcoal or fresh herbs for serving as a table cheese.

WATCH POINTS: A slightly bitter smell, normally accompanied by a greyish brown or thin opaque mould, indicates the cheese is no longer fresh and will taste bitter.

SOFT-WHITE CHEESES
(WHITE, FUZZY PENICILLIUM CANDIDUM RIND)

EXAMPLES: *Camembert, Brie, Bonchester, Pencarreg, Chaource*

The floppy curd is ladled gently into moulds and left to drain in perforated moulds in an atmosphere of high humidity so that the curd does not lose too much whey. After a few hours, the cheeses are turned out of their moulds and left to mature for a few weeks. Their high moisture content, coupled with the high humidity, attracts and encourages the growth of the classic white penicillium mould seen on Bries and Camemberts around the world.

The penicillium moulds help to break down the curd and contribute to the flavour and texture of the cheese. The result is a creamy, smooth, voluptuous interior that when perfect looks as though it is almost ready to run.

Originally, the mould would have existed naturally in the atmosphere, along with other wild moulds and yeasts. Today, these need to be introduced into the cheesemakers' ripening rooms. Artisan cheesemakers encourage the growth of these wild moulds. On their cheeses, the white rinds tend to be dusted or impregnated with red, yellow, grey or pink moulds, all of which add to the depth and uniqueness of flavour. The wild moulds, however, do not stand up to the modern hygiene conditions that exist in factories. Here the mould spores have to be continually sprayed into the ripening rooms or even injected into the cheeses, producing a rather one-dimensional flavour.

COMMON CHARACTERISTICS: Brie is a classic example of a soft-white cheese, with its rich, runny, creamy texture. The taste is reminiscent of soup made from wild mushrooms, with just a dash of sherry. Pasteurized Bries remain white, and smell more like hay and button mushrooms and have a buttery, mushroom taste.

WATCH POINTS: A strong smell of ammonia indicates that the cheese has entered second fermentation or has been kept too damp. Soft-white cheeses with long shelf lives have been stabilized to prevent them running. They will consequently taste sweeter and more buttery and will be elastic rather than runny. Soft-white cheeses made with milk that has been enriched with cream before being coagulated will be higher in fat, more solid and have the richness of cream but will seldom develop a great depth of flavour. However, they will feel like melted butter or ice cream in the mouth and will taste delicious.

EXCEPTIONS: Blue Bries and other flavoured Brie-type cheeses belong in this category as the classification relates to the *rind* first rather than the cheese's interior. Thus, by looking at a soft flat Brie-type cheese you can tell that its overall character will be that of a soft-white cheese even though only a label or a sharp knife will tell you what is inside.

NATURAL-RIND CHEESES
(BLUE-GREY MOULDED RIND, USUALLY GOAT)
EXAMPLES: *Crottin de Chavignol, Saint-Marcellin, Selles-sur-Cher*

The majority of French farmhouse goat's milk cheeses belong in this category, which applies to fresh cheeses that have been left to drain for longer and in a drier atmosphere than the fresh cheeses. These are the cheeses you see piled on wooden trestles in French markets. When young, they have a slightly wrinkled, cream-coloured rind. In time they dry out, the wrinkles become more pronounced and the character and flavour increases, along with the growth of bluish grey mould.

ABOVE: Shelves of unpasteurized Brie de Meaux in a special ripening room where the cheeses will gradually develop their distinctive rind

COMMON CHARACTERISTICS: Initially, the taste is fresh, almost fruity, with undertones of goat; as the cheeses dry out the flavours intensify, becoming rich and nutty and acquiring a decidedly goaty taste. The mould starts as a discrete hue on the surface, gradually covering the entire cheese in greyish-blue blotches. There are few examples of this variety made in Britain, America or Australasia as the majority of consumers are dubious about moulds.

WATCH POINTS: To mature and ripen, these cheeses must be kept dry. Any wetness on the surface should be patted dry immediately or the cheese will become damp and lose its sharp, clean taste.

WASHED-RIND CHEESES
(ORANGEY-BROWN STICKY RIND)
EXAMPLES: *Epoisses, Herve, Milleens, Stinking Bishop, Munster*

The curd, which may or may not be cut depending on how soft the final cheese should be, is scooped into moulds and left to drain. The high moisture of the curd and the humidity of the maturing rooms attracts a bitter-tasting, grey, hairy mould called "cat fur". To discourage this, the newly formed cheese is rubbed with or dunked in baths of salty water, wine or a similar alcoholic liquid. This produces a rather robust cheese and encourages the development of orange, sticky bacteria that help to break down the curd from the outside, gradually becoming an integral part of the interior, rather than just a skin.

Invented by Trappist monks to enhance their otherwise rather meagre diet on fast days, these cheeses are found right across Europe, but mainly in France, Belgium and (more recently) Ireland.

COMMON CHARACTERISTICS: Ranging from rather spicy to outrageously piquant in taste and aroma (and once banned on French public transport for that very reason), they can smell yeasty or can be almost meaty. The interior may resemble Brie or be more supple and elastic.

WATCH POINTS: A dull brownish rind may indicate that the cheese has been kept too long or has been allowed to dry out. Cracking, if noticed early, can be arrested by wrapping the cheese in clear film to conserve the moisture.

SEMI-SOFT CHEESES
(PINKISH/BROWN TO DARK GREY RIND WITH SUPPLE, ELASTIC "FEEL")
EXAMPLES: *Raclette, Desmond, Gubbeens, Edam, Sonoma Jack, Fontina*

To obtain a firmer cheese, the curd is cut up to release some of the whey before the curd is placed in moulds. It is then often lightly pressed to speed up the draining. After a day or so, the cheese is turned out of its mould and washed in brine. This

ABOVE: Fresh, cloth-wrapped Gruyère curd is placed in the massive, traditional, round wooden hoop

ABOVE: Hundred's of Quicke's Cheddars maturing on ceiling-high shelves in the ripening rooms at their farm in Devon

seals the rind before the cheese is placed in cellars or ripening rooms, where other moulds are encouraged to grow. To eliminate the formation of the rind, the cheeses may be sealed in plastic; otherwise the moulds that form are frequently brushed off, gradually building up a leathery rind that may be fine and barely perceptible from the interior, thin orange brown like the rind on raclette or thick grey-brown and leathery like the rind on Tomme de Savoie.

COMMON CHARACTERISTICS: The lower moisture content means the fermentation process is slower, producing cheeses with a round, full-bodied, rather than strong, flavour. Their taste often seems to be embodied with the oils and esters of the wild mountain flowers of Europe. When young, semi-soft cheeses have a firm yet springy, school eraser texture, becoming elastic and supple.

WATCH POINTS: Cheeses that have been dipped in wax to prevent dehydration and splitting may sweat, causing mould to develop under the rind.

EXCEPTIONS: Some semi-soft cheeses are only very lightly pressed and can be eaten within a few days or the cheese may be encouraged to grow a soft-white rind, although this will slowly be corrupted by the more virulent moulds common to this type of cheese.

HARD CHEESES
(THICK RIND, OFTEN WAXED, OILED OR CLOTHBOUND)

EXAMPLES: *Cheddar, Manchego, Cantal, Gruyèye, Cheshire, Parmigiano-Reggiano, Pecorino*

To make a hard cheese the curd must be cut more finely – from small cubes to rice-size pieces – the smaller the pieces, the more whey will be lost from the curd. The curds are then gently heated in a vat to force out more moisture before the whey is drained off. Salt is then added to the curds, which now resemble rubbery, lumpy, cottage cheese. They may be cut again (the process differs for various types of hard cheeses) before being placed in large perforated moulds that are frequently engraved with a unique symbol, logo, pattern or name to identify the finished cheese or its maker.

Most traditional, hard British cheeses are wrapped in cloth, sealed with lard and left to mature for weeks or even years. Hard European cheeses tend to be left in brine overnight (or, in the case of Parmigiano-Reggiano, for up to 21 days) to seal the rind. Then they, like their British counterparts, are placed in "caves" or ripening rooms to mature. Most hard cheeses require at least a

LEFT: Parmigiano-Reggiano – one of the classic hard cheeses

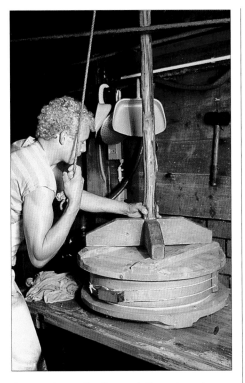

ABOVE: A newly-formed Gruyère cheese is frequently pressed and turned, then it is left in the press overnight

few weeks to mature, if not years, as is the case with good farmhouse Cheddar, Emmental or Cantal.

Hard block cheeses are pressed into shape and then matured in special plastic wrap that allows the cheese to age without the development of either moulds or rind. The moisture that would normally be lost during maturation is also retained. The cheese will mature faster but its texture will be softer than traditionally matured, clothbound cheeses. However, the method for block cheeses is more economical as a hard cheese like Cheddar can lose up to 15 per cent of its original weight if not wrapped.

WATCH POINTS: Hard cheeses are user-friendly. They may grow some surface mould, but this can easily be scraped off. The important thing to remember is to keep the cut surfaces of hard cheese tightly covered with foil or clear film (leaving an opening for the rind to breathe) to prevent the cheese from absorbing any taints from the fridge. Fatty substances, particularly cheeses and fat, absorb smells very easily, which is an advantage when the aroma is acquired intentionally, but a drawback if not.

BLUE CHEESES

(THE RIND VARIES FROM A FINE BLOOM TO A THICK GRITTY RIND LIKE THAT ON STILTON, BUT GENERALLY BLUE CHEESES ARE WRAPPED IN FOIL)

EXAMPLES: *Stilton, Roquefort, Gorgonzola, Cabrales, Maytag Blue, Danish Blue*

Blue cheeses are neither pressed nor cooked. Most frequently the curd is crumbled, eliminating much of the whey, then scooped into stainless steel cylindrical moulds, each with a wooden disk on the top. The curd remains in the moulds for 1–2 weeks and is turned frequently to let the weight of the curds press out more of the whey. Once the cheeses can stand up on their own, they are removed from the moulds, rubbed with salt, then returned to the cellars.

The blue mould is a strain of penicillium that is added to the milk before the rennet is added either in liquid or powder form. The cheese will not turn blue, however, unless it is given air to breathe. This is done by piercing the cheese with rods. The blue then grows along the tunnels and into the nooks and crannies between the loose curd, producing the shattered porcelain look that typifies blue cheese.

Those that are made like Brie have the blue injected into the young curd as the moisture content is so high that any holes made in the cheese would immediately close up, preventing air from penetrating the curd.

WATCH POINTS: Most blue cheeses are normally wrapped in foil to prevent them from drying out. This causes the moisture pumped out by the bacteria during fermentation to gather on the rind. Scrape this off before serving.

SPECIALITY CHEESE

(SIMILAR TO THE ORIGINAL CHEESE USED AS A BASE)

EXAMPLES: *Gouda with Cumin, Sage Derby, Cheddar with Date & Walnut, Red Leicester with Pecans, Raclette with Peppercorns*

These are made from familiar semi-soft or hard cheeses to which flavourings or other ingredients – nuts, fruit, spices, herbs, even fish – have been added . Traditionally

ABOVE: Bleu d'Auvergne curds draining in their stainless steel moulds – they are left for one or two weeks

the flavourings tended to be cumin, cloves or herbs but in the last five years, particularly in Britain, flavoured cheeses have become a significant growth area of the market. Some combinations are successful, others sublime and a few positively ridiculous.

THE ART OF CHEESE TASTING

The most effective way of putting your new knowledge to the test is to taste a selection of cheeses – preferably one of each of the different types. Buy some cheese, wine and bread, then invite a few friends round to compare the flavours and textures of the cheeses against each other. The categories here are roughly in order of strength so use them as a guide, starting from mild to strong, though as with all rules, there are exceptions and reasons for breaking them. Don't lose sight of the object of the exercise, however, which is to enjoy the gentle art of learning that one "lives to eat, not eats to live".

BELOW: Once Bleu d'Auvergne cheeses are removed from the moulds, they are rubbed with salt

WINE AND CHEESE: THE PERFECT MARRIAGE

As a very general rule, the whiter and fresher the cheese the crisper and fruitier the wine should be. The heavier, richer soft cheeses can be partnered with a big white like a Chardonnay or a light red. The harder and darker the cheese, the heavier and richer the style of wine can be. Most blue cheeses, on the other hand, go superbly with sweet wines.

Perfumed or floral reds are too overpowering. So are heavy tannic wines – the tannin tends to steal the nutty richness of the cheese. If asked to select one grape variety over any other to have with a cheeseboard, the author would go for a Pinot Noir from the New World or a soft Burgundian Pinot Noir. However, white wines are often unexpectedly good partners, allowing the cheese and the wine a chance to show their character in a way that a red wine may often fail to do.

FRESH CHEESES

Try fresh light, crisp white wines like Sauvignon or Chenin Blanc; also try Frascati, Soave or Loire whites. Red wines are too heavy, unless the cheese is part of a spicy dish like a pizza.

BELOW: Red wine, especially those made with Pinot Noir grapes, makes an ideal accompaniment to cheese

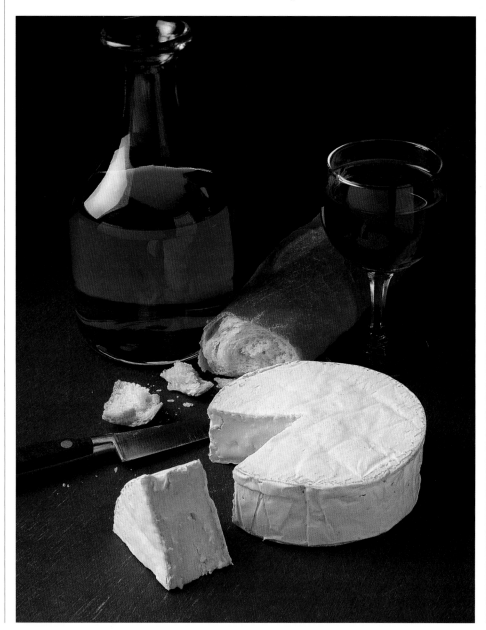

SOFT-WHITE CHEESES

With the mild, slightly sharp, salty style try a slightly sweet wine. Those with a richer, sweeter and more creamy taste need a fruitier wine with a good balance of fruit and acidity. A New Zealand or Chilean Sauvignon Blanc would be ideal. The more meaty Bries prefer a full-bodied, fruity red like a Pinot Noir or even a rich white, such as Chardonnay.

SEMI-SOFT CHEESES

Try a full-bodied gutsy white or a light fruity, red. The firmer, more distinctly flavoured semi-soft cheeses need a Chianti, Rioja or Merlot.

WASHED-RIND CHEESES

The strong, pungent, washed rind cheeses respond well to beer. If you serve wine, make it a spicy Gewurztraminer or a robust red.

HARD CHEESES

They range from the mild to the outrageously tangy, so almost any wine can be a potential match. However a general rule is the stronger the cheese the bigger the wine required.

MILD: something red and fruity – Fitou, Merlot or Chilean reds

MEDIUM: try Côtes du Rhône or a New Zealand Cabernet Sauvignon

STRONG: Californian Cabernet Sauvignon or even an Australian Shiraz

EXTRA STRONG: these can handle the rich sweetness of fortified wines, such as Port or Madeira

BLUE CHEESES

Milder blues need a light fruity white like a Vouvray, Chenin Blanc or a Rosé, while the more piquant blues prefer robust, spicy reds like the Rhônes or a Shiraz. Better still, serve a sweet wine like Monbazillac or some of the sweeter wines from the New World. The classic marriage is of Roquefort with a Sauterne. The sharp, salty tang of the cheese is softened by the wine, while the sweetness of the sheep's milk is underlined.

CREATING THE PERFECT CHEESEBOARD

Use the list of cheese types outlined in the introduction as a guide next time you buy your cheeses. Learn to determine which category you prefer and how to offer a balanced cheeseboard. You should have not only a selection from several categories, but also take care to offer a combination of shapes and provide at least one goat's or sheep's milk cheese.

ACCOMPANIMENTS TO YOUR CHEESEBOARD

BREAD: There are almost as many breads as there are cheeses. The best are home-made or country-style breads. Walnut and raisin breads are favoured by some, but plain breads are often better with cheese.

NUTS: The Europeans often serve their cheese with fresh walnuts, almonds or hazelnuts in the shell. Pre-shelled nuts rarely have the same sweetness.

PICKLES: Serving pickles or chutney with cheese is a very English habit. these accompaniments are suitable for hard, mature cheeses, such as Cheddar, but they can overpower. The best are home-made and sweet, rather than hot and spicy.

FRESH FRUIT: Serve seasonal fruit, preferably local. Citrus is too sharp, and tropical fruit generally too sweet – apples, pears and figs are perfect.

DRIED FRUIT: Dried figs, prunes and raisins are delicious with all style of cheese. The Spanish make a number of delicious fruit pastes or "cheeses" from quinces, figs, almonds and raisins. These are delicious with all their cheeses, particularly the hard cheeses made from sheep's milk.

SAVOURY TOUCHES: Spring onions, olives, celery, fresh beans and crisp greens like rocket (arugula)or long leaf lettuces can be served with, but not on, the cheeseboard.

HONEY: Drizzling blue cheeses lightly with a little wild honey heightens their flavour.

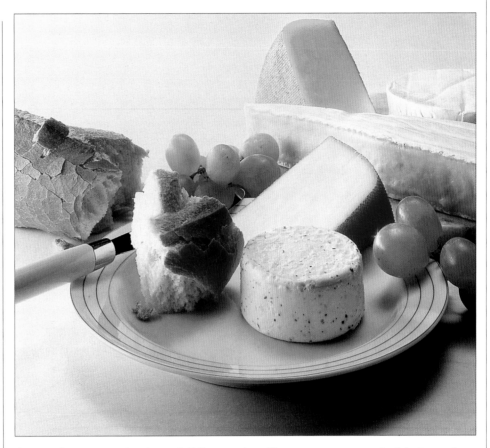

ABOVE: Choose a selection of different cheeses for your cheeseboard and accompany them with bread and fruit

◆ The best cheese board is the one chosen with care and enthusiasm and served on a rough board with chunks of bread, copious quantities of wine and good friends to share it with.

◆ One superb cheese is better than three or four small wedges.

◆ Choosing several cheeses from different categories means you will have a variety of textures. The colours of the rinds will differ, as will the interior of the cheeses.

◆ Colour should come from the rinds of the cheeses and not come from a bunch of grapes or similar fruit. If you want to decorate the board, use chestnut or oak leaves, fresh herbs or wild flowers. Add several different breads.

◆ Biscuits tend to take away from the texture of the cheeses and are often very salty. Try fresh, crusty country-style breads instead.

◆ Serve fresh fruit separately.

◆ There are some wonderful alternatives to the basic round wooden or marble cheeseboard. Experiment with wicker trays, shallow baskets, a piece of driftwood or a tray covered with a linen napkin and grape leaves.

◆ Shapes add interest to your cheeseboard. Where possible avoid having all the shapes of the cheeses the same. Instead, offer pyramids, logs, squares or cylinders. Alternatively, cut the cheese into irregular shapes.

◆ The habit of serving cheese before dessert is practised by the French for the simple reason that this enables the red wine from the main course to be finished with the cheese. The sweet wine can then be served with the blue cheeses (which, because they have the strongest flavour, should be eaten last) and follows through to accompany the dessert.

◆ A cheese board can also be served as a main course for lunch. Serve a selection of cheeses with a lightly dressed mixed leaf salad, pickles or chutney, fresh fruit and nuts and country-style bread. If you like, serve a selection of wines.

CHEESES OF THE WORLD

To taste and record the cheeses of the world would be an impossible, if infinitely pleasureable task. Instead, this reference section includes a cross-section of the world's cheeses. A few are made in huge creameries, but most come from small co-operatives or family-owned farms. Some, such as Roquefort and Cheddar, are found all over the world; others, such as Aorangi from New Zealand, Yerba Santa Shepherd's Cheese from the USA and Cooleeney from Ireland, are recently created, while others use recipes that have remained unchanged for centuries and are rarely found outside the village in which they were first made.

FRENCH CHEESES

France has many of the most fascinating cheeses in the world; over 750 of them. Most are traditional cheeses, cherished and fiercely protected.

The earliest recorded French cheese was Roquefort. Pliny, writing in the first century BC, described it as "the cheese that bears away the prize at Rome where they are always ready to compare and appreciate good things from every land". Roquefort continues to be appreciated to this day – all over the world.

During the Middle Ages the cheese-making tradition was kept alive in the monasteries of France. Monks taught the farmers how to keep their animals healthy and their milk clean. It was they who showed the farmers how to mature cheese, usually the peasants' major source of protein. Their numerous fast days gave them the motivation to invent new recipes and in 960AD the first of the monastery cheeses, Maroilles, was created at an abbey in the Thiérache region of northern France. The monks discovered that rubbing the surface of small, soft cheeses with salt created a pungent and quite meaty aroma and taste. The first of the famous Trappist cheeses was born. Munster, Pont l'Evêque, Epoisses and others were to follow.

French cheeses have retained their individual character, allowing the vagaries

ABOVE: Chevrotin des Aravis (left) and Chèvre Feuille (right)
BELOW RIGHT: Carré de l'Est

of nature, combined with the ingenuity of man, to dictate their type, size and final flavour. In the valleys and on the plains small, fresh cheeses were made that could either be eaten by the family or swiftly sold; in the mountains, where cheeses had to be stored until the shepherds could get them to market, large wheels of cheese were made that would not mature for many months or even years. The numerous limestone caves, like those at Cambalou, where Roquefort is made, proved perfect for the making of blue cheeses.

Most of the vast number of cheeses made in France today are traditional varieties, but even the French have been unable to resist the temptation to create new cheeses. Most of the new cheeses have emerged from the huge dairy companies that now dominate the French market. Some are dismal, bland variations on traditional cheeses, particularly the standardized, pasteurized Bries and Camemberts; others, such as Chaumes, Saint-Agur and Le Roulé, have been made by adapting traditional methods to the modern factory environment, and offer the consumer a stepping stone to the more complex artisan cheeses they might otherwise shy away from trying.

Surprisingly, it is not Camembert that is the most popular cheese in France. That honour goes to Comté (or Comté Jura), the wonderful, hard, fruity mountain cheese from the north-west corner of France. Second favourite is Roquefort. Camembert owes its place as the best-known French cheese outside France to two apparently unrelated events. The first was the manufacture of small wooden boxes that proved perfect for packing the soft, fragile cheeses of Normandy, and the second was the invention of the train. Properly packed and rapidly transported to Paris, and beyond, Camembert soon became a best-seller.

The finest way to discover French cheeses is to travel through France, stopping at markets and fromageries to taste. Failing that, find a good cheesemonger and eat your way to an education.

BELOW:
Vignotte

ABBAYE DE BELLOC (AOC)
REGION: *Pays Basque*
TYPE: *Traditional, farmhouse, unpasteurized, hard cheese*
SOURCE: *Sheep's milk (Manech and others)*
DESCRIPTION: *5kg/11lb fat wheel with natural, crusty, brownish rind with patches of red, orange and yellow. The rind is marked with tiny craters*
CULINARY USES: *Table cheese, grating, grilling, sauces*

The Abbaye de Notre-Dame de Belloc was founded by Benedictine monks. For centuries they have made their cheese from milk produced in the locality. In summer, the shepherds follow the ancient tradition of taking their flocks to mountain pastures. Along with other hard sheep's milk cheeses of the area, Abbaye de Belloc comes under the Ossau-Iraty AOC banner. The cheese has a firm, dense, rich and creamy texture. The taste resembles burnt caramel and there is a distinctive lanolin aroma.

AISY CENDRÉ
REGION: *Burgundy*
TYPE: *Traditional, farmhouse, unpasteurized, semi-soft cheese*
SOURCE: *Cow's milk*
DESCRIPTION: *200–250g/7–9oz round cheese with natural rind covered with a thick coating of ash*
CULINARY USE: *Table cheese*

To make this speciality, a local cheese (usually a young Epoisses) is immersed in a bed of ashes for at least one month. The best the author tasted was made by a winemaker who washed the cheese in his own marc de bourgogne before burying it in ashes. A few days before serving, the winemaker would brush off the ash, soak the cheese overnight in his precious eau-de-vie, then present it along with the rest of the bottle. Slow to ripen, Aisy Cendré has a white, salty, chalky centre surrounded by a softer, earthy-tasting outer layer. Unless you are the sort of person who likes sand with your picnic, you should brush off the layer of ashes before serving the cheese.

Olivet Cendré is a similar cheese.

ARDI-GASNA
REGION: *Pays Basque*
TYPE: *Traditional, farmhouse, unpasteurized, hard cheese*
SOURCE: *Sheep's milk*
DESCRIPTION: *3–5kg/6½–11lb wheel with natural, crusty, yellow rind with greyish moulds*
CULINARY USES: *Table cheese, grating, snacks, desserts*

Ardi-Gasna means "sheep's cheese" in Basque, and this cheese has remained virtually unchanged for centuries. There are still a few local shepherds who make the long journey with their flocks up to the high mountain pastures. Here they make their cheese in stone huts in late spring and early summer. Seldom found outside the region, Ardi-Gasna cheeses are highly prized. The cheese has a hard texture, but feels rich in the mouth. The flavour is clean and fresh with the sweetness of mountain flowers and a nuttiness born of age. The finish has a touch of sharpness that increases as the cheese matures.

Similar cheeses include Laruns and Esbareich.

ARÔMES AU GÈNE DE MARC
REGION: *Lyonnais*
TYPE: *Traditional, farmhouse, unpasteurized, natural-rind cheese*
SOURCE: *Cow's and goat's milk*
DESCRIPTION: *80–120g/3¼–4¼oz small, round cheeses. The whitish rind has some mould. The fermenting lees of the marc are pressed into it*
CULINARY USE: *Table cheese*

Made in various wine-making areas, some two to three months after the grapes have been pressed, these are the result of small immature cheeses such as Rigotte or St Marcellin being macerated or cured in vats of marc (fermenting grape skins and pips). They are then rolled in the marc before being sold. Definitely not for the faint-hearted, the cheeses have a strong, bittersweet, yeasty taste and aroma. When young, the moist, creamy taste of the cheese offers a balance; with age, the cheese becomes hard and flaky, with a formidable pungent taste – not necessarily appreciated by the uninitiated.

Similar cheeses are produced by other villages in the area.

AOC
To preserve and protect the traditions and experience of centuries of French cheesemaking, the AOC (Appellation d'Origine Contrôlée) system was established, as it had been for wine. Each cheese protected by the system must comply with strictly enforced rules that govern the following:

◆ the area where cattle may graze
◆ the origin and type of feed provided
◆ the breed of cattle that furnish the milk
◆ when the cheese is made (what season)
◆ how the cheese is made
◆ the shape and size of the cheese
◆ how the cheese is stored

The regulations often mean that cattle may only graze on permanent pastures that are organically managed, rather than ploughed and re-sown every year. The use of silage or other fermented or man-made feed is prohibited.

The AOC rules guarantee the quality of France's famous cheeses, protecting them against copies and giving the consumer the confidence to buy raw milk cheeses. Some AOC cheeses are made in huge factories, others on tiny farms, but all proudly respect and uphold the traditions of the area.

BELOW: Abbaye de Belloc

ABOVE: Banon

BELOW RIGHT: Beaufort

BAGUETTE LAONNAISE
REGION: *Ile-de-France*
TYPE: *Traditional, creamery,
washed-rind cheese*
SOURCE: *Cow's milk*
DESCRIPTION: *500g/1¼lb oblong loaf
with glossy but crusty,
orange-brown rind*
CULINARY USE: *Table cheese*

Created after the Second World War, Baguette Laonnaise has become a favourite with lovers of strong cheese. The sticky, ridged, orange-brown rind hides a supple, yet dense interior.

As the cheese ages it develops a very pungent, spicy nose and taste, and a finish that is reminiscent of the farmyard. In the wrong hands (or a cold fridge) the rind may dry out and the cheese will become quite bitter and unpleasant to eat.

Similar cheeses include Maroilles, Herve and Limburger.

BANON
REGION: *Provence*
TYPE: *Traditional, farmhouse and
creamery, unpasteurized, natural-
rind cheese*
SOURCE: *Cow's, sheep's or goat's milk,
or a combination*
DESCRIPTION: *100g/3¾oz small, round
cheese, traditionally sold wrapped in
chestnut leaves and tied with raffia*
CULINARY USES: *Table cheese*

This cheese takes its name from the market-town of Banon, where cobbled paths wind up past old, stone cottages to the church. Chestnut trees provide welcome shade and also provide the leaves used for wrapping the cheese. The leaves keep the young, slightly acidic cheese moist and impart a fresh vegetable flavour with a hint of wine. As the cheese ages, blue and grey moulds and yeasts are produced on and under the leaves, which contribute to the taste. Banon cheeses range from firm, mild and lactic to soft, creamy and tart, with a nutty flavour. Although traditionally produced from goat's, sheep's or mixed milks, most are today produced in large creameries, from cow's milk. At the weekly market in Banon, you can buy fresh and aged local cheeses.

The local speciality, Fromage Fort du Mont Ventoux, is produced by placing a young Banon cheese (minus chestnut leaves) in an earthenware crock, seasoning it liberally with salt and pepper and pouring over vinegar or local eau-de-vie. The crock is then placed in a cool cellar and the cheese left to ferment, with just the occasional stir. The longer it is left, the more ferocious it becomes.

BEAUFORT (AOC)
REGION: *Savoie*
TYPE: *Traditional, farmhouse,
unpasteurized, hard cheese*
SOURCE: *Cow's milk*
DESCRIPTION: *Large, concave cartwheel,
about 60cm/24in in diameter and
weighing up to 75kg/165lb. The hard,
brownish-yellow, natural, brushed
rind is slightly rough*
CULINARY USES: *Table cheese, snacks,
fondues, grated, in pies*

A member of the Gruyère family, but with a higher fat content, this ancient cheese dates back to the time of the Roman Empire. Made in mountain chalets, it has an irresistible smoothness, despite its hard appearance. It owes its superb flavour to the flowers, sweet grasses and herbs of the high pastures, where, by AOC rules, the cows must graze. Gruyère gets its name from the time when kings sent their tax collectors, known as "agents gruyers", to collect taxes from the cheesemakers. Also known as Gruyère de Beaufort.

BLEU D'AUVERGNE (AOC)

REGION: *Auvergne*
TYPE: *Traditional, farmhouse and creamery, blue cheese*
SOURCE: *Cow's milk*
DESCRIPTION: *1–3kg/2¼–6½ lb short cylinder. The moist, natural rind has grey and blue moulds*
CULINARY USES: *Table cheese, crumbled in salads (with nuts)*

Named after the magnificent mountainous region where it is made, this is a moist, creamy cheese that resembles Roquefort, although it is made with cow's milk, not sheep's milk. It has a piquant smell and sharp, clean taste with a hint of herbs and melted butter. The cheese is composed of pockets and broken threads of bluish-grey mould. With age, the crust becomes sticky and reddish-orange moulds start to develop. These help to break down the interior, which gradually collapses, intensifying the spicy flavour.

Although Bleu d'Auvergne is now made by large creameries, the AOC regulations ensure that tradition and craftsmanship are retained. Some examples of this cheese are still made in farmhouses from raw milk, but they are seldom found outside the region.

Similar cheeses include Bleu des Causses and Bleu de Laqueuille.

BLEU DE HAUT JURA (AOC)

REGION: *Franche-Comté*
TYPE: *Traditional, farmhouse and co-operative, unpasteurized, blue cheese*
SOURCE: *Cow's milk*
DESCRIPTION: *7.5kg/16½lb wheel with convex edges. The natural rind is dry, rough and thin, with powdery yellow to red moulds*
CULINARY USES: *Table cheese, salads*

Unlike most blue cheeses, this is made in the shape of a large, flat wheel, which speeds the ripening process. The result is a cheese that is more supple and less creamy than other blues, with a mild taste that hints of mushrooms, tarragon and fresh milk. The AOC was granted in 1977. Other blues made in the region, such as Bleu de Gex and Bleu de Septmoncel, are now officially named Bleu de Haut Jura.

BLEU DE LAQUEUILLE

REGION: *Auvergne*
TYPE: *Traditional, creamery, unpasteurized, blue cheese*
SOURCE: *Cow's milk*
DESCRIPTION: *800g–2.5kg/1¾–5½lb cylinder with natural, pale orange rind, on which the more dominant, white penicillium mould battles it out with the greyish moulds common to blue cheeses*
CULINARY USE: *Table cheese*

A statue in Laqueuille reminds visitors to the village that Antoine Roussel created this cheese in 1850 after sprinkling young curd with blue moulds he found growing on rye bread. It rapidly became popular, both locally and in Paris. Like a smaller version of Fourme d'Ambert, it tends to develop a soft, white mould on some or all of the rind. The consistency leans towards that of Brie. The blue is chunky rather than in streaks and the flavour is spicy, fresh and creamy, with a slightly salty tang. The smaller version makes an attractive addition to a cheeseboard.

BELOW: Clockwise from bottom left, Bleu de Laqueuille , Bleu d'Auvergne, Bleu des Causses and Bleu de Gex

BLEU DES CAUSSES (AOC)

REGION: *Auvergne*
TYPE: *Traditional, creamery, unpasteurized, blue cheese*
SOURCE: *Cow's milk*
DESCRIPTION: *2.25–3kg/5–6½lb flat cylinder. The sticky, ivory rind has fine reddish-orange and grey moulds*
CULINARY USES: *Table cheese, salads*

For centuries, this pungent cheese was made in the Rouergue and surrounding areas, using cow's or sheep's milk. However, since 1947 AOC rules have decreed that it must be made with cow's milk to differentiate it from Roquefort, which is made in the same area. Bleu des Causses, like Roquefort, is matured in limestone caves with natural fissures that allow fresh air currents or "fleurines" to circulate and move the natural moulds through the ripening cheese. The result is a cheese that is firm-textured, but more moist and spicy in flavour than other French blues. Fresh-tasting, with a sharp finish, it is an excellent, less salty alternative to Roquefort.

Bleu des Causses cheeses that attain the required standards of quality are stamped with the AOC symbol before being wrapped in silver foil.

BOUGON

REGION: *Poitou-Charentes*
TYPE: *Traditional, creamery,
soft-white cheese*
SOURCE: *Goat's milk*
DESCRIPTION: *80g/3¼oz round with
fine, white penicillium mould rind*
CULINARY USE: *Table cheese*

Although similar cheeses have been made in various forms in France for generations, Bougon was only recently made commercially. Although *bougon* means "grumpy" in French, this is no reflection on the cheese – it is simply named after the town where it is made. It is a smooth and voluptuous cheese with a taste that has been likened to a blend of tarragon, thyme and white wine. The Camembert shape is the most popular, but it also comes in pyramids, cylindrical logs and mini rounds.

BOULETTE D'AVESNES

REGION: *Nord-Pas-de-Calais*
TYPE: *Traditional, farmhouse and
creamery, fresh cheese*
SOURCE: *Cow's milk*
DESCRIPTION: *150–180g/5–6¼oz cone
with natural rind given a dark red
colour by the use of annatto
or paprika*
CULINARY USE: *Table cheese*

This unusual cheese was originally produced from buttermilk and was made on farms as a by-product of buttermaking. Today, creameries use underripe or less-than-perfect Maroilles or Dauphine cheeses. The soft curd is kneaded and mashed with parsley, tarragon, pepper and paprika. The cheese has a fairly doughy texture and a quite outrageously spicy flavour.

ABOVE: Boulette d'Avesnes

BOURSAULT

REGION: *Ile-de-France*
TYPE: *Modern, creamery,
soft-white cheese*
SOURCE: *Cow's milk*
DESCRIPTION: *200g/7oz small
half-cylinder with light, white
penicillium mould rind with
pinkish tones*
CULINARY USES: *Table cheese, canapés*

Invented by Henri Boursault in 1953, about the same time as Boursin, this soft-white-rinded cheese became successful almost overnight. The company is now owned by the cheese giant Van den Berg. The method resembles that used for Brie, but Boursault has a softer and thinner rind. This helps to ripen the cheese, giving off a sweet, mushroomy aroma. The high cream content means that the taste is smooth and almost buttery. The interior is solid rather than supple or runny and the finish is nutty and it has a refreshing citrus tang to balance the richness of the cream. One of the best enriched cheeses, Boursault is also known as Lucullus. Délice de Saint-Cyr is a larger version.

BOURSIN

REGION: *Ile-de-France and Normandy*
TYPE: *Modern, creamery, fresh cheese*
SOURCE: *Cow's milk*
DESCRIPTION: *80g/3¼oz small half-
cylinder without rind, sold in an
attractive, corrugated-foil wrapper*
CULINARY USES: *Table cheese,
baking, spreading*

Founded in 1957 by a Monsieur Boursin and now produced by one of the major French cheese companies (Van den Bergh), this is a moist, yet creamy cheese with a sweet, rich flavour with a hint of acidity. It melts in the mouth like ice cream. The quality has remained consistently good, both as regards the original cheese and the two well-known variations, one with garlic and herbs and the other rolled in fiery cracked peppercorns.

Boursin was the first cheese advertised on French TV and became a sensational success. The wacky, off-the-wall advertisement showed a famous actor being driven from his bed by his desire for the Boursin that was waiting elegantly in his fridge. Boursin – and the catch phrase "*du pain, du vin, du Boursin*" – became part of French culture.

Made only from rich Normandy milk and cream, the cheese is produced without rennet. Only a starter culture is used and much of the processing is still only semi-automated, to ensure that the texture and quality are maintained. Since Van den Bergh took over, it has invented three more exotic variations, but these are nowhere near as good, or as authentic, as the famous three.

ABOVE: Boursin

LEFT: Boursault

ABOVE: Bresse Bleu

BRESSE BLEU

REGION: *Rhône-Alpes*
TYPE: *Modern, creamery, blue cheese*
SOURCE: *Cow's milk*
DESCRIPTION: *125–500g/4¹/₂oz–1¹/₄lb cylinder with soft-white rind with penicillium mould*
CULINARY USE: *Table cheese*

Developed during the Second World War and now owned by the milk processing giant Bongrain, Bresse Bleu became increasingly popular in the 1950s as an alternative to stronger blue cheeses. The interior is rich and buttery. Like Brie, it melts in the mouth, with a sweet, slightly spicy tang. The smooth, white rind has the aroma of button mushrooms. Because of the dense, creamy nature of the cheese, the blue mould must be injected into it, rather than being added to the milk before coagulation. It forms pockets of blue-grey mould rather than fine streaks. Tiny mould spores from the rind may be carried into the cheese when it is injected, forming patches of fluffy, white mould within the cheese.

Individual cheeses are small, so can be sold whole rather than in slices. This fact, together with convenient packaging, means that Bresse Bleu travels well and is therefore widely available outside its country of origin.

Similar cheeses include Blue Brie and Cambazola.

BRIE DE MEAUX (AOC)

REGION: *Ile-de-France*
TYPE: *Traditional, farmhouse, unpasteurized, soft-white cheese*
SOURCE: *Cow's milk*
DESCRIPTION: *2.5–3kg/5¹/₂–6¹/₂lb wheel. The white penicillium mould rind has reddish-brown ferments. The marks of the straw mat on which the cheese matures are visible*
CULINARY USE: *Table cheese*

The father of all soft-white or bloomy-rind cheeses. Brie de Meaux was first recorded in AD774 when the gourmet and soldier Charlemagne tasted it in Brie and ordered two batches to be sent to him annually in Aix.

You will know when you have found the perfect Meaux – it is smooth, voluptuous and not quite runny. The aroma is that of mushrooms with the merest hint of ammonia and the taste is of creamy wild mushroom soup with a dash of sherry.

Although the cheese is now protected by AOC regulations, some critics claim these do not go far enough. Regrettably, the Friesian-Holstein cow continues to replace the old indigenous cattle. The richness and character of the milk is therefore not always what it should be. Fortunately, there remain some superb farm-produced Meaux brought to the point of perfection by talented affineurs.

BRIE DE MELUN (AOC)

REGION: *Ile-de-France*
TYPE: *Traditional, farmhouse, unpasteurized, soft-white cheese*
SOURCE: *Cow's milk*
DESCRIPTION: *1.5–8kg/3–18lb wheel with white penicillium mould forming a fine, white crust with a mix of yellow and red ferments*
CULINARY USE: *Table cheese*

Produced in the same region as Brie de Meaux, Brie de Melun is sharper and more salty. Whereas rennet is used to coagulate Meaux, Melun relies entirely on the action of lactose-loving bacteria. The art of bringing the cheeses to the point of perfection belongs to the affineur. He will watch over row upon row of Bries in various stages of ripeness, each of them sitting on a well-worn wooden shelf lined with a straw mat. The cheese is judged to be ripe when the yellow mould dominates, with just a touch of the red. To attain the perfect balance, the affineur and his team turn as many as 18,000 cheeses twice a week for about two months. They take care not to leave fingermarks and to ensure that no bacteria from their hands are permitted to pass to the cheeses.

A perfect Melun has a supple texture with meadow scents and flavours – quite like an unripe Brie, but with more depth.

BELOW: Brie de Meaux

BELOW: Butte

BRILLAT-SAVARIN
REGION: *Normandy*
TYPE: *Modern, creamery, fresh or soft-white cheese*
SOURCE: *Cow's milk*
DESCRIPTION: *450–500g/1–1¼lb round cheese. There may be a soft-white rind. The cheese will eventually grow a thick, velvety, white crust*
CULINARY USES: *Table cheese, canapés*

Named after the French magistrate, born in 1755, who published a gastronomic tome: *La Physiologie du Goût*. This book bore witness to a lifetime committed to good food. Brillat-Savarin would have approved of this rich triple cream cheese.

Other triple cream cheeses include Le Saulieu, Lucullus and Boursault.

BROCCIU/BROCCIO (AOC)
REGION: *Corsica*
TYPE: *Traditional, farmhouse, unpasteurized, whey cheese*
SOURCE: *Sheep's and goat's milk*
DESCRIPTION: *500g–1kg/1¼–2¼lb cheeses in various shapes, without rind*
CULINARY USES: *Served with herbs as a snack or with fruit for breakfast*

This fresh cheese is made with sheep's milk in winter and goat's milk in summer. Traditionally made from whey, although skimmed milk is often used today. The cheese is drained in woven baskets and has a mild flavour. Some cheeses are salted and dried for six months, when the flavour becomes very sharp and pronounced.

BÛCHETTE D'ANJOU
REGION: *Loire*
TYPE: *Traditional, farmhouse, unpasteurized, natural-rind cheese*
SOURCE: *Goat's milk*
DESCRIPTION: *80–100g/3¼–3¾oz log with natural rind dusted with salt and charcoal*
CULINARY USES: *Table cheese, slicing and grilling, in salads*

These delightful, plain or ash-covered cheeses have been made in the Loire area for centuries. When young they are firm and grainy, with a mild, fresh, citrus taste. Under the watchful gaze of a talented affineur, the interior softens to melting point and the taste becomes redolent of fresh asparagus and wild herbs.

Bûchette de Banon is a similar cheese.

BUTTE
REGION: *Ile-de-France*
TYPE: *Modern, creamery, soft-white cheese*
SOURCE: *Cow's milk*
DESCRIPTION: *350g/12oz brick with thick, smooth, velvety, white penicillium rind*
CULINARY USE: *Table cheese*

This takes its name from the shape, which resembles a small hillock. The cheese owes its buttery texture to cream, which is added to the milk before it is coagulated. The fresh cheese melts in the mouth and has a mushroomy aroma and a salty, bitter tang. If allowed to ripen, the rind develops reddish pigmentation, the interior becomes runny around the edges, the aroma becomes acrid and the taste sharper and (to some) more delicious.

Similar cheeses include Grand Vatel and Explorateur.

RIGHT: From the top, Cabécou de Rocamadour; Camembert and Brillat-Savarin

CABÉCOU DE ROCAMADOUR (AOC)
REGION: *Midi-Pyrénées*
TYPE: *Traditional, farmhouse, unpasteurized, natural-rind cheese*
SOURCE: *Sheep's and goat's milk*
DESCRIPTION: *30–40g/1¼–1½oz disc. The natural, soft rind is cream-coloured and wrinkly. It develops pale blue moulds*
CULINARY USES: *Table cheese, baking, grilling*

These tiny, round discs, with their creamy white rind, have been made in the area for centuries, ever since the locals domesticated the herds of goats and sheep that once roamed wild on the mountainsides. Today, at the height of the season, the cheeses are sold in flat, wooden, slatted trays, which are piled high on market stalls decked with chestnut boughs. The cheeses are sometimes decorated with tiny sprigs of wild herbs, or sold wrapped in bacon strips, ready for grilling and tossing into a salad of frisée lettuce. When the dense, creamy cheese is grilled (perhaps on a crusty baguette), the nutty taste and distinctly goaty aroma intensify – wonderful when washed down with a bottle or two of local wine. Sometimes the cheese is made with sheep's milk, which gives a nuttier taste with a hint of butterscotch.

The cheese is also known simply as Rocamadour.

CAMEMBERT DE NORMANDIE (AOC)

REGION: *Normandy*

TYPE: *Traditional, farmhouse and creamery, unpasteurized, soft-white cheese*

SOURCE: *Cow's milk*

DESCRIPTION: *250g/9oz round with thin, white penicillium mould crust that becomes impregnated with red, brown and yellow pigments as it matures*

CULINARY USES: *Table cheese. Anything else would be sacrilege*

Camembert started life towards the end of the eighteenth century as a dry, yellow-brown cheese made for her family by Marie Harel, a farmer's wife. This was around the time of the French Revolution, and the family gave shelter to a priest from the Brie region. Having often talked to his parishioners while they made their cheeses, he was able to repay the Harels' kindness by imparting his knowledge. As a result, the cheese became softer and more earthy, but it would be some years before it acquired the name by which we know it today.

In 1855, one of Marie Harel's daughters presented Napoleon with one of the cheeses and told him that it came from Camembert. The name stuck, but the cheese might still have remained relatively unknown had it not been for three factors. First, the expansion of the railways opened up new markets. Second, small, wooden cheeseboxes proved perfect for protecting the cheeses on their long journeys. Finally, in the 1920s came the discovery of how to isolate and introduce into the ripening rooms the white penicillium moulds. These virulent moulds were capable of fighting off the less aggressive grey and blue moulds that had previously tainted the young cheeses. As a bonus, they prevented the interior from drying out. The voluptuous texture and mushroom aroma of a classic Camembert was finally achieved.

Today, hundreds of producers in Normandy are permitted to make AOC Camembert. The finest have a fragrant aroma and taste of wild mushroom soup, with a slightly yeasty, almost meaty taste.

ABOVE: Cantal

BELOW: Caprice des Dieux

CANTAL (AOC)

REGION: *Auvergne*

TYPE: *Traditional, farmhouse and creamery, unpasteurized, hard cheese*

SOURCE: *Cow's milk*

DESCRIPTION: *35–45kg/80–100lb tall cylinder with natural, straw-yellow to grey crust, dusted with grey and red pigments*

CULINARY USES: *Table cheese, grating, in soups and in sauces*

One of the oldest French cheeses, Cantal was originally produced by putting the curd into *le formage*, the wooden cylinder that is believed to be the origin of the French word for cheese – *fromage*. Cantal Fermier is produced in mountain chalets during the summer months, while Cantal Laitier is a pasteurized cheese made all year round, using milk from nearby farms in accordance with the AOC regulations. Each cheese has a metal badge embedded in the rind, and is stamped with the official AOC logo.

When young, Cantal is moist, open-textured and springy, with a cheese sauce tang not unlike Lancashire. With age, it becomes more like a mature Cheddar. The cheese is sold as *jeune* when it is at least 30 days old. When it is over six months old and has developed a robust personality, it is categorized as *vieux*. Between two and six months old, the cheese is sold as *entre-deux* (between the two).

CAPRICE DES DIEUX

REGION: *Champagne-Ardenne*

TYPE: *Modern, creamery, soft-white cheese*

SOURCE: *Cow's milk*

DESCRIPTION: *120g/4¹/₄oz oval, with a smooth, velvety, pure white penicillium rind*

CULINARY USE: *Table cheese*

Milky and rather bland, this cheese looks rather more interesting than it tastes. The texture, too, is somewhat disappointing, being more elastic than supple. However, demand has kept the small, oval boxes on the supermarket shelves and no doubt has provided a stepping stone for many would-be cheese connoisseurs.

CARRÉ DE L'EST

REGION: *Champagne and Lorraine*

TYPE: *Traditional, farmhouse, and creamery, washed-rind or soft-white cheese*

SOURCE: *Cow's milk*

DESCRIPTION: *300g/11oz square with either an orange-red, washed-rind or a penicillium mould crust*

CULINARY USE: *Table cheese*

Made in the area for generations, Carré de l'Est is ripened in cellars and encouraged to grow either a soft-white crust or washed in brine and eau-de-vie to produce a pungent, ridged orange rind. Each cheese is turned and washed by hand to spread the colourful bacteria over the cheese. The washed-rind cheeses have a runny interior with a smoky-bacon flavour. The white cheeses have a Camembert-like rind and a flavour reminiscent of melted butter and warm mushrooms.

ABOVE: Chaource

CHABICHOU DU POITOU (AOC)

REGION: *Poitou-Charentes*

TYPE: *Traditional, farmhouse and creamery, unpasteurized, natural-rind cheese*

SOURCE: *Goat's milk*

DESCRIPTION: *120g/4¼oz cylinder with a beautiful, bluish-grey mould that overlays the thin, white mould when mature*

CULINARY USES: *Table cheese, grilling*
The texture is firm and creamy rather than grainy or gluggy, and the cheese has a fresh ground-nut flavour. Mothais, Saint-Maixent and Sainte-Maure are similar.

CHAOURCE (AOC)

REGION: *Champagne*

TYPE: *Traditional, creamery, soft-white cheese*

SOURCE: *Cow's milk*

DESCRIPTION: *250–450g/9oz–1lb cylinder with downy, white penicillium rind*

CULINARY USE: *Table cheese*
Some people prefer the cheese young, when the rind has barely formed and is milky, slightly tart and salty. At this stage, the interior is grainy and coarse, rather than smooth. Other cheese-lovers prefer to wait for the rind to thicken and develop red ferments. The rind of the mature cheese has a slightly bitter flavour with a hint of mushrooms, and the interior is buttery and quite piquant, fruity and sharp. Similar cheeses include Ervy-le-Châtel, and Neufchâtel.

CHAUMES

REGION: *Dordogne*

TYPE: *Modern, creamery, washed-rind cheese*

SOURCE: *Cow's milk*

DESCRIPTION: *2kg/4½lb flattened wheel. The soft, thin rind is deep tangerine in colour with a thin, orange-paper cover*

CULINARY USES: *Table cheese, grilling*
Based upon traditional Trappist-style cheeses, this has proved to be one of the most popular of the modern French varieties. The soft rind is bright tangerine-orange and the interior is smooth, supple and quite rubbery. Although it looks as though it is about to run, the cheese is actually fairly dense and feels wonderfully rich and creamy on the tongue. The nutty, almost meaty taste and aroma are milder than you might suspect. Port Salut is a similar cheese.

LEFT: Chabichou du Poitou – an unpasteurized natural-rind cheese made with goat's milk

ABOVE: Chaumes

CHÈVRE LOG

REGION: *Loire*

TYPE: *Modern, creamery, soft-white cheese*

SOURCE: *Goat's milk*

DESCRIPTION: *3kg/6½lb log with white, velvety rind, which can become damp, acrid and separate from the cheese*

CULINARY USES: *Table cheese, hors d'oeuvres*

First made by a large co-operative in Poitiers and now sold under various brand names, chèvre log, or Bûcheron, is now available throughout Europe. At two days old, it has a lovely, sweet-sour, fruity taste, with just a touch of the almondy character of goat's milk, when the texture is dense with a fine grain. By 10 days, it is firm yet breakable and feels slightly sticky in the mouth. It retains fresh acidity and the aromatic, goaty taste intensifies. It slices easily, so is ideal for grilling.

BELOW: Chèvre log

CHEVROTIN DES ARAVIS

REGION: *Rhône-Alpes*
TYPE: *Traditional, farmhouse, unpasteurized, washed-rind cheese*
SOURCE: *Cow's and goat's milk*
DESCRIPTION: *250–350g/9–12oz round with yellowish-orange, floury-washed rind*
CULINARY USES: *Table cheese, snacks*

One of the few washed-rind goat's cheeses, Chevrotin is produced in the same way as Reblochon, which it resembles in appearance and texture – smooth, melting, rich and sensuous. It has a mild, goaty aroma and a wonderful complexity of character. The taste is nutty and quite savoury.

CÎTEAUX/ABBAYE DE CÎTEAUX

REGION: *Burgundy*
TYPE: *Traditional, farmhouse, unpasteurized, washed-rind cheese*
SOURCE: *Cow's milk (Montbéliard)*
DESCRIPTION: *700g/1lb 9oz wheel. The fine, leathery crust is pale yellow-orange with a dusting of various moulds*
CULINARY USE: *Table cheese*

L'Abbaye de Notre Dame at Cîteaux, near Beaune, was founded in 1098 by the Benedictine monks and became the birthplace of the Cistercian movement. The term "Trappist" was not introduced until the 18th century, and it is now used to describe the monastic-type cheeses.

Set in the heart of wine country, the abbey has a herd of around 200 red and white Montbéliard cows and prefers to keep production small, selling most of its cheese locally. The cheese resembles Reblochon, but because the soil and pastures are very different, so is the taste of the cheese. That great 20th-century cheese-lover Patrick Rance describes it as follows: "Cîteaux has a delicious, melt-in-the-mouth, refreshing character all its own, set off by its fine crust, more even in patina than that of Reblochon. Like the crust of the good bread with which it deserves to be paired, it is an important part of the cheese's savour and consistency against the palate, and should never be cut away and wasted."

COEUR DE CAMEMBERT AU CALVADOS

REGION: *Normandy*
TYPE: *Modern, farmhouse, soft-white cheese*
SOURCE: *Cow's milk*
DESCRIPTION: *250g/9oz round with washed rind covered with fine breadcrumbs soaked in Calvados and decorated with a half walnut*
CULINARY USE: *Table cheese*

For those not satisfied with the delicious taste of a ripe Camembert, there is this variation. The rind is removed from a semi-cured Camembert, which is then soaked in Calvados. Fresh breadcrumbs are then pressed into the cheese and a walnut garnish is added. The cheese absorbs the heady spirit. The faint apple aroma seems to complement the rich, creamy texture of the cheese.

COMTÉ/GRUYÈRE DE COMTÉ (AOC)

REGION: *Franche-Comté*
TYPE: *Traditional, creamery, unpasteurized, hard cheese*
SOURCE: *Cow's milk*
DESCRIPTION: *35–55kg/80–120lb wheel with convex sides. The natural, hard, thick rind is golden-yellow to brown*
CULINARY USES: *Table cheese, snacks, canapés, fondues, gratins*

The French make two Gruyères – Beaufort and Comté, both wonderfully large, impressive wheels. Comté is sweeter than Beaufort and has a convex rather than a concave rind. As with their Swiss counterparts, the quality can be judged by the size, shape and condition of the holes. An experienced affineur, with a gentle tap of a special hammer, can detect their condition by the resonance of the cheese. If you find one with a tiny drop or "tear" in one of the holes, it will be as near perfect as you can get.

Comté is a magnificent, unspoilt, mountain chalet cheese. It is very creamy and has a piquant yet sweet, fruity flavour. The bite is firm, dry and slightly granular, while the acidity is fruity and slightly fizzy – like fermenting pears.

These huge cheeses have been made in co-operatives in the Franche-Comté for centuries. Shepherds, with their small herds, have always spent the summer months in remote mountain huts. Due to their distance from the nearest markets, they needed to make a cheese that required months to mature. So they pooled their milk, creating huge cheeses that were often only taken down the mountain at the end of the season.

When the cattle return to the valleys at the end of summer all production of Comté ceases. Instead, they make the equally delicious but very different Vacherin Mont d'Or, now known as Mont d'Or. Both cheeses are governed by the rules of the AOC.

Similar cheeses include Gruyère, Emmental and Beaufort.

ABOVE: Coeur de Camembert au Calvados

CRÈME FRAÎCHE
REGION: *Various*
TYPE: *Traditional, farmhouse and creamery, matured cream*
SOURCE: *Cow's milk*
DESCRIPTION: *Matured cream, rather than cheese, sold in pots*
CULINARY USE: *Wonderful to cook with as it curdles less easily than double (heavy) cream when heated*

Crème fraîche isn't a true cheese. It is a matured cream made by adding a culture to fresh cream. The bacteria, similar to those used to make yogurt, thicken and ripen the cream. The result is a truly delicious and exceedingly smooth cream that is rich and nutty with just a hint of lemony sourness.

ABOVE LEFT: Crème fraîche

ABOVE RIGHT: Crottin de Chavignol

COULOMMIERS
REGION: *Ile-de-France*
TYPE: *Traditional, farmhouse, unpasteurized, soft-white cheese*
SOURCE: *Cow's milk*
DESCRIPTION: *400–500g/14oz–1¼lb disc with white penicillium mould*
CULINARY USES: *Table cheese, canapés*

Smaller than Brie, Coulommiers ripens more quickly. Some prefer to eat it when the white mould is barely discernible, while others prefer it *affiné* (when the aroma is stronger and more like that of ripe Brie). Commercial versions are pleasant, but lack the depth of an unpasteurized cheese, which can be as good as farmhouse Camembert.

The cheese is also known as Brie de Coulommiers or Petit Brie.

CROTTIN DE CHAVIGNOL (AOC)
REGION: *Loire*
TYPE: *Traditional, farmhouse and creamery, unpasteurized, natural-rind cheese*
SOURCE: *Goat's milk*
DESCRIPTION: *60–100g/2¼–3¾oz cylinder with natural rind that ranges from pale ivory to almost black*
CULINARY USES: *Table cheese, snacks, grilling, in salads*

The young cheese has an off-white, slightly wrinkled rind with a mere suggestion of white and blue moulds. At eight days, the cheese has a gentle, aromatic, yeasty taste and a fine, moist texture. At 11 days, the interior softens; the taste is nuttier and full-bodied. At 20 days, the cheese is denser and creamier and there is a fruity tinge to the taste. The flavour intensifies when the cheese is grilled, as it often is. Grilled crottin is the basis of a delicious chévre salad that is popular all over France. If the cheese is allowed to mature further, blue and grey moulds will cover the rind, drawing out the moisture. The result is a small, hard, dark grey disc that justifies the name: Crottin de Chavignol means "horse droppings". The interior develops a fruity, bitter taste. Most crottins are, however, sold young.

ABOVE: Coulommiers

DAUPHIN
REGION: *Nord-Pas-de-Calais*
TYPE: *Traditional, farmhouse and creamery, unpasteurized, semi-soft cheese*
SOURCE: *Goat's milk*
DESCRIPTION: *300–350g/11–12oz dolphin- or brick-shaped cheese with brick-red, washed rind*
CULINARY USE: *Table cheese*

The cheese is said to derive its name from the unusual shape. Usually this resembles a dolphin or fish, although some are small rectangles. A more likely explanation is that when Louis XIV and the Dauphin visited the region and praised the local cheese, the inhabitants settled on both name and shape accordingly.

The brick-red rind gives way to the firm, yet supple interior. Tarragon and pepper are added to the fresh curd, which is then drained and matured. The cheese has a spicy flavour with a yeasty aroma.

DREUX À LA FEUILLE
REGION: *Ile-de-France*
TYPE: *Traditional, farmhouse, unpasteurized, soft-white cheese*
SOURCE: *Cow's milk*
DESCRIPTION: *300–350g/11–12oz round with white penicillium mould rind, enclosed in a chestnut leaf*
CULINARY USE: *Table cheese*

In size and texture, this cheese, being supple and almost runny when ripe, resembles Coulommiers. The chestnut leaf wrapping imparts a nutty, slightly aromatic taste to the cheese, which is generally a good buy.

EPOISSES DE BOURGOGNE (AOC)
REGION: *Burgundy*
TYPE: *Traditional, farmhouse, unpasteurized, washed-rind cheese*
SOURCE: *Cow's milk*
DESCRIPTION: *250g/9oz round cheese with smooth, shiny, brick-red, washed rind*
CULINARY USE: *Table cheese*

Each cheese is "washed" by hand, using a small brush to spread the bacteria over and into the rind. The final wash is alcohol – usually marc de Bourgogne.

Like many of France's best-loved cheeses, Epoisses are enjoyed at different stages of their maturation by different people. Epoisse Frais (30 days) is a mere shadow of its aged counterpart, being firm, moist and grainy, yet still creamy with a fresh acidity and mild yeasty tang.

At 40 days the rind is orange-brown in colour and very sticky. When the outer edges of the cheese are close to collapse, the interior is not far behind. The pungent, spicy aroma is matched by the strong and strangely meaty taste. Unbelievably good, the cheese deserves to be served with a fine Burgundy or a spicy aromatic white wine. Carré de l'Est, Chambertin, Langres and Soumaintrain are all similar cheeses.

ABOVE: Epoisses de Bourgogne

BELOW: Dauphin

ABOVE: Etorki

ETORKI
REGION: *Aquitaine*
TYPE: *Modern, creamery, hard cheese*
SOURCE: *Sheep's milk*
DESCRIPTION: *4kg/9lb fat wheel with reddish-brown, thin, natural rind*
CULINARY USES: *Table cheese, grating, melting*

Until 1984, most of the sheep's milk in this region went to the makers of Roquefort. However, to comply with the strict AOC rules governing the grazing area and the breed of sheep, the region's milk was excluded after that date. Fortunately, the situation was anticipated by Fromagerie des Chaumes (best known for the cheese of the same name). In 1979, they built a factory that now processes most of the sheep's milk in the area into Etorki. The recipe is based on a cheese that has for centuries been made by the local shepherds.

This factory-made cheese has a bright yellow interior, rich texture and a nutty finish and is more close-textured and supple than the handmade original, but it is nevertheless good, with the burnt-caramel sweetness and creamy texture typical of sheep's milk cheeses. As sheep's milk is abundant only from winter to early summer, the factory makes cow's milk cheese – Lou Palou – for the rest of the year.

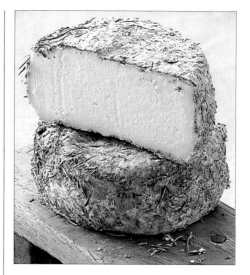

ABOVE: Explorateur

EXPLORATEUR

REGION: *Ile-de-France*
TYPE: *Modern, creamery,*
soft-white cheese
SOURCE: *Cow's milk*
DESCRIPTION: *250g/9oz cylinder with*
soft-white rind
CULINARY USE: *Table cheese*

Invented in the 1950s and named in honour of the first US satellite – Explorer. Explorateur is a firm, creamy cheese with a grainy feel. It has a delicate aroma and a slightly salty, mushroomy tang.

Similar cheeses include Excelsior, Boursault, Brillat-Savarin and Magnum.

FIGUE

REGION: *Aquitaine*
TYPE: *Traditional, farmhouse,*
unpasteurized, fresh cheese
SOURCE: *Goat's milk*
DESCRIPTION: *160–200g/5¼–7oz fresh*
hemispherical cheese
CULINARY USES: *Table cheese, grilling*

Named for its fig shape, this is similar in taste and texture to the wonderful chèvre cheeses found in the Loire, Aquitaine and Périgord areas of France. Mild and pure with a lemony acidity, it is normally dusted with salt and ash, paprika or herbs.

FLEUR DU MAQUIS

REGION: *Corsica*
TYPE: *Traditional, farmhouse,*
unpasteurized, fresh or
natural-rind cheese
SOURCE: *Sheep's milk*
DESCRIPTION: *575–675g/1¼–1½lb*
square cheese with rounded corners.
The natural rind is covered with
chillies, juniper berries, savory
and rosemary
CULINARY USE: *Table cheese*

If the author were asked to identify her favourite cheese, Fleur du Maquis would be near the top of her list. Not merely because it looks so desirable with its covering of wild herbs, peppers and juniper berries, nor because of its aromatic scent, but largely because it is never the same.

Most Corsican cheeses are superb, thanks to the diverse breeds of sheep and goats and the natural grazing. The island is covered with wild thyme, marjoram and the maquis, a scrubby, aromatic bush on which the sheep graze and which gave its name to this exceptional cheese.

When young, Fleur du Maquis is mild, sweet and lemony. Age brings a richness of character (and a string of superlatives): sweet, nutty, aromatic and creamy. The cheese has a melt-in-the-mouth texture.

BELOW: Figue

ABOVE: Fleur du Maquis

FOUGERUS, LE

REGION: *Ile-de-France*
TYPE: *Traditional, farmhouse,*
unpasteurized, soft-white cheese
SOURCE: *Cow's milk*
DESCRIPTION: *1kg/2¼lb thick disc with*
white penicillium mould rind. It is
decorated with a piece of bracken
or fern
CULINARY USE: *Table cheese*

Similar in both size and texture to Coulommiers, this cheese is supple, almost runny when ripe and resembles Dreux à la Feuille. The fern or bracken *fougerus* used to decorate it imparts an earthy charm to the cheese.

FOURME D'AMBERT
REGION: *Auvergne*
TYPE: *Traditional, farmhouse and co-operative, blue cheese*
SOURCE: *Cow's milk*
DESCRIPTION: *1.5–2kg/3¼–4½lb cylinder. The natural, white crust develops patches of red and blue moulds*
CULINARY USE: *Table cheese*

Fourme d'Ambert ("cheese of Ambert") is more supple and dense than most blues. The mould gathers in erratic patches rather than the more usual streaks and the flavour is savoury and nutty. The cheese is easily recognized by its unusually tall, cylindrical shape.

Similar cheeses include Fourme de Montbrison, Bleu de Montbrison, Bleu de Gex and Bleu de Septmoncel.

FRINAULT
REGION: *Orléanais*
TYPE: *Traditional, creamery, unpasteurized, soft-white cheese*
SOURCE: *Cow's milk*
DESCRIPTION: *120–150g/4¼–5oz round with natural rind covered with ash*
CULINARY USE: *Table cheese*

Invented by Monsieur Frinault in 1848 at Chécy, this cheese is similar to a Camembert, but matured in wood ash. It has a slightly firmer, less voluptuous texture and a strong, rather spicy taste. The quality varies, however, and the cheese can be bitter if it is allowed to dry out too much. It is quite difficult to obtain. Also known as Chécy, it is similar to Olivet Cendré.

LEFT: Fourme d'Ambert

RIGHT: Fromage frais

FROMAGE CORSE
REGION: *Corsica*
TYPE: *Traditional, farmhouse, unpasteurized, semi-soft cheese*
SOURCE: *Sheep's and goat's milk*
DESCRIPTION: *500g/1¼lb round. The crusty, washed rind has orange and yellow moulds*
CULINARY USE: *Table cheese*

Made by the local people for the local people, and thus it has remained for centuries. Even the rennet is still obtained by drying the stomach of a young goat, then slicing it and soaking it in water for two days before it is required. This ancient practice, first discovered by nomadic tribes over 2,000 years ago, gives the cheese added depth.

The rough exterior is pungent, with orange and yellow ferments on a pale beige-yellow background. The interior is supple, sometimes almost runny, with small holes. It has a robust flavour redolent of the wild maquis and herbs that grow on the rugged mountains of the island. The cheese is seldom found outside Corsica, except in Paris. It resembles Niolo.

RIGHT: Fromage Corse

FROMAGE FRAIS
REGION: *Various*
TYPE: *Traditional, farmhouse and creamery, fresh cheese*
SOURCE: *Cow's, goat's and sheep's milk*
DESCRIPTION: *Moist, creamy, white, fresh cheese sold in pots*
CULINARY USES: *On fresh fruit, for breakfast, as a spread*

One of the first cheeses made by man, fromage frais is simply milk that has been coagulated using a bacteria culture rather than rennet. High in moisture, it varies little except for the fat content, which ranges from *maigre* (very low) to *allégé* (double) and *triple crème*. The culture used is similar to that for yogurt, but, because it is slower-acting, it produces a citrus tingle rather than an acidic taste. The milk is left for around 12 hours to coagulate, the whey is then drained and the fromage frais is strained for two hours before being potted.

GAPERON
REGION: *Auvergne*
TYPE: *Traditional, farmhouse and co-operative, soft-white cheese*
SOURCE: *Cow's milk*
DESCRIPTION: *250–350g/9–12oz cheese shaped like a small, upturned basin and tied with raffia. It has a soft-white rind dusted with white mould.*
CULINARY USES: *Table cheese, snacks*
Traditionally, this cheese and others like it were made in homes, rather than by cheesemakers. Buttermilk was originally used, although skimmed milk is more often used today. The curds were kneaded with garlic and peppercorns before being pressed into the bowl-shaped moulds, tied with raffia and hung in the kitchen or cellar to dry.

Mild and milky, the cheese has a gentle acidity and spongy, texture. The aroma of the garlic and peppercorns dominate the flavour.

GRATARON D'ARÈCHES
REGION: *Savoie*
TYPE: *Traditional, farmhouse, unpasteurized, washed-rind cheese*
SOURCE: *Goat's milk*
DESCRIPTION: *300–400g/11–14oz thick cylinder with smooth, beige, washed rind*
CULINARY USE: *Table cheese*
Grataron d'Arèches is one of the few washed-rind goat's cheeses of the Savoie, and it is worth looking out for. The leathery, pale beige rind covers an open-textured, white interior with a wonderful scent of almonds and flowers.

RIGHT: Gris de Lille

GRATTE-PAILLE
REGION: *Ile-de-France*
TYPE: *Modern, farmhouse, soft-white cheese*
SOURCE: *Cow's milk*
DESCRIPTION: *300–350g/ 11–12oz brick with natural white mould rind*
CULINARY USES: *Cheeseboards, baked in pastries with chicken and vegetables*
Invented in the 1970s by a creamery in Seine-et-Marne, this cheese takes its name from *gratte* (to scratch) and *paille* (straw), marking the fact that when bales of straw were carried through the narrow streets in summer, pieces of the straw would become wedged in the walls along the way. Some of the cheeses are sold on small straw mats.

The cheese is very good. Rich and exceedingly creamy, it has a pleasant mushroomy flavour. With age comes a slight sharpness.

LEFT: Gaperon

RIGHT: Gratte-Paille

GRIS DE LILLE
REGION: *Nord-Pas-de-Calais*
TYPE: *Traditional, farmhouse, and creamery, unpasteurized, washed-rind cheese*
SOURCE: *Cow's milk*
DESCRIPTION: *700g–1kg/1lb 9oz–2¼lb square with sticky, pinkish-grey, washed rind*
CULINARY USES: *Table cheese, snacks*
Gris de Lille is also known as Puant de Lille or Puant Macéré. The word *puant* means obnoxious or stinking – a term of endearment to those who love the rich flavour of this pungent cheese with its distinctive farmyard aroma. The cheese is similar to Maroilles, although the curing process is different.

LA TAUPINIÈRE

REGION: *Poitou-Charentes*

TYPE: *Traditional, farmhouse, unpasteurized, natural-rind cheese*

SOURCE: *Goat's milk*

DESCRIPTION: *225–250g/8–9oz dome-shaped cheese. The wrinkled, natural rind has a delicate, blue mould*

CULINARY USES: *Table cheese, grilling*

La Taupinière means molehill, which aptly describes this unusually shaped cheese. Quite dense, it is ripened for two to three weeks and is deliciously nutty, with a fresh, lemony tang.

LA VACHE QUI RIT

REGION: *Various*

TYPE: *Modern, creamery, processed cheese*

SOURCE: *Cow's milk*

DESCRIPTION: *Small disc with bright red, waxed rind*

CULINARY USES: *Snacks, lunch boxes*

The slightly supercilious face of La Vache qui Rit – the laughing cow – is seen on the walls of the Metro, and in supermarkets across France. It may well laugh, for it seems so unlikely that this sweet, bland, buttery, processed cheese should have become a household name in a country famous for its magnificent, pungent cheeses. The tiny discs are a favourite snack with children and adults alike.

LAGUIOLE (AOC)

REGION: *Auvergne*

TYPE: *Traditional, farmhouse, unpasteurized, hard cheese*

SOURCE: *Cow's milk*

DESCRIPTION: *30–50kg/65–110lb cylinder. The hard, mottled brown-grey, natural rind carries the distinctive, red lettering proclaiming its AOC status*

CULINARY USES: *Table cheese, snacks, grating, grilling*

With an ancient pedigree (the cheese was certainly made in the fourth century BC and was earlier described by Pliny the Elder), Laguiole has a supple to firm texture. Not as compact as the classic English Cheddar, it has a light, musty aroma that can be quite penetrating when the cheese is fully aged. The straw-yellow interior has

ABOVE: Laguiole

a creamy feel and a taste reminiscent of cheese and onion quiche.

Over the years, economics and the disinclination of sons to follow in the footsteps of their cheesemaking fathers have led to changes in the production of the cheese. The Holstein cow, a prolific milker, was brought in to replace the native Aubrac breed. The number of traditional cheesemakers or *buronniers* has dramatically reduced. At the beginning of this century there were more than a thousand *buronniers*; today there are only four or five producing the cheese.

Laguiole is still a great cheese, especially if you buy one made from *transhumance* milk (produced between late May and mid October, when cows are taken up to the mountain pastures that are covered in gentians, violets, broom and wild herbs). Many people hope that a growing awareness of the need to retain the old ways, coupled with a little assistance from the AOC, will mean that the character of this wonderful, old French cheese will not be lost in the race for progress.

RIGHT: Langres

LANGRES (AOC)

REGION: *Champagne-Ardennes*

TYPE: *Traditional, farmhouse, and co-operative, unpasteurized, washed-rind cheese*

SOURCE: *Cow's milk*

DESCRIPTION: *180g or 800g/6¼oz or 1¾lb concave cone or cylinder with washed rind ranging from orange and sticky to brick-red and dry*

CULINARY USES: *Table cheese, also baked and used as a dip for vegetables*

Monks who passed through the region during the Middle Ages probably introduced this cheese. The shape is unusual – a cone or cylinder with a hollow in the top. To form the hollow, the curd is turned only twice during draining. The weight of the whey, and its movement through the curd, causes the centre to subside.

The brightly coloured rind is the result of continual washing; orange bacteria grow on the surface, as well as some white flora or yeasts.

The cheese is notable for its pungent, smoky-bacon aroma. When young, the texture is firm and grainy. With age, the rind starts to break down and becomes smooth-flowing and creamy. The flavour intensifies. Some affineurs pour eau-de-vie into the crater. This gradually seeps into the cheese, adding a new dimension to an already powerful flavour.

ABOVE: *Laruns*

LARUNS

REGION: *Pyrénées*
TYPE: *Traditional, farmhouse, unpasteurized, hard cheese*
SOURCE: *Sheep's milk*
DESCRIPTION: *5–6kg/11–13lb flattened round loaf with smooth, thin, yellow to ochre, natural rind*
CULINARY USES: *Table cheese, snacks, cooking (when aged)*

Named after the local market town, this cheese has been made by shepherds in mountain huts for generations and is now produced by Ossau Valley. When young, it has a supple texture and is mild and nutty; as it ages it becomes hard and brittle, with a sharper flavour. At six months it is best for grating and cooking.

LE FIUM'ORBO

REGION: *Corsica*
TYPE: *Traditional, farmhouse, unpasteurized, semi-soft cheese*
SOURCE: *Sheep's and goat's milk*
DESCRIPTION: *400–450g/ 14oz–1lb round cheese with natural rind*
CULINARY USE: *Table cheese*

A farmhouse version of Fromage Corse, this has a pungent nose but a more delicate taste, suggesting herbs and flowers. It is an ancient cheese, which has been made by the shepherds for centuries.

LE BRIN

REGION: *Savoie*
TYPE: *Modern, creamery, semi-soft, vegetarian cheese*
SOURCE: *Cow's milk*
DESCRIPTION: *150g/5oz small, hexagonal cheese with natural, thin, reddish-orange rind dusted with white penicillium mould*
CULINARY USE: *Table cheese*

Le Brin was created by Fromagerie Guilloteau in the 1980s as a milder version of the traditional French washed-rind cheeses. It is made by the ultrafiltration method rather than by using rennet to separate the curd from the whey. This gives a higher yield of solids per litre of milk, which means the production costs are lower than when traditional cheese-making methods are employed. *Brin* means a wisp, a breath or a twig – something small or light. The cheese is velvety smooth, like English custard, and has a mild, sweet, almost perfumed aroma and taste. It resembles its soft-white-rinded cousin, Pavé d'Affinois.

Le Terroir is a similar cheese.

ABOVE: *Le Brin*

ABOVE: *Le Roulé*

LE ROULÉ

REGION: *Loire*
TYPE: *Modern, creamery, fresh cheese*
SOURCE: *Cow's milk*
DESCRIPTION: *Logs of various sizes, rolled in fresh herbs*
CULINARY USES: *Table cheese, baking, spreading*

The now familiar logs of Le Roulé with their distinctive green swirl of herbs and garlic, were first introduced in the mid-1980s by Fromagerie Triballat, with the aim of attracting attention to cheese counters in supermarket delicatessens. An overnight success, Le Roulé was rapidly joined by Roulé Light and miniature Roulé logs with numerous exotic combinations: salmon and dill; chives and even strawberry. These may not be to everyone's taste, but attention to quality and an excellent marketing campaign have ensured the success of this new cheese. Its melt-in-the-mouth texture and refreshing herb and garlic layer practically guarantees that first-time consumers will come back for more.

RIGHT: Livarot

MAMIROLLE
REGION: *Franche-Comté*
TYPE: *Modern, creamery, washed-rind cheese*
SOURCE: *Cow's milk*
DESCRIPTION: *500–675g/1¼–1½lb brick. The finely ridged, orange, washed rind can be slightly damp*
CULINARY USES: *Table cheese, grilling*

The author first tasted Mamirolle at Besançon, where she shared it with the cheesemaker, one of the students at the Ecole Nationale d'Industrie Laitière de Besançon-Mamirolle, where it is made as part of their hands-on experience. She reports as follows: "The supple, smooth interior is encased with a fine, orange rind with a sweet-sour, faintly smoked aroma and taste, although the occasional batch can be as robust and enthusiastic as the students, particularly if it is made towards the end of their academic year!"

The cheese is produced in the department of Doubs and is similar to Limburger.

MAROILLES (AOC)
REGION: *Flanders*
TYPE: *Traditional, farmhouse and creamery, unpasteurized, semi-soft cheese*
SOURCE: *Cow's milk*
DESCRIPTION: *700g/1lb 9oz square cheese with brick-red, smooth, washed rind*
CULINARY USES: *Table cheese, snacks and pies, especially the local goyère*

This is regarded as the forefather of all the Trappist cheeses. It was first made in the tenth century at the Abbaye de Maroilles in northern France, where St Hubert, the patron saint of cheese, is buried.

The cheese has a thickish, damp, brick-red rind with fine ridges. The interior is pale yellow, bouncy and porous, not supple and dense like many similar cheeses. The aroma – powerful and aromatic, with a suggestion of fermenting fruit – is stronger than the flavour, which is sweet-sour in character, with perhaps a hint of smoky bacon. The cheeses can be ripened for up to four months, although many are sold too young, when they are still chalky in the centre and have bitter rinds.

Similar cheeses include Baguette Laonnaise, Dauphin and Gris de Lille.

LIVAROT (AOC)
REGION: *Normandy*
TYPE: *Traditional, farmhouse and creamery, unpasteurized, semi-soft cheese*
SOURCE: *Cow's milk*
DESCRIPTION: *250g/9oz or 450g/1lb round cheese. The smooth, glossy, brown, washed rind has some white and occasional bluish moulds*
CULINARY USES: *Table cheese, snacks*

This smooth, supple-textured cheese is washed to encourage the orange ferments to grow. These days the wash is a flavourless natural dye, annatto, which may be one of the reasons the cheese is less pungent than it used to be. Heavy in the mouth, it leaves a spicy taste on the finish.

Livarot is jokingly called "the colonel" because of the stripes of sedge grass (today, more often orange plastic) that encircle the cheese. Originally made by the monks in the area, nowadays most Livarot is produced in factories, but the AOC regulations should help to maintain its ancestry.

MÂCONNAIS
REGION: *Burgundy*
TYPE: *Traditional, farmhouse and co-operative, unpasteurized, natural-rind cheese*
SOURCE: *Cow's and goat's milk*
DESCRIPTION: *50–60g/2–2¼oz truncated cone with natural, fine white to pale blue rind*
CULINARY USES: *Table cheese, grilling, in salads*

Small and elegant, this cheese can be made from cow's or goat's milk – or a mixture – depending on the season. When young, it has a dense, flaky interior with a rind of blue and white moulds. The subtle hint of tarragon in the flavour recalls the fruitiness of a young Chardonnay, and the cheese is the perfect partner for a Mâcon white wine. The locals prefer the cheese when it is brittle, almost rancid, savouring it with a generous glass of the local Burgundy or a Beaujolais.

RIGHT: Maroilles

MIMOLETTE FRANÇAISE

REGION: *Flanders*
TYPE: *Traditional, creamery, hard cheese*
SOURCE: *Cow's milk*
DESCRIPTION: *2–4kg/4 1/2–9lb sphere. The natural rind ranges in colour from yellow-orange to light brown, and is pitted, dry and hard*
CULINARY USES: *Table cheese, snacks, canapés, grating*

This cheese originated in Holland and was probably introduced into France when Flanders was part of that country. Basically, it is a matured Edam that is allowed to ripen for around six to nine months, by which time it becomes so hard and brittle that pieces have to be chiselled off in granite-like chunks. Intensely fruity, with a mouth-puckering tang, it is popular as a cooking cheese, and as a snack to eat with a glass of beer. When young (four to six months), the cheese is firm, compact and slightly oily, with a subtle, fruity aroma and a mellow, nutty taste. Most Mimolette is, however, eaten when aged (*vieux* or *étuvé*).The bright, deep tangerine colour of the cheese is due to the natural dye, annatto.

Mimolette Française is also known as Boule de Lille.

BELOW: Mimolette

MONT D'OR/VACHERIN HAUT-DOUBS (AOC)

REGION: *Franche-Comté*
TYPE: *Traditional, farmhouse and co-operative, unpasteurized, washed-rind cheese*
SOURCE: *Cow's milk (Montbéliard and Pie Rouge de l'Est)*
DESCRIPTION: *500g–1kg/1 1/4–2 1/4lb round with a wrinkled, pale-brownish pink, washed rind, dusted with fine, white mould. The cheese is encircled with a band of spruce bark and set in a wooden box*
CULINARY USE: *Table cheese*

In the days when the borders of France and Switzerland were less well defined, the local soft, washed cheese was called Vacherin Mont d'Or, regardless of which side of the mountain it came from. Later, the Swiss (who produce the pasteurized version) laid claim to the name, and the unpasteurized French Vacherin became simply Mont d'Or or Vacherin Haut-Doubs.

A good Mont d'Or has an aroma of chopped wood and mountain flowers, with a faint hint of fermentation and resin. The texture is full and creamy and the flavour suggests wild herbs. Production begins on 15 August, when the cows return from the mountain pastures. The cheese is available only from the end of September through to 31 March. At the moment it may not be exported. Summer milk is taken to one of the local co-operatives to create another great French cheese – Gruyère de Comté.

To check if the cheese is ripe, press gently on the rind. As the soft, runny cheese flows away from the pressure you should see a gentle wave. Carefully remove the "lid" or rind using a sharp knife, then carefully fold back the "lid", scraping off any soft cheese attached. Scoop a dollop of cheese on to a chunk of country bread, and enjoy a superb treat, preferably with a glass of good wine.

Other French Vacherin cheeses include d'Abondance and des Beauges.

BELOW: Morbier

MORBIER

REGION: *Franche-Comté*
TYPE: *Traditional, farmhouse and creamery, unpasteurized, semi-soft cheese*
SOURCE: *Cow's milk*
DESCRIPTION: *5–9kg/11–20lb wheel. The yellow-brown or pale grey rind is thick, moist and leathery*
CULINARY USES: *Table cheese, snacks, grilling, slicing*

Made during the winter months on the lower reaches of the Jura Mountains, Morbier has a horizontal band of wood ash and salt through its centre. The mixture was originally sprinkled over the fresh curds made from the morning milking, left during the day, then covered with the curds from the evening milking. Nowadays the ash layer is more likely to be food colouring, and is purely decorative.

The cheese is elastic and springy, with a pungent, yeasty aroma and a sweet, fruity taste. Traditionally, a half-wheel of Morbier would be propped up by the fire. As it started to melt, the cheese would be scraped on to crusty bread or hot potatoes.

Factory-made versions tend to be bland and odourless, but are excellent for melting.

RIGHT: Münster (bottom) and the smaller, Münster Géromé (top)

MUNSTER/MUNSTER GÉROMÉ (AOC)

REGION: *Alsace*
TYPE: *Traditional, farmhouse and creamery, unpasteurized, washed-rind cheese*
SOURCE: *Cow's milk (Vosgiennes)*
DESCRIPTION: *120g/4¼oz; 450g/1lb; 1.5kg/3–3½lb rounds. The sticky, washed rind ranges in colour from yellow-orange to russet*
CULINARY USES: *Table cheese, snacks, grilling*

The Vosges mountains are the backbone of Alsace and home to one of the smelliest and most delicious cheeses on earth. Those made in Alsace are called Munster, while the smaller versions from Lorraine are known as Géromé.

The cheese owes its unique character to the unspoilt pastures of Alsace and the Vosgiennes cows, renowned for giving high-protein milk.

The cheese is constantly rubbed with brine over a period of two to three months. This causes the rind to develop its rich colour and the aroma to intensify.

Don't let the smell put you off. The cheese is wonderful – supple, with a flavour that is both sweet and savoury (almost yeasty), and an intense, spicy, aromatic finish. It is traditional to enjoy the cheese with boiled potatoes, cumin seeds and a glass of local wine.

Munster au Cumin is a popular variation. Langres is a similar cheese, as of course is Géromé.

MUROL

REGION: *Auvergne*
TYPE: *Traditional, creamery, semi-soft cheese*
SOURCE: *Cow's milk*
DESCRIPTION: *450–500g/1–1¼lb ring. The thin, smooth, washed rind is mottled pinkish-yellow*
CULINARY USES: *Table cheese, cheese puffs*

This cheese was invented by Monsieur Jules Bérioux, a local affineur. In the 1930s, M Bérioux decided to stamp out a central hole from several young Saint-Nectaire cheeses, ripen the rings and call them Grand Murols, after one of the villages in the area. The cheese is simple and uncomplicated. Supple, creamy and very smooth, it has the sweetness of fresh milk with a delicious, nutty aroma and taste. The unique shape adds a little *je ne sais quoi* to any cheeseboard and the taste appeals to every palate.

The stamped-out holes are not wasted, but are made into Murolait or Le Trou de Murol. These tiny, cork-shaped treats are very soft, but are held in check by a coating of bright red wax. They resemble La Vache qui Rit, but have more flavour.

NANTAIS

REGION: *Brittany*
TYPE: *Traditional, creamery, washed-rind cheese*
SOURCE: *Cow's milk*
DESCRIPTION: *175–200g/6–7oz square cheese with smooth, straw to ochre, washed rind*
CULINARY USE: *Table cheese*

Brittany has no native cheeses and had to wait until the early 1790s for a young priest who was on the run from the French Revolution to introduce cheese-making. This cheese, also known as Curé de Nantais or Fromage de Curé, celebrates that fact. A small, sticky, washed-rind cheese, it has a pungent, yeasty rind. The voluptuous, creamy interior has a rich, smoky-bacon taste and spicy finish. Nantais can be rather good and deserves a weighty Pinot Noir or a strong-tasting Gewurztraminer wine for company.

Carré de l'Est Lavée is a similar cheese.

NEUFCHÂTEL (AOC)

REGION: *Normandy*
TYPE: *Traditional, farmhouse and creamery, soft-white cheese*
SOURCE: *Cow's milk*
DESCRIPTION: *100–200g/3¾–7oz cheeses in various shapes, with natural, downy, white rind, which develops reddish pigmentation*
CULINARY USES: *Table cheese, snacks*

Unlike other soft-white-rinded cheeses, Neufchâtel has a grainy texture. Although it has the aroma and taste of mushrooms, it is also quite sharp and salty. Some lovers of this cheese prefer it when it has been kept until the rind develops reddish pigmentation and a smell of ammonia. At this stage the taste is bitter, salty and acrid.

Neufchâtel is available in various shapes, such as squares, rounds, logs, hearts, loaves and cylinders. Some are available unpasteurized. Gournay is a similar cheese.

LEFT: Neufchâtel – a soft-white cheese with a pleasant, grainy texture

OLIVET AU FOIN
REGION: *Orléanais*
TYPE: *Modern, farmhouse, unpasteurized, soft-white cheese*
SOURCE: *Cow's milk*
DESCRIPTION: *250g/9oz round with soft, dry rind decorated with fine strands of hay*
CULINARY USE: *Table cheese*

Similar to Camembert, but milder and not as soft when ripe, Olivet au Foin is decorated with fine strands of hay *(foin)*, whose scent is absorbed into the cheese.

OLIVET BLEU
REGION: *Orléanais*
TYPE: *Traditional, farmhouse, unpasteurized, blue cheese*
SOURCE: *Cow's milk*
DESCRIPTION: *300g/11oz disc with blue-white, natural rind*
CULINARY USE: *Table cheese*

Slightly grainy, with a distinct aroma and taste of mushrooms and a salty finish, Olivet Bleu resembles a mild Camembert. "Bleu" refers to the rind, which is so white that it has a blue tinge – like whiter-than-white washing!

OLIVET CENDRÉ
REGION: *Orléanais*
TYPE: *Traditional, farmhouse, unpasteurized, soft-white cheese*
SOURCE: *Cow's milk*
DESCRIPTION: *250–300g/9–11oz round with ash-grey, natural rind*
CULINARY USES: *Table cheese, snacks*

Olivet Cendré resembles Olivet au Foin, but is cured for three months in wood ash from vines. This gives it a more supple texture and a fairly pungent, spicy aroma. Similar cheeses include Vendôme Cendré and the Cendrés of Champagne and the Ardennes.

OSSAU-IRATY-BREBIS PYRÉNÉES (AOC)
REGION: *Pyrénées*
TYPE: *Traditional, farmhouse, unpasteurized, semi-soft cheeses*
SOURCE: *Sheep's milk*
DESCRIPTION: *2–7kg/4½–15¼lb wheels with natural rind*
CULINARY USES: *Table cheese, grating, soups*

A number of *fermier* (farmhouse), artisan, co-operative and industrial cheeses made in the rugged and majestic Béarn and Basque regions come under this AOC umbrella. The regulations state that the affinage for the mountain sheep's milk cheeses must be at least 60 days for the small and 90 days for the larger ones. Coagulation can only be from rennet, and no milk may be used until 20 days after lambing. These and other conditions must be met before any cheese can carry the AOC label. Those that do not conform must be sold as simple Fromage de Brebis.

Transhumance (the moving of cows in summer to mountain pastures) is still a way of life for the shepherds of this region. The cheeses are still made in small mountain chalets – *kaiolar* – and the hills ring with the sound of the bells worn by the black-faced Manech sheep as they wander across landscapes of spectacular natural beauty.

Other cheeses in this group include Matocq, Ardi-Gasna and Abbaye de Belloc.

ABOVE: Ossau-Iraty-Brebis Pyrénées

PALET DE BABLIGNY
REGION: *Loire*
TYPE: *Traditional, farmhouse, unpasteurized, soft-white cheese*
SOURCE: *Cow's milk*
DESCRIPTION: *100g/3¾oz oval with fine, white penicillium mould rind*
CULINARY USE: *Table cheese*

This tiny cheese packs a lot of punch for its size. Hard and flaky in texture, it has a flavour like that of a fruity, mature Cheddar, yet it melts like chocolate in the mouth and has a hint of chèvre.

ABOVE: Olivet au Foin (left) and Olivet Cendré (right)

ABOVE: Pavé d'Affinois

RIGHT: Pélardon

PAVÉ D'AFFINOIS
REGION: *Lyonnais*
TYPE: *Modern, creamery, soft-white, vegetarian cheese*
SOURCE: *Cow's milk*
DESCRIPTION: *150g/5oz square with ridged penicillium rind*
CULINARY USE: *Table cheese*

This was one of the first cheeses to be made commercially using ultrafiltration – a method of extracting the solids from liquid milk, which gives a much higher yield of solids than when traditional means are used. No rennet is required for the cheese-making process, only a culture to encourage the lactic fermentation. The technique, together with the packaging and promotion of Pavé d'Affinois and its stablemates Le Brin and Chèvre d'Affinois, has led to excellent sales, but it is to be hoped that this method of preparation is not adopted for the traditional cheeses of Europe.

When young, Pavé d'Affinois is grainy, mildly scented and virtually tasteless apart from a slight hint of mushrooms from the rind. However, if it is allowed to ripen in a warm, humid cellar for two to three weeks, the interior of the cheese literally melts, retaining a firm, slightly chalky centre the size of a quail's egg. The taste is similar to Brie and has hints of Granny Smith apples.

RIGHT: Pavé d'Auge – so-named because it is shaped like "pavé", the squarish French cobble stones

PAVÉ D'AUGE
REGION: *Normandy*
TYPE: *Traditional, farmhouse, unpasteurized, semi-soft cheese*
SOURCE: *Cow's milk*
DESCRIPTION: *675–800g/1½–1¾lb square cheese. The russet-yellow rind can be dry or washed. It is sometimes covered with a white mould*
CULINARY USE: *Table cheese*

Pavé is the name given to the roughly square cobblestones you still see in old marketplaces in France. It is a charming name for this supple, creamy cheese, with its reddish rind. The aroma suggests cool cellars. The flavour is earthy and spicy, but it can be a little bitter.

PÉLARDON
REGION: *Languedoc-Roussillon*
TYPE: *Traditional, farmhouse, unpasteurized, fresh cheese*
SOURCE: *Goat's milk*
DESCRIPTION: *60–100g/2¼–3¾oz disc. The thin, wrinkled, natural rind has white and pale blue moulds*
CULINARY USES: *Table cheese, grilling*

Softer and more mousse-like than most goat's milk cheeses when young, the flavour of Pélardon suggests sour cream infused with walnut oil, balanced by a gentle, salty finish. When aged, the wrinkled, mould-covered rind has a distinct goaty aroma and an intense, Brazil-nut sweetness. The texture is somewhat drier, but the cheese is still very creamy in the mouth.

Pélardon is made in several areas in the Languedoc region and is currently being considered for inclusion among the AOC cheeses of France.

Similar cheeses include Pélardon des Cevennes, Pélardon d'Altières and Pélardon des Corbières.

BELOW: Pérail

PÉRAIL
REGION: *Rouergue*
TYPE: *Traditional, farmhouse, unpasteurized, natural-rind cheese*
SOURCE: *Sheep's milk*
DESCRIPTION: *80–120g/3¼–4¼oz disc. The soft, wrinkled, natural rind is a pale straw colour with a pinkish tinge*
CULINARY USE: *Table cheese*

This *fermier* (farmhouse) or artisan cheese has the softest, most delicate of rinds with a nutty aroma. Inside is an even softer, toffee-like centre with the freshness of meadow flowers. The sweet taste of the sheep's milk makes you wish you had bought two – or even three.

BELOW: Picodon

PETIT-SUISSE
REGION: *Various*
TYPE: *Traditional, farmhouse and creamery, fresh cheese*
SOURCE: *Cow's milk*
DESCRIPTION: *30g/1¼oz cylinder without rind*
CULINARY USES: *Eaten as a snack with fruit, honey or nuts; also used as the basis of several traditional French desserts*

Normally sold in trays of six, this mousse-like fresh cheese was invented in the late nineteenth century by Charles Gervais, a Swiss cheesemaker. He decided to make a variation on the local cheese, Neufchâtel, by adding cream to the fresh curd and selling the result before the soft white rind could develop.

The light, yet creamy texture and charming shape made Petit-Suisse a major success. It is now produced throughout France, although the fat content and quality vary as much as the recipe.

PICODON DE L'ARDÈCHE/PICODON DE LA DRÔME (AOC)
REGION: *Rhône-Alpes*
TYPE: *Traditional, farmhouse and creamery, unpasteurized, natural-rind cheese*
SOURCE: *Goat's milk*
DESCRIPTION: *50–100g/2–3¾oz round with natural rind that ranges in colour from pale ivory to soft white or pale blue-grey*
CULINARY USES: *Table cheese, grilling, baking, fromage fort*

The lower end of the Rhône Valley is too dry for the cultivation of vines, but is ideal for the hardy goats, which attack the tufts of grass and scented scrub with the sort of enthusiasm we might reserve for a gastronomic feast. The milk they yield is the basis of a cheese that varies from area to area, but seldom disappoints. The thin rind has the scent of stone cellars and the hard, compact interior is aromatic. The cheeses are occasionally packed with herbs in jars of the local green olive oil.

Picodon cheeses are very similar to the Pélardon cheeses of the Languedoc-Roussillon region further south.

ABOVE: Pithiviers

PITHIVIERS AU FOIN
REGION: *Orléanais*
TYPE: *Traditional, farmhouse, unpasteurized, soft-white cheese*
SOURCE: *Cow's milk*
DESCRIPTION: *300g/11oz round cheese with soft-white rind rolled in strands of hay or grass*
CULINARY USE: *Table cheese*

Similar to Camembert, Pithiviers au Foin has a mild, milky, caramel flavour. The fine, white rind is delicately rolled in wisps of hay or grass. As such, it resembles Olivet au Foin.

POIVRE D'ANE

REGION: *Provence-Alpes-Côte d'Azur*
TYPE: *Traditional, farmhouse, unpasteurized, natural-rind cheese*
SOURCE: *Cow's, sheep's or goat's milk*
DESCRIPTION: *100–120g/3³/₄–4¹/₄oz round cheese. The natural rind is white with a hint of blue or yellow. It is traditionally covered with a sprig of wild savory*
CULINARY USES: *Table cheese, grilling, fromage fort*

This dense, fine-grained cheese has a lovely, aromatic scent and flavour. Any variation comes from the source of the milk: sheep's milk in spring and early summer; goat's milk from the end of spring to the start of autumn; cow's milk virtually all year round.

Banon is a similar cheese.

PONT L'EVÊQUE (AOC)

REGION: *Normandy*
TYPE: *Traditional, farmhouse and creamery, unpasteurized, semi-soft cheese*
SOURCE: *Cow's milk*
DESCRIPTION: *350–400g/12–14oz finely ridged square with greyish-yellow, washed rind*
CULINARY USE: *Table cheese*

This is probably one of the oldest cheeses of Normandy, an area

RIGHT: Pouligny-Saint-Pierre – due to its shape, this elegant, traditional goat's cheese has earned several nick-names. The two most often used are "the pyramid" or "Eiffel Tower"

renowned for the lushness of its pastures. The small Normandy cow has produced some of the greatest French cheeses, including Camembert, Livarot, Pavé d'Auge and Boursin.

Pont l'Evêque is said to have originated in an abbey, though there appears to be no evidence to substantiate this. Despite being granted its AOC status in 1976 to protect its history and good name, only around 2 or 3 per cent of the cheese is *fermier* (farmhouse) made; the majority comes from just two large producers. To comply with AOC regulations and achieve the authentic taste and texture, the cheese must be regularly washed, brushed and turned to encourage the special bacteria to grow on the rind. The milk used for Pont l'Evêque must come from the local area and the curd must be kneaded before it is drained.

The aroma of the cheese has been likened to damp washing, mouldy cellars and farmyards, but the taste is deliciously savoury and piquant, with just a trace of sweetness and a robust tang on the finish. The texture is springy and open and the cheese glistens, thanks to the richness of the milk.

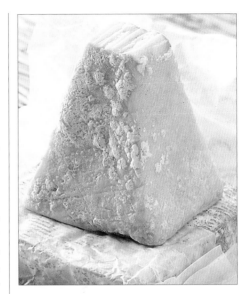

POULIGNY-SAINT-PIERRE (AOC)

REGION: *Berry*
TYPE: *Traditional, farmhouse and creamery, unpasteurized, natural-rind cheese*
SOURCE: *Goat's milk*
DESCRIPTION: *250g/9oz truncated pyramid with soft, wrinkled, ivory-coloured, natural rind. When this dries out, the wrinkles deepen and grey, white and blue moulds gather. A red label indicates that it is made in a dairy, while a green label means it is farmhouse-made*
CULINARY USES: *Table cheese, grilling, in salads*

Named after the eponymous village, this cheese has earned various nicknames because of its shape, the most common of which is "the pyramid". To many people it epitomizes chèvre: wonderfully rustic, yet elegant. The rind is soft and ivory-coloured when the cheese is young. As it ages and dries, the rind becomes reddish-orange and acquires an array of beautiful moulds, providing a magnificent contrast to the firm, pure white, slightly grainy interior.

The first impression is a heady mix of goat, fresh hay and mould. Tasting reveals a complexity of flavours, including herbaceous plants (especially tarragon) and white wine, and a texture that is both creamy and nutty. Like a fine wine, once tasted Pouligny-Saint-Pierre is never forgotten.

ABOVE: Pont l'Evêque

RACLETTE

REGION: *Savoie*

TYPE: *Traditional, farmhouse and creamery, unpasteurized, semi-soft cheese*

SOURCE: *Cow's milk*

DESCRIPTION: *7–8kg/15¹/4–18lb round or square cheese with smooth pink to deep orange, slightly sticky, natural rind*

CULINARY USES: *Sliced and grilled on potatoes or blanched vegetables*

Raclette is an ancient mountain cheese common to the Savoie region in France and the canton of Valais in Switzerland. Although the cheese has a pleasant enough flavour, it is not particularly special until it is heated in front of a fire or under a hot grill. Then the full, nutty, sweet and slightly fruity aroma intensifies and the stringy elasticity of the melting cheese makes it truly magnificent. The rind has a farmyard aroma. When grilled it becomes really crunchy and has a wonderful savoury flavour.

Traditionally, a large cheese was cut in half and leant against a stone with the cut surface facing the open fire. The outer layer of the supple interior was allowed to heat up gradually. As soon as it started to crinkle and change colour, a bowl of steaming potatoes would appear, to be smothered in an avalanche of bubbling cheese. The aroma was irresistible and the rich, nutty, sweet flavour of the cheese was the perfect partner for the potatoes. Nowadays, the dish can be created by heating slices of cheese under the grill.

Bagnes and Conches are similar.

Above: Raclette

Right: Rigotte

RIGHT: Reblochon

REBLOCHON (AOC)

REGION: *Haute-Savoie*

TYPE: *Traditional, farmhouse and creamery, unpasteurized, semi-soft cheese*

SOURCE: *Cow's milk*

DESCRIPTION: *240g/8¹/2oz or 550g/1¹/4lb round cheese. The yellow to orange, natural rind has fine, white, powdery mould*

CULINARY USES: *Table cheese, melting*

Not unlike Saint-Nectaire or Tamie, Reblochon has a supple, creamy texture that flows over and caresses the palate. The cheese, made in the factories or by co-operatives (*fruitières*), has a warm, yeasty aroma, with the sweet flavour of freshly crushed walnuts, whereas the farm- (*fermier*-) made cheese is both more intense and more complex, and has a distinct savour of fresh spring grass and wild alpine flowers. Do not be deterred by the farmyard aroma of the rind.

RIGOTTE

REGION: *Auvergne and Lyonnais*

TYPE: *Traditional, creamery, unpasteurized, fresh cheese*

SOURCE: *Cow's or goat's milk*

DESCRIPTION: *70–90g/2³/4–3¹/2oz cylinder. The rind is very lightly coloured with annatto*

CULINARY USES: *Table cheese, grilling, in salads, fromage fort*

Firm and grainy when a few weeks old, with a mild, lemony freshness and slightly bitter finish, Rigotte becomes quite tart if allowed to dry. Some dry cheeses are marinated in aromatic oils flavoured with peppers and fresh herbs. The cheese absorbs the flavours while becoming creamier, and the result is strangely reminiscent of *saucisson* (sausages) or salami.

Rigottes that are matured in humid conditions develop the classic pale blue moulds. They acquire a more nutty character, but still retain a slight bitterness of taste.

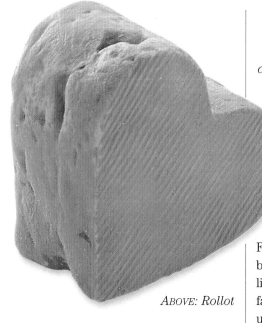

ABOVE: Rollot

ROLLOT

REGION: *Picardy*
TYPE: *Traditional, farmhouse and creamery, unpasteurized, semi-soft cheese*
SOURCE: *Cow's milk*
DESCRIPTION: *280–300g/10¹/₄–11oz round or heart-shaped cheese with grainy, burnt orange, washed rind*
CULINARY USE: *Table cheese*

The cheese takes its name from the village of Rollot. Under the tough, sticky rind, the pale yellow interior is firm yet supple, with a rather pungent, yeasty aroma and taste with a fruity bite on the finish. It can be quite salty and bitter if the rind is allowed to dry out.

BELOW: Roquefort

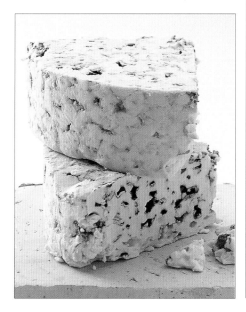

ROQUEFORT (AOC)

REGION: *Rouergue*
TYPE: *Traditional, farmhouse and creamery, unpasteurized, blue cheese*
SOURCE: *Sheep's milk (Lacaune, Manech, Baso-bernaise; also Corsican breeds)*
DESCRIPTION: *2.5–3kg/5¹/₂–6¹/₂lb cylinder with sticky, pale ivory, natural rind. Sold wrapped in foil*
CULINARY USES: *Table cheese, blue cheese dressings, in salads*

For over 2,000 years, shepherds have been maturing their cheeses in the deep limestone caves of Cambalou, which are famous for the blue moulds that exist naturally in the air.

The traditional way of introducing the mould was to allow it to grow on loaves of rye bread placed beside the cheeses in the caves, and a version of this method is still practised by some cheesemakers today. Loaves of the local rye bread are baked especially for the purpose at the start of the season. The bread is left for 70 days to dry and become mouldy, then it is ground to a powder and tiny amounts are sprinkled on the curds before they are placed in the moulds.

Roquefort has a distinct bouquet and a flavour that combines the sweet, burnt-caramel taste of sheep's milk with the sharp, metallic tang of the blue mould. Crumbly, melt-in-the-mouth, refreshing, clean – all these adjectives and more have been used to describe this great cheese.

ROUY

REGION: *Burgundy*
TYPE: *Modern, creamery, washed-rind cheese*
SOURCE: *Cow's milk*
DESCRIPTION: *250g/9oz square cheese with rounded corners. The smooth, terracotta-coloured rind is slightly sticky and may have some white mould*
CULINARY USE: *Table cheese*

This is a commercially made copy of the stronger, more pungent, traditional French washed-rind cheeses like Langres or Epoisses. Nevertheless, it is a good buy.

SALERS (AOC)

REGION: *Auvergne*
TYPE: *Traditional, farmhouse, unpasteurized, hard cheese*
SOURCE: *Cow's milk*
DESCRIPTION: *30–50g/1¹/₄–2oz cylinder with hard, brown, natural rind that becomes rough and crusty with age*
CULINARY USES: *Table cheese, grating, grilling, sauces*

Salers or Fourme de Salers is the *fermier* version of Cantal. Thousands of cheese mites – the sign of a truly great cheese – colonize the thick, brownish-yellow rind, creating a craggy, rock-like surface. The aroma is very meaty, and the rich yellow interior is redolent of wild flowers, including dandelions, and fresh green grass. There is an overlying nutty taste and a strong, savoury, raw-onion bite. Languiole is a similar cheese.

ABOVE: Salers

SANCERRE

REGION: *Loire*
TYPE: *Traditional, farmhouse, unpasteurized, natural-rind cheese*
SOURCE: *Goat's milk*
DESCRIPTION: *120–150g/4¹/₄–5oz round. The natural rind is cream in colour, with soft wrinkles*
CULINARY USES: *Table cheese, grilling, in salads*

This classic chèvre has a fine, wrinkled rind that hardens over time. It has a light, goaty smell and a slightly grainy texture that becomes dense and smooth. There is a fresh "white wine" fruitiness to the young Sancerre and a strong, nutty, goaty taste when aged. The white wine of the region is a perfect partner for the cheese. Similar cheeses include Crottin de Chavignol and Santranges.

SELLES-SUR-CHER (AOC)

REGION: *Loire*

TYPE: *Traditional, farmhouse and creamery, unpasteurized, natural-rind cheese*

SOURCE: *Goat's milk*

DESCRIPTION: *150–200g/5–7oz round cheese. The ash-covered rind gradually develops blotches of grey and blue moulds*

CULINARY USES: *Table cheese, grilling, in salads*

The Loire is famous for its goat's milk cheeses. They come in a wide array of shapes – pyramids, rounds, truncated cones, hearts, logs and cylinders – but all have the same natural, blue-grey rind and many are lightly dusted with wood ash.

Selles-sur-Cher is a classic example. The ash, mixed with coarsely ground salt, is sprinkled over the cheese, adding to its visual appeal while facilitating the draining of the whey. The concept was probably introduced to the Loire in the eighth century, when the Saracen invaders from Spain reached its southern banks. Most of the invaders were later repelled, but some remained with their goats to provide the foundation for these famous chèvres.

SOUMAINTRAIN

REGION: *Burgundy*

TYPE: *Traditional, farmhouse and creamery, unpasteurized, washed-rind cheese*

SOURCE: *Cow's milk*

DESCRIPTION: *350g/12oz round cheese with washed rind. The white of the curd can be seen through the shiny, reddish-brown moulds*

CULINARY USES: *Table cheese, fromage fort*

Quite grainy and moist when young, Soumaintrain has a mild, refreshing lemony flavour. After six weeks in a humid cellar, where it is frequently washed in brine, it begins to resemble its more outspoken cousin, Epoisses. The rind becomes more pungent and it develops a strong, spicy tang and a creamier feel. Soumaintrain is sometimes immersed in ash to make Aisy Cendré, a local speciality. Saint-Florentin is a similar cheese.

BELOW: Sancerre (left) and Selles-sur-Cher (right)

ABOVE: Soumaintrain is often used to make a traditional delicacy called "fromage fort" (strong cheese) – the cheese is steeped in the local wine before if is eaten

SAINT-AGUR

REGION: *Auvergne*

TYPE: *Modern, creamery, blue cheese*

SOURCE: *Cow's milk*

DESCRIPTION: *2kg/4½lb octagonal cylinder with cream-yellow, natural rind with blue-grey moulds*

CULINARY USES: *Table cheese, in salads and dressings*

Created in 1986 by the huge French cheese company Bongrain, Saint-Agur is made from pasteurized milk and has a moist, creamy texture and spicy, blue cheese taste. It is far milder than most other French blue cheeses, with the blue mould evenly spread in patches throughout the cheese. The unique octagonal shape makes this cheese very easy to cut into wedges.

ABOVE: Saint-Agur

ABOVE: Saint-Marcellin

SAINT-NECTAIRE (AOC)

REGION: *Auvergne*
TYPE: *Traditional, farmhouse and creamery, unpasteurized, semi-soft cheese*
SOURCE: *Cow's milk (Salers)*
DESCRIPTION: *1.5kg/3–3¹/₂lb round cheese. The leathery, natural rind is pinkish, with a covering of pale grey mould*
CULINARY USE: *Table cheese*

This soft, voluptuous cheese is cured on a bed of straw for eight weeks, and seems to absorb some of its earthy, pastoral aroma. Like a large version of Reblochon, a cheese from the Savoie, Saint-Nectaire is creamy and rich, redolent of freshly cut grass, sweet hay, wild flowers and herbs.

When selecting a Saint-Nectaire, look out for an oval, green label that declares it to be a *fermier* (farmhouse) cheese made from raw milk. A square, green label is used on factory-made cheeses, which are usually pasteurized.

BELOW: Saint-Nectaire

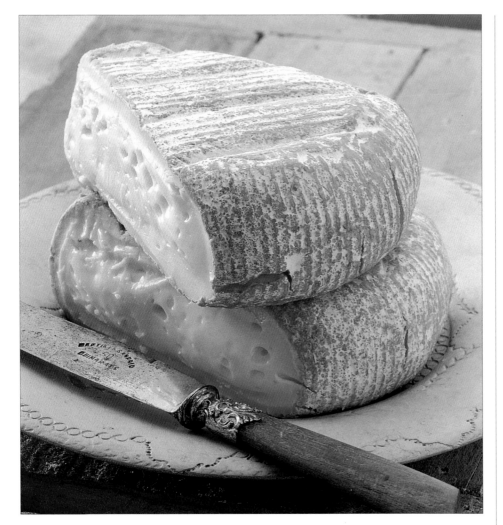

SAINT-ALBRAY

REGION: *Aquitaine*
TYPE: *Modern, creamery, soft-white cheese*
SOURCE: *Cow's milk*
DESCRIPTION: *2kg/4¹/₂lb round cheese with a hole in the centre. The rind is reddish-brown, overlaid with white penicillium mould*
CULINARY USES: *Table cheese, snacks*

Saint-Albray was invented in 1976 to appeal to those who found the flavour of Camembert too strong, but liked that type of cheese. Twenty years later, it is still found in supermarkets around the world. The stable nature of the cheese means that it can survive the rigours of long journeys and cold cabinets.

Ripened for only two weeks, Saint-Albray develops a moist, rubbery texture and has a mild, creamy, undemanding flavour. The shape makes it very practical for serving: round, with a hole in the middle, it is marked into neat sections by indentations in the rind.

ABOVE: Saint-Albray

SAINT-MARCELLIN

REGION: *Rhône-Alpes*
TYPE: *Traditional, farmhouse and creamery, unpasteurized, natural-rind cheese*
SOURCE: *Cow's or goat's milk*
DESCRIPTION: *80g/3¹/₄oz round with wrinkly, natural rind dusted with a coating of white yeast. With age, a delicate, blue mould and red and yellow pigments develop*
CULINARY USES: *Table cheese, fromage fort à la Lyonnaise*

Saint-Marcellin is known to have been served to royalty as early as 1461. In those days it would probably have been made from goat's milk, although cow's milk is often used today. The texture of the young cheese varies from firm to very runny, and it has a mild, slightly salty flavour. When ripe, it is irresistible, with a slightly yeasty taste.

SAINT-PAULIN

REGION: *Various*

TYPE: *Modern, farmhouse and creamery, semi-soft cheese*

SOURCE: *Cow's milk*

DESCRIPTION: *500g–1.5kg/1¼–3½lb or 1.8–2kg/4–4½lb wheel. The thin, washed rind is smooth and leathery. It ranges in colour from pale yellow to bright mandarin orange*

CULINARY USES: *Table cheese, melting, snacks*

Based on the Trappist cheese Port-du-Salut, Saint-Paulin has remained a popular cheese since it was first made in 1930. It was the first French cheese produced from pasteurized milk and has remained so, although one producer decided to buck the trend in 1990 and is making a version made with raw milk. Saint-Paulin has a slightly smoky, sweet-sour aroma and taste.

ABOVE: Tamie

SAINTE-MAURE DE TOURAINE (AOC)

REGION: *Loire*

TYPE: *Traditional, farmhouse, unpasteurized, fresh or natural-rind cheese*

SOURCE: *Goat's milk*

DESCRIPTION: *250g/9oz log rolled in black wood ash. It develops a blotchy, blue-grey rind with age*

CULINARY USES: *Table cheese, grilling, baking*

Saint-Maure is made both on small farms and in large factories throughout Touraine, but the protection afforded by the AOC regulations ensures that the quality is always good. The freshly formed curd is scooped by hand into log-shaped moulds. Farmhouse cheeses have a piece of straw running through the centre. In theory, this makes them easier to pick up; in practice, pulling or lifting the straw often makes the cheese collapse in large chunks.

The ash coating provides a wonderful contrast when the cheese is cut to reveal the stark white interior. Young cheeses are moist and grainy, but as the mould develops the cheese dries, hardens and becomes more dense. Saint-Maure has a lovely musty, citrus flavour that intensifies with age.

ABOVE: Tomme d'Abondance

TAMIE

REGION: *Haute-Savoie*

TYPE: *Traditional, farmhouse, unpasteurized, semi-soft cheese*

SOURCE: *Cow's milk (Montbéliard, La Tarine)*

DESCRIPTION: *500g/1¼lb or 1.3kg/2¾lb round. The fine, leathery, washed rind ranges in colour from pinkish-brown to orange-pink*

CULINARY USE: *Table cheese*

Tamie, made by the monks of the Abbaye de Tamie, has an attractive rind with a sweet, earthy aroma. Underneath, the cheese is a creamy colour. Initially, the taste is sweet, herbaceous and vaguely nutty, followed by a more powerful tang. The rind should be soft and supple; if it is hard and unyielding, the cheese has probably been kept for too long at too low a temperature and will be past its prime. Such a cheese is liable to be highly acidic without the balancing sweetness.

Similar cheeses include Reblochon and Chambarand.

TOMME D'ABONDANCE (AOC)

REGION: *Savoie*

TYPE: *Traditional, farmhouse, unpasteurized, hard cheese*

SOURCE: *Cow's milk*

DESCRIPTION: *5–15kg/11–33lb wheel with brushed, natural, grey rind*

CULINARY USES: *Table cheese, melting*

For centuries, this deep golden cheese has been made in mountain chalets near the border between France and Switzerland. The cheese has a distinct, fruity tang with a hint of yeast. Firm, but supple and slightly grainy, it is made from skimmed milk.

ABOVE: Tamie

TOMME DE ROMANS

REGION: *Dauphine*
TYPE: *Traditional, farmhouse and creamery, unpasteurized, natural-rind cheese*
SOURCE: *Cow's milk*
DESCRIPTION: *200–300g/7–11oz round. The natural rind has fluffy, white and blue-grey mould*
CULINARY USE: *Table cheese*

These attractive little cheeses are traditionally sold in wooden trays lined with straw. They have a slightly sour, grassy flavour with a delicate, nutty finish.

TOMME DE SAVOIE

REGION: *Savoie*
TYPE: *Traditional, farmhouse and creamery, unpasteurized, semi-soft cheese*
SOURCE: *Cow's milk*
DESCRIPTION: *1.5–3kg/3–6¹/₂lb wheel. The thick, furry, grey, natural rind has yellow and orange blotches*
CULINARY USES: *Table cheese, grating, grilling*

An ancient mountain cheese from the Savoie, made in winter when the herdsmen have returned from the summer pastures. In summer, the milk goes with the milk from other herds to become Beaufort, but when the weather worsens and yield drops, the herdsman makes his cheese at home. When searching out the best Tomme, look for "*lait cru*" on the label, the numbers 73 or 74 on an oval, red, casein plaque and the logo of four red hearts and the word "Savoie". Don't be put off by the appearance of the rind. Inside, the pale yellow cheese with its few small holes will be firm, yet supple with a gentle flavour hinting at meadow flowers, milk and walnuts.

ABOVE: Valençay

ABOVE: Tourée de l'Aubier

TOURÉE DE L'AUBIER

REGION: *Normandy*
TYPE: *Modern, creamery, washed-rind cheese*
SOURCE: *Cow's milk*
DESCRIPTION: *200g/7oz or 2kg/4¹/₂lb round. Sticky, leathery, washed rind with powdery, white mould on its orange red surface*
CULINARY USE: *Table cheese*

The spruce bark belt gives this washed-rind cheese a unique flavour. Creamy, sweet, yet pungent, it becomes almost runny when mature. Created as a pasteurized copy of the great French Mont d'Or, it is passable as long as it is ripe.

LEFT: Tomme de Savoie

VALENÇAY

REGION: *Berry*
TYPE: *Traditional, farmhouse and creamery, unpasteurized, natural-rind cheese*
SOURCE: *Goat's milk*
DESCRIPTION: *200–250g/7–9oz truncated pyramid with natural, white rind dusted with charcoal ash. With age, the rind develops blue-grey moulds*
CULINARY USE: *Table cheese*

This elegant pyramid is dusted with fine, black charcoal. When young, the white cheese can be seen through the ash. Gradually, however, the colours merge and blue-grey moulds appear. The taste is at first fresh and citrus-like, but age gives the cheese a nuttier flavour and a distinctly goaty character. The commercially produced version is known as Pyramide.

VIGNOTTE/LES VIGNOTTES

REGION: *Champagne or Lorraine*
TYPE: *Traditional, creamery, soft-white cheese*
SOURCE: *Cow's milk*
DESCRIPTION: *150g/5oz cylinder or 2kg/4¹/₂lb thick disc with thick, velvety, smooth penicillium rind*
CULINARY USES: *Table cheese, grilling*

This very popular, triple-cream cheese has a light, almost mousse-like texture, thanks to the careful ladling of the young curd into the moulds. The flavour is fresh and creamy, slightly lemony and salty.

ITALIAN CHEESES

For more than six centuries Europe was dominated by the Romans. What began as a few farming settlements in the eighth century BC grew into the city of Rome. In the sixth century BC Rome became a republic, governed by a senate, which was made up of representatives from the influential families of the day. The Romans set about conquering the world as they knew it, and by the second century AD the Roman Empire included all the countries that encircled the Mediterranean, stretching as far as the Persian Gulf in the east, to England, France and Spain in the west, and the countries of North Africa.

Cheese played a major role in the diet of the Romans, as it was convenient, compact and travelled well – even in the knapsacks of the legionnaires – and came in numerous forms. One of the earliest mentions of cheeses was by Pliny the Elder, when he referred to the cheesemaking techniques used by shepherds on the outskirts of Rome to make the sheep's milk cheese that was the forefather of Pecorino Romano. In his writings, Columella also referred to cheese and cheesemaking, demonstrating his understanding of the use of rennet, a significant breakthrough in the art.

Cheesemaking skills were recorded and communicated to shepherds and farmers across Europe who, until the arrival of the Romans, had only a rudimentary understanding of the process, and made mainly soft, fermented cheeses preserved in oil or salt.

It was the legions of Julius Caesar who brought the knowledge of how to make hard cheeses to Switzerland in 400BC, laying the foundation for what were to become some of the world's finest cheeses. Some of the classic English and French hard cheeses also owe their origins to Roman cheesemaking skills.

Roquefort was among the earliest cheeses from the provinces to be mentioned by Pliny in around AD40. The stretched curd *(pasta filata)* cheeses, such as Provolone and mozzarella, are thought to have originated, not in Italy, but with the Bedouin tribes of Persia.

LEFT: Bel Paese, one of Italy's most famous semi-soft cheeses, is now also made under licence in the USA

In a recent survey, nearly 400 Italian cheeses were identified. Some have been given the protection of the DOC (a system of control and protection), while others are yet to be included. They rate in quality and diversity alongside the cheeses of France, but whereas in France cheese tends to be served as a separate course, the great Italian cheeses have found fame for the flavour, style and character they give to Italian food. Enormous volumes of Grana Padano, Parmigiano-Reggiano, Provolone and Pecorino are sent around the world.

It is a shame that most consumers use these wonderful hard cheeses purely for cooking. Once you have eaten a freshly cut chunk of Parmigiano-Reggiano or Pecorino Toscano with fresh figs and Parma ham or simply solo, with a glass of Barolo, you will understand why Italians like to refer to these as table cheeses – the implication being that they should be kept on the table to be eaten whenever wanted.

Many of Italy's greatest cheeses are seldom found outside the areas where they are made, let alone beyond Italy's borders, so the best way to discover them is to take a trip through this wonderful country.

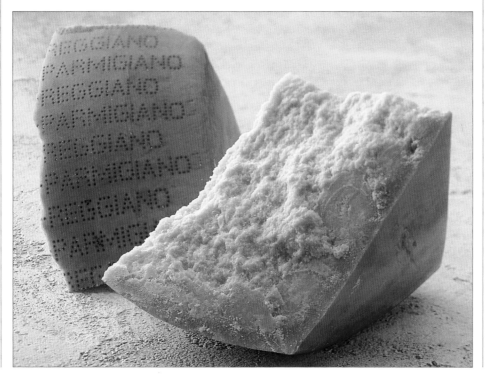

LEFT: Parmigiano-Reggiano

ASIAGO (DOC)

REGION: *Vicenza & Trento*
TYPE: *Traditional, farmhouse and creamery, unpasteurized, hard cheese*
SOURCE: *Cow's milk*
DESCRIPTION: *8–20kg/18–44lb wheel. The natural rind is smooth and glossy. Yellow when young, it deepens to burnt orange*
CULINARY USES: *Table cheese, grating, as a condiment*

Centuries ago, this was a sheep's milk cheese, made by shepherds from the Asiago plateau. However, as sheep gave way to cattle (with their higher milk yields), cow's milk came to be used. There are two distinct types of Asiago. The first is a lightly pressed cheese made from whole milk in small dairies. It is sometimes incorrectly referred to or mistaken for Pressato – a fact that irritates the Asiago producers – and it ripens within 20–30 days. Pale yellow and springy, with a delicate, sweet, undemanding flavour and fragrance, it has achieved

RIGHT: Asiago

significant commercial success with the modern consumer.

Asiago d'Allevo is the mature cheese, and, according to locals, the better form. Although it is made with skimmed milk, the long, slow maturation process creates a fruity, slightly sharp cheese with a compact, granular interior full of small holes. After 12 months it is the colour of liquid honey; after two years it acquires a toffee colour and becomes brittle and intensely flavoured. Like Parmesan cheese, Asiago can, when grated, be used as a condiment.

DOC

Like France, Italy operates a system to protect certain indigenous cheeses. It goes under the acronym DOC (Denominazione di Origine Controllata). In 1955 the Ministry of Agriculture and Forestry, in conjunction with a consortium of cheesemakers, set out to identify suitable candidates for DOC regulation. They agreed standards of production and determined areas where the cheeses in question could be made. So far 26 cheeses have been given the DOC classification, and more will undoubtedly follow.

Identifying and promoting indigenous cheeses in this way helps to protect them from being copied, while guaranteeing the consumer a level of quality. It also brings to the attention of the public artisan cheeses that might otherwise have become extinct.

Inspectors regularly visit the cheesemakers. If a cheese sold under the DOC label fails to comply with the regulations, the producer can be heavily fined and legal action may be taken. The DOC symbol is more than a legal requirement, however. It recognizes that indigenous cheeses and their makers have an important role to play in the nation's history. It also acknowledges the places where the cheeses are traditionally made. DOC status is a matter of pride.

What DOC status does not do is guarantee that every cheese that carries the symbol is perfect (or identical with every other cheese of the same type). The character of an individual cheese will depend upon the grazing, the season and the skills of the cheesemaker. DOC status, however, guarantees an overall standard.

BEL PAESE

REGION: *Lombardy*
TYPE: *Modern, creamery, semi-soft cheese*
SOURCE: *Cow's milk*
DESCRIPTION: *2kg/4¹/₂lb wheel with shiny, golden, waxed rind*
CULINARY USES: *Table cheese, melting; can be used instead of mozzarella*

Dante referred to Italy as "*bel paese*" – beautiful land. This later became the title of a book, which in turn proved the inspiration for Egidio Galbani when he sought a name for his soft and yielding cheese. Bel Paese is ivory in colour and has a delicately sweet flavour that has won the hearts of thousands around the world. The cheese ripens in one to three months. A version is made in the USA under licence.

BRA (DOC)

REGION: *Piedmont*
TYPE: *Traditional, farmhouse and co-operative, unpasteurized, hard cheese*
SOURCE: *Cow's milk*
DESCRIPTION: *8kg/18lb round. The natural rind ranges in colour from pale straw yellow to deep brownish-yellow and has some surface moulds*
CULINARY USES: *Table cheese, grating, melting*

Like Stilton, Bra is named not for where it is made, but for the place where it was originally sold. The people of Bra (in Cuneo, Piedmont) used to buy young cheeses from the herdsmen of the Alpine valleys. These they matured in their own cellars, either for their own consumption or for selling on. If the cheeses were matured for long enough, they could be substituted for the more expensive and less readily available Pecorino.

Today there are two types of Bra, both similar in appearance but cured in different ways. The traditional, hard version is still the most popular. It is matured for three to six months, when the colour darkens and the flavour intensifies.

The cheese is also sold young, at 45 days, when the paste is still soft. This version is made in small dairies, almost always from pasteurized milk; it is disapproved of by traditional producers.

CACIOCAVALLO

REGION: *Southern Italy*
TYPE: *Traditional, farmhouse and creamery, stretched curd cheese*
SOURCE: *Cow's milk*
DESCRIPTION: *2–3kg/4¹/2–6¹/2lb fat, gourd-shaped cheese, tied at the thin end with a cord for hanging. The rind is oily and smooth*
CULINARY USES: *Table cheese, grating, grilling, melting*

This stretched curd (*pasta filata*) cheese is typical of the south of Italy. The origin of the name has long been debated. *Cavallo* means "horse" in Italian, and some say the cheese was originally made from mare's milk. A more logical, but less romantic, explanation is that the name comes from the method of hanging pairs of cheeses over a pole, as if on horseback.

Usually farm-made, the curd is pulled and stretched until it is stringy but no longer breaks. It is then divided into portions, kneaded into shape and matured. At three months the Caciocavallo is sweet and supple and eaten as a table cheese. Some though are matured for up to two years, when they can be grated. The interior is golden-yellow and close-textured, the aroma is intense and lingering, and the taste is full but mellow. Caciocavallo is sometimes made with a lump of butter in the middle, which oozes out when the cheese is cut. There are also smoked versions.

CANESTRATO PUGLIESE (DOC)

REGION: *Foggia*
TYPE: *Traditional, farmhouse, unpasteurized, hard cheese*
SOURCE: *Sheep's milk (Merino or Apulian Gentile)*
DESCRIPTION: *7–14kg/15¹/4–31lb cylinder. The natural, beige to gold rind is embossed with the intricate pattern of the basket in which it is drained*
CULINARY USES: *Table cheese, grating*

Named after the simple, hand-woven reed basket in which it is pressed and drained, Canestrato Pugliese is a flavoursome Pecorino. After being allowed to mature on a wooden shelf for a month or two, the cheese has an aroma reminiscent of wet wool, lanolin and mould. Although hard and grainy, the texture retains the rich, creamy feel and burnt-caramel taste characteristic of sheep's milk cheeses. The cheese can be left to mature for up to a year, and has a fat content of 45 per cent.

BELOW: Casciotta di Urbino

ABOVE: *Caciocavallo*

CASCIOTTA DI URBINO (DOC)

REGION: *Tuscany and Umbria*
TYPE: *Traditional, farmhouse, unpasteurized, semi-soft cheese*
SOURCE: *Sheep's milk (Sardinian and Appennine Brown) plus some cow's milk*
DESCRIPTION: *1.2kg/2¹/2lb round-edged cylinder with thin, polished, yellow to orange, natural rind*
CULINARY USES: *Table cheese, snacks, cooking, in salads*

Casciotta is the name used to describe the many small, artisan cheeses made all over central Italy and in some parts of the south. They can be made with cow's, goat's or sheep's milk (or a mixture) and are popular with both locals and tourists alike. Some have smooth, firm, oiled rinds; others have the basket imprint typical of Pecorinos.

Casciotta di Urbino is said to be one of the best. The yellow rind gives way to a deliciously compact, friable, straw-coloured interior. Sweet-tasting and moist, with the aroma and flavour of warm milk, it is a delicate, subtle cheese with underlying flavours of fresh green grass, nuts and wild flowers.

The makers of Casciotta di Urbino use raw milk and make their cheese only between April and September. It ripens in 15–30 days and has a fat content of 45 per cent. The cheese may be flavoured with garlic, onion or truffles.

CASTELMAGNO (DOC)

REGION: *Cuneo*
TYPE: *Traditional, farmhouse and co-operative, unpasteurized, hard cheese*
SOURCE: *Cow's milk (with goat's or sheep's milk)*
DESCRIPTION: *5–7kg/11–15¼lb cylinder. The reddish-yellow, natural rind is crusty, with some grey moulds and yeasts*
CULINARY USES: *After-dinner cheese; also used to make gnocchi*

The first official record of Castelmagno was in 1277, when it was mentioned as a unit of exchange. Production remained steady for centuries and some even found its way to Paris and London, but by the early 1950s demand had dropped significantly. Recognizing the importance of preserving a part of local history, an association to protect Castelmagno was formed and formalized under the DOC system in 1982.

Castelmagno is made from partially skimmed cow's milk, with some goat's or sheep's milk added. The evening milk is left to ripen overnight. Next day, the morning milk is added, which contributes to its strong taste and unusual texture. This has been described as resembling cotton wool, but lovers of Castelmagno prefer to describe it as flaky or compact, but not dense, not unlike young Lancashire.

The cheeses are left to ripen in damp cellars and drying rooms, occasionally being turned and washed to encourage the development of the natural micro-flora that contribute to the pungent, yeasty aroma. Blue moulds, present in the cellars, sometimes penetrate the rind to form fine, blue streaks that impart a more spicy flavour to the cheese. It ripens in two to five months (today's consumers tend to prefer it younger and milder).

CRESCENZA

REGION: *Lombardy*
TYPE: *Traditional, farmhouse and creamery, fresh cheese*
SOURCE: *Cow's milk*
DESCRIPTION: *1–2kg/2¼–4½lb white square or rectangle*
CULINARY USES: *Baking, grilling, in sauces*

The texture of this Stracchino-style cheese varies considerably from one brand to the next and according to the percentage of fat. The best examples are reputed to come from around Milan or Pavia. Sold within a few days of making, they come wrapped in simple, white, greaseproof paper and are quite luscious. Squidgy and so moist as to be almost wet, they have a fresh, clean acidity not unlike that of yogurt. Other Crescenzas are more rubbery, jelly-like or mushy, with a sour, synthetic taste. Low-fat varieties can be grainy.

Crescenza should be ripened for no longer than 10 days and eaten as soon as possible after that. The fat content varies between 48 and 50 per cent.

BELOW: Dolcelatte

DOLCELATTE

REGION: *Lombardy*
TYPE: *Modern, creamery, blue cheese*
SOURCE: *Cow's milk*
DESCRIPTION: *1–2kg/2¼–4½lb wheel. The moist, natural rind is white, blotched with blue and grey mould*
CULINARY USES: *Table cheese, dressings, in salads and on pasta*

The name means "sweet milk" and the cheese has a luscious, sweet taste. Deliciously soft, it melts like ice cream in the mouth. Created by Galbani, a company already famous for Bel Paese, Dolcelatte appeals to those who find the more traditional blue cheeses, such as Gorgonzola and Roquefort, too strongly flavoured, robust and spicy.

The cheesemaking method is similar to that used for Gorgonzola, except that Dolcelatte is made from the curd of only one milking. Produced in factories, the cheese ripens in two to three months and has a fat content of around 50 per cent. It may also be labelled Gorgonzola Dolce. Similar cheeses include Dolceverde and Torta Gaudenzio.

LEFT: Dolcelatte Torta

FONTINA (DOC)

REGION: *Valle d'Aosta*
TYPE: *Traditional, farmhouse and creamery, unpasteurized, semi-soft cheese*
SOURCE: *Cow's milk*
DESCRIPTION: *8–18kg/18–40lb wheel. The thin, uneven, light brown to terracotta rind is lightly oiled*
CULINARY USES: *Table cheese, melting, grilling*

In the pastures of the Valle d'Aosta, dominated by the highest mountains in Europe, the very dry summers result in a wide variety of high-quality fodder. There has been a cheese industry here since the eleventh century, when the local cheese was known simply as "caseus" to indicate that it was made from cow's milk.

Today, the name Fontina is used exclusively and proudly to identify cheeses produced in the Valle d'Aosta. The best of these are made in mountain chalets between May and September, when the herds graze the alpine meadows.

Fontina is dense, smooth and slightly elastic. The straw-coloured interior, with its small, round holes, has a delicate nuttiness with a hint of mild honey. When melted, as it frequently is (Fontina being the foundation for that superb fondue-style dish, fonduta), the flavour is earthy, with a suggestion of mushrooms and a fresh acidity.

Each cheesemaker has his own favourite location for ripening his cheeses – caves, tunnels, former military bunkers and even an abandoned copper mine. Fontina ripens in about three months and has a fat content of 45 per cent.

DOLCELATTE TORTA

REGION: *Various*
TYPE: *Modern, creamery, blue cheese*
SOURCE: *Cow's milk*
DESCRIPTION: *2–3kg/4 1/2–6 1/2lb rectangle with moist, natural rind covered in grey and blue moulds*
CULINARY USES: *Table cheese; also used in dips and spreads and over pasta*

Created in the 1960s, this cheese consists of thick layers of mascarpone cream alternating with the mild, Italian blue cheese, Dolcelatte. The cream mellows the blue cheese and the feel in the mouth is soft and gentle, more like ice cream than cheese. Spread it on warm toast, melt it over pasta or keep it for a private feast. Dolcelatte Torta is really too rich – the fat content is a hefty 75 per cent – to serve with ordinary wine, but it is delicious accompanied by a smooth fortified wine, such as Madeira, or even a sweet Italian dessert wine to cut the richness.

In the USA it may also be labelled Gorgonzola Torta.

The success of this cheese has led to the creation of other *tortas*, some good, some almost inedible. One of the best has layers of lightly toasted pine nuts and pesto alternating with the mascarpone – a few chunks of this *torta* melted into hot pasta and sprinkled with fresh chopped basil makes an irresistible starter.

FIORE SARDO (DOC)

REGION: *Sardinia*
TYPE: *Traditional, farmhouse and co-operative, unpasteurized, hard cheese*
SOURCE: *Sheep's milk*
DESCRIPTION: *1.5–4kg/3–9lb cylindrical wheel. The hard, ridged, natural rind is golden-yellow to dark brown*
CULINARY USES: *Table cheese, grating, cooking, snacks*

Don't be put off by the sour, damp smell of the rind. This is the sweetest of the Pecorinos. Straw-coloured and compact, this hard and grainy cheese has a wonderfully rich flavour, with a caramel sweetness, a mouthwatering, salty tang and a hint of fruit.

Rennet from lamb or kid (goat) is used to coagulate the milk. The method differs from that used for traditional Pecorino in that the curds are not "cooked" or heated in the whey. Once drained, the curds are scalded in hot water to seal the rind. They are then stored on a woven reed shelf, which hangs over the family hearth, absorbing the sweet smoke as they dry. Ripening continues in another room or the attic and the cheeses are periodically rubbed with olive oil and sheep fat to keep them moist and prevent moulds from forming. Fiore Sardo ripens in three to six months and has a fat content of 45 per cent.

ABOVE: Fontina

GORGONZOLA (DOC)

REGION: *Lombardy*
TYPE: *Traditional, creamery and co-operative, blue cheese*
SOURCE: *Cow's milk*
DESCRIPTION: *6–12 kg/13–26lb drum with red to orange rind covered with powdery patches of grey and blue moulds*
CULINARY USES: *Table cheese, dressings, salads, on pasta or gnocchi*

There are several folk legends to explain how what was originally a winter-made Stracchino cheese became one of the world's first blue cheeses. According to some, it was discovered inadvertently by an innkeeper in Gorgonzola, who found that his young Stracchino cheese had turned "blue" after a few weeks in his cool, damp cellars. Conscious of his profit margin, he decided to dish it up to some passing customers. Far from protesting, they demanded more.

The greenish-blue penicillium mould imparts a sharp, spicy flavour and provides an excellent contrast to the rich, creamy cheese. Gorgonzola is made by over 80 producers – large and small – in the north of Italy. Some use unpasteurized milk and follow the traditional method of allowing the curd to hang overnight so that it can become exposed to the mould naturally, but most Gorgonzola is made with pasteurized milk, to which the mould is added. At about four weeks the cheeses are pierced with thick needles to encourage the spread of the mould. Some are still ripened in the caves at Valsassina and Lodi, which provide ideal conditions for the formation of the mould.

Gorgonzola ripens in three to six months and has a fat content of 48 per cent. The cheese is usually wrapped in foil to keep it moist.

LEFT: Grana Padano

GRANA (DOC)

REGION: *Po Valley*
TYPE: *Traditional, creamery, unpasteurized, hard cheese*
SOURCE: *Cow's milk*
DESCRIPTION: *24–40kg/52–88lb drum with rock-hard, polished, yellow to brown, natural rind*
CULINARY USES: *Table cheese, grating, in sauces, as a condiment*

Grana is the generic name for the hard, grainy cheeses that originated in the Po Valley in Roman times. Magnificent, fruity and full of flavour, Grana must be matured for at least 12 months (longer, if covered by DOC controls).

The most famous examples of Grana are Grana Padano and Parmigiano-Reggiano, which are listed separately in this book. Grana Lodigiano is characterized by a slightly greenish tinge and the flavour is very strong, even bitter. It is unbelievably expensive to buy.

LEFT: Gorgonzola

GRANA PADANO (DOC)

REGION: *Specified parts of Piedmont, Lombardy, Emilia Romagna, Veneto and Trentino*
TYPE: *Traditional, co-operative, unpasteurized, hard cheese*
SOURCE: *Cow's milk*
DESCRIPTION: *24–40kg/52–88lb drum. The smooth, natural rind is extremely hard and thick. Deep yellow and often oily, it carries the official logo*
CULINARY USES: *Table cheese, grating, in starters and sauces, on pasta and salads*

Both Grana Padano and Parmigiano-Reggiano are known to many of us as simply "Parmesan". The cheese should taste fresh, fruity and sweet, with a hint of pineapple; never sour or dull. The pale yellow interior should be hard, grainy and crumbly. Although they are expensive, a little goes a long way. These cheeses freeze very well, you can either grate the cheese first and pack in a freezer container, or simply freeze the piece. It can be grated straight from the freezer – a far better convenience food than the unpleasant-tasting pre-packed pots of grated Parmesan that are available.

Grana Padano ripens in 12–48 months and has a fat content of 32 per cent.

MASCARPONE

REGION: *Various*
TYPE: *Traditional, farmhouse and creamery, vegetarian, matured cream*
SOURCE: *Cow's milk*
DESCRIPTION: *Pale cream and shiny, sold in pots*
CULINARY USES: *Desserts, baking, with pasta, in savoury dishes*

Technically speaking, mascarpone is not a cheese at all, but rather the result of a culture being added to the cream skimmed off the milk used in the production of Parmesan. It is, however, often described as a curd cheese although it is made in much the same way as yogurt.

After the culture has been added, the cream is gently heated, then allowed to mature and thicken. It develops a magnificent, thick, spoonable texture and is extremely versatile.

Famous as the main ingredient of that most sensuous of all Italian desserts, tiramisù, it also makes an excellent alternative to double (heavy) cream in both sweet and savoury dishes. In southern Italy mascarpone is sometimes made from buffalo's milk. It takes only a few days to ripen and has a fat content of 75 per cent.

BELOW: Mascarpone

MONTASIO (DOC)

REGION: *Friuli and Veneto*
TYPE: *Traditional, farmhouse and creamery, unpasteurized, hard cheese*
SOURCE: *Cow's milk (with some sheep's milk)*
DESCRIPTION: *5–10kg/11–22lb wheel. The yellow-brown rind is smooth and springy at first, becomes harder and a darker brown with age*
CULINARY USES: *Table cheese, grating, in sauces*

Developed in the thirteenth century at the monastery of Maggio, Montasio was originally made wholly from sheep's milk. Cow's milk is used today. The evening milk is partially skimmed (the cream being used to make mascarpone) and then mixed with the morning milk. The cheese is the same shape as Fontina, but in texture it resembles a young Asiago. Pale yellow or straw-coloured, the body is firm, with small holes. A good Montasio is creamy, rich and fruity, with a hint of pineapple. It should be quite tangy on the finish – not unlike a medium Cheddar. As it matures, the rind becomes very hard and the interior quite granular, even brittle. The fruity taste intensifies.

Montasio ripens in three to 18 months and has a fat content of 30–40 per cent.

ABOVE: Mozzarella

MOZZARELLA DI BUFALA

REGION: *Various*
TYPE: *Traditional, farmhouse and creamery, stretched curd cheese*
SOURCE: *Water buffalo's milk*
DESCRIPTION: *Spherical or oval cheeses in various sizes – wet, shiny and pure white*
CULINARY USES: *Freshly sliced in salads, baked on pizzas, also grilled*

Like most fresh cheeses, mozzarella is used to add texture rather than a specific taste to a dish. The juices, oils and flavours of the other ingredients are absorbed and intensified by the mild, moist, open layers of spun curd. It is this characteristic, together with the fact that mozzarella melts to become wonderfully elastic, that has made the cheese so popular.

The cheese is sold swimming in whey. It should be floppy rather than rubbery and have moisture trapped between the layers of springy curd. Cow's milk mozzarella is not as delicately flavoured as that from water buffalo's milk, nor as soft in texture, but it can be exceptional if well made. A fresh cheese, it should be eaten within a few days of being made.

If the cheese is lightly smoked, it is called mozzarella affumicata. If the cheese is more heavily smoked (a process that dries it out), it is referred to as scamorza. The hard, rubbery "pizza" cheese sold as mozzarella outside Italy may be perfect for pizzas in terms of texture, but will never equal fresh mozzarella in taste. In Italy, the commercial "block" mozzarella is usually called pizzaiola.

MURAZZANO (DOC)

REGION: *Cuneo*
TYPE: *Traditional, farmhouse and creamery, unpasteurized, fresh cheese*
SOURCE: *Cow's and sheep's milk in 60:40 ratio*
DESCRIPTION: *150–250g/5–9oz round with fine, smooth, yellow rind*
CULINARY USES: *Table cheese, grilling*

Named for the village where it is made, this is a typical Piedmontese *robiola* – a soft, round cheese made from a mixture of cow's and sheep's milk. The texture is delicate and supple and the taste fresh and milky, with a hint of the caramel characteristic of sheep's milk cheese. Although it is delicious as it is, it is usually melted on pizzas or crostini or used in sauces or pastries. Murazzano ripens in four to five days and has a fat content of 45 per cent.

PARMIGIANO-REGGIANO (DOC)

REGION: *Modena, Parma, Reggio Emilia, parts of Bologna and Mantua*
TYPE: *Traditional, co-operative, unpasteurized, hard cheese*
SOURCE: *Cow's milk*
DESCRIPTION: *24–40kg/52–88lb drum with thick, hard, yellow to orange rind*
CULINARY USES: *Table cheese, grating, in sauces and salads, over pasta and risotto*

In Italy, this wonderful cheese is sold in large, rough, grainy chunks chiselled from the shiny drum that carries its name emblazoned on the rind. The aroma is sweet and fruity, the colour fresh yellow and the taste exquisite – fruity (like fresh pineapple), strong and rich, but never overpowering or vicious. It will keep for months in the fridge, but the rough surface may grow some mould. If you have bought a large chunk and use it infrequently – an unthinkable possibility – freeze it. You can grate it straight from the freezer. In 1955 the rules relating to where Parmigiano-Reggiano could be made were tightened and the method of manufacture strictly specified. The cows

RIGHT: Murazzano

ABOVE: Parmigiano-Reggiano

whose milk goes into the cheese may have only fresh grass, hay or alfalfa. Enforcing these rules adds to the production cost, but the result is a cheese whose flavour and quality are guaranteed.

The secret of the continuing success of Parmigiano-Reggiano is the determination of the regulating body to maintain the 800 or so local dairy farms producing it. Only on small farms, where the milk does not have far to travel to the cheesemaker, can the close relationship between each batch of milk and its transformation into cheese be maintained.

A surprising feature of this delicious, robust and full-bodied cheese is that it is made from partially skimmed milk. The evening milk is left to rest in vats overnight. Next morning, the slightly soured cream is skimmed off to make mascarpone and the skimmed milk is combined with the fresh morning milk. It is then poured into conical, copper cauldrons so that the cheesemaking process can begin.

To seal the rind, and protect it from drying out over the next 18–48 months, the cheeses are floated in enormous brine baths for around 21 days, then they are moved to the storerooms. Throughout the maturation process, the huge cheeses are carefully brushed, turned, checked and rechecked before being graded by an official representative of the consortium responsible for determining the quality of each one.

The trademark, Parmigiano-Reggiano, is branded all over the rind, so that even a small piece of the cheese can easily be identified. It is one of the finest cheeses in the world.

PECORINO ROMANO (DOC)

REGION: *Lazio and Sardinia*
TYPE: *Traditional, farmhouse and creamery, hard cheese*
SOURCE: *Sheep's milk*
DESCRIPTION: *22–33kg/48–72lb drum. The smooth, hard rind is pale straw to dark brown in colour*
CULINARY USES: *Table cheese, grating, in sauces, on pasta*

Pecorino is the generic name for cheeses made from pure sheep's milk. Each is characteristic of a specific area and of a particular breed of sheep. For centuries, Pecorino Romano was made in the countryside around Rome, and it remains virtually unchanged to this day.

Since the first century AD the cheese has been widely exported, thanks to its excellent keeping qualities. It was issued to Roman legionaries as part of their rations. Demand continued to grow until the Roman producers could no longer keep up. At that point production spread to Sardinia, where there are now more than 60 factories or dairies compared with only 10 in the area around Rome.

The cheese is made between November and late June, when the sheep graze freely on the natural pastures. Pecorino Romano is larger than most cheeses of this type and must be pressed. It takes eight to 12 months to mature, during which time it develops its characteristic flavour – salty, with a fruity tang that becomes steadily more robust. The rind varies in colour, depending on the age of the cheese, and may have a protective coating of lard or oil. The compact interior is white to pale yellow, with irregular, small eyes. It should feel moist, yet granular and it is a superb grating cheese.

Other Romanos are Caprino Romano made with goat's milk and Vaccino Romano made with cow's milk. Both are hard and have their own individual character.

PECORINO SARDO (DOC)

REGION: *Sardinia*
TYPE: *Traditional, farmhouse, unpasteurized, hard cheese*
SOURCE: *Sheep's milk*
DESCRIPTION: *1–4kg/2¼–9lb cylinder. The natural rind varies in colour from pale straw yellow to deep russet*
CULINARY USES: *Table cheese, grating, in snacks, salads and sauces, on pasta*

Only recently brought under the protective umbrella of the DOC system, this cheese has two distinct styles. The delicate and sweet Pecorino Sardo Dolce is matured for 20–60 days and weighs 1–2.3kg/2¼–5lb. The body is white and firm, with a few scattered eyes.

Pecorino Sardo Maturo is matured for up to 12 months and becomes hard, granular and dry. It develops a robust sharpness and a salty tang. A cornucopia of flavours – sweet, nutty and herbaceous – is released when the cheese is grated on to hot foods such as pasta.

Each season can bring a subtle difference in the flavour of the cheese, depending on the flowers, grasses and herbs favoured by the native Sardinian sheep – the *mouflon* – that range over the rocky hillsides of the island.

BELOW: Pecorino Romano (left), Sardo (top) and Toscano (right)

PECORINO TOSCANO (DOC)

REGION: *Tuscany*
TYPE: *Traditional, farmhouse and co-operative, unpasteurized, hard cheese*
SOURCE: *Sheep's milk*
DESCRIPTION: *1–3kg/2¼–6½lb wheel. The natural rind ranges in colour from pale straw to brown or black*
CULINARY USES: *Pared or grated on pasta or risotto, in sauces and salads*

A young Pecorino Toscano is supple, fruity and aromatic; the complex flavour suggests walnuts and rich, burnt caramel.

Until recently, the name was used to describe any cheese made in Tuscany from sheep's milk or a mixture of milks. New regulations mean that the name is now protected and reserved only for pure sheep's milk cheeses. Mixed milk cheeses are sold as Caciotta.

Generally smaller than other Pecorinos, Toscano ripens more quickly. Those sold young have a yellow rind and are firm, but not hard. The rind darkens to a brownish-red after two to three months. The black-rinded cheese (Pecorino Toscano Crosta Nero) is matured for at least six months and has an intense flavour.

PRESSATO (DOC)

REGION: *Vicenza and Trento*
TYPE: *Traditional, co-operative, hard cheese*
SOURCE: *Cow's milk*
DESCRIPTION: *Various sizes and shapes with pale straw to golden-yellow rind*
CULINARY USES: *Table cheese, melting*

Pressato simply means "pressed" and is a generic name for a family of lightly pressed cheeses made from either skimmed or semi-skimmed milk. These sweet-sour, milky cheeses are sold young, when they are supple and open-textured. Asiago (to the annoyance of the producers) is sometimes wrongly referred to as Pressato.

ABOVE: Provolone

PROVOLONE (DOC)
REGION: *Lombardy*
TYPE: *Traditional creamery stretched curd cheese*
SOURCE: *Cow's milk*
DESCRIPTION: *200g–5kg/7oz–11lb cheeses in various shapes. The thin, hard rind is golden-yellow and shiny. It is sometimes waxed*
CULINARY USES: *Table cheese, grilling, melting*

No one knows precisely where or how this cheese originated, but it was certainly among the earliest cheeses known by the Romans. Local names for Provolone usually reflect the shape or size, which can vary considerably. The cheese can be spherical, pear-shaped, cylindrical or even plaited and the weight depends on the mood of the cheesemaker. The Giganti (monster cheeses), often made for special occasions or trade fairs, can be over 3m/3¼yd long, but the most familiar shape, often found hanging in Italian delicatessens, is the sausage tied with cord.

Dolce (mild Provolone) is aged for two to three months, and it is supple and smooth, with a thin, waxed rind. It is generally used as a table cheese. Picante (piquant) is coagulated with kid's rennet, which gives it a stronger flavour. Aged for six months to two years, it is darker, with small eyes, a hard rind and a strong, spicy flavour. It is often grated as a condiment.

QUARTIROLO LOMBARDO
REGION: *Lombardy*
TYPE: *Traditional, farmhouse and creamery, semi-soft cheese*
SOURCE: *Cow's milk*
DESCRIPTION: *1–3kg/2¼–6½lb square cheese. The tender, pale pink rind hardens with age and acquires reddish-grey moulds*
CULINARY USES: *Table cheese, served with salads and cold meats*

In summer, the abundant grass in the Lombardy valleys was traditionally mown three times. After the final mowing, the cattle would be brought from the mountain pastures to graze on the sweet, new grass (*erba quartirola*) before being turned into the barns for the winter. The cheese made from the rich milk yielded at this time was called Quartirolo Lombardo. Skimmed milk was used (the cream being turned into butter).

Today, the cheese is made all year round, usually from full-cream milk. It looks like a young Taleggio, and has a slightly crumbly, lumpy centre. If eaten within the first few weeks, it has a lemon-fresh acidity and delicate fragrance; after two months it becomes dense, almost runny, and its fruity character is more distinctive. Cheese lovers seek out those made in the mountains – Quartirolo di Monte – which are unpasteurized and slowly ripened. Producers are currently attempting to have the cheese brought under the control of the DOC system to protect its quality and character.

BELOW: Raschera

RAGUSANO (DOC)
REGION: *Sicily*
TYPE: *Traditional, farmhouse and co-operative, unpasteurized, hard cheese*
SOURCE: *Cow's milk (Modicana)*
DESCRIPTION: *10–12kg/22–26lb brick. The thin, smooth, natural, yellow rind is polished*
CULINARY USES: *Table cheese, grilling*

In local dialect, Ragusano (or Caciocavallo Ragusano) is described as a *scaluni* or step. The curd is heated and stretched until it is rubbery. It is then pressed into special rectangular moulds. Once draining is complete, the cheeses are rubbed with salt and left to mature in cellars for up to six months. To stave off insects, they are regularly rubbed with a mixture of oil and vinegar. The pale yellow interior is soft and supple, with a savoury taste that becomes stronger as the cheese hardens and ages beyond six months.

RASCHERA (DOC)
REGION: *Cuneo*
TYPE: *Traditional, farmhouse and co-operative, semi-soft cheese*
SOURCE: *Cow's milk (with sheep's or goat's milk)*
DESCRIPTION: *7–10kg/15¼–22lb round or square. The thin, reddish-yellow crust with white or grey moulds*
CULINARY USES: *Table cheese, grilling*

Named after Lake Raschera, which lies at the foot of Mt Mongioie, this cheese resembles Toma, but is square, the practical shape having been determined in the days when it was transported by mule.

Generally made with the sweet milk of the Piedmontese cow, Raschera has a pale ivory interior scattered with tiny holes which occasionally have a bluish tinge. When young, the cheese is supple and elastic, with a delicate sweet taste that becomes richer, more aromatic and slightly tart. The flavour changes from season to season. Spring and summer cheeses are sweet and fresh, whereas those made in winter tend to be more solid and vibrant. The best is reckoned to be that which comes from the alpine pastures – look for the words "*di alpessio*" on the label.

RICOTTA

REGION: *Various*

TYPE: *Traditional, farmhouse and creamery, whey cheese*

SOURCE: *Cow's milk*

DESCRIPTION: *1–2kg/2¼–4½lb basin-shaped cheese, pure white and wet, but not sticky*

CULINARY USES: *As a dessert cheese with sugar and fruit; also baked in ravioli or pastries*

When cheese is made, the solids in the milk are separated from the liquid by coagulation. Yet, however careful the cheesemaker, some solids are lost to the whey. To retrieve these, the milk is heated until the solids come to the surface as small, white lumps. These are skimmed off and drained in woven baskets until the curd is solid enough to stick together and can be turned out. The result is a soft, moist, basin-shaped cheese.

Good ricotta should be firm, not solid, and consist of a mass of fine, moist, delicate grains, neither salted nor ripened. One of the finest, Fior di Maggio, has a texture not unlike delicate bread and butter pudding. Only vaguely grainy, it melts in the mouth. Unfortunately, much of the ricotta made today uses semi-skimmed milk instead of whey and the texture can vary tremendously. It can be gritty, lumpy or even wet, causing havoc for those trying to use it in a traditional recipe.

In Italy, ricotta appears in a number of guises. Ricotta Romano is made from sheep's milk and is available only from November to June. Ricotta Salata is a salted and dried version that resembles feta, while Ricotta Infornata is a Sicilian speciality that is baked until it is lightly browned. Northern Italians like their ricotta smoked.

Ricotta ripens in one to five days and has a fat content of around 20 per cent.

RIGHT: Ricotta Salata (left) and fresh Ricotta (right)

ROBIOLA DI ROCCAVERANO (DOC)

REGION: *Lombardy*

TYPE: *Traditional, farmhouse and co-operative, fresh cheese*

SOURCE: *Cow's and goat's milk*

DESCRIPTION: *200g/7oz round or square cheese. Pure white when fresh, it becomes pink to orange with reddish ferments if aged*

CULINARY USES: *Table cheese, baking, spreading, in sauces*

Roccaverano is a small, typically Italian hillside town. The local cheese was once made exclusively from goat's milk, but a mixture of milks is now permitted and cow's milk can account for as much as 85 per cent. Some Robiola di Roccaverano is still made on farms for family consumption, but the majority is made in small co-operatives, using pasteurized milk.

The cheese can be eaten fresh, at just a few days old, when it is sweet and very moist. Others prefer it once it has matured for up to 20 days. The mature cheese is sharper, but still retains the subtle, taste characteristic of goat's milk. The pasteurized cheese is spreadable, with a smooth texture. It has a sweet-sour aroma and a taste that resembles melted butter, but can be quite salty. The unpasteurized cheese has a much more complex flavour. Rich and meaty, it has a piquant, yeasty aroma.

ABOVE: Scamorza Affumicate

SCAMORZA

REGION: *Various*

TYPE: *Traditional, farmhouse and creamery, stretched curd cheese*

SOURCE: *Cow's milk*

DESCRIPTION: *Smooth, shiny, white cheese traditionally made in a money-bag shape*

CULINARY USE: *Cooking*

The producers of Caciocavallo make this cheese when milk is abundant. It matures within a few days and it thus provides a good way to boost their income while waiting for the Caciocavallo to ripen.

A stretched curd cheese, Scamorza resembles Provolone. It is rubbery, with a stringy texture, and is drier than mozzarella. Sold young, within two to three days of making, it has a bland, vaguely milky taste. The smoked version, Scamorza Affumicate, is more popular than the plain and is often used in pasta dishes. It is also served with ham, mushrooms or chargrilled vegetables.

STRACCHINO

REGION: *Lombardy*
TYPE: *Traditional, farmhouse and creamery, semi-soft cheese*
SOURCE: *Cow's milk*
DESCRIPTION: *Made in various sizes and shapes (usually square). The thin, natural rind ranges from pale cream to reddish-brown, and can be sticky*
CULINARY USES: *Table cheese, melting, grilling*

Stracchino is a generic term, used to describe a style of soft cheese that has been made in Lombardy since the twelfth century. The quality varies considerably, so it is wise to taste before you buy. A good Stracchino will have a supple, yielding texture and a deliciously fruity flavour.

Well-known Stracchino-style cheeses include Crescenza, Quartirolo, Taleggio and Robiola.

TALEGGIO (DOC)

REGION: *Lombardy*
TYPE: *Traditional, farmhouse and creamery, semi-soft cheese*
SOURCE: *Cow's milk*
DESCRIPTION: *2kg/4¹/₂lb square with distinctive markings. The rough, rosy crust is imprinted with the official stamp of the consortium*
CULINARY USES: *Table cheese, grilling, melting (popular over polenta)*

Taleggio was originally only one of several cheeses referred to as "Stracchino", a term still used to describe the soft, square cheeses of Lombardy. Today, DOC regulations govern both how and where Taleggio is made, and the quality is maintained (as are the basic shape and method of production) despite the fact that the majority of the cheese is now produced in factories from pasteurized milk.

Traditionally, the cheeses were matured in natural caves, which had deep crevices that provided natural air-conditioning and encouraged the spread of the moulds and ferments essential to create Taleggio's unique aroma and taste. Over 30 per cent of the cheeses sold today continue to be matured in these

ABOVE: *Stracchino*

caves, which undoubtedly makes a difference to their flavour.

By the time Taleggio reaches your favourite cheese shop it will have developed its rosy crust. The curd will be very nearly at melting point, while the centre will be elastic, with some eyes. The aroma will be gentle, but insistent, redolent of almonds and sweet hay.

In the hands of a talented affineur, the rind will harden and the ivory interior will reveal its magic – to experience it is like smelling and then eating a rich cream of asparagus soup.

Taleggio ripens in 25–50 days and has a fat content of 48 per cent.

ABOVE: *Taleggio, which is still matured in caves*

TOMA (DOC)

REGION: *Piedmont*
TYPE: *Traditional, farmhouse, semi-hard cheese*
SOURCE: *Cow's milk (or mixed milk)*
DESCRIPTION: *Made in various shapes and sizes. The natural rind ranges from thin and pale yellow to thick, grey and crusty*
CULINARY USES: *Table cheese, cooking*

Toma has been made in the mountains of Piedmont in various shapes and sizes for generations. Although it now comes under the DOC umbrella, there are as many variations as there are small dairy farms in the Valle d'Aosta, where the finest Toma is said to be made. The young cheese is sweet and milky, but if it is allowed to mature for up to 12 months, the flavour becomes more tangy, often sharp. The Toma Piedmontese available in Britain has a soft, leathery rind and supple texture. It tastes fresh and creamy, with a hint of meadow flavours.

UBRIACO

REGION: *Vicenza and Trento*
TYPE: *Traditional, farmhouse, unpasteurized, hard cheese*
SOURCE: *Cow's milk*
DESCRIPTION: *8–12kg/18–26lb wheel. The deep burgundy, natural rind is rough and hard*
CULINARY USES: *Table cheese, grating*

Ubriaco means "drunken" in Italian, and it isn't difficult to see how the cheese got its name. Following local custom, the young cheese is soaked in wine, covered with the crushed grape skins left after pressing and allowed to mature for six to 10 months. The result is a cheese with the heady aroma of fermenting fruit. Ubriaco has a firm, crumbly but open texture that is fairly wet (the moisture tastes distinctly alcoholic and salty) and has a mouth-puckering bite that is reminiscent of ripe pineapple.

ENGLISH CHEESES

Simple cheesemaking implements dating back to the Iron Age have been found in England, but it was the arrival of the Romans in the first century AD – and the sweeping agricultural changes that ensued – that resulted in the introduction of harder, longer-lasting cheeses.

It is possible that Celtic monks from Wales and Ireland introduced the Trappist cheeses, but no records exist until the arrival of William the Conqueror in 1066. William brought with him Cistercian monks from Cîteaux in Burgundy, who taught the shepherds of the Yorkshire Dales how to make sheep's milk cheeses.

The dissolution of the monasteries during the reign of Henry VIII, meant that the monks were forced to find shelter and employment on local farms. Their cheesemaking skills spread further afield. Gradually sheep were replaced by cattle, which yielded far more milk and had longer lactation periods.

England is well suited to dairy farming, and by the sixteenth century nearly every county had its own cheese. Sadly, few of these cheeses exist today. Those that do are known as "territorials", with the best-known example being Cheddar.

The unique texture is obtained by using the traditional "cheddaring" process, whereby the curds are drained, cut into bricks, then pressed numerous times until the texture satisfies the cheesemaker. It is this laborious task that makes farmhouse Cheddar unique.

Unlike the other great cheeses of Europe, neither the name of Cheddar nor its method of production is protected, and the cheese has been copied the world over. The "cheddaring" performed in giant factories means that a generation of Cheddar eaters have grown up without the slightest clue as to what this great cheese should really taste like.

Although the origin of its name is still hotly disputed, it was unquestionably the landlord of the Bell Inn in the village of Stilton who put Stilton on the world map in the 1800s by serving the cheese to travellers journeying on the Great North Road from London to Scotland.

Cheshire, mentioned in the Domesday Book, is one of Britain's oldest cheeses. It derives its distinct character from the salt marshes on which the cattle graze. Port records from 1770 show that over 5,000 tons of Cheshire were shipped to London that year. It was considered to be one of Britain's finest cheeses, and by the 1930s there were more than 400 farms producing Cheshire.

Both Double and Single Gloucester have been made in Gloucestershire since the sixteenth century, originally from the milk of the native Old Gloucester cows.

Although still popular in the north of England, Lancashire has all but lost its way since the last century, when it was considered to be one of England's finest cheeses. Leicester – or Red Leicester as it is now known – was, until the late 1700s, produced in volume. However, the production of farmhouse versions of this russet cheese all but ceased before the Second World War. The same can be said of most of England's farmhouse cheeses, which are made only in limited volume and farmhouse varieties rarely exist.

LEFT: Today, Cheddar accounts for about 70 per cent of all cheese consumed in Britain

ABOVE: Stilton is one of England's best-loved cheeses

Several factors led to the decline and almost fall of these great cheeses. First was the cattle epidemic of 1860, when thousands of cows were slaughtered and tons of mass-produced American Cheddar was imported, paving the way for the industrialization of the cheese industry.

With the increasing demand for milk, many farmers found it easier to sell their milk rather than make cheese, and the number of cheesemakers declined further.

The ravages of the Second World War devastated the industry. With few men to run the farms and severe food shortages, the Ministry of Food ruled that any excess milk be used to make fast-ripening "National Cheese". When rationing ended in 1954 many farming families were without their menfolk and cheesemaking skills had been lost. Before the war there had been 15,000 cheesemakers; by the time it ended, only 126 remained.

In the past 15 years there has been a revolution. Block cheeses have improved, farmhouse cheesemakers are on the increase, old recipes are being revived and old breeds of cow are on the increase. Sheep's and goat's milk cheeses are making their way on to supermarket shelves.

England can now boast over 300 artisan cheeses. At the recent British Cheese Awards, 507 cheeses were entered. Of these, 44 were sheep's milk and 64 were goat's milk – as diverse and distinctive as those found in Europe.

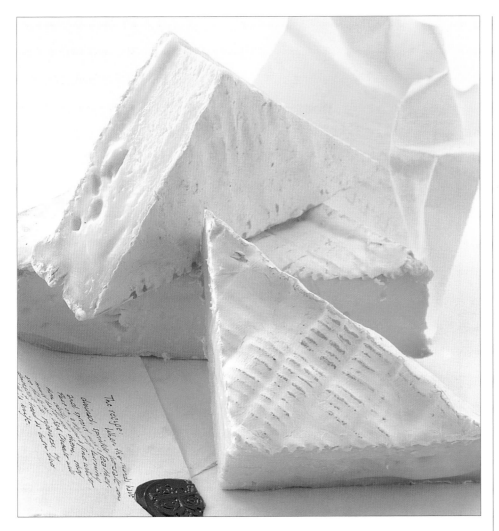

ABOVE: Bath Cheese – one of the many recently created British cheeses that is based on an old recipe

BASING

REGION: *Kent*
TYPE: *Modern, farmhouse, unpasteurized, organic, vegetarian, hard cheese*
SOURCE: *Goat's milk*
DESCRIPTION: *4kg/9lb truckle cheese. The fine natural rind has some moulding*
CULINARY USES: *Table cheese, grating*

Maureen and Bill Browning make this Caerphilly-type cheese with milk from their own goats at Lower Basing Farm. It is lightly pressed, moist and crumbly. The mild and pleasant acidity, with just a hint of the herbaceous goat's milk, becomes smooth and more creamy as it matures. It ripens within two months and has a fat content of 45 per cent.

Basing has been a silver medal winner at the British Cheese Awards.

BATH CHEESE

REGION: *Avon*
TYPE: *Modern, farmhouse, unpasteurized, soft-white cheese*
SOURCE: *Cow's milk (Friesian and Ayrshire)*
DESCRIPTION: *225g/8oz square with smooth, white penicillium rind*
CULINARY USE: *Table cheese*

When young, Bath Cheese has a slightly grainy texture, while the flavour is mild and slightly tart, with a salty finish. When aged, the soft, furry, white rind yields to a soft interior, which oozes on to the plate as it reaches perfection. The flavour has hints of mushroom and warm milk balanced with a peppery, dandelion bite.

The producers, G. and P. Padfield, who also make York Cheese, developed the cheese after reading Patrick Rance's description of a similar cheese made in Bath a century ago.

Bath Cheese ripens in three to four weeks. It has twice been a silver medal winner at the British Cheese Awards.

BEENLEIGH BLUE

REGION: *Devon*
TYPE: *Modern, farmhouse, unpasteurized, organic, vegetarian, blue cheese*
SOURCE: *Sheep's milk*
DESCRIPTION: *3kg/6 1/2 lb cylinder. The rough, crusty, natural rind is slightly sticky and has some patches of blue, grey and white moulds*
CULINARY USE: *Table cheese*

Robin Congdon and Sari Cooper of Ticklemore Cheese are gifted cheese-makers. Their Beenleigh Blue is one of only three blue sheep's milk cheeses made in Britain. A consistent gold medal winner at the British Cheese Awards, it is moist yet crumbly, with the blue appearing as bold blue-green streaks through the white interior. The flavour is steely blue, with the burnt-caramel sweetness characteristic of fine sheep's milk cheese. It melts on the palate, disclosing its strong, spicy character. Don't cook it – eat it. It is wonderful with mead or sweet cider. Beenleigh Blue ripens in six months and has a fat content of 45–50 per cent. It is available from August to January.

Robin and Sari also produce Harbourne – a blue, goat's milk cheese – and Devon Blue, made from cow's milk. Ticklemore, their hard, goat's milk cheese, has a smooth texture and herbaceous character. These cheeses – and others from all over the country – are available from their cheese shop in Totnes.

BELOW: Beenleigh Blue

BERKSWELL

REGION: *West Midlands*
TYPE: *Modern, farmhouse, unpasteurized, vegetarian, hard cheese*
SOURCE: *Sheep's milk (Friesland)*
DESCRIPTION: *3.25kg/7lb flattened round. The deep russet-red, natural rind bears the intricate marks of the basket mould in which it is made*
CULINARY USES: *Table cheese, grating, in soups*

Stephen Fletcher and his mother make their magnificent-looking cheese at Ram Hall, an Elizabethan house in Berkswell, near the Forest of Arden. The milk comes from their flock of East Friesland sheep.

Berkswell is sold at around four months, when the hard, crusty, ridged rind has an aroma of lanolin and damp wool. The cheese is hard and chewy, almost granular, with a fat content of 48 per cent. Each bite reveals more of its complex flavours – roasted nuts, caramelized onions and meadow flowers with a prickly tang.

This is truly one of the great modern British cheeses.

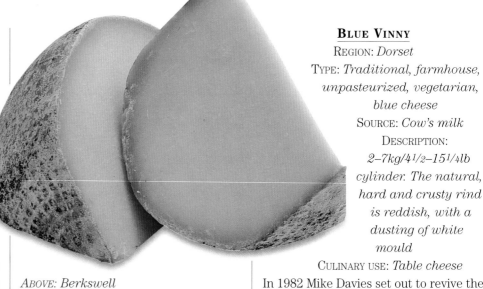

ABOVE: Berkswell

BLUE CHESHIRE

REGION: *Cheshire*
TYPE: *Traditional, farmhouse and creamery, vegetarian, blue cheese*
SOURCE: *Cow's milk*
DESCRIPTION: *9kg/20lb truckle cheese. The natural rind is rough and crusty*
CULINARY USE: *Table cheese*

Traditionally, because of its open, crumbly texture, some Cheshire cheese would develop fine threads of blue during the months spent maturing in cellars. As this occurred naturally it was referred to as "blue fade" and came to be highly prized.

In recent years, the old idea has been revived, particularly by some of the Stilton makers. To guarantee that the blueing occurs, however, the mould is added to the milk before curdling. The young cheese is pierced, which allows in air and encourages the blueing to spread so that it provides an attractive contrast to the orange interior. A dry, dense and crumbly cheese, Blue Cheshire tends to be quite sharp, with a hint of green grass and salt balanced by the creaminess of the milk. The colour, which was originally obtained from carrots or marigolds, is now provided by annatto, a natural dye. Blue Cheshire ripens in two to three months.

LEFT: Blue Wensleydale (front) and Blue Vinny (back)

BLUE VINNY

REGION: *Dorset*
TYPE: *Traditional, farmhouse, unpasteurized, vegetarian, blue cheese*
SOURCE: *Cow's milk*
DESCRIPTION: *2–7kg/4¹/₂–15¹/₄lb cylinder. The natural, hard and crusty rind is reddish, with a dusting of white mould*
CULINARY USE: *Table cheese*

In 1982 Mike Davies set out to revive the old Dorset blue cheese, Blue Vinny, which had all but disappeared, yet about which there were a host of rumours. One claimed the cheese acquired its spidery, blue veining from having had old leather boots placed beside the vats.

Like most rumours, this had little foundation. "Vinny" is the old English word for "veining", and the blue comes from the family of penicillium moulds that occur naturally in the air. These invade the young, moist, open-textured, skimmed milk curd to create what is known as "blue fade". The same mould is attracted to old leather, hence the tall tale.

Today the blueing is not left to chance, and the penicillium mould is added directly to the milk.

Blue Vinny ripens in three to five months. The fat content is 40 per cent.

BLUE WENSLEYDALE

REGION: *North Yorkshire*
TYPE: *Traditional, creamery, vegetarian, blue cheese*
SOURCE: *Cow's milk*
DESCRIPTION: *4kg/9lb clothbound cylinder with hard, dry, brown-orange, rough rind*
CULINARY USE: *Table cheese*

Based on an original recipe that dates back to the eleventh century, this cheese has recently been revived by several creameries in the Yorkshire Dales. Firmer than most blues and slightly crumbly, Blue Wensleydale has a spicy, blue tang with a slightly bitter, dark chocolate and chicory finish. It takes nine to 12 weeks to mature and has a fat content of 45 per cent.

BOSWORTH

REGION: *Staffordshire*
TYPE: *Modern, farmhouse, unpasteurized, vegetarian, soft-white cheese*
SOURCE: *Goat's milk*
DESCRIPTION: *150g/5oz round cheese with very thin, velvety, penicillium rind dusted with a fine layer of ash*
CULINARY USE: *Table cheese*

Made by Hugh Lillington of Innes Cheese, this elegant, soft-white cheese has an unexpectedly firm, breakable texture rather than the usual Brie-like softness. It melts in the mouth like fudge, yielding up its sweet, nutty flavours with just a suggestion of goat's milk. It matures in three to four weeks and has a fat content of 45 per cent.

Hugh and his team at High Fields Dairy make various unpasteurized goat's milk cheeses, including Bosworth Leaf, so called because of the chestnut leaf wrapping that contrasts beautifully with the fluffy, white rind of the cheese. Bosworth Leaf has a fine, grained texture that softens to a velvety smoothness. The taste is reminiscent of vanilla and butterscotch, with a subtle but distinct, almost almondy finish.

BUFFALO

REGION: *Hereford and Worcester*
TYPE: *Modern, farmhouse, unpasteurized, vegetarian, hard cheese*
SOURCE: *Water buffalo's milk*
DESCRIPTION: *2kg/4¹/₂lb wheel with thin, leathery, polished, natural rind*
CULINARY USES: *Table cheese, grilling*

The sight of water buffalo in the rolling Cotswold Hills is an incongruous one, yet these animals have adapted to their new home exceedingly well. Buffalo was released on the market in 1996 and won the British Cheese Awards' Best New or Experimental Cheese that same year. Not surprisingly, it is the only hard buffalo's milk cheese made in Britain, where the smooth, soft, Italian cheese – mozzarella – is better known. Firm yet supple, with a creamy feel, Buffalo has a flavour that hints of almonds and has a citrus tang.

RIGHT: Buffalo is the only hard buffalo's milk cheese made in Britain

BUTTON/INNES

REGION: *Staffordshire*
TYPE: *Modern, farmhouse, unpasteurized, vegetarian, fresh cheese*
SOURCE: *Goat's milk*
DESCRIPTION: *50g/2oz round*
CULINARY USE: *Table cheese*

Voted Supreme Champion at the British Cheese Awards in 1994, Button, or Innes Button, is soft, mousse-like and fragile. It simply dissolves on the palate, trailing a hint of almonds, honey, lemon, white wine and tangerine. One of Britain's finest goat's milk cheeses, it is also available dusted with ash, pink peppercorns, chopped nuts or herbs. Button ripens in five to 10 days and has a fat content of 45 per cent. Like Bosworth it is made by Hugh Lillington of Innes Cheese in Staffordshire.

BUXTON BLUE

REGION: *Derbyshire*
TYPE: *Modern, creamery, vegetarian, blue cheese*
SOURCE: *Cow's milk*
DESCRIPTION: *8kg/18lb clothbound cylinder. The rind is orange-brown and crusty*
CULINARY USES: *Table cheese, crumbled into soups or salads, also blended with soft cheese to make a spread*

The Duke of Devonshire established one of the first creameries in England at Hartington in Derbyshire in the 1870s, using milk from his tenant farmers. The building was virtually destroyed by fire towards the end of the nineteenth century and lay abandoned until Thomas Nuttall, a successful Stilton maker, took it over. The creamery, now part of Mendip Dairy Crest, still concentrates on making Stilton, but created Buxton Blue in 1994 to meet the growing demand from consumers and supermarkets for new cheeses.

Buxton Blue is firmer than Stilton, with fine, blue streaks in the pale orange interior. More crumbly than hard, it is milder than most blues and has a hint of dark chocolate and burnt onions on the finish. It ripens in 10–12 weeks and has a fat content of 45 per cent. The factory also makes Dovedale Blue.

ABOVE: Buxton Blue is one of only nine British cheeses that has been granted PDO status by the EC

CAPRICORN GOAT

REGION: *Somerset*
TYPE: *Modern, creamery, vegetarian, soft-white cheese*
SOURCE: *Goat's milk*
DESCRIPTION: *125g/4¹/₂oz cylinder or 1.2kg/2¹/₂lb square cutting cheese with pure white, soft rind*
CULINARY USE: *Table cheese*

Lubborn Cheese is best known for its Somerset Camembert and Brie cheeses, but Capricorn Goat has made giant strides in convincing the British public that goat's milk cheese can be mild, not vicious, and can have a distinct character without being overwhelming.

The smaller version of this cheese is an attractive cylinder with a delicate, soft-white rind. Slightly chalky, like unripe Camembert when young, it becomes softer around the edges and is sometimes almost runny. The fresh, creamy feel with a background of chicory and nuts is very appealing. The cheese ripens in four to six weeks and has a fat content of 26 per cent. It has twice won bronze medals at the British Cheese Awards.

CERNEY

REGION: *Gloucestershire*
TYPE: *Modern, farmhouse, unpasteurized, vegetarian, fresh cheese*
SOURCE: *Goat's milk*
DESCRIPTION: *240g/8¹/₂oz pyramid dusted with oak ash and salt*
CULINARY USE: *Table cheese*

Like many of Britain's artisan cheese-makers, Lady Angus, creator of this distinctive cheese, maximizes the flavour by using unpasteurized milk. Her cheeses are named after the pretty village of Cerney where they are made. Each has a mild, zingy, citrus taste, with a delicate, goaty finish. The light, moist texture resembles that of fromage frais. Each of the small, truncated cones is hand-made, and over the years a number of interesting variations has emerged. Apart from the original, which is dusted with a fine layer of ash, there is Cerney Smoked, Cerney Pepper and Cerney Village. Cerney Ginger is particularly good, with freshly chopped, spicy, ginger pieces scattered throughout the soft curd. Cerney ripens in seven to 10 days and has a fat content of 43 per cent.

BELOW: Capricorn Goat

CHEDDAR

REGION: *Somerset*
TYPE: *Traditional, farmhouse, unpasteurized, hard cheese*
SOURCE: *Cow's milk*
DESCRIPTION: *26kg/57lb cylinder with natural rind, bound in cloth*
CULINARY USES: *Table cheese; also widely used for cooking in a host of traditional dishes*

Since the sixteenth century, the hard cow's milk cheese made in the Mendip Hills near the Cheddar Gorge has been known as Cheddar. The cheese undoubtedly goes back to earlier centuries, perhaps even to the Romans, who first introduced the people of England to hard cheeses.

Over the centuries, the recipe for this West Country cheese has been taken by emigrants to Canada, the USA, Australia, South Africa and New Zealand. More than any other British cheese, it has been copied and emulated, but it is not really Cheddar unless it comes from the verdant hills of Somerset, Devon and Dorset.

To taste a hand-made, unpasteurized, clothbound Cheddar, made from the milk of cows whose daily diet is fresh green grass, buttercups and daisies, is to taste a piece of magic. The bite is like chocolate, firm and yielding; the aroma is fresh, nutty and slightly savoury. The flavour differs from farm to farm, but there is always the rich sweetness of the milk, a classic acid tang and a long-lingering kaleidoscope of flavours. Cheddar is generally matured for between nine and 24 months, and has a fat content of 50 per cent (34.4 per cent in the dry matter).

Unlike the great cheeses of Europe, Cheddar's name is not protected, so it has been used and abused. Hundreds of tasteless tonnes are churned out in giant factories around the world. Even in Britain, both the consumers and the market have conspired against the farmhouse Cheddar makers. Today there are only six cheesemakers who still make traditional, clothbound Cheddars:

CHEWTON (Chewton, Somerset): Firm and biteable, the cheese has a flavour that

ABOVE: Traditional clothbound Cheddars from top right, Green's, Keen's, Quicke's and Montgomery's

CHESHIRE

REGION: *Cheshire*
TYPE: *Traditional, farmhouse, unpasteurized, hard cheese*
SOURCE: *Cow's milk*
DESCRIPTION: *900g/2lb, 8kg/18lb or 20kg/44lb tall cylinders with natural rind with grey moulding, tightly wrapped in cloth*
CULINARY USES: *Table cheese, grilling, snacks, grating*

Fewer than a handful of cheesemakers still make the traditional clothbound Cheshire, using raw milk. Most of the cheeses are factory-made today and lack any real depth of character. The fine, moist texture that is the hallmark of a good Cheshire (but which also renders the cheese susceptible to cracking, crumbling or blueing) is rejected by many supermarkets in favour of cheeses that are creamier and more solid. Changes are afoot, however, and smaller producers are now being encouraged to return to a more traditional style.

Clothbound Cheshire is produced by several traditional cheesemakers, including the Applebys, H. S. Bourne and V. J. Hares. The Appleby's have been making Cheshire for generations. The current cheesemaker, Mrs Appleby, now in her 70s, is particularly highly regarded. Her Cheshire has a crumbly, flaky texture and a sea-breeze freshness with the tang of orange zest.

Cheshire requires two to six months to mature.

BELOW: Cheshire

explodes on the palate. The rind is nutty, the interior suggests cheese and onion with a hint of butter. The mature, unpasteurized Chewton has twice won the accolade of Best Cheddar at the British Cheese Awards. Both pasteurized and unpasteurized cheeses are available.

DENHAY (Bridport, Devon): Hand-made and matured on the farm, Denhay is nutty, and rich with a strong, savoury tang. All the milk comes from the farm's own herd.

GREEN'S (Glastonbury, Somerset): Made by three generations on the same farm, Green's is matured for 12 months or more. Each cheese is hand turned until all reach their peak. Twice winner of a gold medal at the British Cheese Awards, the cheese is savoury (redolent of cheese and onion) and tangy.

KEEN'S (Wincanton, Somerset): Made on the farm since the turn of the century, using only milk from its own herd, Keen's has a full-bodied flavour. It is complex, with hints of liquorice and a fresh, green tang. Nutty, smooth and creamy, it melts in the mouth. A past winner of a silver medal in the British Cheese Awards, it is both clothbound and larded.

MONTGOMERY'S (Yeovil, Somerset): Twice voted Best Cheddar at the British Cheese Awards, this has a superb richness, a spicy acidity and real depth to the fruity finish. Montgomery's makes only eight or nine cheeses a day.

QUICKE'S (Exeter, Devon): The only traditional cheddarmakers in Devon, the Quicke family have been farming at Newton St Cyres for over 450 years. Their Cheddar is a regular medal winner at the British Cheese Awards. Firm and chewy, with a buttery texture and tangy, nutty, complex aroma, the cheese, when tasted, suggests green grass and fresh hay. Pasteurized and unpasteurized versions are available.

COQUETDALE

REGION: *Northumberland*
TYPE: *Traditional, farmhouse, vegetarian, hard cheese*
SOURCE: *Cow's milk*
DESCRIPTION: *650g/1 1/2lb or 2.2kg/5lb round cheese. The fine, leathery, natural rind has yellowish-grey mould*
CULINARY USE: *Table cheese*

Mark Robinson's cheesemaking urge came in 1985 after he read a book about sheep and their cheeses. At the time he had over 600 ewes on his farm in Northumberland. Over the following five years he built up the herd, changing over to Friesland sheep, then diversifying into cow's milk as well.

On a trip to France, he visited the makers of Saint-Nectaire and decided to develop a similar cheese at home in Northumberland. Once the cheese was placed in his wonderful old caves, however, and came into contact with the natural flora and moulds that live on the walls and roofs, the original recipe began to change. The result is a soft, supple cheese with a wonderful balance of sweet-savoury flavours and a nutty, slightly salty finish.

Coquetdale ripens in 10–12 weeks and has a fat content of 55 per cent. Mark Robinson's Northumberland Cheese Company also produces Northumberland and Redesdale.

ABOVE: Cornish Yarg

CORNISH PEPPER

REGION: *Cornwall*
TYPE: *Modern, farmhouse, vegetarian, fresh cheese*
SOURCE: *Cow's milk*
DESCRIPTION: *500g/1 1/4lb round cheese coated in cracked peppercorns*
CULINARY USES: *Table cheese; also spread or grilled on country-style bread*

Lynher Valley Dairies produces two soft cheeses, Cornish Pepper and Cornish Herb and Garlic. Both are rich, moist cream cheeses. The former is liberally sprinkled with cracked peppercorns; the latter is mixed with herbs and garlic before being rolled in chopped parsley. The cheeses ripen in four to six weeks and have a fat content of 45 per cent. The dairy also produces Cornish Yarg.

ABOVE: Coquetdale is ripened in old caves at the dairy in Northumberland

CORNISH YARG

REGION: *Cornwall*
TYPE: *Modern, farmhouse, vegetarian, hard cheese*
SOURCE: *Cow's milk (Friesian)*
DESCRIPTION: *900g/2lb and 2.75kg/6lb circular cheeses. The natural rind is covered in fresh nettles*
CULINARY USE: *Table cheese*

Cornish Yarg is a hand-made cheese produced from a traditional seventeenth-century recipe discovered and initially made by a couple called Gray. When they were trying to find an authentic Cornish name for it, someone pointed out that Gray spelt backwards had a very Cornish ring to it and so Yarg it became.

Michael Horrell of Lynher Dairies now produces this delicious cheese. The nettle wrapping provides an unusual and attractive contrast to the white interior, and gives a slight flavouring to the cheese. Moist but crumbly, Cornish Yarg is not unlike Caerphilly, and has a lovely freshness. As it matures, a greyish hue covers the nettles, the interior softens and the taste is reminiscent of meadow flowers and creamed spinach. Other cheeses made by Michael Horrell include Cornish Pepper and Cornish Herb and Garlic. Cornish Yarg won a silver medal in the British Cheese Awards of 1995. It matures in 10–15 weeks and has a fat content of 45 per cent.

COTHERSTONE

REGION: *Durham*
TYPE: *Traditional, farmhouse, unpasteurized, hard cheese*
SOURCE: *Cow's milk*
DESCRIPTION: *900g/2lb or 3.5kg/8lb round. The cream-coloured, natural rind has some white or grey moulds*
CULINARY USES: *Table cheese, grilling*

Made by Joan and Alwyn Cross in Teesdale from an old Dales recipe, Cotherstone is a hard, crumbly, open-textured cheese. Yeasty, with a crisp, white wine acidity and a fresh, citrus tang, it is one of the few traditional Dale cheeses still being made in the wild and beautiful Pennines.

Cotherstone matures in two to 10 weeks and has a fat content of 45 per cent.

COVERDALE
REGION: *North Yorkshire*
TYPE: *Traditional, creamery, vegetarian, hard cheese*
SOURCE: *Cow's milk*
DESCRIPTION: *1.5kg/3¼lb clothbound truckle cheese with pale yellow rind*
CULINARY USE: *Table cheese*

A mild, buttery cheese, Coverdale has a sharp, clean taste. The texture is firm and open. In recent years many of the old cheese recipes have been revived and new cheeses created in the same style. Coverdale is one such. It reappeared in 1987 after an absence of 50 years. Originally made in Coverdale, it is now produced in nearby Fountains Dairy. Coverdale matures in four to five weeks.

CURWORTHY
REGION: *Devon*
TYPE: *Traditional, farmhouse, unpasteurized, vegetarian, hard cheese*
SOURCE: *Cow's milk (Friesian)*
DESCRIPTION: *450g/1lb and 1.4kg/3lb truckle cheese with natural, firm, grey rind*
CULINARY USES: *Table cheese, grilling, grating*

In the heart of Devon is Stockbearne Farm. Here Rachel Stevens makes cheeses by hand, using milk from the farm's own Friesian cows. Curworthy, her first cheese, is based on a seventeenth-century recipe. It has a creamy interior with a supple, open texture. The delicate, melted butter taste becomes more rounded with age. Curworthy Cheeses also produce two variations on Curworthy: Meldon (flavoured with Chiltern ale and wholegrain mustard) and Belston. Curworthy is matured for three to four months and has a fat content of 48 per cent. Devon Oke is larger than the Curworthy. Aged for up to six months, it has a richer, more full-bodied flavour.

DENHAY DORSET DRUM
REGION: *Dorset*
TYPE: *Traditional, farmhouse, vegetarian, hard cheese*
SOURCE: *Cow's milk*
DESCRIPTION: *2kg/4½lb clothbound truckle cheese with natural rind*
CULINARY USES: *Table cheese, grilling, grating*

A smaller version of the traditional Denhay Cheddar, Denhay Dorset Drum matures more quickly and has a dense, chewy texture and a delicious, mellow nuttiness. The small size of cylinder, known as a truckle, makes this cheese an excellent gift.

Denhay Dorset Drum is a past silver medal winner at the British Cheese Awards. It matures in six to nine months and has a fat content of 50 per cent.

BELOW: Curworthy is an unpasteurized vegetarian cheese

BELOW: Coverdale – one of the newly revived old cheeses

DERBY
REGION: *Derbyshire*
TYPE: *Traditional, creamery, hard cheese*
SOURCE: *Cow's milk*
DESCRIPTION: *4–13.5kg/9lb–30lb cylinder with natural, pale primrose yellow rind*
CULINARY USES: *Table cheese, grilling*

Originally made on small farms, in 1870 Derby became the first cheese in Britain to be made in a factory, which was tantamount to signing its death warrant. However, the growing interest in Britain's old cheeses may well see a resurgence in its popularity.

Similar in texture to Cheddar, but more open, Derby has a softer, flakier curd and a melted-butter taste . Few, if any, farmhouse examples exist, and those that are sold tend to be too young and lacking in flavour.

Derby ripens in one to six months and has a fat content of 45 per cent More commonly available is Sage Derby, a herb-flavoured version.

DEVON BLUE

REGION: *Devon*
TYPE: *Modern, farmhouse, unpasteurized, vegetarian, blue cheese*
SOURCE: *Cow's milk (Ayrshire)*
DESCRIPTION: *3kg/6½lb cylinder with rough, crusty, natural rind mottled with grey, white and brown moulds*
CULINARY USE: *Table cheese*

Ticklemore Cheeses make three excellent blues, one each from cow's milk, goat's milk and sheep's milk. Available all year round, Devon Blue is milder than the others and has a subtle flavour of new leather overlaid by the spicy blue tang. Smooth, creamy and deliciously herbaceous, it is aged for four to six months, then wrapped in foil to prevent it from drying out.

DEVON GARLAND

REGION: *Devon*
TYPE: *Modern, farmhouse, unpasteurized, vegetarian, speciality cheese*
SOURCE: *Cow's milk*
DESCRIPTION: *4kg/9lb wheel. The natural rind is firm and smooth, with a grey-brown crust*
CULINARY USES: *Table cheese, grilling, grating*

This old West Country cheese was revived by Hilary Charnely and is now made by the Peverstone Cheese Company Limited at Cullompton, near Exeter. When young, it resembles Caerphilly. The "garland", or layer of fresh herbs, from which it gets its name, is added to the cheese before it is placed in cellars to mature for up to eight weeks. The aroma of the herbs permeates the loosely packed, lemon-fresh curds and the resultant taste is fresh, clean and savoury. Devon Garland matures in six to eight weeks and has a fat content of 45 per cent.

DOUBLE GLOUCESTER

REGION: *Gloucestershire*
TYPE: *Traditional, farmhouse and creamery, unpasteurized, hard cheese*
SOURCE: *Cow's milk*
DESCRIPTION: *3.5–8kg/8–18lb deep round. The hard, natural rind has some grey-blue moulds and bears the marks of the cloth in which it is matured*
CULINARY USES: *Table cheese, grating, grilling, sauces*

Both Double and Single Gloucester have been made in Gloucestershire since the sixteenth century and were originally clothbound, round cheeses made from the milk of the native Old Gloucester cows. Single Gloucester is smaller, made from skimmed milk and meant to be eaten young. The full-cream milk in Double Gloucester gives it its characteristic, rich, buttery taste and flaky texture. It is firm and biteable, like hard chocolate. The colour is a pale tangerine. It has a wonderful, savoury flavour of cheese and onions. Not as firm as Cheddar, it has a mellow, nutty character with a delicious, orange-zest tang.

Few of these cheeses are made by traditional methods today, but those that are are well worth trying. Traditional makers include Appleby, Quicke and Smart.

ABOVE: Mellow and nutty Double Gloucester

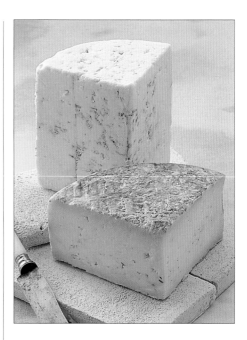

ABOVE: Devon Blue (back) and Devon Garland (front)

DOUBLE WORCESTER

REGION: *Worcester*
TYPE: *Modern, farmhouse, unpasteurized, hard cheese*
SOURCE: *Cow's milk (Holstein/Friesian)*
DESCRIPTION: *4kg/9lb cylinder. The hard, natural rind is yellow with some moulding*
CULINARY USES: *Table cheese, grilling, sauces*

A smaller version of Double Gloucester, this is made by Anstey's in the neighbouring county of Worcester. It develops a firm, breakable, flaky texture and deep tangerine-orange interior with a rounded, mellow character and a flavour that is reminiscent of citrus zest. Hand milking contributes to its unique flavour.

The farm on which the cheese is made has been in the Anstey family for four generations. Colin and Alyson Anstey decided to diversify into cheese-making in 1995 and won a silver medal at the British Cheese Awards that same year. Their Double Worcester matures in five to seven months and has a fat content of 45 per cent.

Another cheese created by the Ansteys is Old Worcester, flavoured with Worcestershire sauce. They have a farm shop and mail order service.

DUDDLESWELL

REGION: *East Sussex*
TYPE: *Modern, farmhouse, unpasteurized, vegetarian, hard cheese*
SOURCE: *Sheep's milk*
DESCRIPTION: *2kg/4¹/₂lb truckle cheese with hard, finely ridged, polished, natural rind*
CULINARY USES: *Table cheese, grating (can be substituted for Pecorino)*

The producers of this cheese, Sussex High Weald Dairy, are based at Putlands Farm in the heart of Ashdown Forest, the hunting ground of the kings of England since 1372. Mark Hardy and his father Guy have been making a range of sheep's products for over 10 years, including yogurt and a fresh cheese called Sussex Slipcote that comes in various flavours.

Duddleswell is a cheerful-looking truckle whose firm, almost flaky texture seems to melt in the mouth, releasing a sweet, caramel flavour with a hint of Brazil nuts and fresh hay. It is a past winner of a silver medal at the British Cheese Awards. The cheese ripens in 10–12 weeks and has a fat content of 45 per cent. Sussex High Weald Dairy also produces halloumi and feta cheeses.

EMLETT

REGION: *Avon*
TYPE: *Modern, farmhouse, unpasteurized, soft-white cheese*
SOURCE: *Sheep's milk*
DESCRIPTION: *150g/5oz disc with fine crusty penicillium rind dotted with reddish-brown ferments*
CULINARY USE: *Table cheese*

Emlett is a firm, smooth and cream cheese produced by Mary Holbrook of Sleight Farm. As it ages, the cheese softens like ice cream. Quite earthy, it has a delicious, yeasty aroma that penetrates the cheese and enhances the sweet acidity and characteristic nuttiness. The cheese requires four to six weeks to mature.

Little Rydings, another of Mary Holbrook's cheeses, is made from the same curd, but because it is bigger, it drains and matures at a different rate to produce a cheese that is distinctly different. Also in the Sleight Farm range are Tyning, Tymsboro and feta.

ABOVE: *Exmoor Blue*

EXMOOR BLUE

REGION: *Somerset*
TYPE: *Modern, farmhouse, unpasteurized, vegetarian, blue cheeses*
SOURCE: *Cow's, goat's or sheep's milk*
DESCRIPTION: *Various sizes and shapes, all with natural rind*
CULINARY USE: *Table cheeses*

Alan Duffield makes five blue cheeses from cow's, goat's and sheep's milk, each with its own unique character and style. The Jersey milk cheeses – Somerset Blue and Jersey Blue (a soft white) – are made with milk from two local herds. Both these cheeses are a distinctive, Monet yellow colour. The goat's milk comes from the same area, but the sheep's milk is from the Quantocks. Cheesemaking takes place in the original dairy at Willett Farm. All the cheeses are made with raw milk.

FINN

REGION: *Hereford and Worcester*
TYPE: *Modern, farmhouse, unpasteurized, vegetarian, soft-white cheese*
SOURCE: *Cow's milk*
DESCRIPTION: *225g/8oz round with thick, white penicillium rind*
CULINARY USES: *Table cheese, baking*

Produced by Charlie Westhead of Neal's Yard Creamery, this is the only triple cream cheese made in England. It is firm and amazingly rich, with a mild, fresh, creamy acidity and just a hint of mushrooms. Finn ripens in two to four weeks and has a fat content of 75 per cent.

LEFT: *Duddleswell (bottom) and Emlett (top)*

FLOWER MARIE

REGION: *East Sussex*
TYPE: *Modern, farmhouse, unpasteurized, vegetarian, soft-white cheese*
SOURCE: *Sheep's milk*
DESCRIPTION: *200g/7oz or 1.5kg/3¼lb square cheese. The thin, soft-white rind has a mushroomy-pink tint*
CULINARY USE: *Table cheese*

Produced by Kevin and Alison Blunt at Greenacres Farm, Flower Marie has a gentle fragrance like that of fresh mushrooms and a soft rind that envelops the firm yet moist interior. It melts like ice cream in the mouth to reveal a lemony freshness under the characteristic sweetness of the sheep's milk. It ripens in five to six weeks.

FRIESLA

REGION: *Devon*
TYPE: *Modern, farmhouse, vegetarian, hard cheese*
SOURCE: *Sheep's milk*
DESCRIPTION: *2.5kg/5½lb boulder-shaped cheese. Hard natural rind*
CULINARY USE: *Table cheese*

Friesla is an excellent hard sheep's milk cheese. Sweet and fragrant, the flavour suggests elderflowers with a hint of blackcurrants and a delicious, almond finish. Its creamy, melt-in-the-mouth feel appeals to a wide range of palates and it provides the perfect introduction to sheep's milk cheeses. Based on the original Gouda recipe, it takes its name from the Friesland Islands, where both the world's finest milking sheep and this cheese originate. Friesla matures in six to 10 weeks and has a fat content of 45 percent.

GOLDEN CROSS

REGION: *East Sussex*
TYPE: *Modern, farmhouse, unpasteurized, vegetarian, soft-white cheese*
SOURCE: *Goat's milk*
DESCRIPTION: *225g/8oz log with mould-ripened rind dusted with salted ash*
CULINARY USE: *Table cheese*

Based on the traditional, French, artisan cheese Sainte-Maure, Golden Cross is lightly dusted with ash. At first firm and slightly grainy, the cheese softens with age to a texture more like ice cream. The flavour is a careful blend of sweetness and acidity: vanilla and caramel combine with the bitterness of celery and green grass, and there is a barely detectable goaty finish.

Produced by Kevin and Alison Blunt, Golden Cross ripens in four to six weeks.

ABOVE LEFT: Flower Marie

BELOW: Gospel Green (back) and Golden Cross (front)

GOSPEL GREEN

REGION: *Surrey*
TYPE: *Modern, farmhouse, unpasteurized, vegetarian, hard cheese*
SOURCE: *Cow's milk*
DESCRIPTION: *900g–3.25kg/2–7lb clothbound truckle cheese. The fascinating range of moulds that impregnate the fine, leathery crust are essential to the final flavour*
CULINARY USES: *Table cheese, grilling, grating, sauces*

A small, Cheddar-style cheese, Gospel Green is slightly softer and less dense than classic Cheddar, with a taste reminiscent of meadow flowers and lush grass. The name comes from the hamlet where it is made by James and Cathy Lane. The cheese is left to mature for four to eight weeks. Its flavour and texture reflect unashamedly the seasonal changes; some suggest that in late summer, the cheese absorbs the fruity aroma of apples crushed in the old cider press outside the dairy.

Gospel Green has a fat content of 48 per cent.

HARBOURNE BLUE
REGION: *Devon*
TYPE: *Modern, farmhouse, unpasteurized, vegetarian, blue cheese*
SOURCE: *Goat's milk*
DESCRIPTION: *5kg/11lb round. Crusty, natural rind with some moulding*
CULINARY USE: *Table cheese*

This smooth, yet crumbly blue is one of the great, modern, British cheeses. Like Beenleigh Blue, it is made by Robin Congdon and Sari Cooper of Ticklemore Cheeses and has twice won medals at the British Cheese Awards.

Available all year round, Harbourne Blue is one of only three English, hard, blue, goat's milk cheeses. The aroma suggests tropical fruit, and it finishes with the hot, spicy tang associated with blues. Harbourne Blue needs three to four months to ripen and has a fat content of 48 per cent.

HEREFORD HOP
REGION: *Gloucestershire*
TYPE: *Traditional, farmhouse, vegetarian, speciality cheese*
SOURCE: *Cow's milk*
DESCRIPTION: *2.2kg/5lb round cheese. The flaky, natural rind of toasted hops is yellow to brown*
CULINARY USE: *Table cheese*

Charles Martell, a cheesemaker renowned for his love of tradition and local history, revived this old Hereford cheese in 1988. The recipe came from local archives and is made using Hereford hops and milk from his own herd. Supple and Caerphilly-like, with the unusual rind of lightly toasted hops, the cheese makes an attractive addition to any cheeseboard. The hops are crunchy, with the slightly yeasty taste associated with beer, while the cheese is mellow, sweet and buttery. It requires one to three months to mature and has a fat content of 45 per cent.

Hereford Hop is also produced by Malvern Cheese-wrights, although each cheese has its own distinct style.

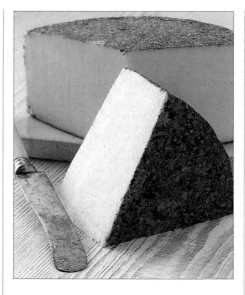

HERRIOT FARMHOUSE
REGION: *North Yorkshire*
TYPE: *Modern, farmhouse, vegetarian, hard cheese*
SOURCE: *Sheep's milk*
DESCRIPTION: *1.4kg/3lb and 3.25kg/7lb truckle cheese. The rough, dry rind has some moulds and yeasts*
CULINARY USE: *Table cheese*

Judy Bell and her husband Nigel decided to diversify from farming, and in 1988 turned to cheesemaking. They now make a range of sheep's milk cheeses, including Herriot Farmhouse, which is based on a nineteenth-century recipe. It is an unpressed "hard" cheese, firm, moist and crumbly, with a zesty taste and a soft sweetness that hints at misty hills. It is matured for eight to 12 weeks.

LANCASHIRE
REGION: *Lancashire*
TYPE: *Traditional, farmhouse and creamery, hard cheese*
SOURCE: *Cow's milk*
DESCRIPTION: *4–18kg/9–40lb clothbound cylinder. The hard, thin, natural rind is pale gold. It bears the marks of the cloth and has some grey-blue mould*
CULINARY USES: *Table cheese, snacks, grilling, grating (a superb melting cheese)*

Few of these historic cheeses are produced in Lancashire today – and fewer still are made on farms. During the Industrial Revolution, Lancashire cheese was the staple food of the mill workers. The first factory-made Lancashire appeared in 1913, and today most of this cheese comes from creameries that are scattered throughout Britain.

When young, the traditional cheese is described as "Creamy Lancashire". At this stage the texture is moist and crumbly – rather like scrambled egg – with a cheese and chive finish and an excellent balance of fat and acidity. As the cheese matures, the flavour intensifies and the cheese becomes known as "Tasty Lancashire".

One of the finest of these is Kirkham's Tasty Lancashire, which was declared Supreme Champion at the British Cheese Awards in 1995. A superb example of a genuine farmhouse Lancashire, it had been matured for nearly six months by Neal's Yard Dairy.

Mrs Kirkham's and Dew-Lay are the only two Lancashire makers who use a combination of three days' curd to give a unique, slightly mottled texture. As the curds ripen at different times, it acquires a three-dimensional flavour that is sharp and peppery, with a mouth-puckering finish.

Acid or "crumbly" Lancashire, introduced in the 1970s is a faster-ripening cheese that has the bite of true Lancashire, but lacks the depth.

ABOVE: Hereford Hop

LEFT: Mrs Kirkham's Tasty Lancashire

LEAFIELD

REGION: *Oxfordshire*
TYPE: *Modern, farmhouse, vegetarian, hard cheese*
SOURCE: *Sheep's milk*
DESCRIPTION: *2kg/4¹/₂lb wheel. The hard, natural rind is imprinted with a pattern that resembles the tread on a nineteenth-century steam wheel*
CULINARY USE: *Table cheese*

Before the dissolution of the monasteries in the 1530s by King Henry VIII, the monks of Abingdon Abbey owned the farm where Rodney Whitworth now produces his sheep's milk cheese. It was recorded that, at that time, the monks made three "ponders" (tons) of sheep's milk cheese a year.

The history of Abbey Farm obviously captured Rodney Whitworth's imagination and in the late 1980s he faithfully revived the sixteenth-century recipe for Leafield.

It is a hard, dense, chewy cheese, with a delightful medley of flavours. There is a certain fruitiness (rather like fresh pineapple) coupled with a nutty taste with hints of hawthorn and aniseed. The cheese matures in three to four months and has a fat content of 48 per cent.

Abbey Farm also produces Tubney, which is the size and shape of a cricket ball. Smooth and creamy, Tubney has a sweet aroma and a lemon-zest tang that balances the smoky background and the burnt-caramel flavour of the sheep's milk. These small cheeses are mainly made for the Christmas market.

ABOVE: Little Rydings

BELOW: Lincolnshire Poacher (top) and Leafield (bottom)

LINCOLNSHIRE POACHER

REGION: *Lincolnshire*
TYPE: *Modern, farmhouse, unpasteurized, hard cheese*
SOURCE: *Cow's milk (Holstein)*
DESCRIPTION: *20kg/44lb cylinder. The brown rind resembles granite in appearance*
CULINARY USES: *Table cheese, grating, grilling*

Lincolnshire is not an area generally known for its dairy farming. This fact did not deter Simon Jones when he decided to turn the abundant spring milk from his herd of Holsteins into cheese. One morning the cheese legend, Dougal Campbell, arrived at Simon's farm with a bottle full of rennet. Together they made the first batch of Lincolnshire Poacher. On the following day, Simon found himself in charge of the cheesemaking. That was in 1992. A few years later, his cheese was declared to be the Supreme Champion at the British Cheese Awards. It had been chosen from a field of 480 entries.

LITTLE RYDINGS

REGION: *Avon*
TYPE: *Modern, farmhouse, unpasteurized, soft-white cheese*
SOURCE: *Sheep's milk*
DESCRIPTION: *250g/9oz round with fine, uneven, whitish penicillium rind covered with red-brown pigmentation*
CULINARY USE: *Table cheese*

This irresistible cheese is made from March to November by Mary Holbrook, one of Britain's leading cheesemakers. The slightly uneven Camembert-like rind encloses a unpasteurized, soft cheese that is deep creamy yellow around the edge. If young, it may be slightly chalky and white in the centre. Like good Camembert, Little Rydings simply melts in the mouth to reveal distinct yet subtle layers of flavour: the sweetness of caramel, a hint of Brazil nuts and a slightly "sheepy" taste that is reminiscent of soggy lambswool sweaters or lanolin. Little Rydings matures in three to five weeks and has a fat content of 48 per cent.

Mary Holbrook also produces Tyning, Emlett and Tymsboro.

MALVERN

REGION: *Hereford and Worcester*
TYPE: *Modern, farmhouse, unpasteurized, vegetarian, hard cheese*
SOURCE: *Sheep's milk (Friesland)*
DESCRIPTION: *2.5kg/5½lb wheel with smooth, polished, yellow rind that is slightly greasy*
CULINARY USES: *Table cheese, grating, grilling*

Malvern Cheesewrights were the first of the new generation of English cheese-makers to make a sheep's milk cheese in sufficient volume to sell in the supermarket. Cheesemaker Nick Hodgetts modified the recipe for Wensleydale, which was made with sheep's milk in the seventeenth century. Malvern is ideal for people allergic to cow's milk. Firm and dry, yet dense and creamy in the mouth, it has a definite, sweet, butterscotch taste infused with a hint of thyme. The finish is salty and the aroma is of wool or lanolin. Malvern matures in 16 weeks and has a fat content of 50 per cent. At the 1997 British Cheese Awards it won a silver medal.

Malvern Cheesewrights also produce Hereford Hop, Buffalo and Duchy Originals Herb and Garlic.

RIGHT: Malvern

MENALLACK FARMHOUSE

REGION: *Cornwall*
TYPE: *Modern, farmhouse, unpasteurized, vegetarian, hard cheese*
SOURCE: *Cow's milk*
DESCRIPTION: *2kg/4½lb truckle cheese with hard, greyish-brown, natural, crusty rind*
CULINARY USES: *Table cheese, grilling, sauces*

Menallack at two months old is mild, smooth and creamy. At four months, the texture is firm and biteable, the colour has deepened to a golden yellow and there is a wonderful, rich, savoury tang to balance the acidity. It has a fat content of 45 per cent. In 1995, Menallack Farmhouse won a bronze medal at the British Cheese Awards. Variations include Nanterrow and Menallack with Chives and Garlic.

LODDISWELL AVONDALE

REGION: *Devon*
TYPE: *Modern, farmhouse, unpasteurized, vegetarian, semi-soft cheese*
SOURCE: *Goat's milk*
DESCRIPTION: *1.4kg/3lb round with brownish-orange, washed rind*
CULINARY USE: *Table cheese*

Jocelyn and Bill Martin won the British Cheese Awards' 1994 Cheese Lover's Trophy with this impressive cheese.

Firm, almost dry, it has a fragrant, almondy nose that carries through as it melts in the mouth, leaving behind an unusual hint of aniseed and a sweet, sherbet-like zing. It matures in two months and has a fat content of 45 per cent.

Jocelyn and Bill make several goat's milk cheeses, including Hazelwood and the soft, fresh Loddiswell Bannon.

NORTHUMBERLAND

REGION: *Northumberland*
TYPE: *Modern, farmhouse, vegetarian, hard cheese*
SOURCE: *Cow's milk*
DESCRIPTION: *2.2kg/5lb round. The firm, natural rind is pale yellow, dusted with greyish mould*
CULINARY USE: *Table cheese*

In 1987 Mark Robertson started making Northumberland, basing it upon a European washed curd recipe. It matures slowly in the old, stone cellars of a farm where cheesemaking is reputed to have been going on since 1296. Northumberland is a moist, firm cheese with a sweet, fruity nose. The flavour is robust, with a tart bite that lasts. It matures in 10 weeks and has a fat content of 50–55 per cent.

OLDE YORK

REGION: *North Yorkshire*
TYPE: *Modern, farmhouse, vegetarian, fresh cheese*
SOURCE: *Sheep's milk*
DESCRIPTION: *450g/1lb round with waxed rind*
CULINARY USES: *Table cheese, grilling, in salads and on baked potatoes*

Loosely based upon an authentic York recipe for a cheese originally made by farmers' wives, Olde York resembles feta without being salty. It is more moist than feta – almost wet – coming apart in layers, rather than crumbling. Creamy, soft and high in "acid", it has a lemony zest offset by the subtle sweetness of sheep's milk. At the 1996 British Cheese Awards, Olde York won a silver medal. The cheese matures in 10–22 days and has a fat content of 45 per cent. Cheesemaker Judy Bell of Shepherd's Purse makes several medal-winning variations, including Green Peppercorns, Garlic and Parsley, and Mint.

ORANGE GROVE

REGION: *Leicestershire*
TYPE: *Modern, creamery, vegetarian, speciality cheese*
SOURCE: *Cow's milk*
DESCRIPTION: *2kg/4¹/2lb round cheese. It looks rather like a cheesecake, with the surface decorated with rings of candied orange*
CULINARY USE: *Table cheese/dessert*

Created in 1964 by Millway Foods, best known for their Stilton, this is the answer for those who are uncertain as to whether to end a meal with dessert or cheese. Decorated with candied orange rings, Orange Grove has a layer of finely chopped orange peel through the middle of the slightly tart, creamy cheese. The cheese matures in two to six weeks and has a fat content of 50 per cent.

Orange Grove is a past winner of a British Cheese Awards bronze medal. The producer, Millway Foods, also makes Pineapple Grove.

BELOW: Orange Grove

OXFORD BLUE

REGION: *Oxfordshire*
TYPE: *Modern, creamery, vegetarian, blue cheese*
SOURCE: *Cow's milk*
DESCRIPTION: *2.5kg/5¹/2lb round, wrapped in silver foil. The moist rind is cream-coloured and has some grey-blue moulds*
CULINARY USE: *Table cheese*

Baron Robert Pouget is well known to visitors to Oxford's famous covered market, where he has a wonderful, old-fashioned

BELOW: Perroche can be plain (centre), or flavoured with dill (left) or rosemary (right)

cheese shop. Always searching for something new, he decided to create his own cheese in the style of the French blues, as a distinct alternative to Stilton. After months of experimentation in conjunction with a well-known blue cheesemaker, Oxford Blue was born in 1993. Three years later it won a silver medal at the British Cheese Awards.

When ripe, the cheese is a luscious, creamy blue with a distinct but not strong, blue flavour. Aromatic and spicy, it has a hint of dark chocolate and white wine, with tarragon on the finish. It matures in 14–16 weeks and has a fat content of 30 per cent.

PERROCHE

REGION: *Hereford and Worcester*
TYPE: *Modern, farmhouse, unpasteurized, vegetarian, fresh cheese*
SOURCE: *Goat's cheese*
DESCRIPTION: *150g/5oz round or 450–900g/1–2lb log*
CULINARY USES: *Table cheese, toasting, grilling*

Perroche, produced by Charlie Westhead of Neal's Yard Creamery, has a subtle, goaty taste that is clean and slightly almondy. The high moisture gives it a light, almost fluffy feel, but a short shelf life. It ripens in less than two weeks and has a fat content of 45 per cent. It is also made with herbs, such as tarragon, dill, rosemary and thyme.

ABOVE: Red Leicester

RED LEICESTER

REGION: *Leicestershire*
TYPE: *Traditional, farmhouse and creamery, hard cheese*
SOURCE: *Cow's milk*
DESCRIPTION: *4–18kg/9–40lb wheel. The bright orange-red rind has fine, powdery moulds*
CULINARY USES: *Table cheese, grilling, grating*

Leicester was produced in volume by the late eighteenth century. The cheese owed its bright orange-red colour to the natural dye, annatto. During the Second World War, however, all cheese producers had to make National Cheese, a moist, Cheddar-like variety, and the practice of adding annatto to Leicester was banned. When the colour was eventually returned to the pale, wartime version of Leicester cheese, it became known as Red Leicester to distinguish it from the tasteless imposter.

Traditional makers of Red Leicester include Quicke and Overton Hall. A good Red Leicester has a firm body and a close, flaky texture. The flavour is delicately sweet and improves with keeping. There is a mere suggestion of green-grass bitterness behind the more distinct butterscotch and nut flavours.

Red Leicester can be eaten young, but it should ideally be left to mature for six to nine months. It has a fat content of 48 per cent.

RIBBLESDALE GOAT

REGION: *North Yorkshire*
TYPE: *Modern, farmhouse, unpasteurized, vegetarian, hard cheese*
SOURCE: *Goat's milk*
DESCRIPTION: *2kg/4½lb wheel with smooth rind covered with white wax*
CULINARY USES: *Table cheese, grating, grilling*

Created in 1982 by Iain and Christine Hill, this cheese is sought after for its fresh, delicate flavour. The texture is rather like a young Gouda, and the taste suggests chicory and almonds, with a trace of misty hills and wild herbs. The sharp whiteness of the cheese is further enhanced by the distinctive, white, wax coating. Ribblesdale Goat won a bronze medal at the 1996 British Cheese Awards. It matures in six to eight weeks and has a fat content of 45 per cent. Ribblesdale is also made with cow's milk.

BELOW: *Rosary Round (front right), Rosary Herb Log (back) and Rosary Dazel (front left)*

ABOVE: *Ribblesdale Goat*

ROSARY PLAIN

REGION: *Wiltshire*
TYPE: *Modern, farmhouse, vegetarian, fresh cheese*
SOURCE: *Goat's milk (Saanen)*
DESCRIPTION: *275g/10oz round or 1kg/2¼lb log – stark white and decorated with a sprig of fresh herbs*
CULINARY USES: *Table cheese, melting, spreading*

Made by Claire Moody, Rosary Plain won a bronze medal at the 1996 British Cheese Awards. Delicate, moist, soft and creamy, the cheese is subtly flavoured by the sprig of fresh herbs that is used as a decoration. Rosary Plain matures in one to two weeks and has a fat content of 45 per cent. Flavoured versions, including Rosary Herb Log and Rosary Dazel, are also available.

ABOVE: Shropshire Blue

SHROPSHIRE BLUE

REGION: *Nottinghamshire*
TYPE: *Traditional, creamery, vegetarian, blue cheese*
SOURCE: *Cow's milk*
DESCRIPTION: *8kg/18lb cylinder. The deep orange-brown, natural rind has a cocktail of colourful moulds and yeasts*
CULINARY USE: *Table cheese*

Despite its name, this cheese was invented in Scotland earlier this century, and was then introduced to the Stilton makers. It is similar in style to Stilton, but is distinguished by the wonderful, orange colour, created by adding a few drops of annatto, a natural dye, to the vat. The royal blue of the mould provides a distinct colour contrast. The cheese maintains its wonderful blue taste, while the annatto seems to create an underlying hint of rich, buttery, burnt caramel. Shropshire Blue matures for 10 weeks and has a fat content of 34 per cent.

NOTE: When a blue cheese appears to be lopsided or is wider at the bottom than at the top, it has "soggy bottom". This indicates that it has not been turned often enough during the maturation process. The moisture has dropped to the bottom, leaving the top of the cheese to dry out. Avoid any cheese like this.

BELOW: Sage Derby – this version has a central layer of sage-speckled cheese

SAGE DERBY

REGION: *North Yorkshire*
TYPE: *Traditional, creamery, vegetarian, speciality cheese*
SOURCE: *Cow's milk*
DESCRIPTION: *4–13.5kg/9–30lb cylinder flecked with tiny flakes of sage*
CULINARY USES: *Table cheese, grilling*

In the seventeenth century, the custom of adding sage (a herb valued at the time for its health-giving properties) to Derby cheese was begun. As the cheese aged, the savour of the herbs was gradually incorporated. Today, however, most Sage Derby unfortunately consists of reconstituted cheese blended with spinach juice or green vegetable dye and colourless dried sage. The effect is to give the cheese a green-and-white-marbled appearance.

Sage Derby ripens in one to three months and has a fat content of 45 per cent.

SHARPHAM

REGION: *Devon*
TYPE: *Modern, farmhouse, unpasteurized, vegetarian, soft-white cheese*
SOURCE: *Cow's milk (Jersey)*
DESCRIPTION: *250g/9oz; 500g/1¼lb or 1kg/2¼lb round or square cheese with smooth, soft, velvety-white rind*
CULINARY USE: *Table cheese*

The Sharpham estate's permanent pastures undoubtedly give its Jersey milk a unique flavour. This Brie-type cheese is hand-ladled into moulds to retain the soft feel of the smooth Jersey milk, which is so thick that it feels more like clotted cream. It has just a hint of acidity and a whiff of mushrooms. The cheese is made from March to December, ripens in six to eight weeks and has a fat content of 45 per cent.

SOMERSET BRIE

REGION: *Somerset*
TYPE: *Modern, creamery, vegetarian, soft-white cheese*
SOURCE: *Cow's milk*
DESCRIPTION: *2.5kg/5¹/₂lb cylinder with soft, velvety, smooth, white rind*
CULINARY USE: *Table cheese*

Probably the best-selling British soft cheese, Somerset Brie has a delicious "set custard" texture. The aroma and taste suggest mushrooms with a hint of green grass, with some acidity to give the cheese depth. It does not pretend to be like a French Brie, which is richer and more robust, due to the differences in climate, soil, breed of cattle and production methods. Somerset Brie matures in six weeks, with a fat content of 50 per cent. It is made by Lubborn Cheese Ltd, which also produces Somerset Brie and Capricorn Goat.

SPENWOOD

REGION: *Berkshire*
TYPE: *Modern, farmhouse, unpasteurized, vegetarian, hard cheese*
SOURCE: *Sheep's milk*
DESCRIPTION: *2kg/4¹/₂lb round cheese. The natural rind is firm and crusty. The colour is yellowish-grey*
CULINARY USES: *Table cheese, grating, grilling*

Made by Anne Wigmore of Village Maid Cheese, Spenwood was not only awarded a gold medal at the 1996 British Cheese Awards, but also took the Cheese Lover's Trophy. Hard and seemingly dry, the cheese is creamy in the mouth, melting to release its distinct sweet, caramel flavour, which is superbly balanced with acidity. With age, the flavour of ground nuts becomes more pronounced. Spenwood ripens in six months and has a fat content of 50 per cent.

SINGLE GLOUCESTER

REGION: *Gloucestershire*
TYPE: *Traditional, farmhouse and creamery, unpasteurized, hard cheese*
SOURCE: *Cow's milk*
DESCRIPTION: *3.25kg–5.5kg/7–12lb millstone shapes or 1.4kg/3lb truckles. The hard, smooth, natural rind bears the marks of the cloth*
CULINARY USES: *Table cheese, grilling*

Traditionally made from skimmed milk from the evening milking, which was then mixed with the morning's whole milk, Single Gloucester is lighter, more crumbly and lower in fat than Double Gloucester. Only two traditional cheesemakers produce this firm, biteable cheese. The buttery flavour has hints of vanilla and ice cream. Mild, but with character, it has some sweetness on the finish to balance the slight acidity. Charles Martell's Single Gloucester is made from milk from a rare breed of cow – Old Gloucester. Smart's version is chewy, with the richness of cream toffee and just a hint of liquorice. Since 1997, Single Gloucester can only be made in Gloucester.

ABOVE: Spenwood

RIGHT: Somerset Brie

ABOVE: Staffordshire Organic

STAFFORDSHIRE ORGANIC

REGION: *Staffordshire*
TYPE: *Modern, farmhouse, unpasteurized, vegetarian, organic, speciality cheese*
SOURCE: *Cow's milk*
DESCRIPTION: *3.5–18kg/8–40lb cylinder with firm, Cheddar-like rind*
CULINARY USES: *Table cheese, grilling, grating*

Smooth and creamy, yet firm, this is one of the few hard, pressed, organic cheeses in the UK. Herb and Chive varieties are available, but the most interesting addition is wild garlic. Whereas some farmers scour their fields to remove any trace of wild garlic, Michael Deaville harvests his, then minces and freezes it so that it retains its zingy freshness when added to the cheese. Staffordshire Organic matures in six to eight weeks and has a fat content of 48 per cent.

RIGHT: The perfect Stilton will have blue mould spreading out to the rind

STILTON

REGION: *Nottinghamshire, Derbyshire, Leicestershire*
TYPE: *Traditional, creamery, vegetarian, blue cheese*
SOURCE: *Cow's milk*
DESCRIPTION: *2.5kg/5½lb or 8kg/18lb drum. The rough, crusty rind formed by a multitude of moulds gives the cheese the appearance of a rock covered in lichen*
CULINARY USES: *Table cheese, snacks, soups*

Who first made Stilton has been debated for centuries, but it remains one of Britain's best-loved cheeses, thanks to the foresight of the Stilton makers. In the early 1900s they formed themselves into an association to control how the cheese should be made. As with the AOC system in France, they also specified where Stilton could be made – only in the three counties of Nottinghamshire, Derbyshire and Leicestershire.

The rind of good Stilton exudes wonderful aromas of cellars, stone walls and moulds. It is punctuated with tiny holes where it has been pierced by stainless-steel needles to allow air to penetrate the interior. The perfect Stilton should have the blue mould spreading out to the rind so that it looks like shattered porcelain, while the taste should suggest old leather, dark chocolate and an intense spicy "blue" quality, with a hint of white wine and herbs. It should be rich and creamy, not dry and crumbly, with a clean, lasting, tangy finish.

The mistake some producers and retailers make is to sell Stilton too young, when it can be bitter and dry. It matures in nine to 15 weeks, with a fat content of 55 per cent.

Over the years, some unusual rules of etiquette have developed around Stilton – especially the habit of "digging" pieces out with a spoon. This tradition arose when a whole Stilton used to be served at banquets, or in a pub, where it would be consumed quickly. If you are given a whole or even a half Stilton, don't dig into it unless you are planning to eat all of it within a week, or it will dry out. Instead, work your way down gradually, keeping the surface as flat as possible.

Stilton producers include Colston Bassett Dairy, Millway, Long Clawson, Websters, Cropwell Bishop, Mendip Dairy Crest and Tuxford & Tebbutt.

STINKING BISHOP

REGION: *Gloucestershire*
TYPE: *Modern, farmhouse, vegetarian, washed-rind cheese*
SOURCE: *Cow's milk*
DESCRIPTION: *1.8kg/4lb round with glistening, orange-yellow, slightly sticky rind washed in brine*
CULINARY USE: *Table cheese*

This wonderfully eccentric cheese was created by Charles Martell. It looks a little like Munster and is washed and rubbed with perry, an alcoholic drink made with a local variety of pear called "Stinking Bishop". Wonderfully aromatic, pungent, almost meaty and probably over-the-top for most people.

At the British Cheese Awards in 1994 and 1996 it was awarded gold and bronze medals respectively and at a recent tasting in France, this velvety-smooth, almost spoonable cheese was greeted with amazement. It seems the French still labour under the misconception that the only cheeses made in England are Cheddar and Stilton – a view unfortunately shared by many of the British.

Stinking Bishop requires six to eight weeks to mature and has a fat content of 48 per cent.

SUSSEX SLIPCOTE

REGION: *Sussex*
TYPE: *Modern, farmhouse, unpasteurized, vegetarian, fresh cheese*
SOURCE: *Sheep's milk*
DESCRIPTION: *115g/4oz round or 900g/2lb log. The pure white cheese may form a fine clear "skin"*
CULINARY USES: *Table cheese, baking, spreading*

The recipe is said to date back to the time of Shakespeare, when the young curd would mature too fast and slip out of its cheesecloth coat – hence the name. Today the curd is carefully ladled into moulds so that sufficient whey is retained to give the finished cheese its light, mousse-like texture and refreshing, citrus acidity. Light and creamy, with a suggestion of sweetness from the sheep's milk, Sussex Slipcote is available in three varieties: plain, garlic and herb, and cracked peppercorn. The cheese takes 10 days to mature and has a fat content of 45 per cent.

SWALEDALE

REGION: *North Yorkshire*
TYPE: *Modern, farmhouse, vegetarian, hard cheese*
SOURCE: *Cow's or sheep's milk*
DESCRIPTION: *2.5kg/5½lb round. The hard, natural rind has a blue-grey mould*
CULINARY USE: *Table cheese*

Swaledale is a classic Yorkshire cheese, made by David Reed in the valley of the Swale River. It is soaked in brine before being left to mature in humid cellars, where the rind acquires the attractive mould that prevents the interior from drying out. Softer than Wensleydale and a little more moist, it has the freshness of the misty Yorkshire Dales and wild bracken, along with the typical acidity associated with Dale cheeses.

A frequent medal winner at the British Cheese Awards, Swaledale matures in one month and has a fat content of 48 per cent. Variations of the cow's milk version include cheeses flavoured with fresh chives, garlic and apple mint, and another that is soaked in Old Peculiar ale.

TOP RIGHT:
Stinking Bishop

ABOVE: Swaledale Cow

TALA

REGION: *Cornwall*
TYPE: *Modern, farmhouse, unpasteurized, vegetarian, hard cheese*
SOURCE: *Sheep's milk (Dorset and Friesland cross)*
DESCRIPTION: *400g/14oz and 1.8kg/4lb drum. The smooth, hard, brushed rind is yellowish-grey and sometimes has beautiful pinkish moulds*
CULINARY USE: *Table cheese*

Hans and Heather White took up cheese-making in 1989 after Hans retired from teaching. Their delightful, small, drum cheese is a past bronze medal winner at the British Cheese Awards. Although firm, the cheese melts in the mouth. Creamy and full-bodied, it has the sweet, aromatic, burnt-caramel taste and suggestion of lanolin and aromatic rosemary that is so typical of sheep's milk. Gentle smoking seems to underscore the sweet caramel nature of the cheese, and the smoked version of Tala is a gold medal winner.

Tala matures in five months and has a fat content of 48 per cent.

ABOVE RIGHT: Tyning – a former "Best English Cheese"

RIGHT: At the 1997 British Cheese Awards, Tymsboro was voted Best Soft-white Cheese

TORVILLE

REGION: *Somerset*
TYPE: *Modern, farmhouse, unpasteurized, washed-rind cheese*
SOURCE: *Cow's milk*
DESCRIPTION: *3.25kg/7lb round with fine pink to orange, natural rind with speckles of chopped herbs*
CULINARY USE: *Table cheese*

Making traditional, farmhouse Caerphilly has been an integral part of the lives of the Duckett family for decades. The sweet, musty aroma of ripening cheese seems to envelop you as you step into their large, farmhouse kitchen. Ten years ago, Chris Duckett decided to turn his hand to something a little different and began washing some of the fresh Caerphilly in the local scrumpy cider and herbs. As the bacteria in the alcohol attack the young curd, the outer edge rapidly softens and absorbs some of the tart apple flavour – an excellent foil for the slightly salty, sweet Caerphilly. Torville can be difficult to find, but the search is well worth the trouble.

Torville ripens in 15–30 days and has a fat content of 45 per cent.

TYMSBORO

REGION: *Avon*
TYPE: *Modern, farmhouse, unpasteurized, vegetarian, soft-white cheese*
SOURCE: *Goat's milk*
DESCRIPTION: *250g/9oz flat-topped pyramid. The natural rind, dusted with black ash, is covered with a fine, white mould*
CULINARY USE: *Table cheese*

When Mary Holbrook's elegant-looking cheese is cut, a fine layer of black ash is revealed between the centre and the crust. The taste is of lemon sorbet, elderflowers and apples; the finish suggests crisp, fresh fruit with a gentle, spicy tang. Tymsboro ripens in two to four weeks.

TYNING

REGION: *Avon*
TYPE: *Modern, farmhouse, unpasteurized, hard cheese*
SOURCE: *Sheep's milk*
DESCRIPTION: *2.25–3.25kg/5–7lb cheese shaped like a flying saucer and with a natural rind in various shades of brown and grey*
CULINARY USES: *Table cheese, grating*

Tyning is hard, almost brittle and slightly oily. Intensely fruity and spicy, and full of contrasting flavours, it seems to get better every year. Even when young, it has a burnt-caramel sweetness with a fresh, pineapple tang. Made by Mary Holbrook of Sleight Farm, Tyning was judged Best English Cheese and Best Modern British Cheese at the British Cheese Awards in 1995. It matures in three to 12 months and has a fat content of 45 per cent.

VULSCOMBE

REGION: *Devon*
TYPE: *Modern, farmhouse, unpasteurized, vegetarian, fresh cheese*
SOURCE: *Goat's milk*
DESCRIPTION: *170g/6oz round, decorated with a bay leaf or crushed peppercorns*
CULINARY USE: *Table cheese*

Twice winner of a bronze medal at the British Cheese Awards, Vulscombe is produced by Joyce and Graham Townsend. The cheese is unusual in that rennet is not used to separate the milk; coagulation occurs purely through the acidity of the curd. Vulscombe is small, round and elegantly packaged, its stark white appearance offset by a bay leaf or crushed peppercorns. Moist but creamy, it has a fresh, lemon-sorbet taste and just the merest hint of goat's milk. It matures in one to three weeks and has a fat content of 45 per cent. Vulscombe is available plain, with fresh herbs and garlic, or with crushed peppercorns and garlic.

WATERLOO

REGION: *Berkshire*
TYPE: *Modern, farmhouse, unpasteurized, vegetarian, semi-soft cheese*
SOURCE: *Cow's milk (Guernsey)*
DESCRIPTION: *900g/2lb round. The thick natural, pinkish rind is dusted with white moulds. With age it becomes grey, crusty and wrinkled*
CULINARY USE: *Table cheese*

Made by Anne and Andy Wigmore, Waterloo is a washed curd cheese: sweet, supple and smooth, it is full-bodied in flavour and a rich yellow colour. It starts life mellow and fruity, but time and nature break down the proteins and fat. As the interior reaches the point where it starts to run, the cheese acquires a vegetal taste like young celery leaves and dandelions. These somewhat peppery tastes are balanced by the richness of the milk.

Waterloo matures in four to 10 weeks and has a fat content of 45 per cent. It is a past silver medal winner at the British Cheese Awards.

ABOVE: Vulscombe, with fresh herbs and garlic (left), with crushed peppercorns and garlic (right), and plain (centre)

WELLINGTON

REGION: *Berkshire*
TYPE: *Modern, farmhouse, unpasteurized, vegetarian, hard cheese*
SOURCE: *Cow's milk (Guernsey)*
DESCRIPTION: *2kg/4¹/₂lb round. The natural, crusty rind has moulds in various shades of grey and brown*
CULINARY USES: *Table cheese, grating*

Wellington is a superb, modern, British cheese. Made in a similar way to a Cheddar, but much smaller, it owes its Monet-yellow colour to Guernsey milk. Initially smooth and creamy, the cheese progesses to a more intense, sharp, Cheddar bite and has a finish reminiscent of parsley, celery and chives. Wellington matures in six to 10 weeks and has a fat content of 45 per cent.

WHITE STILTON

REGION: *Leicestershire*
TYPE: *Traditional, creamery, vegetarian, hard cheese*
SOURCE: *Cow's milk*
DESCRIPTION: *8kg/18lb drum with pale primrose-yellow, natural rind*
CULINARY USES: *Table cheese, salads*

White Stilton is a younger version of the King of the Blues, Stilton, without the blue. It is mild and crumbly with a lemon-fresh acidity and none of the punch of its more mature, blue cousin. Pleasant but rather unexciting, it is made by most of the Stilton makers. It matures in six to eight weeks and has a fat content of 45 per cent.

WIGMORE

REGION: *Berkshire*
TYPE: *Modern, farmhouse, unpasteurized, vegetarian, semi-soft cheese*
SOURCE: *Sheep's milk*
DESCRIPTION: *500g/1¼lb or 2kg/4½lb round. The thick natural rind ranges from pink to grey-brown and is uneven and wrinkled*
CULINARY USE: *Table cheese*

This is produced by Anne Wigmore of Village Maid Cheese. The curd is washed to remove excess whey, then packed in moulds to drain. This creates a low-acid cheese, which retains the sweetness of the milk and develops a voluptuous consistency. The rind is washed and has a yeasty aroma that penetrates the supple interior of the cheese. The result is a taste sensation, combining floral flavours with burnt caramel, macadamia nuts and roast lamb. Wigmore, consistently wins gold medals at the British Cheese Awards.

WENSLEYDALE

REGION: *Yorkshire*
TYPE: *Traditional, farmhouse, hard cheese*
SOURCE: *Cow's milk*
DESCRIPTION: *4.5kg/10lb or 21kg/46lb clothbound cylinder with natural rind*
CULINARY USES: *Table cheese; also traditionally eaten with apple pie*

The most famous of all the Yorkshire Dales cheeses, Wensleydale is now made by several small creameries and cheesemakers, including some who have revived the tradition of using sheep's milk. Based on a recipe that can be traced back to the Cistercian monks who came over with William the Conqueror in the 11th century, it is wrapped in cheesecloth and matured in cellars.

The best-known example of this cheese is made by the Wensleydale Creamery in

ABOVE: Wensleydale (top), Wellington (left) and Baby Waterloo (right)

Hawes, where it has been produced for almost a century. Production almost ended in the mid-1990s when the owners decided to close down the creamery. They reckoned without the determination of the local community, workers and management, who fought the closure and have revitalized the company.

Good Wensleydale has a supple, crumbly, moist texture and resembles a young Caerphilly. The flavour suggests wild honey balanced with a fresh acidity. It matures in two to four months and has a fat content of 45 per cent.

RIGHT: White Stilton

THE BRITISH CHEESE AWARDS

The British Cheese Awards, sponsored by Tesco, is an annual event which rewards excellence within the British cheese industry. Created by the author, the awards are endorsed by the media, respected specialists and the dairy industry and aim to stimulate awareness of the diversity and quality of cheeses being produced in Britain.

Each year, British cheesemakers are invited to submit their cheeses to a carefully chosen panel of judges including food writers and experts from the cheese, hospitality, retail and food industries. In 1997, over 500 cheeses (including 64 goat's milk cheeses and 46 sheep's milk cheeses) were entered for the awards.

Each cheese is judged alongside others produced in the same way. There are no guaranteed prizes, only those cheeses that attain a level of excellence are awarded gold, silver or bronze medals. The award for Best of Category is chosen from the gold medal winners in each category, and a Supreme Champion is chosen from the 12 category winners.

A national compaign, The British Cheese Festival, runs for two weeks after the award announcements, not only to promote the winners, but also to increase awareness of all British cheese and its regional diversity.

Winners of the awards include: Peroche – Best Fresh Cheese; Tymsboro and St Killian – Best Soft-white Cheese; Croghan and Wigmore – Best Semi-soft Cheese; Montgomery's Cheddar and Chewton's Cheddar – Best Traditional British Cheese; Milway Shropshire Blue and Cropwell British Blue – Best Blue Cheese; and Hereford Hop – Best Speciality Cheese. Milleens, Mrs Kirkham's Lancashire and Lincolnshire Poacher have been Supreme Champion.

YORKSHIRE BLUE

REGION: *North Yorkshire*
TYPE: *Traditional, farmhouse, vegetarian, blue cheese*
SOURCE: *Sheep's milk*
DESCRIPTION: *3.5kg/8lb cylinder with moist, yellow-white, crusty, natural rind*
CULINARY USE: *Table cheese*

Judy Bell of Shepherd's Purse developed this excellent cheese using traditional methods dating back to the early Yorkshire cheeses of the eleventh century. It was introduced in 1995 and won a British Cheese Awards gold medal in 1997. A creamy, sweet, moist blue, it is mellow but not mild. When young, it is typical of a young Wensleydale – crumbly and flaky with a subtle "blue" flavour – but maturity brings softness and a more pronounced taste. It matures in eight to 10 weeks and has a fat content of 48 per cent.

BELOW: Wigmore is one of only a handful of washed-rind cheeses made in Britain

IRISH CHEESES

There is a certain magic in the hand-made cheeses of Ireland that is indefinable yet almost tangible. Perhaps it is the touch of the leprechaun or the passion of the Irish for life that comes through the soil. For despite all the past and present problems that are a part of Irish life, the land is still rich and green and fertile.

Since ancient times, the people of this natural dairy land have valued butter and milk, but, curiously, there is no early record of cheesemaking. Even the monks who were responsible for so many of the great European cheeses never inspired in the Irish a love of cheese nor much desire to make it. Most of what is produced today is rather unexciting block Cheddar, mainly made in large factories in Northern Ireland and exported.

The situation is changing, however. A new generation of cheesemakers has arisen, rediscovering old recipes and creating new ones.

There must be something in the West Cork air that has led four of Ireland's best-loved cheese-makers to produce the Trappist-style washed-rind cheese. Perhaps it is the rugged coastline battered by the Atlantic or the gentle mist and rain that have inspired Milleens, Gubbeen, Ardrahan and Durrus. Certainly the presence of Cashel Rock must have influenced the Grubbs to make their robust and spicy Cashel Blue.

The cheese revolution has barely crossed the border into Northern Ireland, where production remains highly industrialized. However, Blue Rathgore, a goat's milk cheese produced by Woodford Dairies in South Belfast is hopefully the first of many modern specialist cheeses.

ARDRAHAN

REGION: *West Cork*
TYPE: *Modern, farmhouse, vegetarian, washed-rind cheese*
SOURCE: *Cow's milk*
DESCRIPTION: *400g/14oz and 1.5kg/3¼lb wheel. The ridged, brine-washed rind is encrusted with brown, ochre, grey and yellow moulds*
CULINARY USE: *Table cheese*

A silver medal winner at the 1995 British Cheese Awards, Ardrahan is made by Eugene and Mary Burns. It has a distinctive, earthy aroma. Beneath the brine-washed rind, the deep yellow interior is firm and slightly chalky. It exudes a wonderful complexity of flavours, the zesty acidity underscoring the buttery, savoury, meaty character. The finish is reminiscent of a young Gruyère. Ardrahan matures in four to eight weeks.

LEFT: Cashel Blue (left) and Ardrahan (right)

ABOVE: Coolea

CASHEL BLUE

REGION: *Tipperary*
TYPE: *Modern, farmhouse, blue cheese*
SOURCE: *Cow's milk*
DESCRIPTION: *1.5kg/3¼lb cylinder. The wet, crusty rind has rampant, grey moulds*
CULINARY USES: *Table cheese; also excellent spread thickly on warm walnut bread*

Jane and Louis Grubb are descendants of buttermakers and millers expelled from England in the seventeenth century. Ten years ago they started making the only Irish blue cheese, under the shadow of the Rock of Cashel, a bold outcrop overlooking the Tipperary plains. The milk comes from their own pedigree herd.

When young, Cashel Blue is firm yet moist, with just a hint of fresh tarragon and white wine. With age, its true character emerges, mellowing to a rounder, more spicy style. The interior softens, then – when the cheese is at the peak of perfection – it gives up the battle of the bulge and collapses, providing a challenge for the retailer but a treat for the connoisseur.

Cashel Blue is available pasteurized, unpasteurized, vegetarian and non-vegetarian. It matures in eight to 14 weeks and has a fat content of 45 per cent.

COOLEA

REGION: *West Cork*
TYPE: *Modern, farmhouse, unpasteurized, hard cheese*
SOURCE: *Cow's milk*
DESCRIPTION: *900g/2lb, 5.5kg/12lb and 9kg/20lb cheeses shaped like millstones, with smooth, shiny, orange, natural rind*
CULINARY USES: *Table cheese, snacks, sauces*

Coolea is made by the Willems family, immigrants from Holland. Their Gouda-style cheese is widely considered to be as good as any made on Dutch farms, while having its own unique character. The rich grazing of this isolated part of Cork produces a rich, nutty cheese with a fruity tang on the finish.

Coolea matures in six to 12 months. Occasionally, the family makes a larger cheese that can be matured for up to two years, when its fruity character intensifies, the colour deepens and the small holes gather drops of moisture. The fat content is 45 per cent.

COOLEENEY

REGION: *Tipperary*
TYPE: *Modern, farmhouse, unpasteurized, soft-white cheese*
SOURCE: *Cow's milk*
DESCRIPTION: *200g/7oz or 1.5kg/3 1/4lb round with soft-white rind*
CULINARY USE: *Table cheese*

Breda Maher makes this Camembert-style cheese by hand. Full-flavoured and grassy, with a distinct aroma of mushrooms when ripe, Cooleeney's rich, semi-liquid interior benefits from the lush pastures for which Tipperary is famous. The cheese ripens in four to eight weeks and has a fat content of 45 per cent.

BELOW: Doolin

ABOVE: Cooleeney (bottom) and, Croghan (top)

CROGHAN

REGION: *Wexford*
TYPE: *Modern, farmhouse, unpasteurized, organic, vegetarian, semi-soft cheese*
SOURCE: *Goat's milk*
DESCRIPTION: *1.2kg/2 1/2lb round, shaped like a flying saucer. The smooth, brine-washed, leathery rind is brown-pink to terracotta in colour and has some mould*
CULINARY USE: *Table cheese*

Luc and Anne Van Kampen who make this cheese live in an idyllic part of the world with their small herd of goats. Croghan is loosely based on Gouda. The intensity of flavour is the result of inspired cheesemaking coupled with superb coastal grazing. The flavour suggests grass and hay, while the finish is aromatic without being pungent. Croghan matures in four to 12 weeks. Made only from spring to autumn, it can be difficult to find, but is worth searching for.

DOOLIN

REGION: *Waterford*
TYPE: *Modern, co-operative, vegetarian, hard cheese*
SOURCE: *Cow's milk*
DESCRIPTION: *11kg/24lb wheel with smooth, hard, golden-yellow, waxed rind*
CULINARY USES: *Table cheese, grating, grilling, sauces*

The vintage version of this Gouda-style cheese made a spectacular debut on to the market when it won both the Cheese Lover's Trophy and the Best Irish Cheese at the 1995 British Cheese Awards. Although Doolin is made in a creamery, it is turned by hand and matured slowly to bring out the best from the wonderful, local milk. There are three versions of the cheese. Young Doolin, which is sold after only two months, is pleasant enough, but dull; Mature Doolin has a more distinctive, fruity character; and Vintage Doolin has a deep golden paste, fine grainy texture and layers of flavour – rich, wonderfully buttery and fruity. The tangy finish is long and lingering. Doolin has a fat content of 45 per cent.

ABOVE: Gubbeen

RIGHT: Durrus (top) and Gabriel

GUBBEEN

REGION: *Cork*
TYPE: *Modern, farmhouse, vegetarian, semi-soft cheese*
SOURCE: *Cow's milk (Friesian, Kerry and Brown Swiss)*
DESCRIPTION: *1.5kg/3¼lb round. The terracotta, brine-washed rind has fine, white and pale blue moulds*
CULINARY USE: *Table cheese*

Tom and Gina Fergusson's washed rind cheese has twice won silver medals at the British Cheese Awards. There is a wonderful, earthy sweetness to Gubbeen, as the yeasts and moulds work to produce the rugged rind. The taste of this dense, full-bodied cheese is rich and savoury. The finish is of burnt onions and grilled cheese.

LAVISTOWN

REGION: *Kilkenny*
TYPE: *Modern, farmhouse, unpasteurized, vegetarian, hard cheese*
SOURCE: *Cow's milk*
DESCRIPTION: *1.4kg/3lb and 3.5kg/8lb cheeses in the shape of millstones. The natural rind is smooth and firm*
CULINARY USE: *Table cheese*

Crumbling and fine, Lavistown resembles a Cheddar but is less compact. Made by Olivia Goodwillie to a Swaledale recipe, it has a sharp acidity and green, leafy taste.

DURRUS

REGION: *West Cork*
TYPE: *Modern, farmhouse, unpasteurized, vegetarian, semi-soft cheese*
SOURCE: *Cow's milk*
DESCRIPTION: *1.4kg/3lb round. The zipper-patterned, washed rind is fawn in colour, with blotches of blue, grey and white moulds*
CULINARY USE: *Table cheese*

The milk for Durrus comes from a neighbouring farm each morning and is processed in a magnificent copper vat in Jeffa Gill's charming dairy. Over the next few weeks the natural moulds and yeasts in the air gradually form a coat, which both protects the cheese and helps in the ripening process.

When young, Durrus is buttery, mild and slightly acidic, mellowing out to a silky-smooth, compact cheese that resembles a French Tomme. There is the smell of the earth on the rind and the medley of flavours includes caramel toffee, tart apples and a hint of smoke, with a nutty creaminess on the finish. The cheese matures in four to eight weeks and has a fat content of 45 per cent.

Durrus has twice won a bronze medal at the British Cheese Awards.

GABRIEL

REGION: *West Cork*
TYPE: *Modern, farmhouse, unpasteurized, hard cheese*
SOURCE: *Cow's milk*
DESCRIPTION: *6.75–27kg/15–60lb wheel with sharp edges. The natural rind is smooth, dark brown or khaki and very hard*
CULINARY USE: *Table cheese*

This wonderful, Gruyère-type cheese is full of flavour and has a strong, fruity zing. Lightly salted in brine, it is cured for many months with neither wax nor plastic to hinder its path to maturity. It seems the climate of this part of West Cork lends itself particularly well to these slow-ripening, hard cheeses. Bill Hogan and Sean Ferry of West Cork Natural Cheese Limited produce two more: Desmond, which is similar to Gabriel but smoother, with a sharp, resonant finish; and Mizen, a huge cheese, often over 45kg/100lb in weight, hard, almost brittle and not unlike the Swiss cheese Sbrinz or Italian Parmesan.

MILLEENS

REGION: *West Cork*
TYPE: *Modern, farmhouse, unpasteurized, semi-soft cheese*
SOURCE: *Cow's milk*
DESCRIPTION: *225g/8oz or 1.4kg/3lb rounds, with wrinkled, rather uneven, pinkish-orange, brine-washed rind*
CULINARY USE: *Table cheese*

Veronica and Norman Steele have been making Milleens on the Beara Peninsula for more than 10 years, and it is seldom the same twice, though never disappointing. The aroma is of farmyard, wet rocks and heather, the heather recurring in the flavour of the firm, supple, sweet cheese, which also has hints of cream and butterscotch. At its peak, the paste becomes almost fluid, and the taste is yeasty and savoury, with a strong, herbaceous tang and a suggestion of sea breezes. Milleens has the sweet-sour taste associated with genuine Trappist cheeses. It matures in four to 10 weeks and has a fat content of 45 per cent. It was Supreme Champion at the 1997 British Cheese Awards.

BELOW: Mine-Gabhar (back) and Milleens (front)

MINE-GABHAR

REGION: *Wexford*
TYPE: *Modern, farmhouse, unpasteurized, organic, vegetarian, soft-white cheese*
SOURCE: *Goat's milk*
DESCRIPTION: *225g/8oz round with mould-ripened, dove-grey coat*
CULINARY USE: *Table cheese*

Another award-winning cheese from Luc and Anne Van Kampen, Mine-Gabhar was declared Best Irish Cheese and Best Soft White Rind Cheese at the 1996 Cheese Awards. It matures in three weeks.

ORLA

REGION: *Cork*
TYPE: *Modern, farmhouse, unpasteurized, organic, vegetarian, semi-hard cheese*
SOURCE: *Sheep's milk*
DESCRIPTION: *2kg/4 1/2lb round with fine, orange, brine-washed crust*
CULINARY USES: *Table cheese, grilling, snacks*

One of the cheeses that sits between semi-soft and hard, depending on the degree of maturity, Orla is supple and decidedly semi-soft when young. After being aged in cellars for up to six months, it more closely resembles Manchego in texture, although it is less oily. The mature cheese is sharp and salty, while retaining the earthy, burnt-sugar flavour so typical of sheep's milk. The texture is firm and breakable, with some holes.

ST KILLIAN

REGION: *Wexford*
TYPE: *Modern, farmhouse, vegetarian, soft-white cheese*
SOURCE: *Cow's milk*
DESCRIPTION: *250g/9oz hexagonal cheese with velvety, smooth, soft, white rind*
CULINARY USE: *Table cheese*

Attractively boxed, this Camembert-style cheese has taken the market by storm. Although the rind can be a little whiffy, the prevailing smell is of mushrooms and cellars, while the soft, nearly melting interior has the rich flavour of warm butter, with a bite that suggests green grass. St Killian is produced by Patrick Berridge.

BLUE RATHGORE

REGION: *Antrim, Northern Ireland*
TYPE: *Modern, creamery, vegetarian, blue cheese*
SOURCE: *Goat's milk*
DESCRIPTION: *2.2kg/5lb wheel. The natural crust is creamy white, fine and wet*
CULINARY USES: *Table cheese, dressings and salads*

Blue goat's milk cheeses are seldom made anywhere in the world. But Britain can boast several: Harbourne Goat, Clawson's Blue Goat, Brendon Blue and, of course, Rathgore, which was created in 1989 for the local and American markets. Problems with supply meant that production almost ceased until 1995, when the producer decided to start again. That same year, Blue Rathgore gained a gold medal in the New and Experimental Class at the British Cheese Awards. The cheese is moist and crumbly, with the smattering of blue giving it a spicy, slightly burnt taste. Through the blue you can still identify the almondy freshness of the goat's milk. Blue Rathgore matures in three to six months.

SCOTTISH CHEESES

Scotland has only a small number of indigeous cheeses. A harsh climate and rugged terrain are not conducive to the development of a cheese industry, although some soft cheeses were made by the crofters (tenant farmers). Caboc, the oldest of these, can be traced back to the fifteenth century. Crowdie, another soft cheese, is thought to have been introduced by the Vikings, although there is no record of it by name until the eighteenth century, possibly because it was usually made for home consumption.

Dunlop, the only indigenous hard cheese, was first made in the time of James II by Barbara Gilmour, the most influential figure in Scottish cheese history. She learnt how to make cheese in Ireland, where she was driven at the time of the religious troubles. On her return to Scotland around 1688, she started making a sweet, milk cheese, which was named after the village in which she lived. The making of Dunlop went on to become a flourishing industry in the eighteenth and nineteenth centuries, then all but died out until Anne Dorward revived the tradition in the mid-1980s.

In the last 15 years there has, however, been a revolution in the Scottish cheese industry. Today there are over 30 different artisan cheeses. Ironically, the very qualities that mitigated against the industry in the past have become its strength. It is the toughness of the climate and terrain and the hardy nature of the milking animal that makes the new Scottish cheeses worthy of mention.

ABOVE: Bonchester

RIGHT: The wash for Bishop Kennedy includes a generous dash of whisky

BISHOP KENNEDY

REGION: *Perthshire*
TYPE: *Modern, creamery, unpasteurized, vegetarian, semi-soft cheese*
SOURCE: *Cow's milk*
DESCRIPTION: *1.4kg/3lb disc with sticky, orange-yellow, brine-washed rind*
CULINARY USE: *Table cheese*

It was not the Vikings, the Romans or the monks who introduced washed-rind cheese to Scotland, but a young French cheesemaker lured to Howgate Cheese in 1992. With his first success, St Andrews, under his belt, he set about creating a washed-rind cheese with a more Scottish attitude. He finally perfected a secret concoction that included a generous dram of whisky. This is rubbed or smeared over the cheese during maturation.

Bishop Kennedy – named after a fifteenth-century bishop of St Andrews – is smooth and velvety, with a spicy finish. The distinctive odour, typical of a washed-rind cheese, has been likened to damp washing or old socks, although more polite people describe it as yeasty. When the cheese is mature, it almost runs and virtually hums with flavour. No doubt it would make an excellent hangover cure. It ripens in eight weeks; the fat content is about 45 per cent.

BONCHESTER

REGION: *Roxburghshire*
TYPE: *Modern, farmhouse, unpasteurized, soft-white cheese*
SOURCE: *Cow's milk (Jersey)*
DESCRIPTION: *275g/10oz round cheese with soft, white crust*
CULINARY USE: *Table cheese*

John and Christian Curtis created this unique, Camembert-style cheese using the milk from their own herd. Theirs is one of the few farms to retain the old practice of resting the herd: the cows are milked from March to December, then dried off until the spring. The Jersey milk gives the cheese its rich, butter-yellow colour and velvety texture. If cut when still "under age", the curd will be slightly chalky. It needs a few weeks to soften to a custard-like consistency, take on a richer colour and acquire a more rounded flavour. There is a hint of mushrooms from the rind and the interior has a fresh, grassy taste.

Bonchester is a past bronze medal winner at the British Cheese Awards and was Champion Cheese at the Royal Highland Show. It ripens in four to eight weeks and has a fat content of 48 per cent.

CABOC

REGION: *Ross and Cromarty*
TYPE: *Traditional, farmhouse, vegetarian, fresh cheese*
SOURCE: *Cow's milk*
DESCRIPTION: *900g/2lb chubby log rolled in oatmeal*
CULINARY USES: *Table cheese; also spread on oatcakes*

Made with cream-enriched milk, Caboc is buttery and wickedly rich. The toasted oats give it a nutty, yeasty flavour. This is one of Scotland's indigenous cheeses, made to an ancient recipe. According to legend it was created by Mariota de Ile, daughter of a fifteenth-century Mac-Donald, Lord of the Isles. When she was 12 years old, Mariota was in danger of being abducted by the Campbells, who planned to marry her to one of their own and seize her lands. Mariota escaped to Ireland, learned how to make cheese and brought the knowledge back to her people. Caboc was popular for many years, but then went into decline. It was revived by Susannah Stone, a descendant of Mariota de Ile, in 1962.

Caboc ripens in five days and has a fat content of 69 per cent.

CAIRNSMORE

REGION: *Dumfries and Galloway*
TYPE: *Modern, farmhouse, unpasteurized, hard cheese*
SOURCE: *Sheep's milk (East Friesland)*
DESCRIPTION: *1.4kg/3lb truckle. The hard, crusty rind has rusty red ferments. Available with natural rind or clothbound*
CULINARY USE: *Table cheese*

A past winner of a bronze medal at the British Cheese Awards, this delicious sheep's milk cheese from Galloway Farmhouse Cheese looks irresistible with its sometimes slightly lopsided shape. The rind develops a series of wonderful, furry moulds as it reaches maturity. The aroma hints at old leather and moss and the texture is firm, rather like Cheddar but more moist. Aromatic and decidedly nutty, with the sweetness of caramel and burnt toffee, Cairnsmore ripens in seven to nine months. The cheese is made only from April to October.

CROWDIE

REGION: *Ross and Cromarty*
TYPE: *Traditional, farmhouse, vegetarian, fresh cheese*
SOURCE: *Cow's milk*
DESCRIPTION: *125g/4½oz log; also packed in tubs*
CULINARY USES: *Table cheese, baking, snacks and breakfast*

The author's wonderful Scottish granny, one of many pioneers to brave the long sea voyage to New Zealand in the late nineteenth century, used to make her own hand-churned butter by skimming the cream off the milk. The buttermilk went into her exquisite scones and from the skimmed milk she would make Crowdie. The fresh, unpressed curd would be ready to eat the following day.

Crowdie is thought to have been introduced into Scotland by the Vikings in the eighth century. It is called Gruth in Gaelic. Slightly sour-tasting, it has a creamy yet crumbly texture and collapses gently on the palate.

Cheesemaker Susannah Stone recently introduced a blend of Crowdie and double cream called Gruth Dhu (Black Crowdie). This is formed into oval shapes and covered in toasted pinhead oats and crushed peppercorns.

BELOW: Cairnsmore (left) and Caboc

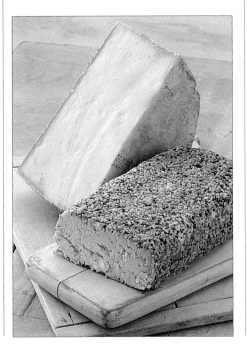

DUNLOP

REGION: *Ayrshire*
TYPE: *Traditional, farmhouse, unpasteurized, vegetarian, hard cheese*
SOURCE: *Cow's milk (Ayrshire)*
DESCRIPTION: *250g/9oz round with pale yellow, natural, rind finely dusted with moulds*
CULINARY USE: *Table cheese*

Anne Dorward started making traditional Dunlop 10 years ago at the farm where it was first established. Firm yet springy, it is very mild and buttery, with the sweetness of fresh milk and a gentle acidity on the finish. It ripens in six months. The producer, Dunlop Dairy, also makes Bonnet and Swinzie.

BELOW: Dunlop

DUNSYRE BLUE

REGION: *Lanarkshire*
TYPE: *Modern, farmhouse, unpasteurized, vegetarian, blue cheese*
SOURCE: *Cow's milk (Ayrshire)*
DESCRIPTION: *1.4–1.8kg/3–4lb cylinder wrapped in foil. The moist, white rind attracts a variety of moulds*
CULINARY USE: *Table cheese*

Dunsyre Blue is wrapped in foil to keep its rind moist. When aged, the smooth, creamy-coloured interior is penetrated by chunky streaks of blue-green mould that impart a spicy flavour to the cheese. The flavour is strongly suggestive of the clover and grasses of the pastures where the cows graze. Dunsyre Blue ripens in six to 12 weeks and has a fat content of 45 per cent. It is made by Humphrey Errington, who also produces Lanark Blue.

GALLOWAY GOAT'S MILK GEMS

REGION: *Dumfries and Galloway*
TYPE: *Modern, farmhouse, unpasteurized, fresh cheese*
SOURCE: *Goat's milk*
DESCRIPTION: *20g/³/₄oz spheres*
CULINARY USES: *Table cheese, grilling, spreading, salads*

These tiny, pure white balls of fresh goat's cheese are marinated with fresh herbs and garlic in jars of olive oil. Although garlic is the overriding flavour, you can still identify the freshness of the herbs and the herbaceous, lemony character of the milk.

The same cheese is available as a 450g/1lb round, coated in yellow wax. Very moist and crumbly, it melts in the mouth and has a subtle, goaty aroma and taste, with a slightly smoky finish. The producer, Galloway Farmhouse Cheese, also makes Cairnsmore.

GOWRIE

REGION: *Perthshire*
TYPE: *Modern, farmhouse, hard cheese*
SOURCE: *Cow's milk*
DESCRIPTION: *27kg/60lb cylinder with natural rind, bound in cloth*
CULINARY USES: *Table cheese, grating, in sauces*

Wrapped in locally made linen to produce a natural rind, Gowrie is a large and impressive cheese. It is made using traditional Cheddar techniques, but is softer and less dense, more closely resembling Scotland's famous hard cheese, Dunlop. It ripens in seven to 12 months.

ABOVE: Lairobell

ISLE OF MULL

REGION: *Isle of Mull*
TYPE: *Traditional, farmhouse, unpasteurized, hard cheese*
SOURCE: *Cow's milk*
DESCRIPTION: *25kg/55lb cylinder. The pale yellow rind bears the marks of the cloth in which it is bound*
CULINARY USES: *Table cheese, grating, grilling*

The milk from this part of Scotland produces a pale cheese, but its taste does not suffer from a lack of colour. Jeff Reade uses traditional methods but with a local twist: his herd, mainly Friesians with the odd Ayrshire and Jersey, are fed with hops in the winter months. The cheeses, having been bound in cloth, are matured for up to 12 months in the Tobermory Distillery. The cheese is very dense and packs a powerful punch – the classic Cheddar tang being laced with savoury overtones of garlic and onions, and a barely perceptible flavour of parsley and coriander. A headstrong cheese, Isle of Mull is also available in a gift size, with such flavourings as herbs, caraway seeds and peppers.

RIGHT: Isle of Mull

LAIROBELL

REGION: *Orkney*
TYPE: *Modern, farmhouse, unpasteurized, vegetarian, hard cheese*
SOURCE: *Goat's milk*
DESCRIPTION: *1.8kg/4lb cylinder. The firm, smooth, natural rind is beige in colour*
CULINARY USE: *Table cheese*

The cheesemakers are Jock and Hattie Bell, a retired policeman and his wife, who moved from Glasgow to the remote island of Shapinsy in the Orkneys. Lairobell is slightly open in texture and has a dry, crumbly feel. The unspoilt, natural meadows of the island, with their wild flowers and grasses, give the milk a subtle herbaceous flavour with a hint of almonds and a slightly goaty tang.

In the capable hands of an experienced affineur like Iain Mellis, Lairobell can become quite strong and goaty. It ripens in two to eight weeks.

LANARK BLUE

REGION: *Lanarkshire*
TYPE: *Modern, farmhouse, unpasteurized, vegetarian, blue cheese*
SOURCE: *Sheep's milk*
DESCRIPTION: *1.4–1.8kg/3–4lb cylinder wrapped in foil. The moist, white rind has some grey and blue mould*
CULINARY USE: *Table cheese*

Cheesemaker Humphrey Errington, who also makes Dunsyre Blue, was the first person this century to milk sheep commercially in Scotland (they had been replaced by higher-yielding cows). His flock of 400 graze the wild heather pastures some 300 metres above the Clyde Valley. The unique grazing, coupled with Humphrey's skill and enthusiasm, produces an aromatic, slightly sweet yet pungent, Roquefort-style cheese. The superb, green-blue veins spreading through the cheese are the result of a Roquefort mould having been sprinkled into the milk vat before the cheese is curdled. It is then moulded by hand and allowed to mature for three months.

Lanark Blue is a past winner of a silver medal at the British Cheese Awards. It has a fat content of 45 per cent.

LEFT: Loch Arthur Farmhouse is a traditionally made clothbound Cheddar produced using organic milk

LOCH ARTHUR FARMHOUSE

REGION: *Dumfries and Galloway*
TYPE: *Modern, farmhouse, unpasteurized, organic, vegetarian, hard cheese*
SOURCE: *Cow's milk*
DESCRIPTION: *9kg/20lb clothbound cylinder with pale brown-grey, natural rind*
CULINARY USE: *Table cheese*

Made by Loch Arthur Creamery, part of the Loch Arthur Community and Camphill Village Trust, this is a traditionally made, clothbound Cheddar. Firm and quite dry, it melts in the mouth like hard chocolate, revealing a wonderful, nutty character overlaid by fresh, green shoots and a strong, fried-onion tang on the finish. Loch Arthur Farmhouse is less aggressive than mature Cheddars, so the fragrance and subtleties of the organic milk are able to come through.

Loch Arthur Farmhouse ripens in six to nine months and has a fat content of 48 per cent.

The creamery also produces their own Quark and Crannog. A recent addition to the range is Cebuck, a Dales-style cheese, made by putting the fresh curd into a cloth and then hanging it up so that it dries and matures in the shape of a teardrop.

ORKNEY EXTRA MATURE CHEDDAR

REGION: *Orkney*
TYPE: *Traditional, creamery, hard cheese*
SOURCE: *Cow's milk*
DESCRIPTION: *20kg/44lb block cheese, without rind; also made in smaller rounds*
CULINARY USES: *Table cheese, grating, salads, snacks, sauces*

Produced on the island of Orkney, which is renowned for the richness and flavour of its milk, this was declared Best Scottish Cheese at the British Cheese Awards in 1996. An excellent example of a creamery-made cheese, it is strong-bodied and biteable, with the tiny crystals of calcium lactate sometimes found in well-aged, hard cheeses like Parmesan. Orkney Extra Mature is nutty and creamy, with a savoury, burnt-onion taste. It is no surprise that it has achieved around 9 per cent of the UK market, despite the distance it must travel.

Orkney Extra Mature is matured for at least 12 months and has a fat content of 50 per cent.

ABOVE: Orkney Extra Mature Cheddar

SERIOUSLY STRONG CHEDDAR

REGION: *Dumfries and Galloway*
TYPE: *Traditional, creamery, hard cheese*
SOURCE: *Cow's milk*
DESCRIPTION: *20kg/44lb block cheese, without rind*
CULINARY USES: *Table cheese, grilling, grating, sauces*

This blockbuster of a Cheddar is aged from 18 to 24 months and the flavour is strong and savoury, with a mouthwatering tang to balance the creamy richness. The texture is sometimes slightly crunchy, due to the calcium lactate crystals that form in old, hard cheeses. For the Scottish market it is coloured with annatto, while a "white" version is available for those on the English side of the border.

BELOW: St Andrews

ST ANDREWS

REGION: *Perthshire*
TYPE: *Modern, creamery, unpasteurized, semi-soft cheese*
SOURCE: *Cow's milk*
DESCRIPTION: *2.2kg/5lb disc or small square with sticky, deep orange, brine-washed rind*
CULINARY USE: *Table cheese*

This is one of only two Trappist-style, washed-rind cheeses made in Scotland. It has a supple, "holey" texture and a sweet-sour, slightly yeasty taste.

WELSH CHEESES

The most famous Welsh cheese – and the only traditional one still made – is Caerphilly, named after the Welsh mining village where it was first produced in 1831. With its high moisture content and raised salt content, it was the ideal cheese for the miners, replacing the salt lost as they sweated far below the pastures.

The economic advantages of this quick-ripening cheese were quickly recognized by the major Cheddar makers of Somerset. Cheddar, which was made in huge cylinders, took months to mature, occupying valuable space and creating cash-flow problems in the interim. Caerphilly, on the other hand, weighed less and, thanks to its high moisture content, it ripened in a week, but would keep for two to three months. The Somerset cheesemakers could make the small, Welsh cheeses in the summer months when milk was abundant, and still produce their Cheddars.

By the end of the Second World War production had all but ceased in Wales, having been taken up by the large factories in England. Uniformity of feed and pasteurization eroded the subtleties of Caerphilly, and in its block form it became almost indistinguishable from the other "crumblies" – Wensleydale, Lancashire and Cheshire.

Fortunately, with the revival of the old ways by a new generation of cheese-makers, including recent immigrants from Italy and Holland, authentic Welsh farmhouse Caerphilly is back on the shelves. New cheeses, such as Llangloffan and Pant ys Gawn are there too, together with Teifi, a buxom Gouda. Sheep's and goat's milk cheeses are on the increase and the fire is back in the Welsh dragon's tail.

ACORN

REGION: *Cardiganshire*
TYPE: *Modern, farmhouse, unpasteurized, vegetarian, hard cheese*
SOURCE: *Sheep's milk (East Friesland)*
DESCRIPTION: *1.8kg/4lb truckle with golden, crusty, natural rind*
CULINARY USES: *Table cheese, grating*

Acorn is loosely based on an old-style Wensleydale. Firm yet crumbly, it melts in the mouth, releasing the flavours of cream caramel and crushed nuts, with a citrus finish. The cheese ripens in three to six months. It has a fat content of 52 per cent.

In addition to Acorn, cheesemakers Karen and Don Ross produce Skirrid, which is soaked in mead.

CAERPHILLY

REGION: *South and West Wales*
TYPE: *Traditional, farmhouse, unpasteurized, vegetarian, hard cheese*
SOURCE: *Cow's milk*
DESCRIPTION: *900g/2lb and 3.25kg/7lb wheels, with ivory-white rind dusted with fine flour. As the cheeses are aged in a moist cellar, the white and grey moulds become thicker and more leathery*
CULINARY USES: *Table cheese, grilling, grating*

One of the four British cheeses fondly known as "the crumblies", Caerphilly is only lightly pressed and has a higher moisture content than other traditional British cheeses. It was first made in Caerphilly (Castle Town) in about 1831. The brine baths in which the cheese was soaked overnight sealed in the moisture, and the cheese proved popular with Welsh miners who had lost salt during their labours.

One of the best-known producers today is the Duckett family of Walnut Farm in Somerset, who have been making traditional Caerphilly for generations. When young, their Caerphilly has a fresh, citrus taste with a background of crushed bracken and riverside reeds. The texture is moist, friable yet supple, like a school eraser. With maturity, the edges become wonderfully creamy, and the flavour becomes more rounded. Duckett's Caerphilly won a silver medal at the 1996 British Cheese Awards.

Other traditional makers include Caws Cenarth, Glynhynod Farmhouse Cheese, Nantybwla and Abergavenny Fine Foods. Caws Cenarth has converted an old barn into a cheese room with a special viewing gallery for visitors.

While a good factory-made Cheddar can still retain some of the character of a traditionally made cheese, the same cannot be said of Caerphilly. It is worth seeking out the traditionally made cheese, which is not only delectable in its own right, but also makes a marvellous ploughman's lunch or Welsh rarebit.

ABOVE: Caerphilly

CELTIC PROMISE

REGION: *Carmarthenshire*
TYPE: *Modern, farmhouse, unpasteurized, vegetarian, semi-soft cheese*
SOURCE: *Cow's milk*
DESCRIPTION: *500g/1¼lb round. The smooth, brine-washed rind ranges from orange to terracotta and has a dusting of moulds*
CULINARY USE: *Table cheese*

John and Patrice Savage-Ontswedder only recently started making this small, dumpling-shaped, washed-rind cheese under the guidance of the "inventor", James Aldridge. James is one of Britain's most talented cheesemakers, who willingly passes on his legendary knowledge to those willing to work hard and listen attentively.

Once drained, the young, freshly shaped curds are washed, rubbed or smeared with brine to encourage and spread the growth of the orange-pink moulds that contribute to the taste and texture of the final cheese. Supple, smooth, spicy, aromatic and pungent, Celtic Promise is absolutely delicious and is a past winner of a bronze medal at the British Cheese Awards. Available only from some specialist cheese shops, it ripens in about eight weeks.

ABOVE: Llangloffan Farmhouse

CWMTAWE PECORINO

REGION: *Swansea*
TYPE: *Modern, farmhouse, unpasteurized, vegetarian, hard cheese*
SOURCE: *Sheep's milk*
DESCRIPTION: *1.8kg/4lb tall round. The hard, ridged rind is brine-washed and is brownish in colour*
CULINARY USES: *Table cheese, grating*

It is rare to find an Italian cheesemaker outside Italy, but to find one in Wales is unique. Giovanni Irranca farms his flock of 140 ewes on the wild grasses and bracken of the Brecon Beacons. His Pecorino-style cheese is redolent of their aromatic, vaguely almondy aromas. When young, the cheese is creamy, not grainy like its world-famous Italian cousin. The finish is rich and grassy. The cheese ripens in three months. A smoked version is also available.

In keeping with tradition, the sheep are milked only from April to November.

LEFT: Celtic Promise

LLANBOIDY

REGION: *Pembrokeshire*
TYPE: *Modern, farmhouse, unpasteurized, vegetarian, hard cheese*
SOURCE: *Cow's milk (Red Poll)*
DESCRIPTION: *4.5kg/10lb wheel. The crusty, wrinkled, yellow rind has some mould*
CULINARY USES: *Table cheese, grilling*

Sue Jones, the cheesemaker, is a past winner of a silver medal at the British Cheese Awards for this Cheddar-like cheese. It is firm yet crumbly and has a dense and creamy consistency. The aroma is of fresh cut hay and meadows and the cheese has a mouthwatering, sharp, green and grassy tang. Llanboidy ripens in two to four months.

LLANGLOFFAN FARMHOUSE

REGION: *Pembrokeshire*
TYPE: *Modern, farmhouse, unpasteurized, vegetarian, hard cheese*
SOURCE: *Cow's milk (Brown Swiss and Jersey)*
DESCRIPTION: *4.5kg/10lb wheel. The natural rind is quite rough and pitted. It has a stone-like texture with some moulds, along with the imprint of the cloth in which it is moulded*
CULINARY USE: *Table cheese*

In Castle Morris, near Fishguard, Leon and Joan Downey have been making cheese for 20 years, ever since Leon retired from the Hallé Orchestra. A born entertainer, Leon has created a dairy where he can make cheese for an audience.

Llangloffan Farmhouse is a traditional, hand-made cheese with a rich yet dry, almost crumbly texture that melts in the mouth. Fruity and slightly grassy, it has a hint of fire on the finish. It has twice been declared Best Welsh Cheese at the British Cheese Awards and won the Dougal Campbell Memorial Trophy.

The cheese ripens in two to six months and has a fat content of 45 per cent.

A chive and garlic version of the cheese, coloured with the natural red dye, annatto, is also available.

PANT YS GAWN

REGION: *Monmouthshire*
TYPE: *Modern, farmhouse, vegetarian, fresh cheese*
SOURCE: *Goat's milk*
DESCRIPTION: *100g/3¾oz disc or log*
CULINARY USES: *Table cheese, snacks, grilling, spreading, salads*

This small, delightful, goat's milk cheese has a very clean, fresh, citrus flavour with a tantalizing suggestion of tarragon. The texture resembles that of fromage frais.

The soft, moist curds are carefully drained in tiny moulds and are ready for sale in only a few days, yet with clever packaging the cheeses have a remarkably long shelf life. Pant ys Gawn is now sold quite extensively in supermarkets throughout Britain – its mild, goaty flavour has a wide appeal. Varieties of the cheese include mixed herbs, cracked black peppercorns, and garlic and chives. The producer, Abergavenny Fine Foods Limited, also makes Castle Meadow Caerphilly, Welsh Goat's Log (a log-shaped version of Pant ys Gawn), St David's (a spicy semi-soft cheese), and a number of blended or speciality cheeses.

RIGHT: Pant ys Gawn has a clean, fresh, citrus flavour

PENBRYN

REGION: *Carmarthenshire*
TYPE: *Modern, farmhouse, unpasteurized, organic, vegetarian, hard cheese*
SOURCE: *Cow's milk*
DESCRIPTION: *2.25kg/5lb round. The natural rind has a dusting of blue and white moulds and wild yeasts*
CULINARY USE: *Table cheese*

Penbryn, an organic cheese based on Gouda, is firm yet really creamy, with a host of flavours. Nutty, fruity, sweet and grassy. All these adjectives have been used to describe a cheese that also tastes of melted butter. It ripens in two months.

ABOVE: Pencarreg, a modern Brie-style cheese, is one of a range of organic cheeses made by Welsh Organic Foods

PENCARREG

REGION: *Cardiganshire*
TYPE: *Modern, farmhouse, organic, vegetarian, soft-white cheese*
SOURCE: *Cow's milk (Ayrshire, Shorthorn and Friesian)*
DESCRIPTION: *200g/7oz oval or 1.8kg/4lb round, each with a thick, soft-white penicillium rind*
CULINARY USE: *Table cheese*

Pencarreg is a Brie-style cheese with a texture that feels like solid, whipped cream as it melts in the mouth. The aroma is of mushrooms, while the slightly bitter, green-grassy character is balanced by a buttery sweetness. Pencarreg ripens in two to eight weeks.

The cheese was developed by the late Dougal Campbell, who fell in love with cheese while on holiday in Switzerland. He stayed to learn about cheesemaking, then brought his new-found skills and passion home to create Tyn Grug, a hard, cow's milk cheese.

As more organic milk became available, Dougal embarked on an ambitious project to set up a small creamery, Welsh Organic Foods, and developed a range of organic Welsh cheeses, of which Pencarreg was the first. This was followed by Pencarreg Blue, in which the blue is dotted through the cheese to give a gentle, spicy, blue flavour that becomes more pronounced with age. Pencarreg Blue has a fine, white, Camembert-style crust.

Sadly, Dougal was killed in a tragic farm accident in 1995, but his memory and vision lives on with the cheesemakers at Welsh Organic Foods.

St David's

REGION: *Monmouthshire*
TYPE: *Modern, farmhouse, vegetarian, semi-soft cheese*
SOURCE: *Cow's milk*
DESCRIPTION: *2kg/4¹/₂lb round. The orange, brine-washed rind is smooth and slightly moist*
CULINARY USE: *Table cheese*

One of only two Welsh washed-rind cheeses, St David's has a pungent, yeasty taste, with an undercurrent of smoked bacon. The texture of this semi-soft, vegetarian cheese is quite supple and squidgy, with tiny holes.

Bryson Craske and his team at Abergavenny Fine Foods also produce Pant ys Gawn and Castle Meadow Caerphilly. The company's speciality cheeses include Tintern and Y Fenni.

Teifi

REGION: *Carmarthenshire*
TYPE: *Modern, farmhouse, unpasteurized, organic, vegetarian, hard cheese*
SOURCE: *Cow's milk*
DESCRIPTION: *450g/1lb, 900g/2lb and 3.5–4.5kg/8–10lb millstones with smooth, polished, natural rind*
CULINARY USES: *Table cheese, snacks, grating*

Similar to a Gouda in both shape and texture, Teifi has a deep sunshine-yellow interior. Firm, dense and fairly fruity when young, the cheese becomes hard and almost flaky when mature. The flavour intensifies and tingles the taste buds with a suggestion of bitter chocolate and young celery.

Made by John and Patrice Savage-Ontswedder, Teifi ripens in two to nine months. A smoked version of the cheese is also produced, as are versions flavoured with nettles and cumin.

RIGHT:
St David's

Tyn Grug

REGION: *Cardiganshire*
TYPE: *Modern, farmhouse, unpasteurized, organic, vegetarian, hard cheese*
SOURCE: *Cow's milk*
DESCRIPTION: *7.5kg/16¹/₂lb and 15kg/33lb clothbound cylinders. The rough, deep golden-yellow rind bears the faint outline of the cloth and has some greyish moulds*
CULINARY USE: *Table cheese*

Loosely based on Cheddar, with a Swiss influence, Tyn Grug is dense, firm and slightly grainy. It has a wonderful complexity of flavours that are gradually released on to the palate. At first there is a hint of young celery leaves, then a rich Gruyère nuttiness and finally a delicious, peppery acidity on the finish. One of the author's favourites, it has won bronze medals at the British Cheese Awards.

Tyn Grug ripens in five months.

BELOW: Tyn Grug (left) and Teifi (right) are both unpasteurized, organic cheeses

SPANISH CHEESES

Wherever you go in Spain, from the vast, barren plains of Extremadura to the majestic beauty of the Sierra Nevada, you will find wonderful cheeses. At the last count, there were more than 600, many owing their idiosyncratic nature to the numerous varieties of indigenous sheep, cows and goats that have developed over the centuries.

In 1988, aware that this marvellous heritage could easily be lost as a new generation of Spaniards turned its back on tradition and moved to the cities, the government initiated an ambitious survey. Its aim was to catalogue every cheese made in Spain. Much of the survey had to be carried out on horseback or on foot, in order to reach artisan cheesemakers in isolated, mountain regions whose cheeses had been made for centuries, but were unknown in the wider world.

Recipes were compared, and eventually 81 distinct varieties of cheese were identified. A national quality-control system, Denominación de Origen (DO) was introduced. This regulates where a specific cheese must be made, which breed of animal must supply the milk, exactly how the cheese must be made and what size it must conform to. It also details any distinguishing characteristics. Similar to the systems that exist in France and Italy, it protects producers and consumers from inferior or foreign copies, as only those cheeses that meet the criteria may carry the official stamp on their rind.

Discovering this astonishing bounty can be a wonderful pilgrimage for the cheese lover. Northern Spain, from Galicia on the Atlantic coast to Catalonia on the Mediterranean, offers the most extensive choice, but the Basque Country, with over 40 different cheeses, should not be neglected. Follow St James' Way, a network of byways that stretches for about 800km/500 miles over Roman causeways, medieval cattle tracks, through ruins and walled cities, and discover delectable cheeses that have been made in virtually the same way for over a thousand years.

The Spanish are warm and welcoming. The food is fascinating and enjoying it amounts to a way of life. Stop in one of the many tapas bars and sample slivers of the local cheese with slices of air-dried Serrano ham, a dish of marinated red peppers and some fresh anchovies. Add a glass of fino sherry – heaven!

BELOW: Mahon

AFUEGA'L PITU
REGION: *Asturias*
TYPE: *Traditional, farmhouse, unpasteurized, fresh cheese*
SOURCE: *Cow's milk*
DESCRIPTION: *500g/1¼lb cone or pumpkin-shape. The rind is buff to deep orange in colour and has a dusting of white mould*
CULINARY USE: *Table cheese*

When the author was first offered a taste of this innocent-looking cheese in a tapas bar, she was unaware of its reputation. Local Asturians hooted with laughter as she took a bite – then reached for a glass of fruity León wine to quench the fire. It was only then that they translated the name: Afuega'l Pitu means "a fire in the gut". Fresh red chilli pepper is added to the cheese and more is rubbed into the rind as the cheese is allowed to mature. The pumpkin or bishop's mitre shape is obtained by straining the cheese in a cloth that is knotted at the top, rather than folded. A plain version of the cheese is also made. Both are well worth trying.

BURGOS
REGION: *Castile-León*
TYPE: *Traditional, farmhouse and creamery, unpasteurized, fresh cheese*
SOURCE: *Cow's and sheep's milk*
DESCRIPTION: *1–2kg/2¼–4½lb wheel with corrugated grooves down the sides and ridged wedges marked on the top and bottom*
CULINARY USES: *Baking; also often eaten for dessert, with sugar and honey*

This fresh cheese takes its name from the Castilian city that used to hold a weekly market. Throughout the winter and spring, farmers from the surrounding areas would gather at the market to sell their sheep's milk cheese. Ready within hours of being made, Burgos, also known as Requeson, is pure white, smooth and slightly rubbery. It tastes of fresh milk, with a hint of acidity and salt. If you can, find a hand-made example. The markings on the cheese come from the moulds into which the fresh curd is pressed.

CABRALES (DO)
REGION: *Asturias*
TYPE: *Traditional, farmhouse, unpasteurized, blue cheese*
SOURCE: *Cow's, sheep's or goat's milk*
Description: *3kg/6¹/₂lb cylinder with natural rind, wrapped in either maple leaves or foil*
CULINARY USES: *Table cheese; also served for dessert, with honey*

This, Spain's best-known blue cheese, is made by hand in the north-east corner of the Picos de Europa (Peaks of Europe) where rugged mountain peaks tower above beech, oak and birch forests. The best cheeses are produced in spring and summer, when the shepherds take their animals to the high pastures and the cheese is made from a mixture of cow's, goat's and sheep's milk. In winter, when only cow's milk is available, the cheese lacks the wonderful complexity of the mixed-milk version.

The cheese was traditionally wrapped in maple or plane tree leaves, which covered the coarse, sticky, orange-yellow rind, with its pervasive aroma. Today, foil is used as it holds the cheese together better. The inside can be off-white or yellow, with brown around the edges. It is streaked like a banana cake, with irregular lines and patches of crunchy, grey-green to purple-blue mould. The texture is unusually complex: soft and creamy, yet grainy and almost crumbly. The pungent smell suggests fermenting fruit, moulds and yeast, and the cheese has a spicy, lip-smacking finish.

Cabrales is ripened in natural limestone caverns for two to three months. The rind is penetrated with rods to encourage the blue mould naturally present in the caves (*Penicillium glaucum*) to penetrate the rind. The locals are said to prefer the cheese at six months old, when it is almost totally blue and *con gustano* (with maggots). This the author has not experienced, nor does she intend to!

Similar cheeses include Picos de Europa and Valdeon.

CASTELLANO
REGION: *Castile-León*
TYPE: *Traditional, farmhouse and creamery, unpasteurized, hard cheese*
SOURCE: *Sheep's milk (Churro and Castilian)*
DESCRIPTION: *1–3kg/2¹/₄–6¹/₂lb round (half cylinder). The pale fawn, natural rind is marked with the zigzag pattern of the draining hoop*
CULINARY USES: *Table cheese: serve with the classic Spanish quince cheese – membrilla – whose fruity tang makes it the perfect companion*

Castile-León is now the largest cheese-making region in Spain, accounting for 85 per cent of pure sheep's milk cheeses. Like Manchego, Castellano is a hooped cheese, which means that the fresh curds are drained in special plastic hoops, which leave distinctive zigzag marks on the rind. The top and base of the artisan cheeses also carry a motif or design from the carved wooden or plastic bases, which are placed below the cheese as it drains in the hoops. The motif (a flower, geometric pattern or pair of initials) identifies the cheesemaker – or did. Today, as more of the cheeses are made in factories or co-operatives, the size and shape of Castellano is becoming more uniform, confusing shoppers accustomed to recognizing their favourite cheese by the markings on the rind.

Extremes of climate, the distinctive milk of the Churro and Castilian sheep and the origin of the individual cheese-maker's recipe all contribute to the character of the artisan cheese. The pale yellow interior of a good Castellano is firm and dense. Compared to Manchego, it is quite moist, and has a few rice-sized holes. The wonderfully delicate, cream-caramel taste is perfectly offset by the fresh acidity and hint of salt.

CUAJADA
REGION: *Various*
TYPE: *Traditional, farmhouse and creamery, fresh cheese*
SOURCE: *Sheep's and goat's milk*
DESCRIPTION: *Sold in pots of various sizes*
CULINARY USES: *Use instead of yogurt; often served with honey or fruit for breakfast*

Cuajada originally came from northern Navarre, where the shepherds used the local thistle rather than animal rennet to coagulate the milk. This gave the traditional cheese a unique and more floppy consistency than the modern equivalent, which is made, like junket, by adding rennet to fresh milk and then heating it gently. The mixture is poured into small, earthenware or plastic pots, where it sets lightly.

LEFT: Cuajada – this fresh cheese is widely available in Spanish supermarkets

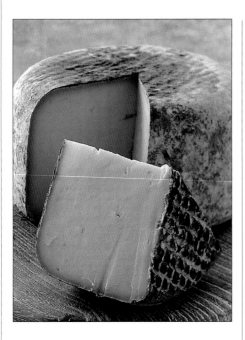

ABOVE: Garrotxa

GARROTXA

REGION: *Catalonia*
TYPE: *Modern, farmhouse, unpasteurized, hard cheese*
SOURCE: *Goat's milk*
DESCRIPTION: *1kg/2¼lb round with natural rind covered in thick, furry, grey mould*
CULINARY USE: *Table cheese*

Disillusioned with the stress of city life, a steady stream of professionals in many industrialized countries have moved to the country, bringing their entrepreneurial skills to a range of enterprises, including cheesemaking.

Although this cheese is based on an old recipe, it has been developed and marketed using modern methods by several groups of what the Spanish people refer to as "neo-rurals" working together as a co-operative in a village north of Barcelona.

Garrotxa is one of the author's favourites. The pure white milk seems to have absorbed the flavour of fresh walnuts and the scent of mimosa, while retaining the fresh crispness of young grass. The texture is firm yet springy, becoming smooth and velvety as you reach for more.

RIGHT: Idiazabal

IDIAZABAL (DO)

REGION: *Basque and Navarre*
TYPE: *Traditional, farmhouse and co-operative, unpasteurized, hard cheese*
SOURCE: *Sheep's milk (Lacha and Carranzana)*
DESCRIPTION: *1–3kg/2¼–6½lb cylinder. Pale yellow to amber in colour, the natural rind is smooth and hard*
CULINARY USES: *Table cheese, grilling, grating, tapas*

For centuries Idiazabal has been made by shepherds in the high mountain pastures of the Urbia and Aralar mountains. It was traditionally sold at the end of September, when the shepherds and their herds of sheep were forced down from the mountains by the first snows of winter.

The cheese has a compact texture, with a few pinprick holes. It is dry, but not crumbly, and feels pleasantly oily in the mouth. The rind carries the marks of the wooden moulds in which it is drained.

The characteristic, smoky flavour was originally the result of the cheeses having been stored near the shepherds' night fires. There were no chimneys in the simple mountain huts, so the cheeses absorbed the sweet, aromatic smoke.

Artisan cheesemakers continue to make the cheese in the way their fathers and grandfathers did, but Idiazabal is also produced industrially. Producers wishing to carry the DO stamp of approval must, however, adhere to traditional methods.

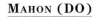

MAHON (DO)

REGION: *Minorca*
TYPE: *Traditional, farmhouse and creamery, unpasteurized, hard cheese*
SOURCE: *Cow's milk (Friesian)*
DESCRIPTION: *1–4kg/2¼–9lb square with rounded edges. The hard, orange rind carries the imprint of the cheesecloth and tends to be greasy*
CULINARY USES: *Table cheese, grating (especially over pasta), snacks*

This cheese comes from Minorca, one of the Balearic Islands off the north-east coast of Spain. It was originally made from the local sheep's milk, but during the brief British occupation in the eighteenth century, cattle were shipped in and the local cheesemakers were persuaded to change to cow's milk.

Although the unpasteurized cheese is sold fresh, a few days after being made, it is at its most bold and delicious when age has given it a hard and slightly granular texture, like that of Parmesan. The ivory interior, with its small, irregular holes, contrasts with the bright orange rind whose colour comes not from bacteria, but from being rubbed with butter, paprika and oil. The taste is sharp, with a salty tang due to the proximity of the grazing to the sea. Some of the traditional cheesemakers add a small proportion of sheep's milk to their cheese.

The curd is piled in the centre of a cloth square, alternate corners are knotted and twisted together and the cheese is pressed for a few days. This gives the cheese its characteristic "cushion" shape and the indentation in the centre.

Mahon is sold at various stages of maturity. If fresh, it must be consumed within 10 days. The semi-cured cheese has been matured for at least two months, while the cured cheese has been matured for five months and the aged cheese for 10 months. Pasteurized Mahon is also available. It is usually sold young, when the texture is smooth and supple and the aroma is sweet and fruity.

MANCHEGO (DO)
REGION: *La Mancha*
TYPE: *Traditional, farmhouse and creamery, hard cheese*
SOURCE: *Sheep's milk (La Mancha)*
DESCRIPTION: *2–3.5kg/4¹/₂–8lb cylinder with flat surfaces. The natural rind is distinctively patterned*
CULINARY USES: *Table cheese, grating, grilling*

The plains where the legendary Don Quixote tilted at windmills and protected the shepherds from attack by marauding bandits are now irrigated. There are vineyards where once only the hardy La Mancha sheep survived. Much has changed, but the sheep are still there, grazing on the shrubs and grasses of the Dahesa and producing the thick, aromatic milk that gives Manchego its character.

This remarkable cheese has been made in La Mancha since the time of the Romans. However, it is now produced in large, modern co-operatives and the milk is frequently pasteurized, but this has not markedly altered the flavour.

To qualify for the famous Manchego label, the cheese must be firm and dry, yet rich and creamy. Only sheep's milk from La Mancha may be used. The distinctive pattern on the waxed rind – originally the result of encircling the curd with a plaited

BELOW: Manchego, from left, aged for 4 months, 6 months and 10 months

(braided) band of esparto grass – must be visible. (The colour of the wax denotes the age of the cheese.) The interior should be ivory in colour, with small, irregular eyes. The complexity of the flavour will depend on the age of the cheese, but there should be a richness, reminiscent of Brazil nuts and burnt caramel, with a slightly salty finish. The aroma should suggest lanolin and roast lamb.

Manchego is sold at various stages of maturity: at the age of 13 weeks, it is described as *curado* (cured) and when over three months old, it is referred to as *viego* (aged). There is a peppery bite to cheeses that have reached a great age.

MATO
REGION: *Catalonia*
TYPE: *Traditional, farmhouse, fresh cheese*
SOURCE: *Goat's and cow's milk*
DESCRIPTION: *1–2kg/2¹/₄–4¹/₂lb bowl-shaped cheese; also sold in pots*
CULINARY USES: *Cooking, as a breakfast cheese, snacks*

This fresh cheese resembles fromage frais. It has a delicate citrus and herb tang. No salt is added before it is potted or drained in basketweave moulds shaped like pudding basins, so it does not keep long. Often made at home, it is used for both savoury and sweet dishes, and is freqently served with honey, aniseed and fruits.

PENAMELLERA
REGION: *Asturias*
TYPE: *Traditional, farmhouse and co-operative, natural-rind cheese*
SOURCE: *Cow's, goat's or sheep's milk*
Description: *500g/1¹/₄lb disc. The thin, wrinkled, yellowish-orange crust has a dusting of fine, white mould*
CULINARY USES: *Table cheese, snacks*

Named after the high peak that rises behind the village where the cheese has been made for centuries, Penamellera has a slightly greasy appearance and oddly meaty smell. The interior is more elegant. Supple and dense, with a few small, irregular holes, it has a mellow, vaguely nutty taste. The finish is fresh and lemony.

Similar cheeses include Quesuco, Porua and the locally produced Rozagas. In 1984 concern that the number of local producers was gradually dwindling led some Asturian farmers to form a co-operative to market their unique cheese. Production has increased and Penemellera is now well known throughout northern Spain.

PICOS DE EUROPA (DO)
REGION: *Cantabria*
TYPE: *Traditional, farmhouse and creamery, blue cheese*
SOURCE: *Cow's milk*
DESCRIPTION: *3kg/6¹/₂lb cylinder with natural rind wrapped in plane tree leaves*
CULINARY USES: *Table cheese, often eaten with wild honey*

The recipe for this creamy, moist cheese is thought to have been brought to Spain by early French pilgrims as they followed St James' Way to the Atlantic coast.

Picos de Europa is usually made from cow's milk, but farmhouse cheesemakers will add a little goat's or sheep's milk, as available. The cheese has blue-green veins, a pungent aroma, a pleasantly salty bite and a clean, piquant finish. Wrapped in plane leaves, it gives a cheeseboard a rustic yet elegant look. If the rind darkens and becomes sticky, pat it dry and leave it in a cool place to breathe for a few hours.

Also known as Valdeon, Picos de Europa ripens in two to three months and has a fat content of 45 per cent.

QUESO IBERICO (DO)

REGION: *Central Spain*
TYPE: *Modern, creamery, hard cheese*
SOURCE: *Cow's, goat's and sheep's milk*
DESCRIPTION: *3kg/6½lb wheel. The hard, dry rind bears the marks of the esparto (plaited/braided grass) bands used in the draining process*
CULINARY USES: *Table cheese, grating, grilling, snacks*

The mixture of cow's, goat's and sheep's milk gives this modern, uniquely Spanish cheese a truly three-dimensional character. Regulations require that it contain not less than 25 per cent and not more than 40 per cent of any one type of milk, and the flavour has elements of all three.

The creamy texture melts in the mouth gradually, releasing a rich, full-bodied nuttiness before delivering a fruity tang on the finish. It is made by large consortiums, in much the same way as Manchego. It is sometimes mistaken for Manchego, partly because the cheese looks very similar and also because the words "Manchego Blend" appear on some labels. Queso Iberico ripens in one to six months.

QUESO IBORES

REGION: *Extremadura*
TYPE: *Traditional, farmhouse and co-operative, unpasteurized, hard cheese*
SOURCE: *Goat's milk (Retinta and Verata)*
DESCRIPTION: *3kg/6½lb round. The smooth, reddish-brown, natural rind is rubbed with oil and paprika*
CULINARY USES: *Table cheese, tapas*

Queso Ibores takes its name from the area in Extremadura – Los Ibores – where it has been made since Roman times. The unusual, deep red of the rind provides a wonderful contrast to the pure white interior. The aroma of the paprika is distinctive and penetrates the cheese as a subtle spicy tang. This is offset by the aromatic and creamy nature of the goat's milk.

QUESO MAJORERO

REGION: *Fuerteventura*
TYPE: *Traditional, farmhouse and co-operative, unpasteurized, hard cheese*
SOURCE: *Goat's milk*
DESCRIPTION: *5–7kg/11–15¼lb cylinder. The pale amber, natural rind has a geometric pattern printed at top and bottom*
CULINARY USES: *Table cheese, grilling*

Also known as Queso Fuerteventura, from the barren yet beautiful island on which it is made, this cheese is one of the author's favourites. Firmly pressed to create the hard texture, its tough rind bears the traditional marks typical of many Spanish cheeses. Although the interior seems dense, it melts in the mouth to leave a trail that suggests wild honey, the scent of wild thyme and almonds. The finish is peppery and rounded, like a fine, red wine. It is excellent with a fino sherry or robust red wine.

Fuerteventura, like all the Canary Islands, is short of water, yet the prickly pear, thistles, cacti and straggly bushes provide the native goat with a veritable feast. The arid conditions mean a reduced milk yield, but the flavour of the milk is intensely aromatic, almost perfumed.

BELOW: Queso Iberico

ABOVE: Queso Majorero

QUESO DE MURCIA

REGION: *Murcia*
TYPE: *Traditional, farmhouse and co-operative, fresh cheese*
SOURCE: *Goat's milk*
DESCRIPTION: *1–2kg/2¼–4½lb pure white, round cheese with indented ridges from the wooden bases on which it drains*
CULINARY USES: *Table cheese, cooking*

Driving through hot, barren Murcia, one could be forgiven for wondering what the straggly flocks of sheep and goats find to eat in the gravelly soil. Closer inspection reveals tough scrub and intensely scented wild thyme, oregano, rosemary and other hardy plants, each contributing to the flavour of the milk. The low moisture content of the grazing also means that the yield of milk is low, but rich and thick and ideal for cheesemaking.

Queso de Murcia is pure white, with innumerable small holes. The texture is spongy and the cheese is subtly flavoured with rosemary and tarragon, balanced by a refreshing acidity. The fresh cheese has been made in the same way for centuries, but because it has a short shelf life and does not travel well, the local government decided to create a cured or aged local cheese that would keep well and have a wider appeal outside the region and abroad. The result was Queso de Murcia al Vino, a delicious and highly successful cheese, made by washing the cheese in the local red wine. The naturally porous rind takes on a deep burgundy colour and the cheese absorbs the fruity, slightly spicy flavour and aroma of the wine.

QUESO DEL MONTSEC

REGION: *Catalonia*
TYPE: *Modern, farmhouse, unpasteurized, vegetarian, soft-white cheese*
SOURCE: *Goat's milk*
DESCRIPTION: *2kg/4¹/2lb round with rustic-looking, patchy rind coated with wood ash*
CULINARY USE: *Table cheese*

Like Garrotxa, this was developed by a group of young professionals who were looking for a more meaningful lifestyle for themselves and their families. The press dubbed them "neo-rurals" and did not always take them seriously, but had to reconsider when they successfully made and marketed Montsec.

The cheese has a dense, fairly grainy texture that feels very creamy in the mouth, yet has a definite bite. The distinctive taste of goat's milk is instantly apparent, and the cheese has a strong, herbaceous, spicy finish.

Queso del Montsec requires two to three months to ripen. It is also known as Cendrat.

QUESO DEL TIETAR

REGION: *Avila*
TYPE: *Traditional, farmhouse, unpasteurized, fresh or hard cheese*
SOURCE: *Goat's milk*
DESCRIPTION: *Fresh – in pots; aged – in 2.5kg/5¹/2lb cylinders. The natural rind on the aged cheese is blue-grey*
CULINARY USES: *Table cheese, cooking (fried with the local pequilla peppers, garlic and plum tomatoes, it makes a perfect partner for pasta)*

Seldom found outside Avila, Queso del Tietar comes in two distinct styles. The fresh cheese is called Cabra del Tietar. Sold when it is only a few days old, the cheese is pure white and rindless, with a lemon-fresh flavour that hints at the aromatic goat's milk. It is often mixed with wild thyme, oregano and rosemary or paprika.

If the cheese is aged for two to three months, the texture hardens. It resembles Sierra de Zuheros and is firm but spongy, with a pronounced, nutty flavour.

RONCAL (DO)

REGION: *Navarra*
TYPE: *Traditional, farmhouse and cooperative, unpasteurized, hard cheese*
SOURCE: *Sheep's milk (Lacha and Aragon)*
DESCRIPTION: *2kg/4¹/2lb wheel with hard, natural rind covered with a velvety-smooth layer of blue-grey mould*
CULINARY USES: *Table cheese, tapas, grating, grilling*

Roncal was the first Spanish cheese to be awarded the protection of the Denominacion de Origen, but regulation of its production goes back to the thirteenth century, when the local council controlled the movement of the indigenous Lacha and Aragon sheep. In July, the animals were taken to the summer alpine pastures, returning at the end of September. On 13 October they were on the move again, this time to the winter pastures in the south of Navarre, where they remained until 15 May.

This migratory pattern (transhumance) is still practised by a few shepherds, but change of ownership or usage of the land makes it difficult. In 1974 a cheese factory was set up near Pamplona to ensure that this delicious cheese would continue to be produced.

Roncal is aged for at least four months and has a fat content of 45 per cent. The firm, elastic interior is slightly grainy, with small, irregular holes. The flavour owes much to the richness of the milk. Distinctly "sheepy" and quite pungent, it retains a sweet, herbaceous flavour, thanks to the natural pastures of wild grasses, herbs and flowers on which the sheep graze.

ABOVE: *San Simon*

SAN SIMON

REGION: *Galicia*
TYPE: *Traditional, farmhouse and creamery, semi-soft cheese*
SOURCE: *Cow's milk (Galicia)*
DESCRIPTION: *1–2kg/2¹/4–4¹/2lb pear shape with glossy, honey-coloured, natural rind*
CULINARY USE: *Table cheese*

Another quirky Spanish cheese, this has the shape of a bullet or a pear. Enquiries as to the origin of its shape provoke wide grins or unprintable stories, but it has been made for generations on the western tip of Spain, where the lush, green pastures nourish the Galacia cows.

San Simon is lightly pressed, then smoked. It has a supple, open consistency and an attractive, polished rind, which ranges in colour from honey to reddish-brown. The smoke gives the cheese a woody taste to add to the buttery quality and slight acidity from the milk.

ABOVE: *Queso del Montsec – also known as Cendrat*

ABOVE: Zamorano

SIERRA DE ZUHEROS

REGION: *Andalusia*
TYPE: *Traditional, farmhouse and creamery, hard cheese*
SOURCE: *Goat's milk (Murcia)*
DESCRIPTION: *1kg/2¹/₄lb cylinder with smooth, pale yellow, hard rind*
CULINARY USES: *Table cheese, tapas*

Sierra de Zuheros is made from the milk of the Murcia goat on small farms and co-operatives near the old town of Trujillo. Like many Spanish cheeses, it was traditionally moulded in hoops made of plaited (braided) esparto grass. Today, these are slowly being replaced by plastic moulds, which have the distinctive pattern imprinted on the inside. They look rather incongruous hanging up against ancient stone walls.

The cheese is dry, fine and almost crumbly. It has a discernible but not pervasive goaty character, with hints of sweet smoke, wild thyme and lemon zest. The rind of Sierra de Zuheros is sometimes rubbed with paprika and oil, which gives the cheese a spicy finish.

TETILLA (DO)

REGION: *Galicia*
TYPE: *Traditional, farmhouse and creamery, semi-soft cheese*
SOURCE: *Cow's milk*
DESCRIPTION: *750g–1.5kg/1³/₄–3¹/₄lb pear-shaped cheese with pale yellow, ridged rind*
CULINARY USE: *Table cheese*

Tetilla looks like a large, finely ridged fig or breast – hence the name. Made from cow's milk, it has a mellow, fresh, lemony taste with a hint of green grass. The consistency is supple, with a creamy feel on the palate. It ripens in two to three weeks.

TRONCHON

REGION: *Aragon*
TYPE: *Traditional, farmhouse and creamery, semi-soft cheese*
SOURCE: *Sheep's, cow's or goat's milk*
DESCRIPTION: *600g–1.5kg/1¹/₃–3¹/₄lb flattened globe with deep crater. The natural rind is smooth, glossy and the colour of butter*
CULINARY USES: *Table cheese, grilling, snacks*

In terms of texture, Tronchon resembles a young Caerphilly. The taste is aromatic, with a background of white wine acidity. The origin of the shape is obscure, but it is replicated today with special moulds.

ULLOA

REGION: *Galicia*
TYPE: *Traditional, farmhouse, semi-soft cheese*
SOURCE: *Cow's milk (Galicia and Friesian)*
DESCRIPTION: *1kg/2¹/₄lb round with smooth, waxy, pale yellow, natural rind*
CULINARY USE: *Table cheese*

Ulloa is almost identical to Tetilla, differing only in the shape and the area where it is made. Ulloa is round, with convex sides. It has a fat content of 45 per cent and ripens in about one month.

ZAMORANO (DO)

REGION: *Castile-León*
TYPE: *Traditional, farmhouse and co-operative, hard cheese*
SOURCE: *Sheep's milk (Churro)*
DESCRIPTION: *2 or 3kg/4¹/₂ or 6¹/₂lb drum. The hard, dry, natural rind is covered in a thin, grey mould*
CULINARY USE: *Table cheese*

A hard sheep's milk cheese, Zamorano has something in common with both Castellano and Manchego, but is less grainy. It is matured in conditions of high humidity in order to encourage the growth of the natural, grey mould rind. The flavour has the appealing intensity of burnt caramel and green grass, balanced by the buttery nature of the milk.

Until late this century, Zamoran shepherds and their families were itinerant cheesemakers, trekking from farm to farm with their rennet, hoops, hand-carved wooden boards and curdling vats. The cheeses they made were often matured in the deep, humid, underground "caves" of neighbouring vineyards, which imparted a musty yet fruity character to the cheese and encouraged the growth of a thick, grey mould rind. This practice is frowned upon by modern winemakers.

Zamorano ripens in three to nine months and has a fat content of about 50 per cent.

PORTUGUESE CHEESES

Unlike Spain, Portugal avoided invasion by the Goths, Vandals and Moors, thanks largely to the Atlantic ocean on one side and the high mountains of the east. This led to the development of a proud, independent race, who to this day value and preserve the old ways.

With a long expanse of coastline, it was inevitable that the Portuguese would become great sailors. In the fifteenth and sixteenth centuries they led the search for new trade routes. The Azores, off the coast of Portugal, were the last port of call for the great explorers on their long journey to the New World. In the fifteenth century, a small settlement was established on the islands. The climate was more temperate than that of the mainland, and a herd of cows was soon established to provide hard, long-lasting cheese, similar to Cheddar, for the seafarers and the islanders. The cheese is known as Queijo da Ilha (island cheese).

The climate on mainland Portugal does not lend itself to cheesemaking and dairy products play a very minor role in the national cuisine. Those cheeses that are made, however, are outstanding: ancient cheeses produced on small farms or dairies in the isolated valleys and mountainsides, where agile, tenacious goats thrive on a diet of wild herbs, scrub, gorse blossoms and brambles. Their milk is thick, luscious and aromatic, and makes superb cheese. The milk from the woolly sheep of the magnificent Serra da Estrela in the centre of Portugal is equally rich and fragrant and shepherds have for centuries used it to make Queijos de Serra. Several similar cheeses, including Queijo Serpa, are made in other areas.

As in other parts of Europe, milk was a precious commodity, and the whey was made into a ricotta-type cheese called Requeijao. Wrapped in fig or cabbage leaves and sold fresh in local markets and small village shops, it is equally useful in desserts or savoury dishes.

During the 1960s and 70s, Portugal underwent rapid social and economic change. The tourist industry boomed and there was a vast migration of people from rural areas to the new coastal developments. This stimulated a need for a more sophisticated dairy industry and large factories were built to bottle fresh milk and produce yogurt and copies of foreign cheeses, such as Camembert, chèvre and Edam.

In the last decade, however, the Portuguese have seen the Spanish revive and revitalize their cheese industry, and have started a drive to do something similar in their own country. 10 Portuguese cheeses recently qualified for Protected Designation of Origin (PDO) and Protected Geographical Indication (PGI) status in Europe (a scheme to recognize and preserve indigenous cheeses, introduced by the European Community and based on the French AOC system). Some, like Queijo Evora, are small discs made with goat's milk; others are made from cow's milk, like Queijo de São Jorge; while others, such as Serra da Estrela, are made with sheep's milk or a blend, like Queijo Rabacal, a fresh cheese.

There is no doubt that, in the next few years, these wonderful Portuguese cheeses will become more readily available outside their country of origin.

SÃO JORGE/ILHA DE SÃO JORGE
REGION: *Azores*
TYPE: *Traditional, farmhouse, unpasteurized, hard cheese*
SOURCE: *Cow's milk*
DESCRIPTION: *8–12kg/18–26lb cylinder. The hard, natural rind is yellowish-brown and slightly mottled*
CULINARY USES: *Table cheese, grating, sauces*

São Jorge is a small island in the Azores. The high plateaux and craters, reminders of the island's violent volcanic past, give way to lush pastures, vibrant local flora and fertile soil.

A Flemish settlement was established on the nearby island of Faial in the fifteenth century. Isolation from the mainland made it necessary for the islanders to become self-sufficient. Cows were brought over and traditional cheese-making was established both here and on neighbouring islands.

The Azores were the last stop for explorers *en route* to the New World, so the cheeses were much sought after. Like Gouda or Edam, São Jorge improves with age and keeps well, so it continues to prove popular with seafarers like the trans-atlantic yachtsmen who call at the Azores today for provisions. Over the centuries the recipe has been adapted to the local climate and conditions: the result is a unique cheese with the look of Gouda but the savoury tang of Cheddar.

SERRA DA ESTRELA
REGION: *Beira*
TYPE: *Traditional, farmhouse, washed-rind cheese*
SOURCE: *Sheep's milk*
DESCRIPTION: *900g/2lb flat round. The fine, leathery, washed rind is orange-brown and slightly sticky. When aged, it becomes smooth and firm*
CULINARY USE: *Table cheese*

Described as the king of Portuguese cheese, Serra da Estrela has been made for centuries by shepherds in the mountains of Serra da Estrela in the Beira region. Most is still made by small cheesemakers, who used the flowers or leaves of a wild thistle to coagulate the sheep's milk. This gives the cheese a subtle but distinct character, and is a contributing factor in the final texture. The curds are broken by hand rather than cut, and matured in caves for one to four months.

The cheese is so soft and voluptuous that it is almost spreadable. It has a rich, perfumed intensity as a result of the superb grazing, and the sweet, slightly burnt toffee character of the sheep's milk comes through on the finish, which is certainly discernible, but not as strong as you might expect.

When the cheese is allowed to age, the rind toughens and the interior becomes denser and more supple. It can then be sliced with ease.

SWISS CHEESES

Switzerland is a tiny country, whose success is largely due to the commitment of the Swiss to quality, hard work and co-operation. Other nations look with envy at their strong economy, efficiently run cities and excellent road system.

Originally known as Helvetia, Switzerland was home to a Celtic tribe, which in 58BC invaded the southern part of Gaul until the Romans forced them back. From the Romans they learnt the art of cheesemaking.

In the fifth century, Helvetia was invaded by tribes from northern Germany, who ruled the area until three of the cantons (provinces) joined forces in 1291 and defeated their foreign rulers. Eventually other cantons joined the battle and in the fifteenth century independence was won and the foundations for the Swiss Federation were laid.

Today Switzerland is a confederation consisting of 22 cantons, each with its own parliament, courts of law and education system. The people are very much involved in governing their own regions. This ability to work together is seen all over Switzerland, but nowhere is it more effective than in the dairy industry, where most of the cheese is made in mountain chalets or in small co-operatives owned by farmers or cheesemakers.

The primary objective of the Swiss agricultural policy is to uphold this system to ensure that the large number of meadows and pastures are maintained and the beauty of the countryside remains unchanged. This is essential in a country where tourism is a major source of revenue. With only 25 per cent of the land suitable for grazing, many of the cows, even in summer, are fed indoors so that the grass is not trampled down. Except in the relatively inaccessible mountain pastures, you will seldom see cows grazing in Switzerland; instead farmers cut and gather the fresh grass in a system known as zero grazing.

Early in its history, cheese was used as currency in Switzerland. Much of what was made was taken over the Alps to be exchanged with the Romans for rice, spices and wine.

Cheese is still a vital part of the Swiss economy, and the Swiss guard its quality fiercely. All hard cheeses have to be purchased by the Swiss Cheese Union. The price of the cheese is laid down by the government, as is the price of the milk. Although Swiss cheeses can be extremely expensive, their quality is guaranteed. None of the foreign copies can compare with the originals, which include some of the best-loved cheeses in the world.

BELOW: Tilsiter

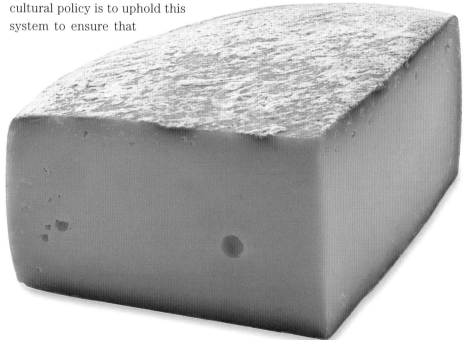

ABOVE: Appenzeller

APPENZELLER
REGION: *Appenzell and St Gallen*
TYPE: *Traditional, farmhouse and creamery, unpasteurized, hard cheese*
SOURCE: *Cow's milk*
DESCRIPTION: *5–6.75kg/11–15lb convex wheel. The hard, brushed rind is pale yellow to burnt orange*
CULINARY USES: *Table cheese, melting, grilling*

One of Switzerland's oldest cheeses, Appenzeller dates back to the time of Charlemagne. As the name suggests, it originated in the Appenzell region, but today it is also made in the canton of St Gallen. Its quality and character are protected by rules similar to those operated by the AOC system in France, and it is at its best when made in mountain chalets from the milk of the summer pastures.

The dry, flat, pale yellow to orange rind derives its colour from being washed in a secret concoction of spices, white wine and salt. The aroma hints at spicy, fermenting fruit. If the cheese has been wrapped in plastic, it may sweat and develop a less than appealing, farmyard whiff. The cheese is firm and dense, yet retains a certain suppleness. A few peanut-sized holes are scattered throughout the yellow interior. At first, the taste is buttery, with fruity overtones. As it matures, the flavour becomes fuller and is reminiscent of hot toast and yeast extract. Appenzeller ripens in three to four months, with a fat content of 45 per cent.

BELOW:
Emmental

EMMENTAL

REGION: *Central cantons*
TYPE: *Traditional, farmhouse, unpasteurized, hard cheese*
SOURCE: *Cow's milk*
DESCRIPTION: *60–130kg/132–286lb wheel with convex rim and slightly concave sides. The thin, hard, natural rind is a beige-yellow and is covered by paper identifying the producer*
CULINARY USES: *Table cheese, grilling, fondue*

The history of Emmental can be traced back to 1293, but it was first mentioned by name in 1542, when it was given to the people of Langehthal whose lives had been devastated by fire. It takes its name from the valley of the upper Emme River, but is now made throughout Switzerland, wherever there are high pastures.

Although Emmental resembles Gruyère, the aroma is sweeter, with hushed tones of fresh-cut hay. Squeeze the rind to savour the wine-like aroma. Smoother and more elastic than Gruyère, Emmental has holes the size of hazelnuts or even walnuts. The promise of the aroma is fulfilled in the flavour, which is very fruity, with a mouth-tingling acidity.

FRIBOURGEOIS

REGION: *Fribourg*
TYPE: *Traditional, farmhouse, hard cheese*
SOURCE: *Cow's milk*
DESCRIPTION: *8kg/18lb wheel. The dry, pale beige, natural rind is covered with a fine, orange, plastic coat*
CULINARY USES: *Table cheese, fondues, grilling*

Like most traditional Swiss cheeses, Fribourgeois can trace its family history back through the centuries to a significant event. According to local documents, it was served to the wife of Duke Sigismund of Austria in 1448. Firm but breakable, it has a very full-bodied, slightly cloying feel, a delicious, meaty quality and a lingering savoury tang. A traditional, hard, mountain cheese, it resembles a small Gruyère, with a spicy rather than nutty taste that intensifies when the cheese is grilled or melted. It is sometimes referred to as Fribourgeois Vacherin, but should not be confused with the better-known Vacherin Mont d'Or, which is much softer.

Fribourgeois is matured for at least three months.

FROMAGE À RACLETTE

REGION: *Various*
TYPE: *Traditional, farmhouse, hard cheese*
SOURCE: *Cow's milk*
DESCRIPTION: *8–11kg/18–24lb cylindrical wheel. The smooth, natural rind varies in colour from pale yellow to orange-brown and can be dry or slightly sticky and rough*
CULINARY USES: *Table cheese, grilling*

Until the nineteenth century, this wonderful melting cheese was known as Valais. It acquired its modern name from the French verb *racler*, meaning "to scrape". The cheese was traditionally cut in half and placed with the cut surface facing the fire. As the cheese started to bubble, it would be scraped on to boiled potatoes to make a delectable treat.

Raclette is very supple. The pale golden interior has a sweet, earthy taste and a pleasant, citrus tang that deepens to a savoury bite. When heated, the cheese bubbles, melts and intensifies in flavour. Also known as Bagnes or Conches, Fromage à Raclette (or simply Raclette) is available in both raw and pasteurized versions, and can be purchased ready-sliced for easy grilling. Some Raclette are made with peppercorns providing a hot, peppery finish to the cheese. It ripens in three to four months and has a fat content of 45 per cent.

ABOVE: Fromage à Raclette – this cheese melts extremely well

GRUYÈRE

REGION: *Gruyère*

TYPE: *Traditional, co-operative and creamery, unpasteurized, hard cheese*

SOURCE: *Cow's milk*

DESCRIPTION: *20–45kg/44–99lb wheel. The natural, rusty brown rind is hard, dry and pitted with tiny holes*

CULINARY USES: *Table cheese, grilling, fondue*

Gruyère is part of the canton of Fribourg and Gruyère cheese has been made here for centuries. In 1115 a quantity of Gruyère was recorded as the tithe paid by local farmers to the monks of Rougement Abbey. Each of the enormous cheeses is made by a group of farmers or by a co-operative, since it takes 400 litres/ 88 gallons of milk to produce a single 35kg/80lb wheel.

The cheese is a darker yellow than Emmental and has a hint of brown in the colouring. The texture is dense and compact, yet flexible. It is this density that makes it stronger and less stringy than Emmental when heated, so it is better for gratins, grilling and in soups.

When Gruyère is first cut, the aroma suggests a million meadow flowers trapped in rich, creamy milk. Slightly grainy, the cheese has a wonderful complexity of flavours – at first fruity, then revealing more earthy, nutty characteristics that linger on the palate.

ROYALP-TILSITER

REGION: *St Gallen*

TYPE: *Traditional, unpasteurized, hard cheese made in small creameries*

SOURCE: *Cow's milk*

DESCRIPTION: *4kg/9lb wheel with smooth, polished, yellow, natural rind*

CULINARY USES: *Table cheese, melting, grilling, breakfast*

Compared with Switzerland's ancient cheeses, this is a relative newcomer, having been introduced in the latter half of the nineteenth century by a Swiss cheesemaker who had learnt to make Tilsiter while in eastern Prussia after the Franco-Prussian war. The rich, creamy milk of the alpine pastures produced a cheese with a robust smooth texture and small, distinct holes, unlike the original Tilsiter, which had irregular cracks running through it.

Royalp-Tilsiter is smaller than other Swiss cheeses and has a fat content of 45 per cent. It is lightly pressed and ripened for at least two months, but is better after six months. To distinguish it from the other Tilsiter cheese, it is known as Royalp abroad.

BELOW: Royalp-Tilsiter

ABOVE: Gruyère

SAANEN

REGION: *Fribourg*

TYPE: *Traditional, farmhouse, hard cheese*

SOURCE: *Cow's milk*

DESCRIPTION: *20–40kg/44–88lb wheel. The natural, very tough rind is brushed and oiled*

CULINARY USE: *Cooking cheese*

Saanen is a very hard, brittle cheese, with a deep yellow interior that is intensely fruity. It resembles Parmesan or Sbrinz and is a good grating cheese that will keep almost indefinitely. Saanen was traditionally reserved for special occasions, when pieces of the cheese would be shaved off and served with a glass of fruity, local wine.

SAPSAGO

REGION: *Glarus*

TYPE: *Traditional, farmhouse and creamery, hard cheese*

SOURCE: *Cow's milk*

DESCRIPTION: *150g/5oz truncated cone. Pale green and rindless. Sold in foil*

CULINARY USES: *Grating, as a condiment*

Sapsago owes its unusual, pale lime green colour to the addition of fenugreek. Very hard and gritty, it melts like Parmesan when heated. It is astringent, salty, sour – and mouthwatering. The aroma suggests warm cows and farmyards, with exotic, spicy overtones. Not a cheese to be taken lightly. Also known as Schabziger.

VACHERIN MONT D'OR

REGION: *Vaud*

TYPE: *Traditional, farmhouse and co-operative, washed-rind cheese*

SOURCE: *Cow's milk*

DESCRIPTION: *500g/1¼lb or 3kg/6½lb round cheese. The supple, undulating, brownish-pink rind has a dusting of white mould. The cheese is girdled with a band of spruce bark and sold in a pine box*

CULINARY USE: *Table cheese*

During summer, the milk produced by the cows in the upper and lower reaches of the Jura Mountains is used to make Gruyère. When winter sets in, the animals are confined to their warm, cosy barns and fed on hay, and the richer, thicker milk is pasteurized and used to make Vacherin Mont d'Or. The same cheese, produced on the other side of the mountains in France, is simply called Mont d'Or and is made with raw milk.

When ripe, Vacherin Mont d'Or is so smooth and runny it can be eaten with a spoon. The aroma of resin from the bark girdle is absorbed by the cheese, and the taste is reminiscent of the flowers and herbs of the mountain pastures. The cheese ripens in four to six weeks.

If you can afford it, buy a whole Vacherin Mont d'Or. Enjoy the cheese with a bottle of full-bodied, fruity white wine or a smooth Pinot Noir.

SBRINZ

REGION: *Various*

TYPE: *Traditional, farmhouse, hard cheese*

SOURCE: *Cow's milk*

DESCRIPTION: *Flat, cylindrical wheel, 60cm/24in in diameter*

CULINARY USES: *Table cheese, grating*

Sbrinz is thought to be the cheese Pliny the Elder referred to as *Caseus Helveticus* in his writings in the first century AD. The method of production is similar to that for Parmesan and the cheeses share similar traits. Sbrinz has the same fresh, pineapple taste and aroma. It has a lovely fruitiness, against a background of ground nuts, and a deliciously spicy finish. Not as potent as Parmesan, it makes a good and generally significantly cheaper alternative.

Sbrinz is matured for two to three years and has a fat content of 45 per cent.

TÊTE-DE-MOINE

REGION: *Bern*

TYPE: *Traditional, farmhouse and creamery, hard cheese*

SOURCE: *Cow's milk*

DESCRIPTION: *600g–2kg/1½–4½lb drum. The hard, ochre to terracotta rind tends to be smelly and sticky*

CULINARY USES: *Table cheese, also shaved over salads as a garnish*

It is often thought that the name of this cheese – which translates as "head of the

ABOVE: Tête-de-Moine

monk" – derives from its shape, but there is a rather more prosaic explanation. The cheese was originally called Bellelay, after a monastery in the Jura Mountains. Following the French Revolution it was renamed Tête-de-Moine, after the monks who made it.

Tête-de-Moine has a strong, earthy flavour, like burnt toast with yeast extract. It is usually served in thick strips or ruffles, made by passing it through a special machine called a girolle. The ruffles are used to garnish salads, platters of cooked meats and other dishes.

Tête-de-Moine ripens in three months and has a fat content of 45 per cent.

ABOVE: Sbrinz can only be made in Switzerland

THE CHEESES OF HOLLAND

More than half the land in Holland is below sea level, and the sea is held back only by the intricate system of dykes and canals that was begun by the Romans. The superb grazing on this reclaimed land, known as the Polders, is the foundation on which the cheeses of Holland were built. Surprisingly, unlike other major cheese-producing countries of Europe, which produce a vast range of different cheeses, Holland concentrates on only two – Edam and Gouda – on which all the other Dutch cheeses are based.

Edam and Gouda played a major role in the economy of Holland in the Middle Ages, when their smooth texture and long-lasting qualities made them highly desirable. In 1621, the founding of the Dutch East India Company gave Holland a powerful trading base, as it held the monopoly on the spices from Indonesia. Cloves, aniseed, cumin and caraway were much sought after, and were soon incorporated into cheeses. Kruidkaas, which includes either caraway or cumin, is still made today, as is Nagelkaas (with cloves) and Leidsekaas (with cumin or aniseed).

By about the middle of the seventeenth century, Edam and Gouda were being exported to virtually every country in Europe. In France in the time of Louis XIV, the passion for Dutch cheese was so great that when the Treasury banned its importation on grounds of cost, the French started developing their own (the forerunner of Mimolette Française).

Artists of the day included cheeses in many masterpieces and it is rumoured that in 1841 the Uruguayan fleet, under American command, defeated the British by substituting Dutch Edams for cannonballs when their supply ran out.

With nearly a third of Holland dedicated to dairy farming, cheese plays a significant role in the economy and over 75 per cent of the annual production is exported. Most cheese is made in highly mechanized factories, a necessary development that has sadly led to a decline in the number of artisan cheesemakers. The few that remain largely make farmhouse Goudas, while some sheep's milk cheeses are produced on the island of Texel and in the province of Friesland, which gave the Friesian cow its name.

Copies of Gouda and Edam are now made all over the world, both in factories and by artisan cheesemakers, often Dutch emigrants seeking a better quality of life and a less regimented environment. To identify authentic Dutch cheeses – and ensure that their quality is maintained – production is governed by strict rules. Each cheese must carry a label that includes detailed information on origin, producer and fat content.

ABOVE: Boerenkaas

BOERENKAAS

REGION: *Various*
TYPE: *Traditional, farmhouse, unpasteurized, semi-hard cheese*
SOURCE: *Cow's milk*
DESCRIPTION: *8–40kg/18–88lb wheel with convex rim and glossy, brushed, natural rind*
CULINARY USES: *Table cheese, often sliced for breakfast; also melted in sandwiches*

Though most of Holland's cheese manufacture is highly mechanized, some farmhouse Gouda is still made by artisan cheesemakers using raw milk. This cheese gets its name – Boerenkaas – from the Dutch words for farmer (*boer*) and cheese (*kaas*). It is quite difficult to obtain in Holland today, due to the decline in the numbers of artisan cheesemakers, which in turn is linked to the scarcity and cost of agricultural land.

Boerenkaas is, however, made in the traditional way. The only modern touch is the porous plastic coating, which is "painted" on to the newly formed cheese to protect it during the months of slow ageing. When young, it is nutty and rich, with a dense, creamy texture and a fragrance reminiscent of meadow pastures and fresh hay. With age, its flavour intensifies, becoming strong and fruity. Tiny calcium crystals, like those in Parmesan, develop in well-aged cheeses.

ABOVE: Maasdam – one of the newer cheeses

BELOW: *Gouda (left), and Edam (right), the majority of which is exported, because the Dutch prefer the stronger flavour of Gouda*

DUTCH MIMOLETTE/ COMMISSIEKAAS

REGION: *Various*
TYPE: *Traditional, farmhouse and creamery, hard cheese*
SOURCE: *Cow's milk*
DESCRIPTION: *3–4.5kg/6–9lb ball. The natural, pitted rind ranges from light brown to deep orange*
CULINARY USES: *Grating, in sauces and pastries, snacks*

Seldom seen outside northern Europe, this magnificent, fruity cheese looks like a giant orange with rough, pitted skin. Known as Commissiekaas in Holland and Dutch Mimolette everywhere else, the cheese is actually a matured Edam coloured with carrot juice.

At around five months Dutch Mimolette is firm, compact and slightly oily, with a fruity aroma and nutty flavour. The best is yet to come, however. When aged, the colour darkens to a deep orange, the texture becomes rock hard, granular and brittle and the flavour is pronounced. It is fruity, with a hint of orange zest (real or imagined). The nutty flavour intensifies to reach a mouth-watering crescendo.

This cheese ripens in six to 12 months and has a fat content of 45 per cent.

EDAM

REGION: *Various*
TYPE: *Traditional, creamery, semi-soft or hard cheese*
SOURCE: *Cow's milk*
DESCRIPTION: *1.5kg/3¹/₄lb ball with barely perceptible rind covered in distinctive, red wax*
CULINARY USES: *Table cheese, popular for breakfast and in sandwiches, also grilled*

Named after the small port of Edam, just north of Amsterdam, this is a pressed, semi-soft or hard cheese in the shape of a ball. The red wax coat, first used in the fourteenth century, makes it a distinctive sight in delicatessens and supermarkets the world over. Most Edam is still produced from skimmed or semi-skimmed milk and has a fat content of between 30 and 40 per cent. Authentic Edam is mostly sold young, when the texture is still supple and elastic, and the flavour is mild, sweet and nutty. Imitations can be bland and rubbery.

A black wax coat indicates an Edam has been aged for at least 17 weeks. Some of the cheese is aged for up to 10 months, when it becomes strong, nutty and excellent for cooking.

FRIESEKAAS

REGION: *Various*
TYPE: *Traditional, creamery, semi-hard cheese*
SOURCE: *Cow's milk*
DESCRIPTION: *Large round, at least 10kg/22lb in weight, with waxed, natural rind*
CULINARY USES: *Table cheese, snacks, breakfast, grilling*

A spiced Dutch cheese, this is similar to Leyden, but is flavoured with a combination of cumin and cloves. It ripens in three to 12 months and has a fat content of 40 per cent.

GOUDA

REGION: *Various*
TYPE: *Traditional, creamery, hard cheese*
SOURCE: *Cow's milk*
DESCRIPTION: *5–10kg/11–22lb round with very smooth, yellow, waxed rind. Mature cheeses are hard and slightly granular, with a black wax coating*
CULINARY USES: *Table cheese, snacks, breakfast, grilling*

Gouda accounts for more than 60 per cent of the cheese produced in Holland. An ancient cheese, its history dates from the sixth century, when it was made on small farms around the village of Gouda. It has been exported since the thirteenth century and is now enjoyed worldwide.

Other European countries, notably Sweden, have adopted the Dutch style of cheesemaking, and produce cheeses that are similar to Gouda. Since the last century, Dutch immigrants in America and Australia have been making farmhouse versions by meticulously adhering to the old methods, although regulations prevent many of them from using raw milk.

When only a few months old, Gouda is firm, smooth and supple, with a scattering of small holes. The flavour is sweet and fruity. As time passes, the taste intensifies and becomes more complex. Mature Gouda (18 months plus) is coated in black wax, which provides a stark contrast to the deep yellow interior. At this age, the texture of the cheese is granular, and it can be grated. Gouda has a fat content of 40–45 per cent.

LEYDEN/LEIDSEKAAS

REGION: *Leiden*
TYPE: *Traditional, farmhouse,*
hard cheese
SOURCE: *Cow's milk*
DESCRIPTION: *3–10kg/6¹/2–22lb boulder-*
shaped cheese with brushed, natural
rind which is either rubbed with
annatto or "painted" with red plastic
CULINARY USES: *Table cheese, grilling*

Made on farms around Leiden, the famous
university city, this cheese is similar in
texture to Gouda, but because it is made
with semi-skimmed milk it feels slightly
drier. The curd is coloured with annatto
and mixed with cumin seeds before being
pressed and washed in brine. The cumin
provides an aromatic flavour that contrasts well with the creamy, nutty
character of the cheese.

A genuine Leyden will be identified as
such by having the imprint of the city's
emblem, the famous crossed keys, on the
rind. To further distinguish the cheese,
the rind is rubbed with annatto until it
acquires a shiny reddish-orange colour.

The traditional custom of treading the
spices into the curd has, needless to say,
been replaced by machine.

Leyden is also called Komijnekaas.

ABOVE: Leyden

BELOW: Leerdammer is one of the
best-known brand names
for Maasdam

LEERDAMMER

REGION: *Zuid-Holland*
Modern, creamery,
semi-hard cheese
SOURCE: *Cow's milk*
DESCRIPTION: *6–12kg/13–26lb*
boulder-shaped cheese. The
smooth, natural rind is
polished and may
be waxed
CULINARY USES: *Table*
cheese, grilling

Most of the large
cheesemaking fac-
tories in Holland
have begun to
produce their own
branded versions
of Maasdam. Leer-
dammer is one of
the better-known,
along with Ronduer,
Goyweter and Fricotal.

MAASDAM

REGION: *Various*
TYPE: *Modern, creamery,*
semi-hard cheese
SOURCE: *Cow's milk*
DESCRIPTION: *6–12kg/13–26lb boulder-*
shaped cheese. The smooth, natural
rind is polished and may be waxed
CULINARY USES: *Table cheese, grilling*

Created in the early 1990s as an alternative to the more expensive Swiss
cheese Emmental, Maasdam has
attracted a large following. The market continues to increase, and it is
already being copied in other countries.

Although there are similarities with
Emmental, it is higher in moisture and
therefore more supple. It ripens faster
than other Dutch cheeses, being ready in
four to 12 weeks. The flavour is sweet and
buttery, with a fruity background, making
it ideal for serving as a snack or breakfast
cheese. It can also be grilled.

GERMAN CHEESES

The Germanic tribes, originally from Scandinavia and the Baltic, gradually expanded east of the Rhine and by 200BC were beginning to invade the Roman Empire. It was not, however, until the arrival of the Franks and the rule of Charlemagne that the cheeses of Germany began to emerge. Charlemagne's love of food is legendary, a fact that helped to shape German cuisine, which has a reputation for being both hearty and substantial.

Germany's dairy industry is huge, now rated fourth or fifth in the world, yet surprisingly its cheeses are far less well known beyond its borders than are its sausages, beers and breads. One of the main reasons for this is that many of the cheeses are either processed varieties, or copies of other European cheeses.

Quark is the notable exception. Now found all over Europe, it is a fresh curd cheese with a sharp, yogurt-like taste. Thought to have originated in the Iron Age, it led to the development of other types of *Sauermilchkäse* (sour milk cheese), which are often very pungent.

Limburger, adopted by the Germans from Belgium, is a Trappist-style cheese, as is Münster. Both have a strong, robust flavour that appeals to the German love of rich, spicy food.

As in Switzerland, the quality of German cheeses is very strictly controlled. Labelling must be precise, which is helpful for the informed local consumer, but not necessarily for the visitor.

ALLGÄUER EMMENTALER
REGION: *Bavaria*
TYPE: *Traditional, creamery and co-operative, hard cheese*
SOURCE: *Cow's milk*
DESCRIPTION: *40–90kg/88–198lb wheel with smooth, waxed, natural rind*
CULINARY USES: *Grilling, melting, snacks, breakfast*

The mountain pastures of Allgäu in southern Bavaria resemble those of their Swiss neighbours, and the cattle are similar, so it is not altogether surprising that the Bavarians produce a cheese that has much in common with that made on the other side of the mountains. Allgäuer Emmentaler is a sweet, fruity cheese, with holes the size of walnuts. It is less expensive than the Swiss original.

Since the end of the last century, when the makers of Allgäuer Emmentaler adopted the same stringent standards of quality maintained by the Swiss, it has been hard to tell the two cheeses apart, although lovers of Swiss Emmental would claim that their cheese has the edge in terms of flavour.

Determined to maintain their unique identity, the Swiss ensure that the rinds on their exported cheeses are completely covered with the words "Switzerland" and "Emmental", leaving the consumer in no doubt about where the cheese is made.

BAVARIAN BERGKÄSE
REGION: *Bavaria*
TYPE: *Traditional, farmhouse and creamery, unpasteurized, hard cheese*
SOURCE: *Cow's milk*
DESCRIPTION: *20–50kg/44–110lb wheel with natural rind, similar to but darker than Emmental*
CULINARY USES: *Table cheese, grilling, melting*

Bergkäse simply means "mountain cheese" and is a smaller version of the popular Allgäuer Emmentaler. Firm but supple, and almost chewy, Bergkäse is a superb melting cheese. More aromatic than Emmental but still fruity, Bergkäse is made only in the summer months from the milk of cows grazing the mountain pastures, which explains why it is also known as Alpenkäse.

Control is less strict than for the Allgäuer Emmentaler and quality can vary from maker to maker, but it is nonetheless a good buy.

Bergkäse ripens in three to nine months and has a fat content of 45 per cent.

BRUDER BASIL
REGION: *Bavaria*
TYPE: *Modern, creamery, semi-soft cheese*
SOURCE: *Cow's milk*
DESCRIPTION: *1kg/2¼lb flattened brick with convex sides. The natural rind is dark mahogany in colour and is waxed*
CULINARY USES: *Grilling; also used in snacks and sandwiches, often served with beer*

This is a traditionally made version of the Bavarian smoked cheese (Rauchkäse) found almost everywhere. The smooth, firm, yellow cheese has small holes. The taste is creamy and pleasantly smoky, but can be rather "plastic".

Bruder Basil ripens in one month and has a fat content of about 45 per cent. A version flavoured with chopped ham is also available.

RIGHT: Bruder Basil

ABOVE: Cambazola, which as the name implies, is based on Camembert and Gorgonzola, appeals to those who find other blue cheeses too ferocious. Bavarian Blue and Blue Brie are similar cheeses

BUTTERKÄSE
REGION: *Various*
TYPE: *Traditional, creamery, semi-soft cheese*
SOURCE: *Cow's milk*
DESCRIPTION: *1–4kg/2¹/4–9lb rectangular loaf or wheel with golden to red, natural rind*
CULINARY USES: *Snacks, breakfast*
Made in both Germany and Austria, this cheese lives up to its name and has a buttery taste and colour. Very supple, but odourless and rather bland, it needs pickles and beer to give it life.

Also called Damenkäse (ladies' cheese), Butterkäse ripens in one month and has a fat content of 50 per cent.

CAMBAZOLA
REGION: *Various*
TYPE: *Modern, creamery, blue cheese*
SOURCE: *Cow's milk*
DESCRIPTION: *2kg/4¹/2lb flat round with penicillium rind*
CULINARY USES: *Table cheese, snacks*
Cambazola is a modern success story. Since its creation in the 1970s, others have tried to copy it, but few have achieved the

consistency of quality and texture, which are responsible for Cambazola's success. The smooth, rich texture is achieved by adding cream to the milk, and the taste is mildly spicy and slightly sweet-sour.

LIMBURGER
REGION: *Various*
TYPE: *Traditional, creamery, washed-rind cheese*
SOURCE: *Cow's milk*
DESCRIPTION: *200–675g/7oz–1¹/2lb brick. The smooth, sticky, washed rind is reddish-brown, with corrugated ridges*
CULINARY USES: *Table cheese, grilling, melting over potatoes*
The aroma is unmistakable – powerful, outspoken and impossible to ignore. The yellow interior hints at sweetness, but the overwhelming taste is spicy and aromatic, almost meaty. Despite its robust nature, Limburger has its limits and passes these if it is allowed to become runny, with a slimy rind. It is best when the texture is firm, yet yielding.

Limburger undoubtedly originated with the cheese-loving Trappist monks in Belgium, but was hijacked by German cheesemakers in the nineteenth century. It is now so popular that most Germans and even some Belgians believe it to be a German cheese.

The cheese ripens in six to 12 weeks and has a fat content that fluctuates between 20 and 50 per cent. A milder version is popular in the United States, having been introduced by German immigrants.

LEFT: Limburger has an unmistakable odour

AUSTRIAN CHEESES

BERGKÄSE

REGION: *Voralberg Massif*
TYPE: *Traditional, creamery, unpasteurized, hard cheese*
SOURCE: *Cow's milk*
DESCRIPTION: *6–30kg/13–65lb wheel with smooth, dark yellow, natural rind*
CULINARY USES: *Table cheese, melting, grilling, fondue*

Closely resembling the Bavarian Bergkäse, this has a creamy, fudge-like flavour with a hint of hazelnuts. The holes in the paste are smaller than those in the German cheese and the cheese is matured for six months or longer.

KUGELKÄSE

REGION: *Danube*
TYPE: *Traditional, creamery, fresh cheese*
SOURCE: *Cow's milk*
DESCRIPTION: *Speckled, white balls in various sizes*
CULINARY USES: *Added to local dishes; also served solo, with beer*

This is a simple local speciality. Once the fresh curd has formed – and while it is still warm – pepper, caraway seeds and paprika are added so that the curd becomes infused with their aroma and character. The cheese is then rolled into balls, which are salted and dried for weeks or even months.

MONDSEER

REGION: *Salzburg*
TYPE: *Traditional, creamery, semi-soft cheese*
SOURCE: *Cow's milk*
DESCRIPTION: *500g–1kg/1¼–2¼lb round. The soft, washed rind is deep orange, dusted with powdery, white mould*
CULINARY USES: *Grilling, snacks*

Firm yet moist, Mondseer is open-textured with a few irregular eyes. It has a slightly spicy aroma and a sweet-sour taste. Although it is related to other washed-rind cheeses, it tends to be milder and less pungent.

Mondseer ripens in about two to three months and has a fat content of 45 per cent.

MÜNSTER

REGION: *Schwarzwald*
TYPE: *Traditional, creamery, washed-rind cheese*
SOURCE: *Cow's milk*
DESCRIPTION: *125–500g/4½oz–1¼lb round cheese with sticky, orange, washed skin*
CULINARY USE: *Table cheese*

Münster is a smooth, fairly soft, yellow cheese with a thin, orange skin and a mildly piquant flavour that can become quite pungent with regular washings. In the Middle Ages the cheese was made by the monks at Munster Abbey in modern-day Alsace. When Alsace became part of Germany, the name of the cheese gained an umlaut, and it became Münster, after the Westphalian town. Ownership of Alsace switched from Germany to France several times after that, but the cheese continued to be made on both sides of the border. Today, it is also produced in the USA, where it is known as Muenster.

QUARK

REGION: *Various*
TYPE: *Traditional, creamery, vegetarian, fresh cheese*
SOURCE: *Cow's milk*
DESCRIPTION: *Moist, white cheese sold in pots*
CULINARY USES: *Cooking, spreading, in dips and cheesecakes, with fruit for breakfast*

Quark simply means "curd" in German, and the cheese is said to date from the Iron Age, when nomadic tribes discovered the means of fermenting milk without the use of rennet.

Quark can be made from whole, skimmed or semi-skimmed milk or even buttermilk. Soft and moist, like a cross between yogurt and fromage frais, it should taste lemon-fresh. Some versions have skimmed milk powder added and can be rather gritty. Quark ripens within a few days.

RIGHT: Quark

ROMADUR/ROMADURKÄSE

REGION: *Various*
TYPE: *Traditional, creamery, washed-rind cheese*
SOURCE: *Cow's milk*
DESCRIPTION: *200–500g/7oz–1¼lb rectangular loaf with yellowish-orange, washed rind*
CULINARY USE: *Table cheese*

Similar to Limburger, but milder and smaller, Romadur has a sweet-sour flavour with a hint of smoke. It can be made with whole or semi-skimmed milk and has a fat content between 20 and 60 per cent.

TILSIT

REGION: *Various*
TYPE: *Traditional, co-operative or creamery, semi-hard cheese*
SOURCE: *Cow's milk*
DESCRIPTION: *4.5kg/10lb wheel. The thin, dry, yellow-beige crust has some moulds*
CULINARY USES: *Table cheese, grilling, snacks*

The original Tilsit was apparently discovered accidentally by Dutch cheese-makers living in Tilsit, which was then in East Prussia. At the time, they were trying to make their beloved Gouda, but various factors combined to create a cheese that was markedly different, especially in relation to the rind.

The cheese is washed and brushed regularly for the first two months so that the crusty rind forms. This protects the smooth, supple interior, with its tiny, irregular holes, from drying out. The aroma is mildly pungent, while the taste is buttery and fruity, with a spicy tinge.

BELGIAN CHEESES

Belgium's cheeses are virtually unknown outside her borders, being overshadowed by those of her famous neighbour, France, yet the country produces over 250 varieties of cheese.

There is evidence that the Belgae, a Celtic people, had some knowledge of basic cheesemaking, and although the Romans introduced more sophisticated techniques, it was the Franks who were to have the most influence on cheesemaking in Belgium. Between AD771 and 800, their king, Charlemagne, developed an extensive empire, and encouraged the building of over 50 abbeys. The monks not only set about spreading the word of God, but also worked with the people to improve their herds and their cheesemaking skills.

The records kept by Charlemagne provide us with an insight into his world. At Aachen, his seat of power, cellars were dug to store and ripen his cheeses. As Charlemagne's empire faded, the country split into independent duchies and trade brought wealth and prosperity. Despite being governed in turn by the Austrians, Spanish and Dutch, Belgium emerged in 1831 as an independent kingdom, with its own culture and cuisine.

Respect for the past, and a determination not to allow the older varieties of cheese to become extinct, led several

LEFT: Herve is Belgium's most famous cheese

cheesemakers in 1960 to embark on a campaign to rediscover old recipes. Their research, in monasteries, farms and libraries, has revitalized the industry, creating a new identity for Belgian cheese, based on its rich and varied history.

Regrettably, the majority of cheeses produced in Belgium today are factory-made copies of traditional Belgian and other European cheeses, but those described here can be found and savoured in the many elegant restaurants and cafés for which Belgium is famous.

BEAUVOORDE

REGION: *Various*
TYPE: *Traditional, creamery, semi-hard cheese*
SOURCE: *Cow's milk*
DESCRIPTION: *3kg/6¹/₂lb or 6kg/13lb hexagonal cheese with grey, natural rind*
CULINARY USES: *Table cheese, also used in snacks and sandwiches*
Beauvoorde cheese was created in the early 1900s by Arthur Djes, innkeeper of Beauvoorde village. His family continued to make the cheese until the Second World War forced them to abandon production. Recently revived, it is now made in creameries. Firm yet supple and open-textured, Beauvoorde has a mild flavour and a spicy aroma.

BRUSSELSE KAAS/FROMAGE DE BRUXELLES

REGION: *Brabant*
TYPE: *Traditional, creamery, washed-rind cheese*
SOURCE: *Cow's milk*
DESCRIPTION: *150g/5oz flattened rounds, sold in tubs*
CULINARY USES: *Spreading, snacks*
Made with skimmed milk, Brusselse Kaas is smooth, sharp and citric, with a bite that is surprisingly strong and salty. This is the result of the cheese having been regularly washed and dried over a period of at least three months. It is shaped into rough rounds and packed in tubs.

HERVE

REGION: *Liège*
TYPE: *Traditional, farmhouse and creamery, washed-rind cheese*
SOURCE: *Cow's milk*
DESCRIPTION: *200g/7oz brick with glossy, orange-brown rind*
CULINARY USES: *Table cheese, snacks*
Belgium's most famous cheese, Herve, has an autumn-coloured crust that is pungent and yeasty. Beneath it, the supple, tender interior ranges from sweet to powerful and spicy, depending on how long the cheese has been ripening. Small quantities of unpasteurized cheese are still made, and there is a double-cream version.

BELOW: Beauvoorde

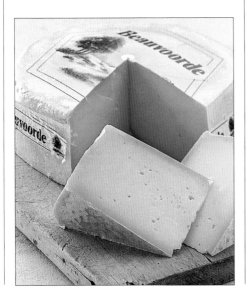

MAREDSOUS

REGION: *Various*
TYPE: *Traditional, farmhouse and creamery, washed-rind cheese*
SOURCE: *Cow's milk*
DESCRIPTION: *1kg/2¼lb or 2.5kg/5½lb loaf-shaped cheese. The firm, orange, washed rind sometimes has a fine dusting of white mould*
CULINARY USES: *Table cheese, grilling*

This is another of Belgium's Trappist-style cheeses and is made by the monks at Maredsous Abbey. It is lightly pressed, then washed in brine to create the firm, orange crust and pungent aroma. The supple, smooth interior is pale yellow with a slightly smoky tinge. Not as aggressive as Herve, it has perhaps more in common with France's Saint-Paulin.

PASSENDALE

REGION: *Flanders*
TYPE: *Modern, creamery, semi-soft cheese*
SOURCE: *Cow's milk*
DESCRIPTION: *3kg/6½lb round, shaped like a country loaf and with a dusting of fine, white mould that resembles flour*
CULINARY USES: *Table cheese, grilling, snacks, breakfast*

With its warm, brown crust lightly dusted with white mould, this looks like a loaf of country bread. A modern cheese, based on an old monastic recipe, it is firm, with small holes. The flavour is mild and creamy. The cheese takes its name from the Flemish village of Passchendaele, where thousands of British soldiers lost their lives in the First World War.

PLATEAU DE HERVE

REGION: *Herve*
TYPE: *Traditional, creamery, washed-rind cheese*
SOURCE: *Cow's milk*
DESCRIPTION: *1.5kg/3¼lb dome with sticky, orange, washed rind wrapped in foil*
CULINARY USES: *Table cheese, snacks*

This lightly pressed cheese has a pale yellow interior with a creamy consistency. Washed regularly in brine, it has the flavour without the pervasive aroma of Herve. It ripens in two to three months.

POSTEL

REGION: *Various*
TYPE: *Traditional, farmhouse, washed-rind cheese*
SOURCE: *Cow's milk*
DESCRIPTION: *4kg/9lb rectangular cheese with orange, washed rind*
CULINARY USE: *Table cheese*

The monks at the Abbey of Postel resumed making this classic Trappist cheese in the 1960s, using the milk from their herd of 160 cows. Volume is small, but those who have discovered this cheese willingly travel to the abbey to buy it.

PRINC'JEAN

REGION: *Various*
TYPE: *Modern, creamery, fresh cheese*
SOURCE: *Cow's milk*
DESCRIPTION: *150g/5oz rindless round*
CULINARY USE: *Table cheese*

This triple cream cheese has a wonderfully rich texture. There is a peppercorn version as well as a softer type, which has a white rind and creamy flavour. The cheese is packed into small, wooden crates for sale.

LEFT: Maredsous

REMEDOU

REGION: *Liège*
TYPE: *Traditional, farmhouse and creamery, washed-rind cheese*
SOURCE: *Cow's milk*
DESCRIPTION: *200–675g/7oz–1½lb square with shiny, moist, red-brown, washed rind*
CULINARY USE: *Table cheese*

Also known as Piquant, which is something of an understatement, this is a larger and particularly aggressive version of Herve. Its size means that it takes longer to ripen, which gives the surface bacteria time to exude the powerful aroma for which the cheese is famous. It is known locally as "stinking cheese" and is best eaten in the open air with a glass of robust, red wine or local beer.

The name of the cheese is said to come from *remoud,* which was an old Walloon word for the rich milk produced towards the end of a cow's lactation period.

ABOVE: Rubens

RUBENS

REGION: *Lo*
TYPE: *Traditional, farmhouse and creamery, semi-soft cheese*
SOURCE: *Cow's milk*
DESCRIPTION: *3kg/6½lb oval with firm, smooth, red-brown, washed rind*
CULINARY USE: *Table cheese*

A chubby, wholesome-looking cheese with a rich, smooth, subtle taste, Rubens is covered with a smooth, reddish-brown, protective coat. One of many old Belgian cheeses revived in the 1960s, it carries a label bearing a portrait of the Flemish painter after whom it is named.

DANISH CHEESES

Denmark's maritime climate and flat meadowlands make it an ideal environment for the comfort-loving cow that becomes a familiar sight as you travel through the picturesque countryside.

Thanks to its geographical position and its Viking past, Denmark has always been a trading nation. The cheese industry was originally based upon varieties made in neighbouring Germany and Holland – cheeses like Gouda, valued for the way it withstood the rigours of sea travel, and Limburger. There are few original Danish cheeses: most are highly efficient copies, many of which now carry Danish names as a result of the Stresa Convention of 1951.

The classic example of Danish cheese is Samso, which was developed in the nineteenth century along the lines of a Swiss-style cheese. Outside Denmark, its best-known cheese is, however, Danish Blue (Danablu), which is based on the French blues.

Danish Feta, a popular cheese that is even exported to the Middle East, was recently at the centre of a controversy over the name. A fierce battle is now brewing between Greece and the European Parliament as to whether Greece should be allowed sole rights to use the name feta for its own cheese.

Over 60 per cent of all cheese made in Denmark is exported, and its Ministry of Agriculture is fiercely protective of the industry. It demands very high standards and has banned the production of raw milk cheeses. Although the cow is by far the most important dairy animal, some goat's milk cheese is made, but mainly for home consumption.

BLA CASTELLO/BLUE CASTELLO

REGION: *Various*
TYPE: *Modern, creamery, blue cheese*
SOURCE: *Cow's milk*
DESCRIPTION: *150g/5oz and 1kg/2¼lb half-moon-shaped cheese. The moist, natural rind may develop some grey, brown or white moulds*
CULINARY USE: *Table cheese*

Developed in the 1960s to meet the growing demand for mild, creamy blues, Bla Castello has a Brie-like texture, with the the blue in fairly thick, horizontal lines. Enriched with cream, it has a fat content of 70 per cent. The aroma is of mushrooms and the taste is mildly spicy. A popular cheese, but one which some regard as rather bland.

DANABLU/DANISH BLUE

REGION: *Various*
TYPE: *Modern, creamery, blue cheese*
Source: *Cow's milk*
DESCRIPTION: *3kg/6½lb drum or block. The sticky, yellow, natural rind has some brownish-grey or blue moulds*
CULINARY USES: *Table cheese, snacks, also crumbled in salads*

This cheese was invented in the early twentieth century by Marius Boel as an alternative to Roquefort, although the two cheeses are very different. It is now known throughout the western world and sales show no signs of abating. The name Danablu is protected by the Stresa Convention; Danish Blue, however, is not.

The appeal of the cheese lies in its sharp, almost metallic taste, salty bite and creamy feel in the mouth. The interior is very white and makes an attractive contrast to the blue-black mould, which is rather gritty and salty (additional salt is added to some exported cheeses).

Danablu ripens in two to three months and has a fat content of 50–60 per cent. It is also known as Marmora.

LEFT: Danish Blue (top) and Mycella

DANBO

REGION: *Various*
TYPE: *Traditional, farmhouse and creamery, semi-soft cheese*
SOURCE: *Cow's milk*
DESCRIPTION: *Rectangular cheese with smooth, dry, yellow rind, sometimes covered in red or yellow wax*
CULINARY USES: *Snacks, breakfast, grilling*

One of the most popular Danish cheeses, it is similar to Samso. Mild and slightly aromatic, it has a pale, elastic interior with a few peanut-sized holes. Occasionally, the cheese contains caraway seeds.

Danbo ripens in six weeks to five months and has a fat content of 45 per cent. Similar cheeses include Fynbo, Elbo, Svenbo and Molbo. Danbo is also called King Christian or Christian IX, by which names it is known in the USA.

RIGHT: Danbo

LEFT: Esrom

RIGHT: Havarti

ESROM

REGION: *Various*
TYPE: *Traditional, creamery, semi-soft cheese*
SOURCE: *Cow's milk*
DESCRIPTION: *200g–2kg/ 7oz–4 1/2lb rectangular cheese with smooth, sticky, pale yellow, washed rind*
CULINARY USES: *Table cheese, snacks, open sandwiches*

Made from an old recipe that was rediscovered by the Danish Cheese Institute in 1951, this cheese is mild and buttery when young. As it ages, it develops a fuller, more robust flavour. The interior, which is scattered with small, irregular-shaped holes, is supple, elastic and generally quite sweet, although it can be pungent.

Esrom ripens in about three weeks and has a fat content of between 45 and 50 per cent. It is named after the ancient monastery of Esrom, and is protected by the Stresa Convention.

HAVARTI

REGION: *Various*
TYPE: *Traditional, creamery, semi-soft cheese*
SOURCE: *Cow's milk*
DESCRIPTION: *2–4.5kg/4 1/2–10lb blocks or drums*
CULINARY USES: *Table cheese, slicing, grilling, snacks*

In the middle of the last century, Hanne Nielsen, a cheese "evangelist", undertook a one-woman crusade to learn about cheesemaking from some of Europe's best artisan cheesemakers. On her return to Denmark, she set about introducing new ideas and methods to the industry, which at that time was rather uninspired. Havarti, named after the farm where Hanne first made the cheese, was her greatest success.

It is a simple, washed-rind cheese with irregular holes throughout. Fairly full-flavoured and creamy at about three months old, it becomes more outspoken with age.

There is an enriched version, with added cream, which is softer and feels more luxurious in the mouth. There is also a version with caraway seeds.

BELOW: Maribo

MARIBO

REGION: *Various*
TYPE: *Traditional, creamery, semi-hard cheese*
SOURCE: *Cow's milk*
DESCRIPTION: *9–14kg/20–31lb round or block. The natural rind has a pale yellow, wax coating*
CULINARY USES: *Table cheese, grilling, breakfast*

Named after the town on the island of Lolland, Maribo is widely available in Denmark, but is seldom exported. More full-flavoured than Danbo, it resembles Gouda and has a firm, dry interior scattered with numerous irregular holes. It is usually coated with yellow wax and is sometimes flavoured with caraway seeds.

It ripens in four months and has a fat content of between 30 and 45 per cent.

MYCELLA

REGION: *Various*
TYPE: *Traditional, creamery, blue cheese*
SOURCE: *Cow's milk*
DESCRIPTION: *5kg/11lb drum with natural, pale orange-brown crust*
CULINARY USES: *Table cheese, snacks, spreading, salads*

Once known as Danish Gorgonzola, this cheese takes its name from the mould that gives it its thin strands or streaks of greenish-blue: *Penicillium mycellium*. The veins in the cheese provide an attractive contrast to the very pale, creamy, almost buttery interior. The flavour of Mycella is relatively mild for a blue cheese.

SAMSØ

REGION: *Various*
TYPE: *Traditional, creamery, semi-hard cheese*
SOURCE: *Cow's milk*
DESCRIPTION: *14kg/31lb wheel or rectangle without rind*
CULINARY USES: *Table cheese, grilling, grating, snacks, fondue*

In the early nineteenth century, the Danish king saw the potential for diversifying the cheesemaking in his country and invited a Swiss cheesemaker to advise the Danish farmers. The result was Samsø, named after the island of Samsø, and forefather of many Danish cheeses.

Looking rather like a pale Emmental, Samsø has a supple, elastic texture with a few irregular-sized holes. When young, it tastes mild and buttery. However, the Danes seem to prefer it aged, when it develops a definite sweet-sour pungency and a distinct, hazelnut flavour. It is the classic cheese to use for the Danish open sandwich.

Samsø ripens in two to three months and has a fat content of 45 per cent.

BELOW: Samsø

NORWEGIAN CHEESES

Less than one per cent of the long, narrow strip of land bordering the Norwegian Sea is grazing land. Most of Norway consists of native forest and rugged mountains. In the north, the magnificent tundra is home to the reindeer, a few Laplanders and little else.

Yet the Vikings chose Norway as the base for their frequent forays across the sea. Around the ninth century, with the help and determination of Irish monks, they turned their ferocious energy to conquering the land and to making cheese. It would seem that some of the more eccentric cheeses the Norwegians have since created continue to reflect the intrepid sense of adventure of their ancestors!

GAMMELOST

REGION: *Various*
TYPE: *Traditional, farmhouse and creamery, blue cheese*
SOURCE: *Goat's milk*
DESCRIPTION: *3kg/6¹/₂lb drum. The hard, pitted, natural crust is greenish, brown, with some mould*
CULINARY USES: *Table cheese, served after dinner with aquavit or gin; also grated*

Gammelost is extremely robust, sharp and aromatic. There is erratic blueing throughout the brownish-yellow paste. The texture starts soft, but is extremely hard, almost brittle, when the cheese is aged.

The name – Gammelost – means "old cheese" and stems from the fact that the rind grows a green-brown mould and looks old before its time. To encourage the mould, the young Gammelost was traditionally wrapped in straw soaked in gin and juniper berries, which added to the flavour.

Gammelost has a fat content of only 5 per cent.

RIGHT: Gjetost

GJETOST

REGION: *Various*
TYPE: *Traditional, farmhouse and creamery, semi-hard cheese*
SOURCE: *Cow's and goat's milk*
DESCRIPTION: *250–500g/ 9oz–1¹/₄lb block, deep honey-brown in colour, without rind*
CULINARY USES: *Snacks; often served as a dessert, with coffee*

A fudge-coloured whey cheese, originally made entirely from goat's milk (*gjet* means goat), but is now more often made with a blend of goat's and cow's milk. It is sweet, with an unusual, aromatic quality.

Gjetost is not to everyone's taste, but Norwegians love it. It is their most popular cheese, available in various versions. When made from pure cow's milk it is called Mysost, while the pure goat's milk version is called Ekta Gjetost.

It is traditionally eaten for breakfast.

JARLSBERG

REGION: *Various*
TYPE: *Traditional, creamery, hard cheese*
SOURCE: *Cow's milk*
DESCRIPTION: *10kg/22lb wheel with smooth, yellow, waxed, natural rind*
CULINARY USES: *Table cheese, melting, grilling, snacks*

This old Norwegian cheese, based on Emmental, was all but forgotten before its discovery in the mid-1900s. Today it is extremely popular and a great deal is exported, particularly to the USA.

Made from the rich milk of the high summer pastures, Jarlsberg is sweeter and less nutty than Emmental. Although it lacks the depth of that great cheese, Jarlsberg has a pleasant flavour. The paste is golden yellow, with holes of various sizes.

ABOVE: Jarlsberg

NÖKKELOST

REGION: *Various*
TYPE: *Traditional, creamery, semi-hard cheese*
SOURCE: *Cow's milk*
DESCRIPTION: *5–12kg/11–26lb white wheel or block, flecked with cumin seeds and marked with the imprint of crossed keys*
CULINARY USES: *Table cheese, grilling, melting over potatoes*

This mild, factory-made version of the Dutch cheese Leiden has been made in Norway since the seventeenth century. The crossed keys (*nökkel* in Norwegian) that appear on both Leiden and Nökkelost are the emblem of the city of Leiden. Nökkelost ripens in three months.

RIDDER

REGION: *Various*
TYPE: *Modern, creamery, semi-soft cheese*
SOURCE: *Cow's milk*
DESCRIPTION: *3.25kg/7lb wheel with sticky, orange, washed rind*
CULINARY USE: *Table cheese*

Invented by Sven Fenelius, a Swedish cheesemaker, this cheese spread to Norway and is now made and copied the world over. It is open textured and elastic, not unlike the French Saint-Paulin, with a buttery feel and a sweet-savoury taste. The aroma can be quite pungent if the cheese is left wrapped in plastic for too long. Ridder ripens in three months.

FINNISH CHEESES

Finland is a land of vast pine forests and thousands of lakes. One third of it lies within the Arctic Circle and the weather is often inhospitable. Despite these circumstances, dairy farming is the most important form of agriculture. Cows survive the winter in barns, and there is a tradition of cheesemaking dating back to the Middle Ages.

Many traditional cheeses share common ground with those made in neighbouring countries. More recently, with the help of Swiss cheesemakers, large, high-tech factories have created Finnish Swiss, a remarkably good copy of Emmental, which outsells all other types of Emmental in the United States.

Inside the Arctic Circle, some Laplanders still live the simple life of their ancestors, herding the reindeer that supply skins, meat and the milk from which Laplanders make their own unique cheese. Reindeer milk is exceptionally rich, containing nearly four times the amount of fat of cow's milk, and so coagulates easily. The cheese has a rather gamey, earthy flavour, which is said to intensify when it is dipped into hot coffee.

JUUSTOLEIPÄ
REGION: *Various*
TYPE: *Traditional, farmhouse, fresh cheese*
SOURCE: *Cow's or reindeer's milk*
DESCRIPTION: *White, round cheeses in various sizes, charred from the fire*
CULINARY USES: *Generally served for breakfast or as a dessert with jam*

Juustoleipä is traditionally made on farms from cow's or reindeer's milk. The curds are drained and pressed into a flat, wooden platter with a rim. This is then held or placed in front of a fire until the outer layer is "toasted" – hence the name, which means "cheese bread". A speciality of Finland and Lapland, it is mild, creamy and smooth under the slightly charred, crusty surface. Today, most Juustoleipä is factory-made. It ripens in a few days.

BELOW: Juustoleipä

MUNAJUUSTO/ILVES
REGION: *Various*
TYPE: *Traditional, farmhouse and creamery, fresh cheese*
SOURCE: *Cow's or reindeer's milk*
DESCRIPTION: *Pale yellow, flattened balls in various sizes, some with brownish pigments*
CULINARY USES: *Snacks, grilling*

This rather eccentric, farmhouse cheese is made by adding one or two eggs to milk, which is then heated until it curdles. The whey is drained off and the curd lightly pressed into hand-woven baskets. The result is a firm, moist, fresh cheese with a cheerful, sunshine-yellow colour. The surface becomes speckled with brown pigments. Like Juustoleipä, it can be roasted in front of a fire or grilled before being left to age. The factory version is called Ilves.

TUTUNMAA
REGION: *Various*
TYPE: *Traditional, farmhouse and creamery, semi-hard cheese*
SOURCE: *Cow's milk*
DESCRIPTION: *6–10kg/13–22lb drum, pale yellow in colour, without rind*
CULINARY USE: *Table cheese*

A breakfast cheese, Tutunmaa was probably introduced in the sixteenth century and was first made in the great manor houses in Turku, Finland's ancient capital. The cheese is smooth and creamy, with a richness and depth of flavour that owes much to the excellent grazing. The texture is firm and open and the flavour is aromatic, with a slightly sharp tang on the finish.

Tutunmaa is matured for two months or more and has a fat content of 50 per cent. Korsholm is a similar cheese.

ABOVE: Munajuusto/Ilves

SWEDISH CHEESES

Unless you have been to Sweden in spring or summer, it is hard to imagine that this land of ancient glaciers and deep fjords could also be home to comfort-loving cows. Yet without them, and the hardy goats, survival would not have been possible during the long periods of winter isolation, when whole towns were cut off from supplies of fresh meat for months at a time.

Cheesemaking was introduced to Sweden in the ninth century AD by Benedictine monks, sent by Louis I, King of the Franks and Charlemagne's son, in an attempt to convert the warmongering Vikings to a more peaceful, God-fearing way of life. The monks set up dairies, encouraged the peasants to tend their goats and cows, and taught them how to make cheese. To avoid wasting the precious whey, still rich in milk sugars, minerals and protein, the Swedes came up with an ingenious way of converting it into a golden-brown, fudge-like cheese, which is known variously as Getost, Mesost and Getmesost.

Most cheesemaking in Sweden has now passed out of the hands of wives and families to become a national industry with stringent quality control. Sadly, much of the individuality and regional nature of the cheeses has been lost, although dairy products now represent a significant part of the Swedish economy.

Aria Ost, which is now one of the 10 largest cheese-makers in Europe, is a Swedish-based company producing more than 80,000 tonnes of cheese annually. Most of its output is semi-soft cheese, which may help to explain why Swedes consume more semi-soft cheese than any other people in the world. Most of this is served either at breakfast or as part of a smorgasbord.

ADELOST
REGION: *Various*
TYPE: *Modern, creamery, blue cheese*
SOURCE: *Cow's milk*
DESCRIPTION: *2.5kg/5 1/2lb drum with pale cream, natural rind lightly dusted with mould*
CULINARY USE: *Table cheese*

This moist, creamy cheese is not unlike Bleu d'Auvergne. The streaks of blue-grey mould are well distributed and it has a sharp, salty tang. Adelost ripens in two to three months and has a fat content of 50 per cent.

GRÄDDOST
REGION: *Various*
TYPE: *Modern, creamery, semi-soft cheese*
SOURCE: *Cow's milk*
DESCRIPTION: *1kg/2 1/4lb truckle without rind*
CULINARY USES: *Table cheese, grilling, slicing*

This modern Swedish cheese was created in 1961 and soon became popular. Similar to Havarti, it is a firm cheese with small, evenly distributed holes. The flavour is mild and very creamy, with a fresh acidity. Gräddost has a fat content of about 60 per cent.

RIGHT: Grevé is a Swedish copy of Emmental

GREVÉOST/GREVÉ
REGION: *Various*
TYPE: *Modern, creamery, semi-hard cheese*
SOURCE: *Cow's milk*
DESCRIPTION: *14kg/30lb wheel with smooth, polished, pale yellow, natural rind*
CULINARY USES: *Table cheese, grating, melting*

A milder, more commercial copy of Swiss Emmental, Grevéost is supple and dense, with a few large holes. The pale interior is sweet and nutty, and feels very creamy. With age, the flavours become more pronounced, but it lacks the depth of flavour and character of genuine Emmental.

Grevéost ripens in 10 months and has a fat content of 45 per cent.

HERRGÅRDSOST
REGION: *Various*
TYPE: *Traditional, creamery, semi-hard cheese*
SOURCE: *Cow's milk*
DESCRIPTION: *12–18kg/26–39lb round cheese. The smooth, pale yellow, natural rind is usually covered with yellow wax*
CULINARY USES: *Snacks, salads, sandwiches, grilling, breakfast*

The name means "manor house" in Swedish. Herrgårdsost is an all-round, family cheese, created at the beginning of the century as an alternative to imported Gruyère. Although there are some similarities with the original – like Gruyère, Herrgårdsost melts easily and keeps well – it is a much softer and more supple cheese, with smaller, round holes. Herrgårdsost has a mild nuttiness and fresh, zingy tang. It is ripened for up to seven months and has a fat content of around 45 per cent. There is also a low-fat version made with skimmed milk, which has 30 per cent fat. It is ripened for four months.

HUSHÅLLSOST
REGION: *Various*
TYPE: *Traditional, creamery, semi-soft cheese*
SOURCE: *Cow's milk*
DESCRIPTION: *3kg/6¹/₂lb drum with natural rind*
CULINARY USES: *Snacks, grilling, sandwiches*

The history of Hushållsost can be traced back over 700 years. The name simply means "household cheese", and its versatility has made it one of Sweden's best-known cheeses. The pale, straw-coloured interior has a smooth, open texture and small, irregular holes. The flavour is mild and creamy, with a lemon-fresh finish.

Unlike most Swedish cheeses, Hushållsost is made with whole milk, rather than skimmed. It has a fat content of 45 per cent and ripens in about one to three months.

MESOST
REGION: *Various*
TYPE: *Traditional, farmhouse and creamery, whey cheese*
SOURCE: *Cow's milk*
DESCRIPTION: *1–8kg/2¹/₄–18lb block, smooth and pale tan to dark coffee in colour, without rind*
CULINARY USE: *Snacks*

Caramelized whey cheeses are peculiar to Scandinavia, and grew out of the need to utilize and preserve every element of the milk, a vital resource in a country where isolation is a way of life. The whey is heated, which causes the residual proteins and fat to separate out. Gradually the liquid evaporates to leave a sticky, toffee-like mass of caramelized milk sugars. This is poured into moulds and left to set, before being cut into blocks and wrapped in foil for sale.

The texture is dense and can be slightly brittle. Mesost looks like fudge and has a creamy, caramel flavour with a strangely bitter aftertaste. It is not as sweet as Norwegian Gjetost, which is made from whole milk.

Mesost has a fat content of between 10 and 20 per cent. The commercially made cheese usually has whole milk or cream added to ensure a greater yield and sweeter taste.

PRÄSTOST
REGION: *Various*
TYPE: *Traditional, creamery, semi-hard cheese*
SOURCE: *Cow's milk*
DESCRIPTION: *12–15kg/26–33lb wheel with a pale yellow rind covered in fine cloth and with a yellow wax coat*
CULINARY USE: *Table cheese*

The origin of Prästost ("priest's cheese") dates back to the sixteenth century, when farmers paid a tithe to the local pastor in milk. It was then his wife's lot to make it into cheese to be sold at the local market. Success at the marketplace was said to be as much a reflection of her husband's popularity as her cheesemaking skills.

Today, Prästost is made only in factories. The cheese is supple, with a slightly mushy texture and many irregular, rice-sized holes. It has a mellow to robust, sweet-sour, lactic flavour that leaves a sharp, fruity tingle on the palate. It is matured for at least two months and has a fat content of 45 per cent.

Prästost washed in whisky is called Saaland Pfarr and has the robust character of the French washed-rind cheeses.

BELOW: Prästost

SVECIAOST
REGION: *Various*
TYPE: *Modern, creamery, semi-hard cheese*
SOURCE: *Cow's milk*
DESCRIPTION: *12–16kg/26–35lb wheel without rind*
CULINARY USES: *Table cheese, grating, grilling*

Svecia is the Latin name for Sweden and is here used to describe a range of cheeses in the traditional Swedish style which were introduced to compete on the international market with the cheeses of the Netherlands, such as Edam and Gouda. Available in different sizes and at different stages of maturity, the cheeses are frequently waxed and are sold in a variety of flavours, including cloves, cumin and caraway. Their fat content ranges from 30 to 45 per cent.

Semi-hard Sveciaost looks like Herrgårdsost, but is smaller. The texture is moist and supple and the cheese has a number of small holes. It has a pleasant, fresh acidity that matures to a more assertive piquancy.

VÄSTERBOTTENOST
REGION: *Various*
TYPE: *Traditional, creamery, semi-hard cheese*
SOURCE: *Cow's milk*
DESCRIPTION: *20kg/44lb wheel with smooth, orange, waxed rind*
CULINARY USES: *Table cheese, grilling, grating*

Firm and very crumbly, Västerbottenost has small, irregular eyes and some trapped moisture. The cheese was invented in the mid-nineteenth century in West Bothnia and is still exclusive to the area. Excellent for grating and melting in sauces, this cheese has a biteable, somewhat granular texture and a very definite, sharply fruity bite.

GREEK CHEESES

The ancient Greeks regarded cheese as the food of the gods, as well as sustenance for mere mortals, and there are countless references to the subject in their literature. One of the earliest and most significant of these is in Homer's *Odyssey*, written around 700BC. In describing the meeting between Odysseus and the Cyclops Polyphemus in Sicily, Homer writes: "There it was that our human monster had his shelter. We entered into the caravan and looked around it: racks laden with cheese, lambs and kid goats in crowded pens – one stall for every age – metal pots, all filled with milk, earthenware vessels, buckets used for milking." Later, Homer describes Polyphemus making fresh cheese and turning "half his white milk into a curd, which he strained and placed in his rush basket". The baskets were called *formoi*,

from which stems several modern words for cheese, such as the French *fromage* or the Italian *formaggio*.

In remote parts of Greece, women still weave by hand the reed baskets used for draining the cheese. Goats graze on wild, herb-scented hillsides, and the bray of the shepherd's donkey can be heard as flocks of sheep pass through the villages early in the morning on their way to new pastures.

A climate of strong contrasts, coupled with terrain that is inhospitable to all but the hardiest sheep and goats, has meant that meat has always been regarded as a luxury in Greece. Milk and its derivatives have therefore played a significant role in Greek cuisine.

The Greeks consume more cheese per head than even the French. For breakfast they enjoy semi-hard cheeses or bowls of fresh fruit covered with dollops of superb,

creamy yogurt and wild honey. Lunch is the ubiquitous but unbeatable Greek salad of sun-ripened tomatoes, olives, cucumber, olive oil and feta. At other times of the day cheese appears in a wide range of guises – in pies, tarts, pastries, soups, bakes and toasted sandwiches.

Large modern factories and co-operatives are now established in the main dairy areas, producing Graviera, Kaseri and feta. Such is the demand for feta that much is now made from cow's milk or even imported from northern Europe.

Cheeses of all shapes and varieties are available in supermarkets and tiny cheese shops, but the best cheeses are often those the shepherds make themselves.

BELOW: The shape of feta is dictated by the containers used – pottery bowls, woven baskets or wooden trays

ANTHOTIRO/ANTHOTYROS

REGION: *Various*
TYPE: *Traditional, farmhouse, unpasteurized, whey cheese*
SOURCE: *Sheep's and goat's milk*
DESCRIPTION: *Made in various sizes and shapes, particularly balls and truncated cones. Dry and white, the cheese has no rind*
CULINARY USES: *For breakfast with honey or fruit; in desserts; in savoury dishes with oil and wild herbs*

Milk was, and still is, a valuable commodity to Greek shepherds and their families. It was important that none should be wasted, so the ancient Greeks – like the Romans in respect of ricotta – developed numerous ways of converting whey into delicious cheeses. Anthotiro has been made for centuries. The name means "flower cheese", so called because the aroma and flavour carry a hint of the wild flowers and herbs on which the animals graze. Smooth, hard and moist, the cheese has a fine, crumbly texture. The pure white interior is delicate, and the famed floral flavour has a smoky tinge.

Ripening between two and five days, the cheese has a fat content of between 20 and 30 per cent. Milk is sometimes added to the whey to make a slightly richer cheese.

FETA

REGION: *Various*
TYPE: *Traditional, farmhouse and creamery, unpasteurized, fresh (brined) cheese*
SOURCE: *Cow's, goat's and sheep's milk*
DESCRIPTION: *Made in various sizes, often as a loaf-shape, feta is smooth and white and has no rind*
CULINARY USES: *Baking, especially in pastries; also in salads*

One of the simplest forms of cheese, feta grew out of the necessity for shepherds long ago to preserve the milk of their nomadic herds. In the *Odyssey*, Homer gives a detailed description of how the cheese is made. Virtually the same recipe is used today: fresh milk is heated to about 35°C/95°F, the rennet is added and the mixture left to coagulate. Once the milk has curdled or separated, the curd is cut or broken and the whey drained off. The moist, lumpy curds are then put in a cloth bag, twisted or pressed, then hung for a few hours to dry out. When the curd is firm enough, it is cut into slices, liberally sprinkled with salt (the more salt added, the harder the cheese will be) and left to dry for about 24 hours before being packed in wooden barrels and covered with brine. The cheese is ready to eat in about a month and will keep almost indefinitely if submerged in salt or brine.

Feta is solid but crumbly, with some fissures. Pure white, it has a milky, fresh acidity. Today, most feta is made with pasteurized milk and tastes of little besides salt. In parts of Greece, Turkey and Bulgaria, however, it is still possible to find excellent feta that reflects the diversity and character of the rich, concentrated milk from animals that graze the wild and rocky mountain pastures.

Some people are put off by the strong salt content, but the salt is intended only as a preservative and is not supposed to overpower the taste of the cheese. Feta can be soaked in fresh, cold water or milk for a few minutes or longer, if necessary, to make it less salty.

Feta has a fat content of 40–50 per cent.

GRAVIERA

REGION: *Dodoni, Naxos and Crete*
TYPE: *Traditional, farmhouse and co-operative, unpasteurized, hard cheese*
SOURCE: *Cow's, goat's or sheep's milk*
DESCRIPTION: *2–8kg/4½–18lb wheel. The hard, cooked rind has a criss-cross pattern derived from the cloth in which the cheese was drained*
CULINARY USES: *Table cheese, snacks, pastries*

After feta, this is the most popular of the Greek cheeses, ideal for all occasions. Like many Greek cheeses, it can be made from cow's, goat's or sheep's milk, depending on the season, although the majority is today made from cow's milk. Much like Gruyère, from which it is copied, it is sweetish and fruity, with a firm yet supple texture, tiny holes and a rich, creamy feel. Graviera from Crete, made from sheep's milk, is much sought after for its delicate fragrance and burnt-caramel taste, which becomes richer and nuttier when the cheese is baked. The island of Naxos produces a wonderfully nutty, cow's milk Graviera in a small local co-operative.

LEFT: Graviera

RIGHT: Kefalotiri is made from sheep's milk

KASERI

REGION: *Various*

TYPE: *Traditional, farmhouse and co-operative, unpasteurized, stretched curd cheese*

SOURCE: *Sheep's and goat's milk*

DESCRIPTION: *1–9kg/2¼–20lb wheel. There is no rind, but the white crust is smooth, creamy and springy*

CULINARY USES: *Table cheese, melting, grilling, baking (in pastries)*

Kaseri must be at least 80 per cent sheep's milk, with the remainder goat's milk. It is a young version of Kefalotiri, which has been immersed in hot brine to create the characteristic, rubbery, stringy texture. As such it resembles the Italian Provolone Dolce, but has a much stronger flavour. Quite salty and pungent, with a dry feel in the mouth, it has an underlying sweetness due to the sheep's milk. Kaseri is used in Greece in place of mozzarella and appears in numerous local dishes.

KEFALOTIRI/KEFALOTYRI

REGION: *Various*

TYPE: *Traditional, farmhouse and co-operative, unpasteurized, hard cheese*

SOURCE: *Sheep's milk*

DESCRIPTION: *6–8kg/13–18lb drum with thin, hard, natural rind ranging in colour from white to rich yellow*

CULINARY USES: *Breakfast cheese, grating, baking, snacks*

Kefalotiri was already well known and respected by the time of the Byzantine era. It is said to take its name from *kefalo*, a Greek hat. Historically, it was the first cheese to be made at the start of the new season. As soon as the young lambs were weaned, the sheep's milk was used to make this popular cheese. The colour varies from white to yellow, depending on the mix of milk and the grazing, and the firm, dry cheese has numerous irregular holes. The flavour is pleasantly fresh, with a distinct taste of sheep's milk and a slightly sharp finish, not unlike a very fruity, herbaceous olive oil.

Kefalotiri is described as a "male" or "first" cheese to indicate that it is made with full-cream milk; the more delicate whey cheeses (like Manouri, Myzithra or Anthotiro) are called "female" or "second" cheeses. The cheese ripens in two or three months and has a fat content of 40–55 per cent.

MANOURI

REGION: *Crete and Macedonia*

TYPE: *Traditional, farmhouse, unpasteurized, whey cheese*

SOURCE: *Sheep's or goat's milk*

DESCRIPTION: *Made in various sizes, in shapes ranging from large, tapered logs to truncated cones, this smooth, white cheese has no rind*

CULINARY USES: *Mainly used in pastries such as spanakopita or drizzled with honey and served for breakfast as a low-fat alternative to Greek yogurt*

An ancient cheese, made from the whey from feta or Kefalotiri, Manouri is creamy and white, with the texture of a light cheesecake. It melts in the mouth and has a fresh, milky, slightly citrus flavour. Firmer than Myzithra, it is also known as Manoypi.

MYZITHRA/MITZITHRA

REGION: *Various*

TYPE: *Traditional, farmhouse and co-operative, unpasteurized, whey cheese*

SOURCE: *Sheep's milk*

DESCRIPTION: *Rindless rounds of various sizes, showing the imprint of the cloth in which they were drained.*

CULINARY USES: *Baked in light pastries or with vegetables. Also eaten fresh*

Myzithra is a mild, refreshing cheese with a fine, crumbly texture. It was originally made with the whey from Kefalotiri or feta, to which some milk or cream was added. It can be eaten after a few days or ripened for several months. Where milk is abundant, Myzithra may be preserved in salt and dried as a firm, grating cheese. A sour form is sold as Xinomyzithira.

XYNOTYRO

REGION: *Various*

TYPE: *Traditional, farmhouse, unpasteurized, whey cheese*

SOURCE: *Sheep's and goat's milk cheese*

DESCRIPTION: *Made in various shapes and sizes and marked by the reed baskets in which they are drained, these cheeses do not have any rind*

CULINARY USES: *Baking, salads*

The name means "sour cheese", which is a rather inadequate description for a hard, flaky cheese that melts in the mouth to leave a distinct, sweet-sour sensation on the palate. The flavour of Xynotyro is a combination of sweet, burnt caramel, lanolin (typical of sheep's milk cheeses) and the sour taste of the whey. It ripens in a few days and has a fat content of 20 per cent.

LEFT: Kaseri has a similar texture to Italian Provolone Dolce

TURKISH CHEESES

The forefathers of the modern Turks migrated from Central Asia and arrived in Anatolia in the tenth century. Like many nomadic tribes, they travelled with the sheep on which they depended for their survival, and which provided them with wool for their clothing and rugs, meat and – most important – fresh milk for both their yogurt (*sivi tas*) and cheese (*peynir*).

In parts of Turkey, shepherds still wander the hills with their flocks and cheeses are still made from recipes handed down over many years from one generation to the next. Milking is done in ancient, stone enclosures, and cheeses can still be seen hanging over open fires, or draining in bags made from goat skins slung under the branches of trees.

In local markets, you may encounter the soft, white, sheep's milk feta (Beyaz Peynir) alongside Gravyer Peynir (Turkish Gruyère) and rustic cheeses, but the majority of cheese is now made in factories, from cow's, goat's or sheep's milk.

Other cheeses you may come across as you travel through this fascinating country include Taze Kaser (fresh cheese), which, despite its name, is a hard cheese, mainly used as a filling for the delicious Turkish-style toasted sandwiches. Another favourite is Eski Kaser (old cheese), which is rather like a Pecorino, though less salty. Firm, dry and white, it becomes softer and a turns a deep yellow with age. Eski Kaser is often served with honey for breakfast. Alternatively, it can be cut into blocks and preserved in brine.

Made from sheep's milk, Kasar Peynir is a hard, tangy cheese that is pale lemon in colour; Los Peynir is a light, creamy whey cheese, which resembles yogurt; Tulum is a cheese that is made and stored in the stomach or skin of a goat; Mihalic Peynir is a rich, unsalted sheep's milk cheese and Dil Peynir is a mild, stretched-curd cheese.

LEFT: Beyaz Peynir

One of the simplest cheeses, Koy Peynir, is made in village homes throughout Anatolia. Milk is warmed to blood heat, salt and rennet are stirred in, and the mixture is then pulled off the heat, covered and left overnight. Next morning, the coagulated milk is tipped into a cloth-lined sieve and left for six hours to drain. The cheese that remains in the sieve should be soft and creamy. It is either eaten as it is or used in cooking.

BEYAZ PEYNIR
REGION: *Various*
TYPE: *Traditional, farmhouse and co-operative, unpasteurized, vegetarian, fresh cheese*
SOURCE: *Sheep's milk*
DESCRIPTION: *Pure white and rindless, the cheese has a grainy appearance. It is usually sold in blocks or slices*
CULINARY USES: *Fresh in salads, cooked in pastries and many local dishes*
The most popular Turkish cheese, Beyaz Peynir is made in factories and co-operatives and by shepherds. Vegetable rennet is used to clot the milk. The curds are pressed for a few hours, then roughly chopped and strained, sometimes in attractive wooden or woven moulds. After draining, the cheese is cut into slices before being salted and covered with brine. Beyaz Peynir is usually stored in brine for more than six months. It resembles feta and has a fat content of about 45 per cent. It is usually soaked in cold water or milk before use, to remove the excess salt.

MIHALIC PEYNIR
REGION: *Bursa*
TYPE: *Traditional, farmhouse, unpasteurized, vegetarian, hard cheese*
SOURCE: *Sheep's milk*
DESCRIPTION: *Made in various sizes and shapes – often as balls or slices – the cheese is smooth and white with no rind*
CULINARY USES: *Fresh in salads, also used in baked dishes*
The fresh curd is divided into small portions, which are placed in hot water, which is then stirred. The curds are left in the water to harden and acquire a firm, slightly elastic texture, then they are tied in a cloth, which is twisted to force out the whey. Finally, the curds are rolled into small balls, or shaped and sliced, then salted and dried. Mihalic Peynir is stored in brine to preserve and protect the cheese until it is needed. It often goes by the name of the village where it is made.

THE CHEESES OF CYPRUS

—

Traces of civilization dating back to the fifteenth century BC have been discovered in Cyprus. The modern city of Larnaca was once the centre of the Phoenician civilization and the island was for centuries an important trading post for the Aegean sea and the eastern Mediterranean. The discovery of rich copper deposits in the third century BC brought considerable wealth to the country and attracted often uninvited attention from a succession of invaders, including the Romans, the Byzantines and the Ottoman Turks.

Through all the centuries of conflict, the shepherds in the rugged interior continued to herd their goats and sheep, making cheese in the same way as their fathers and forefathers had before them. Feta, Kaskavali, which is similar to the Bulgarian Katschkawalj or the Italian Caciocavallo, and Halloumi are the most common varieties. Despite the on-going battle between the Greek and Turkish communities, Cyprus is an increasingly popuar holiday destination.

HALLOUMI
REGION: *Various*
TYPE: *Traditional, farmhouse and creamery, stretched curd cheese*
SOURCE: *Sheep's, cow's or goat's milk*
DESCRIPTION: *Small, rectangular block or loaf shapes in various different sizes. The cheese is shiny, white and smooth, without rind*
Culinary uses: *Frying, grilling, barbecuing*

Originally a sheep's or goat's milk cheese, Halloumi is now more often produced from cow's milk. The curd is heated in hot water, then kneaded. Chopped mint is usually added and the elastic, squeaky curd is rolled out like pastry and cut into small blocks. These are stored in light brine until needed.

Halloumi has a fibrous, rubbery texture and its otherwise bland, milky taste is heightened by the herby flavour of the chopped fresh mint and the salt from the brine. Denser than mozzarella, it is fundamentally a cooking cheese, whose true character is only revealed when it is heated. Halloumi is one of the few cheeses that will hold its shape when it is fried or grilled. If thin slices of the cheese are placed in a hot, non-stick pan, the outside will rapidly become crisp and slightly charred, while the centre melts deliciously, rather like mozzarella.

In recent years Halloumi has become more popular, particularly amongst the young chefs of Australia, New Zealand and the West Coast of America. To respond to their demands, this traditional Cypriot cheese has begun to be made by cheesemakers in Australia where it is called Halloumy, and by Pelusso Cheese in California who call their version Haloumi.

Halloumi is also made in Romania and the Lebanon.

LEFT: Halloumi is a cooking cheese similar to mozzarella

EASTERN EUROPEAN CHEESES

Eastern Europe has been in turmoil since AD552, when the original settlers, the Slavs, were forced from what is now the Ukraine, by the tribesman of the Russian Steppes. The Slavs crossed into Romania and Bulgaria during the sixth century BC taking with them their knowledge of farming and how to preserve milk in the form of yogurt and Sirene (a cheese similar to feta). Later, Roman occupation lead to the introduction of the style of cheese preferred by the Roman forces, although the only obvious survivors today are Katschkawalj and Halloumi.

Hungary, too, has few indigenous cheeses, although Turkish invaders introduced Brynza, a soft feta-like sheep's milk cheese. In Poland in the tenth century BC Polish cheesemakers began producing and exporting copies of European cheeses. Tylzscki, based on Tilsit, is one of the few that is still made.

By the end of the Second World War artisan cheesemaking had all but died out and throughout Eastern Europe, huge factories were constructed to produce bland, industrial copies of European cheeses like Gouda, Cheddar, Camembert. Emmental, Tilsit and Limburger. However, in the late 1980s small cheese production began to flourish and artisan cheeses began to be made again.

ABERTAM
COUNTRY: *Czech Republic*
TYPE: *Traditional, farmhouse and co-operative, hard cheese*
SOURCE: *Sheep's milk*
DESCRIPTION: *500g/1¼lb irregular ball with thin, yellow to orange, natural rind*
CULINARY USES: *Table cheese, melting, grilling*
Abertam is made in Karlovy-Vary (formerly Carlsbad), the famous spa town. The natural pastures of this mountainous part of Bohemia provide the native sheep with a rich diet that is revealed in the robust flavour of the hard, pressed cheese. Abertam ripens in two months and has a fat content of 45 per cent.

BALATON
COUNTRY: *Hungary*
TYPE: *Traditional, farmhouse and creamery, hard cheese*
SOURCE: *Cow's milk*
DESCRIPTION: *9–12kg/20–26lb loaf shape with thin, greasy, natural rind*
CULINARY USES: *Table cheese, grilling*
Named after the beautiful Lake Balaton, this Hungarian cheese has a firm, compact texture with a scattering of small holes. The flavour is mild, with a pleasant acidity.

BRINZA/BURDUF BRINZA
COUNTRY: *Romania*
TYPE: *Traditional, farmhouse and co-operative, fresh cheese*
SOURCE: *Sheep's milk*
DESCRIPTION: *White, slightly grainy cheese made in blocks*
CULINARY USES: *Cooking cheese*
Brinza is the local name for cheese in the Carpathian region. Its origins go back to Roman times and beyond, and similar cheeses have been made for centuries. It is mild, moist, creamy and crumbly. Usually eaten within a day or two of being made, it has a delicate, sweet, aromatic character. Some of it is also preserved in salt for use during winter, when it more closely resembles feta.

BRYNDZA
COUNTRY: *Slovakia*
TYPE: *Traditional, farmhouse and co-operative, fresh cheese*
SOURCE: *Sheep's milk*
DESCRIPTION: *Stark, white cheeses in various shapes and sizes, without rind*
CULINARY USES: *Spread on rye bread, used in salads, baking*
Made throughout Eastern Europe, particularly in the Carpathian Mountains, this is a subtly flavoured sheep's milk cheese, which is cut into cubes and stored in brine. Crumbly and moist, it resembles feta, but is not as salty.

Bryndza can also be made with cow's or goat's milk, either of which will result in a different consistency. The cheese can range from soft and spreadable to firm and crumbly. As the shepherds and their flocks are often some distance from the co-operatives, they turn their milk into simple curds, press these into cloth sacks and leave them to drain. They are then taken to the dairies, where the curds are broken up, salted, milled and remoulded into blocks. Bryndza is also sold in wooden barrels, packed with yet more salt.

Bryndza is matured for four weeks or more. It has a fat content of around 45 per cent. Similar cheeses include the Romanian Brinza, Hungarian Brynza, Sirene from Bulgaria and Greek feta.

LEFT: Hermélin, made in the Czech Republic, is a soft-white Camembert-style cheese – just one of the many copies of the better-known European cheeses produced in Eastern Europe

HALLOUMI

COUNTRY: *Romania*
TYPE: *Traditional, farmhouse and creamery, stretched-curd cheese*
SOURCE: *Cow's milk*
DESCRIPTION: *300–675g/11oz–1¹/₂lb plaited cheese with smooth, shiny, pale yellow, natural rind*
CULINARY USES: *Frying, grilling, melting*

Like many Eastern European cheeses, Halloumi's origins are blurred by the migratory nature of the ancient peoples who once roamed this area. It seems likely that the Romans learned the stretched-curd technique from the Indo-Europeans who, before the Iron Age, spread over Europe from the Russian steppes. Their language and influence can be traced through Persia, Greece, Eastern Europe, the Middle East and down through Turkestan and northern India.

Halloumi is supple and stringy, becoming harder the longer it remains in the brine in which it is traditionally cured. It is also made in Cyprus and Lebanon.

KATSCHKAWALJ

COUNTRY: *Bulgaria*
TYPE: *Traditional, farmhouse and creamery, stretched-curd cheese*
SOURCE: *Sheep's milk*
DESCRIPTION: *6–9kg/13–20lb irregular round, with thin, pale yellow to yellowish-brown, natural rind*
CULINARY USES: *Table cheese, snacks, also fried or baked in local dishes*

Katschkawalj is a *pasta filata* (stretched-curd) cheese made from sheep's milk and found right across Eastern Europe and into Central Asia. It is thought to have originated before the days of the Roman Empire, and may have been the progenitor of the Italian Caciocavallo. Like all *pasta filata* cheeses, it is made by kneading and stretching the fresh curd before it is salted and aged. It keeps well and is valued for its versatility in cooking. Originally made principally by shepherds for their own consumption, it is now largely produced in factories.

Although the best Katschkawalj is made from sheep's milk, mixed milk and pure cow's milk versions are on the increase. The texture of the sheep's milk cheese is firm but flexible and crumbly. Underneath the pale yellow rind (which deepens in colour as the cheese matures), the cheese is salty, sharp and slightly bitter. The flavour has a hint of caramelized onion. Both eaten as a table cheese, and used extensively in cooking, Katschkawalj is sometimes referred to as the "Cheddar of the Balkans". It matures in two months and has a fat content of 45 per cent.

LAJTA

COUNTRY: *Hungary*
TYPE: *Traditional, farmhouse and co-operative, unpasteurized, semi-soft cheese*
SOURCE: *Cow's milk*
DESCRIPTION: *1kg/2¹/₄lb rectangular cheese with moist, deep orange, washed rind*
CULINARY USE: *Table cheese*

This was undoubtedly introduced to Hungary by some order of intrepid monks, determined to convert the local populace, but missing the cheeses of Western Europe. The slightly sticky, washed rind covers a supple interior containing numerous small, irregular holes created as a result of the starter culture used and the ensuing vigorous fermentation process. Lajta has the robust aroma and taste characteristic of washed-rind cheeses. It ripens in four to six weeks and has a fat content of 50 per cent.

LIPTAUER

COUNTRY: *Hungary*
TYPE: *Traditional, farmhouse and co-operative, unpasteurized, fresh cheese*
SOURCE: *Sheep's or cow's milk*
DESCRIPTION: *Spiced, white cheese sold in pots*
CULINARY USE: *Forms the basis of numerous local dishes*

The Hungarians developed Liptauer from a simple, white, sheep's milk cheese called Liptoi, which was made by shepherds in their mountain huts. The curd was hung in cloth sacks for up to a week before being taken to a small dairy, where it was mixed with paprika and salt.

Each family has its own recipe for what has become known as Liptauer cheese.

Onions, caraway seeds, capers, anchovies or other ingredients whose proportions are often secret are added to the curd, together with varying amounts of paprika. Hungarians have a great love of spicy food, so Liptauer can be exceedingly hot, even vicious. It has a fat content of around 50 per cent.

LIPTOI

COUNTRY: *Hungary*
TYPE: *Traditional, farmhouse and co-operative, unpasteurized, fresh cheese*
SOURCE: *Sheep's milk*
DESCRIPTION: *White, mousse-like cheese sold in pots*
CULINARY USES: *Snacks, hors d'oeuvres, salads*

For centuries, this simple cheese has been made by shepherds in the Tatra mountains. Fine and mousse-like, with the subtle, sweet taste of sheep's milk and rosemary, it is mixed with various spices and herbs. There are as many recipes for this cheese as there are makers, as the recipes are handed down from one generation to the next.

Liptoi is the basis for Liptauer, the best-known cheese of Eastern Europe, which combines paprika, caraway, onions and capers in a heady, sometimes wickedly hot spread. This is most often served as a dip, with celery – and copious amounts of the local beer.

MANUR/MANDUR

COUNTRY: *Serbia*
TYPE: *Traditional, farmhouse and creamery, unpasteurized, hard cheese*
SOURCE: *Sheep's or cow's milk*
Description: *2–3kg/4¹/₂–6¹/₂lb sphere with thin, white or straw-coloured, natural rind*
CULINARY USES: *Grating – as a condiment or in soup*

This unusual cheese is unique to Serbia. The fresh milk (cow's or sheep's, depending on the season) is gradually heated until it boils. It is then cooled to hand-hot and a mixture of buttermilk, fresh whey and rennet is added. Once set, the curd is drained in a cloth before being salted, shaped and dried. It ripens in a few days and has a fat content of 40 per cent.

ABOVE: Koliba from the Czech Republic. Like this modern factory-made cheese, many of the traditional cheeses, which were made in what was once known as Czechoslovakia, had intricate designs carved into the moulds by the cheese-maker – giving each a unique pattern

OSCHTJEPKA

COUNTRY: *Slovakia*
TYPE: *Traditional, farmhouse, unpasteurized, semi-hard cheese*
SOURCE: *Cow's and sheep's milk*
Description: *500g/1¼lb round cheese with natural rind marked with slight indentations from the cloth used for draining and drying*
CULINARY USES: *Table cheese, grilling, melting*

Supple and elastic, Oschtjepka is similar to Bulgarian Katshkawalj. It has been made for centuries in the magnificent Carpathian Mountains, a mecca for sheep, with its fresh mountain streams and natural pastures.

Most of the cheese is still made by the shepherds themselves. The soured milk is pressed into balls, each the size of a small melon, and hung to dry from the ceilings of their mountain chalets. The sweet, aromatic smoke from the shepherds' fires gradually dries the cheese and adds to its flavour. Similar cheeses, which are also produced in Eastern Europe, include Parenica, which is made in Slovakia, and the Polish cheese, Oszczpek.

Oschtjepka ripens in about two to three months and has a fat content of around 45 per cent.

OSZCZPEK

COUNTRY: *Poland*
TYPE: *Traditional, farmhouse and co-operative, unpasteurized, semi-hard cheese*
SOURCE: *Cow's and sheep's milk*
DESCRIPTION: *Made in various sizes and shapes (usually oval), with smooth, polished, pale lemon, natural rind which can be chocolate brown if the cheese is heavily smoked*
CULINARY USES: *Table cheese, grilling, melting*

Oszczpek is one of the few remaining traditional cheeses to be found in Poland. Most of the other cheeses on sale there are factory-made imitations of the more popular European cheeses.Made in the Tatra Mountains, Oszczpek belongs to the same family as the Slovakian Oschtjepka.

The curd is kneaded, then pressed into hand-carved, wooden moulds. Once drained, the young cheeses are traditionally stored in the eaves of the house, where they gradually absorb the smoke from the fire.

Oszczpek ripens in one to four weeks and has a fat content of 45 per cent.

PODHALANSKI

COUNTRY: *Poland*
TYPE: *Traditional, farmhouse and creamery, unpasteurized, semi-hard cheese*
SOURCE: *Cow's and sheep's milk*
DESCRIPTION: *500g/1¼lb brick or loaf shape with hard, pale yellow, natural rind that darkens to burnt orange if smoked*
CULINARY USES: *Table cheese, grilling*

Firm, but supple, Podhalanski has tiny holes throughout the pale yellow interior. Some cheeses are lightly smoked in the style of earlier times. Podhalanski ripens in two months.

SIRAZ

COUNTRY: *Serbia*
TYPE: *Traditional, farmhouse, unpasteurized, semi-hard cheese*
SOURCE: *Cow's milk*
DESCRIPTION: *200–400g/7–14oz flat disc. The rough, yellow, natural rind has some yeasts*
CULINARY USES: *Table cheese, baking; often crumbled into local dishes*

To make this unusual Serbian cheese, the young curd is pressed into flat discs, about 15cm/6in in diameter. The cheese is then left in the sun to dry, often on a balcony wall, until the fat begins to ooze. The surface is rubbed and salted several times over the next few days until a crust forms, when the cheeses are stored in wooden containers of brine. The cheese ripens in a few weeks. It has a mellow, slightly sour, salty tang and a compact body.

SIRENE

COUNTRY: *Bulgaria*
TYPE: *Traditional, farmhouse and creamery, unpasteurized, fresh cheese*
SOURCE: *Sheep's and cow's milk*
DESCRIPTION: *White, slightly grainy cheese without rind, sold in blocks*
CULINARY USES: *Salads, spreads, baking; also as a table cheese, with fresh herbs*

The most popular and most widely produced Bulgarian cheese. Moist, crumbly, fresh and lemony, it is stored in barrels or tins of brine. Sirene is richer and creamier than many similar cheeses, and has a fat content of 45–50 per cent.

THE CHEESES OF INDIA AND THE MIDDLE EAST

The culture and climate of India, and of many of her neighbours, have inadvertently conspired against the development of a dairy industry. The combination of high temperatures and humidity causes rapid growth of moulds, cracking of the cheese surface, excessive drying out and rapid putrefaction. Installation of equipment to alter the environment is expensive and inappropriate where the volume of available milk is low and the potential producers and customers widespread and isolated.

Such indigenous cheeses as do exist are generally very simple, and are dried over fires, often fuelled by cattle dung rather than wood, which is scarce, particularly in the Himalayas. Karut is a very dry, hard, skimmed-milk cheese made in Afghanistan and north-west India, while Krutt is made by the nomadic tribes in the middle Asiatic steppes, using skimmed milk from cows, goats, sheep or camels. The milk is coagulated by natural souring, and the curd is hung up in sacks to drain.

Elsewhere, milk is normally coagulated using rennet obtained from a young milk-fed calf, but this is not possible in India, where the cow is a sacred animal. Non-animal rennet can be used, but seldom is. Instead, the practice is to make simple, quick-ripening cheeses, which are coagulated by the action of the acid in milk, and not by bacteria or moulds.

In the mid-1990s, milk consumption in India has more than doubled; it is said to be the fastest-growing market in the world. Production of some of the popular cheeses of European origin is developing. Herds of cows and water buffalos are increasing, but the milk yield is still insufficient to meet the demand and it is necessary to import milk products.

Paneer, a simple cheese made in the home and eaten within a few days of being made, is very popular. It is used in various traditional Indian dishes, including meat and vegetable curries and spicy vegetable dishes.

To make your own paneer, bring 2 litres/3½ pints fresh whole milk to the boil. Stir in 30ml/2 tbsp vinegar or lemon juice and set aside. When the milk has curdled, pour it into a clean, scalded muslin cloth set in a strainer. Rinse with fresh water and drain well, then bring up the sides of the cloth to enclose the curd and shape it into a ball. Place under a heavy saucepan or similar weight and press for 10–15 minutes. This makes about 225g/8oz paneer.

BELOW: Paneer is one of the few cheeses that can easily be made at home

THE MIDDLE EAST

Centuries ago in Iran, simple dried cheeses were produced, then, when milk was abundant, the people made a softer sheep's milk cheese, similar to feta, which was preserved in brine to last through the leaner months. The nomadic bedouins, too, made a soft cheese that was either eaten fresh or preserved in salt.

Nowadays, the most common cheese found in the region are small balls of fresh curd, sometimes rolled in herbs or spices, and served at breakfast time. They are called Lebneh in the Lebanon and Israel, Lebney in Syria, Gibne in the Arabic countries and Labaneh in Jordan. A similar cheese, Serat, made in the high mountains of Iran and Afghanistan, is smoked and dipped in beeswax to help preserve it.

Although most exported Halloumi comes from Cyprus, this cheese was originally made by the Bedouin tribes from sheep's milk. It is still made today, popular because of its ability to hold its shape even when grilled on a skewer.

Kashakawan, found in the Lebanon and Syria, is similar to both Bulgarian Katshkawalj and Turkish Kasar Peynir. The name means "cheese on horseback", and is thought to originate from when the cheeses were tied in pairs and slung acrss a pole like saddle bags to dry. A kosher version of the cheese is made in Israel, where they also make the smaller, Smoked Basna.

Most other cheeses from Israel are copies of popular European cheeses. One of the most common, Bulgarian cheese, is actually feta, but is so-called because the best feta was considered to come from Bulgaria where the cheese is softer and less salty than the Greek varieties. Other cheeses include Bin-Gedi, a Camembert-type cheese; Galil, a sheep's milk cheese modelled on Roquefort; Golan, a hard Provolone-style cheese; Tal Ha'emek, a hard cheese with holes like Emmental; and Gilead, which is similar to mozzarella.

THE CHEESES OF THE USA

All too often, the prevailing attitude to cheese in the USA appears to be that it is something you have to cook, grate or melt for it to be useful. There is also a widely held belief that cheese is too fattening and too high in salt to indulge in more than occasionally. Unfortunately, the supermarket shelves reflect public opinion. They are laden with ready-to-go shredded or sliced Jack, Cheddar, Swiss or processed cheese, kept "fresh" with preservatives. Sanitized, sterilized and standardized – who can blame Americans for thinking cheese is just a commodity that you have to do something with?

How did this happen in a country where, by 1890, nearly a third of the population were European-born immigrants? Ironically, it was the enormous influx of immigrants that helped to create the situation. Mass production was seen as the only way to feed the soaring population. There was no time to invent new cheeses, and distribution of small-volume farmstead cheeses was impossible in such a huge country, so milk was processed, mainly into Cheddar, and "big" was the byword. By 1900, a thousand cheese factories had grown up along the East coast alone.

The first all-American cheese was Brick, set apart from European cheeses as much by name as by the process by which it was made. In 1877, John Jossi, a Wisconsin cheesemaker of Swiss

RIGHT: New York State Cheddar

extraction, discovered that if he squeezed fresh curd between two bricks, the result was a brick-shaped cheese similar to the popular German Limburger, but firmer and more rubbery. His cheese was ideal for cutting, and had a mild aroma and taste. Today, Brick is vacuum-packed in slices, strings or blocks and is sold right across the USA.

Next (in 1882) came Colby, named after a town in Wisconsin. Similar to Cheddar, but softer and more elastic, it also matured more quickly and could be eaten within weeks rather than months. Sweet and bland, Colby was soon accepted as an all-purpose, family cheese. It remains a favourite.

The origin of Monterey Jack, although attributed to the Scot, David Jacks, can actually be traced back to the Spanish Franciscan monks who came north during the early days of the missions, when California was still part of Mexico. Finding themselves with surplus milk, they set about making *queso blanco*, a delicate, creamy cheese that originated in Spain and which had spread to South America.

David Jacks' contribution was to recognize its potential. He set up factories, and by the mid 1880s was producing his own cheese. To distinguish it from others on the market, it was known as Jack's cheese and ultimately Jack. To differentiate this cheese from the firmer, industrially produced Jack, it is usually referred to as Monterey, Sonoma or California Jack.

Like many great cheeses, Dry Jack was created by accident rather than design. In 1915 another San Franciscan found himself with a surplus of young Jack

BELOW: Dry Jack

cheese. Needing the shelf space for other cheeses, he stored the Jack cheese on the floor, hand-salting each one in the hope that it would survive. Weeks later, he found that the Jack cheese had become fruity, rich and hard, not unlike Parmesan. Dry Jack proved instantly popular and has been a favourite ever since.

By 1930 most of the familiar European cheeses were being produced. However, the paranoia over raw milk in the 1950s closed down all but the most intrepid cheesemakers. The few remaining artisans relied on the loyalty of the local community to survive, while those in more isolated areas found success through mail-order sales.

The influence of the Vietnam War, coupled with the growth of the hippie movement, were just two of the catalysts that spawned a new generation of farmstead cheesemakers who had decided to embrace a different way of life.

By the late 1970s, production had moved into the hands of large companies. Small co-operatives disappeared as cheese became another commodity to be distributed as cheaply and efficiently as possible to the increasing number of supermarkets.

A new era of American cooking was emerging, with young chefs turning their backs on the imported cheeses in favour of seeking out regional produce. Mediterranean-style menus called for fresh mozzarella, ricotta and goat's milk cheeses. Delis and fancy food shops were on the increase and the wonderful farmers' markets, with their emphasis on quality rather than quantity, provided a showcase from California to New York for the American farmstead cheeses.

Many of the new generation of cheesemakers turned to goats or sheep. They were easier to handle, required less investment and there was a better return on their milk. The strict laws enforcing pasteurization had been relaxed, and raw cheese could be sold so long as it was matured for more than 60 days.

The consumers' attitude has also changed. When people buy farmstead cheeses, they feel they are supporting the old ways and encouraging those who practise sustainable farming methods. Today there are more than 80 producers of American farmstead cheeses. Seek them out, give them support and enjoy them.

ABOVE:
Monterey Jack

In addition to the smaller cheesemakers, the USA has large manufacturers producing different types of cheese, which are often versions of European varieties. In this section of the book, you will find entries for individual cheeses, as well as listings for companies whose entire range sets a standard that makes them worth looking out for.

BEL GIOIOSO CHEESES
REGION: *Wisconsin*
TYPE: *Various unpasteurized, Italian cheeses*
SOURCE: *Cow's milk*
DESCRIPTION: *Various sizes and shapes, including bell, wheel, pear and wedge*
CULINARY USES: *Various*
Bel Gioioso is the name given to a range of Italian cheeses that have their origins in the Auricchio Cheese Company, which was founded near Naples in 1877. The company flourished, ultimately becoming the world's largest producer of aged Provolone. In 1979, they set up a factory in Wisconsin, using Italian equipment and cheesemakers.

Today, Bel Gioioso Cheeses produces Fontina, Parmesan, Romano, Asiago and Gorgonzola as well as mascarpone and fresh mozzarella, plus the Provolone with which they began. Adherence to traditional Italian cheesemaking methods has given Bel Gioioso cheeses authenticity. However, the differences in climate and grazing, together with the need to meet the demands of the local market, has subtly altered the flavour and texture of the various cheeses. Fortunately, their fundamental character has not been lost.

BERGÈRE BLEUE
REGION: *New York State*
TYPE: *Modern, farmhouse, organic, blue cheese*
SOURCE: *Sheep's milk*
DESCRIPTION: *Cylindrical cheese, 16cm/6¹/₂in in diameter and 10cm/4in tall. The sticky, moist, natural rind has occasional blotches of natural yeasts and moulds*
CULINARY USES: *Table cheese, omelettes and salads*
Bergère Bleue is a Roquefort-style cheese with a rich aroma of lanolin and yeast. It melts in the mouth like butter, releasing the flavour of burnt caramel. The blue-green streaks of *Penicillium roquefortii* give a spicy piquancy to the pale lemon-coloured cheese, which is moist and slightly crumbly. The more mature cheese is spreadable.

The cheesemaker is Jane North, who learnt her craft in the French and Spanish Pyrenees. When she returned to the USA, she and her husband Karl built their farm at Freetown. Eight years later, in 1988, they established Northland Sheep Dairy and started cheesemaking. In addition to Bergère Bleue, the dairy also produces Tomme Bergère and Folie Bergère.

BRIER RUN CHEESES
REGION: *West Virginia*
TYPE: *Traditional, farmhouse, organic, fresh and aged cheeses*
SOURCE: *Goat's milk (Nubian, Alpine and Saanen)*
DESCRIPTION: *Various sizes and shapes, ranging from 115g/4oz to 1kg/2¹/₄lb in weight*
CULINARY USES: *Table cheeses, also used in salads and for grilling*
Goats are hardy creatures, producing their best milk when conditions are tough and varied. The narrow valley, scrub-covered grey crags and herbaceous pastures of the Appalachian foothills provide Greg and Verena Sava's goats with the perfect environment. Their natural existence also means that they breed at their own whim, not man's, so there are times when milk is in short supply and the cheese can be difficult to find. Greg and Verena handle the flavoursome milk with care, hand-ladling the curd to give a creamier, fuller flavour. Their goat's milk cheeses are among America's finest.

BULK FARM CHEESES
REGION: *California*
TYPE: *Various traditional, farmhouse, European-style cheeses*
SOURCE: *Cow's milk*
DESCRIPTION: *Various*
CULINARY USES: *Table cheese, grating, grilling*
Dutch cheesemakers are among the finest exports from Europe, adapting the traditional recipes of their native cheeses to their new pastures and climates. The Bulk family have been cheesemakers for generations, and Walter and Lenneke are doing a fine job of upholding the family tradition at their farm in California.

Those who have sampled the cheeses sold at their small retail store tend to come back, impressed by the quality. To ensure their Gouda has the authentic taste and texture, they import the traditional starter culture and rennet from Holland. This affects every stage of the cheesemaking process and has a direct bearing on the rich, nutty flavour of Gouda. Bulk Farm also produces its own Leyden, Edam and Quark.

CAPRIOLE BANON

REGION: *Indiana*
TYPE: *Traditional, farmhouse, fresh cheese*
SOURCE: *Goat's milk (Alpine)*
DESCRIPTION: *180g/6¼oz disc wrapped in marinated chestnut leaves*
CULINARY USE: *Table cheese*

Judy Schad's cheeses are exceptional in quality and character. Not only do the shapes and names reflect her wicked sense of humour – Wabash Cannonballs and Fromage à Trois are just two of the cheeses from her list – but her concentration on ageing the cheeses to the point of perfection demonstrates her belief that the American palate loves to experience new flavours.

Her Capriole Banon looks like an exquisitely wrapped gift, with its covering of interwoven chestnut leaves that have been marinated in brandy and white wine. Their aroma permeates the soft, creamy curd to devastating effect – a sensational blend of flavours.

Judy's company, Capriole Inc., also makes Mont St Francis, Old Kentucky Tomme and Festiva, which is a wonderful combination of a Jack-style goat's milk cheese with pine nuts, basil and flavoursome sun-dried tomatoes.

CHÈVRE DE PROVENCE

REGION: *Alabama*
TYPE: *Modern, farmhouse, organic, fresh cheese*
SOURCE: *Goat's milk (mixed breeds)*
DESCRIPTION: *Various shapes and sizes, without rind*
CULINARY USES: *Table cheese, grilling or baking, spreading, salads*

Like great pastry chefs, some cheesemakers seem to possess an almost arcane touch. The judges at the 1994 and 1995 American Cheese Society conference certainly recognized Liz Parnell's talents, awarding both her Chèvre de Provence and her fromage frais first place.

Liz's chèvre has been described as an American treasure. The subtle flavour of the tiny discs of fresh, lemony, goat's milk cheese is enhanced by the mixture of olive oil and fresh herbs in which it is packed.

COACH FARM CHEESES

REGION: *New York State*
TYPE: *Modern, farmhouse, fresh and soft-white cheeses*
SOURCE: *Goat's milk (French Alpine)*
DESCRIPTION: *Various shapes and sizes, textures and tastes*
CULINARY USES: *Table cheeses, grilling, baking as filling for pastries, sauces and salads*

From fresh, mild and lemony to creamy, aromatic and mushroomy, Coach Farm Cheeses are of a consistently high quality. They set the standard by which many small farms match themselves, and it is not surprising that nowadays they are among the most widely distributed cheeses in America.

Miles, Lilian and Susan Cahn are perfectionists, taking as much trouble with the varied diet of their 800 goats as they do in finding a wrapping that will protect the cheese while allowing it to breathe.

Their fresh cheeses are ready to eat within days. The aged varieties grow a soft-white penicillium mould and are best eaten when still firm and flaky. Mild, but not bland, they dissolve like ice cream. Both types are available in a variety of flavours. One of their best-known cheeses is Pyramid, in which the young curd is flavoured with aromatic and spicy green peppercorns.

COTTAGE CHEESE

REGION: *Various*
TYPE: *Modern, creamery, fresh cheese*
SOURCE: *Cow's milk*
DESCRIPTION: *Creamy, lumpy cheese sold in pots*
CULINARY USES: *Table cheese, snacks, salads, baking*

Americans have come to think of cottage cheese as their own invention, but it originated with the rural labourers of Europe, who had been making it for centuries before it crossed the Atlantic.

Cottage cheese is an acid curd cheese, relying on the natural tendency of warm milk to curdle, rather than requiring the addition of rennet. Once the soft, floppy curd has formed, it is cut into pea-sized cubes and heated gently in the whey until it reaches the desired texture and body. The whey is then drained off and the lumpy curd is rinsed in cold water to remove the excess whey and lactose. What remains is cottage cheese. Salt and a little milk or cream are routinely added, and many varieties are flavoured to lift what is essentially a bland and often rather boring flavour.

Cottage cheese accounts for nearly 25 per cent of all cheese consumed by weight-conscious Americans. It is produced in factories across the country, each fighting for their share of the market. The cheese ripens in one or two days and has a fat content of five to 15 per cent.

ABOVE: A young Capriole Banon

RIGHT: Cream cheese

COUGAR GOLD

REGION: *Washington State*
TYPE: *Modern, creamery, semi-soft cheese*
SOURCE: *Cow's milk*
DESCRIPTION: *1kg/2¼lb round cheese without rind, packed in a can*
CULINARY USES: *Table cheese, snacks*

Established in 1948 by Washington State University to encourage the growth and quality of cheesemaking in the state, Cougar Gold remains popular – partly, no doubt, due to the novelty of buying a cheese that is packed in a can.

Cougar Gold is creamy, smooth and rich, with a mellow cheese-and-onion-sauce aroma and taste. An enthusiast once sent the author two cans, one 12 months old and the other two years old, in order to prove that cheese in a can could be good and could be aged. The author was suitably impressed but not necessarily converted.

CREAM CHEESE

REGION: *Various*
TYPE: *Modern, creamery, fresh cheese*
SOURCE: *Cow's milk*
DESCRIPTION: *White, rindless cheese sold in pots*
CULINARY USES: *Spreads, baking, dips, cheesecakes*

Like cottage cheese, this is an acid curd cheese, but requires a starter culture to curdle the milk, which it does by turning the milk sugar (lactose) into lactic acid. Low-fat varieties may require the addition of a little rennet to help the milk to coagulate. The freshly formed, soft curd is poured into close-weave linen cloth (or a sack of woven plastic), the ends are knotted together and the bundle is left to drain. After two to three hours, the curd on the sides of the cloth is scraped into the centre, the cloth is re-tied and the bundle is placed on a draining tray under a weight and pressed for two to three hours. At this stage, salt is added. Theoretically, the cream cheese could now be packed into tubs for immediate use, but it is more often heated and extruded before being poured into moulds for sale.

Cream cheese is generally mild and velvety, with a fresh, lemony zing balanced by the buttery richness of the cream. Low-fat versions may contain whey powder, which gives them a slightly grainy feel. Cream cheese made at home must be eaten within a few days, but the commercially produced product can have a shelf life of up to 60 days depending on the method used to make and preserve it. Stabilizers are seldom used, but some manufacturers use a gum of sorts to hold the cheese together and improve its keeping qualities.

CROWLEY

REGION: *Vermont*
TYPE: *Traditional, farmhouse, semi-hard cheese*
SOURCE: *Cow's milk*
DESCRIPTION: *Cylindrical or oblong cheeses in various sizes. The natural rind carries the imprint of the cheesecloth and has some natural mould*
CULINARY USES: *Table cheese, grating, grilling*

This farmhouse cheese is made by washing the freshly cut curd with cool spring water. This removes much of the acidic whey, creating a cheese that is similar to but sweeter than Cheddar. The curd is then salted, loosely packed to allow the small holes to develop, then placed in wooden presses and hand-cranked for just long enough to ensure it develops a firm, yet moist texture. When aged for between three and six months, the cheese is magnificent; at around six months, while retaining some sweetness, it has the pungent, cheese-and-onion tang of mature Cheddar; at over 12 months and labelled "extra sharp" it is Crowley's best-seller.

The story of the cheese starts in the family kitchen, where Winfield and Nellie Crowley made cheese for friends and family. In 1882 they built their creamery. Demand soon grew for their cheese, which was made from a combination of recipes, modified over the years to suit the preferences of individual family members.

Although officially designated as a Colby cheese, Crowley was actually made decades before Colby cheese existed. Nor is it a Cheddar, as the cheesemaking process is different.

In 1967 the factory was in serious danger of closing. Randolph Smith, who had come to Vermont to retire, heard the rumours, stepped in and saved Crowley from extinction. His sons continue to produce this simple, farmhouse cheese by hand in the original wooden barn, often watched by the many thousands of visitors who come every summer to view the cheesemaking.

CYPRESS GROVE CHEVRE
REGION: *California*
TYPE: *Modern and traditional, farmhouse, vegetarian, fresh and aged cheeses*
SOURCE: *Goat's milk (Alpine)*
DESCRIPTION: *Various shapes and sizes*
CULINARY USES: *Table cheese, salads and sauces, grilling and baking*

Consistent quality and distinctive packaging have spelt success for cheesemaker Mary Keehn and her daughter Malorie. Their fresh cheeses are made in the traditional, French, farmhouse style. Light and mousse-like, they have a pleasant acidity and herbaceous finish. When aged, the cheeses develop a white penicillium mould that forms a shell. The herbaceous character becomes more pronounced and the mushroom aroma of the rind penetrates the cheese. Although harder than the young cheeses, the aged cheeses melt in the mouth. Their other cheeses include Chèvre Log, Pee Wee Pyramid, Goat's Milk Cheddar, Tomme and feta.

ABOVE: Dry Jack

CANADIAN CHEESES

Canada's early settlers, from Britain and France, were mainly trappers, traders and foresters with little interest in either cheesemaking or farmsteading, so it is not surprising that cheesemaking was slow to develop in this beautiful, but often inhospitable land. When cattle were introduced, it was for meat, not milk. Cheese was hardly a consideration, since game and meat were plentiful sources of protein. Only in winter, when snow and isolation prevented fresh supplies from reaching large farms, were some rudimentary cheeses made.

It was the arrival of French Trappist monks that really began Canada's cheesemaking tradition. Their first monastery was in Quebec, and by 1881 they were producing a semi-soft, washed-rind cheese, Oka, which has been made commercially since 1960. The Benedictine monks at the abbey of Saint Benoit du Lac in Quebec created Canada's first blue cheese, Ermite (Hermit) in 1943. It, too, is still being made.

British immigrants gradually established dairy herds. They set up co-operatives to process the milk into Cheddar, as they have done in Australia, America and New Zealand.

Canadian Cheddar made its presence known in a big way when a 10-ton Cheddar was made in Ontario for the 1893 World Exhibition in Chicago. The cheese finally ended up in a London restaurant. As a marketing exercise, it was extremely successful, and Canadian Cheddar was placed firmly on the map – and in the minds of the British. It continues to sell well in supermarkets across Britain, industrially made but often aged to a mouth-puckering degree of acidity, a taste staunch supporters insist is the mark of the perfect Cheddar. Epicures who prize the firm, rich nuttiness of traditional British Cheddar, with its final savoury bite, might disagree, however.

Cheddar continues to dominate the Canadian cheese market, although the growth of tourism and the skiing industry has brought about a dramatic increase in sales of Canadian Raclette and Oka. So far, the revival of artisan cheesemaking, which has had such a beneficial affect in America and Great Britain, has scarcely begun in Canada, but cannot be too far away, as a few small cheesemakers scattered across the provinces are already finding a market for their hand-made cheeses.

LEFT: Canadian Cheddar

DRY JACK
REGION: *California*
TYPE: *Traditional, farmhouse, unpasteurized, vegetarian, hard cheese*
SOURCE: *Cow's milk*
DESCRIPTION: *4kg/9lb square with rounded edges. The natural rind is hand-rubbed with oil, cocoa and pepper*
CULINARY USES: *Table cheese, grating, salads*

Like many great cheeses, Dry Jack was created by accident rather than design. In 1915 a San Francisco wholesaler found himself with an over-abundance of young Jack cheese. To clear shelf space for new arrivals, he reluctantly stacked the Jack on the floor, hand-salting each one in the hope that it would survive.

Weeks later, he found that the cheeses were fruity, rich and hard, not unlike the Pecorino and Parmesan he had run out of at the time. Necessity being the mother of invention, he coated each cheese with oil, pepper and cocoa, to imitate the lamp black being used on imported Italian cheeses at that time, and offered "Dry Jack" to his customers. A star was born.

Today the cheese, made by the Vella Cheese Company, is among the finest in the world. The rind looks like chocolate icing. Underneath, the deep yellow cheese is hard and when cut, the cheese shatters rather than breaks, releasing layer upon layer of flavour: sweet and fruity; sharp and mouth-watering, rich and full-bodied like a fine wine.

FRESH JACK

REGION: *California*
TYPE: *Traditional, farmhouse and creamery, semi-soft cheese*
SOURCE: *Cow's milk*
DESCRIPTION: *Rounds in various sizes. The straw-coloured, natural rind is fine and springy*
CULINARY USES: *Table cheese, snacks, melting, salads*

Another cheese from the famous Vella Cheese Company, Fresh Jack resembles Edam in texture, but is creamier and more springy. It has a distinctive taste: aromatic, with a hint of green-grass bitterness. Factory-made Jack tends to be bland, mild and milky, with a rubbery feel compared to this excellent cheese.

GRAFTON VILLAGE CHEDDAR

REGION: *Vermont*
TYPE: *Traditional, farmhouse, unpasteurized, hard cheese*
SOURCE: *Cow's milk*
DESCRIPTION: *Blocks of various sizes, without rind*
CULINARY USES: *Table cheese, grating, melting, grilling, in sauces*

By keeping to small-batch production and traditional methods, Grafton continues to produce excellent white (uncoloured) Cheddars, with the depth of flavour and character possible only with raw milk and long ageing.

The Grafton Village Cheese Company was established in 1890 in the village of Grafton, now meticulously restored. It draws its milk from local dairy farms, where cattle graze the rich grasslands of the southern Vermont mountains. The result is milk that is high in butterfat, with a consistent quality and texture, qualities that are essential for the production of cheeses that will develop real character and depth as they mature.

Grafton Village Cheddar ripens in six to 24 months and has a fat content of 50 per cent. The company makes several flavoured Cheddars (with sage, garlic or dill), plus a version that is smoked over corn cobs.

HOLLOW ROAD CHEESES

REGION: *New York State*
TYPE: *Traditional, farmhouse, organic, fresh and aged cheeses*
SOURCE: *Sheep's milk (also mixed Sheep's and cow's milk)*
DESCRIPTION: *Various shapes and sizes*
CULINARY USES: *Table cheeses, snacks, salads*

Joan Snyder and Ken Kleinpeter produce a range of excellent cheeses, each of which offers a wonderful insight into the character of sheep's milk, with its burnt-caramel sweetness and rich, nutty finish.

Joan and Ken adhere strictly to the principles of organic farming, aiming to produce "healthy food from well cared for and humanely raised animals". In addition to producing fresh sheep's milk cheese logs, ricotta, feta and Camembert, they make their own yogurt, using a mixture of sheep's and cow's milk when sheep's milk is in short supply.

HUBBARDSTON BLUE COW

REGION: *Massachusetts*
TYPE: *Modern, farmhouse, fresh cheese*
SOURCE: *Cow's milk*
DESCRIPTION: *Small round with natural rind covered in blue-grey mould*
CULINARY USE: *Table cheese*

Not a conventional blue, this is so called because of the soft, fuzzy rind of blue-grey mould that helps to speed up the ripening process, softening the cheese close to the rind to the point where it almost runs. The flavour is gentle and aromatic, with a hint of almonds.

Hubbardston Blue Cow is made by Westfield Farm, who also make some goat's milk cheeses.

IDAHO GOATSTER

REGION: *Idaho*
TYPE: *Modern, farmhouse, hard cheese*
SOURCE: *Goat's milk (Saanen)*
DESCRIPTION: *2kg/4½lb wheel with natural, waxed rind*
CULINARY USES: *Table cheese, grating, grilling*

Exchanging their potters' wheels and artists brushes for milking machines and curd cutters seems to have been a natural progression for Charles (Chuck) and Karen Evans, who have turned cheese-making into almost an art form. Their Idaho Goatster looks very attractive, with its annatto-rubbed and waxed rind. The hard, almost dry texture of the cheese is similar to that of an Italian Pecorino, while the flavour of the goat's milk gives it a nutty, almond-like quality.

Chuck and Karen also make Bleu Age, a surface-ripened cheese with the blue mould on the outside. Here it differs from traditional blue cheeses, which blue from the inside out. Bleu Age is creamy and quite sharp, with a spicy quality not unlike Stilton's. At the American Cheese Society's 1990 conference it was judged Best of Show and also took a gold award.

Cranberry Torta consists of alternate layers of plain chèvre and chèvre mixed with cranberries and lemon zest, liberally sprinkled with walnuts. The company also makes Idaho Goatster with Porcini.

ABOVE: Grafton Village Cheddar – an excellent uncoloured Cheddar made in Vermont using raw milk. It is aged for up to a year

LAURA CHENEL'S CHÈVRE
REGION: *California*
TYPE: *Various fresh and aged, traditional, farmhouse cheeses*
SOURCE: *Goat's milk*
DESCRIPTION: *Various sizes and shapes*
CULINARY USES: *Table cheese, salads*

Laura Chenel is to chèvre what Pavarotti is to opera. She has brought these simple yet complex cheeses to the attention of the people of America, and in doing so she has destroyed the myth that goat's cheese is harsh and only for sophisticated palates. Her cheeses are hand-made and matured to the point where the subtlety of the milk is at its most revealing. Inspired by the French artisan cheesemakers she worked with in 1979, Laura adheres to the ancient traditions while allowing the vagaries of the Sonoma climate, the soil and her goats to influence each cheese.

She makes a range of shapes and sizes, from the tiny Cabecou in oil to the aged Tomme. All are highly sought after, not only by the thousands of visitors to the wine-growing region of Mendocino, but also by chefs and restaurateurs. When Alice Waters of the famous Chez Panisse restaurant put the cheeses on her menu and cheeseboard, it was like receiving the royal seal of approval.

MAYTAG BLUE
REGION: *Iowa*
DESCRIPTION: *Traditional, farmhouse, unpasteurized, vegetarian, blue cheese*
SOURCE: *Cow's milk*
DESCRIPTION: *2kg/4¹/₂lb cylinder. The ivory-coloured, natural rind has some grey, blue and white moulds*
CULINARY USES: *Table cheese, blue cheese dressing, dips, salads*

Since 1941 the name Maytag has become synonymous in America with the unlikely combination of washing machines and blue cheese. The link began in the 1920s when the sons of the founder of Maytag Appliances decided to demonstrate their own entrepreneurial skills and started the family farm. They gradually built up a pedigree herd of black and white Holstein/Friesian cows. Selling milk proved to be high in effort and low in profit, so they turned to cheesemaking. Since 1941 they

RIGHT: Maytag Blue

have not looked back, thanks largely to their recognizing the potential of the mail-order business: today, close to 50 per cent of their cheese is sold that way.

You might expect that a cheese that is as well known as Maytag Blue would be produced in huge volumes, but the makers have kept production small to ensure that they retain the quality only achievable when the cheese is made by hand. Maytag Blue has a dense, crumbly texture. Like Roquefort, it melts in the mouth, revealing a very spicy flavour from the fine streaks of blue-grey mould that are scattered throughout the creamy, moist cheese. The finish is hot, with a delicious bite that tempts you to try another piece.

Part of Maytag Blue's success is due to the company's "caves" or cellars, built into the side of a hill. Here the natural moulds and yeasts reside. The temperature and humidity are controlled by nature rather than pure technology, and the cheeses are permitted to ripen slowly over six months. This ensures a creamy texture and a depth of flavour comparable to that achieved by some of the famous European blues.

In addition to Maytag Blue, Maytag Dairy Farms also make White Cheddar and Edam.

MOSSHOLDER CHEESE
REGION: *Wisconsin*
TYPE: *Modern, farmhouse, semi-soft cheese*
SOURCE: *Cow's milk*
DESCRIPTION: *Supple cheese with tiny holes*
CULINARY USES: *Table cheese, melting, grilling*

Like Crowley, Mossholder was invented on the kitchen stove. Grandfather Mossholder's ambition to make a cheese with a bit of punch became something of an obsession, but his patience paid off when he invented Mossholder, which was loosely based on the Trappist cheeses of Europe. Aromatic, pungent and meaty, the supple cheese is full of tiny holes that positively ooze flavour – it is almost as good to breathe in as eat. It is regarded by cheese-lovers as one of the great American farmhouse cheeses.

ABOVE: One of Sally Jackson's sheep's milk cheeses

MOZZARELLA

REGION: *Texas*

TYPE: *Traditional, creamery, vegetarian, stretched-curd cheese*

SOURCE: *Cow's and goat's milk*

DESCRIPTION: *Small, irregularly shaped balls in various sizes*

CULINARY USES: *Salads, baking, pizzas and pastries*

Paula Lambert started the Mozzarella Company when she returned to America after living in Italy and really missed the cheeses she left behind. Undaunted, she set out to make her own. That was in 1982. Today she produces over 20 different cheeses. In addition to Italian specialities, she makes classic French and Mexican-style, soft and semi-soft cheeses. At the annual conferences of the American Cheese Society in 1992, 1994 and 1995, her Scamorza was voted number one in its category.

Paula's mozzarella di bufala was virtually indistinguishable from the classic Italian cheese, but the supply of buffalo's milk dried up and another source has not yet been found. Fortunately, both the cow's milk mozzarella and Capriella (made from a mixture of cow's and goat's milk) are equally delicious.

MUENSTER

REGION: *Wisconsin*

TYPE: *Traditional, creamery, washed-rind cheese*

SOURCE: *Cow's milk*

DESCRIPTION: *Loaf-shaped cheese without rind, coloured with paprika*

CULINARY USES: *Table cheese, grilling*

If you are expecting something which runs across your cheese-board, trailing a strong, pungent aroma and meaty, nutty flavour – in other words, a typical French Munster – you are likely to find disappointment at the end of your knife. American Muenster is closer to the Dutch or German copies, which are decidedly less formidable than the French. It has a supple, springy texture and sweet-sour, savoury tang, but is still a weak copy, best used for cooking as it melts superbly.

PEEKSKILL PYRAMID

REGION: *New York State*

TYPE: *Modern, farmhouse, fresh cheese*

SOURCE: *Cow's milk*

DESCRIPTION: *Pyramid-shaped cheese without rind*

CULINARY USES: *Table cheese, snacks*

Peekskill Pyramid has a rich, wickedly buttery taste and a texture like creamy caramel. Whipped into a pyramid shape, it looks as impressive as it tastes, and has a delicious roundness on the finish.

The cheesemaker is Jonathan White. Like so many newcomers to the world of artisan cheeses, he came not from a rural background but was a disillusioned computer engineer with a fascination for making his own cheese. In 1994, Charles Palmer, the New York restaurateur, suggested he turn his hobby to real purpose. Together they set up Egg Farm Dairy, which neither sells eggs nor is a farm. If the name of the dairy is quirky, so is the setting, next door to a hair salon in a row of small shops. Step inside, however, and you will discover a real haven for cheese and cheese-lovers.

In addition to Peekskill Pyramid, Jonathan makes Muscoot, Amawalk, Hudson and Wild-ripened Cheddar. Muscoot has a rich, creamy feel and a sweet, buttery taste that becomes more complex as it melts in your mouth, while Amawalk is an aged cheese, with a more distinctive, nutty style.

ABOVE: One of Sally Jackson's goat's cheeses

PLYMOUTH CHEESE

REGION: *Vermont*

TYPE: *Traditional, creamery, unpasteurized, hard cheese*

SOURCE: *Cow's milk*

DESCRIPTION: *Granular cheese with smooth, golden-yellow, natural rind, sold in various sizes and flavours*

CULINARY USES: *Table cheese, melting, baking*

The supple, granular texture of this traditional New England cheese is achieved by washing the newly formed curds, then kneading them by hand. The elastic curd is then salted, pressed and matured for several months. It is at its best after six months, when maturity has allowed the distinct fruity tang to come through.

The Plymouth Cheese Company is a family business, dating back to 1890. It was founded by John Coolidge, father of President Calvin Coolidge, in the small, village of Plymouth, now lovingly restored. During the recession it was forced to close, but young John, the President's son, reopened the factory in 1960, using the original recipe to make the cheese. Today it is as successful as a tourist attraction as it is for its cheese, which is sold mainly through the shop and by mail order.

SALLY JACKSON CHEESES

REGION: *Washington State*

TYPE: *Modern, farmhouse, unpasteurized, aged cheeses*

SOURCE: *Goat's and sheep's milk*

DESCRIPTION: *Various shapes and sizes*

CULINARY USES: *Table cheeses, cooking*

Sheep's milk cheeses seem to be emerging as the new stars of the cheese world, and Sally Jackson makes some of the best. Her mild, nutty, sheep's milk cheese wrapped in brandy-soaked chestnut leaves has a wonderful texture – it glides like silk across the palate, and the chestnut leaf wrap gives a vegetal, earthy, vaguely alcoholic subtlety to the final flavour.

RIGHT: The rind of Sonoma Dry Jack has a coating of cocoa

SEA STARS GOAT CHEESES

REGION: *California*
TYPE: *Modern, farmhouse, fresh cheeses*
SOURCE: *Goat's milk (Alpine)*
DESCRIPTION: *Small rounds and logs, garnished with edible flowers*
CULINARY USE: *Table cheese*

Cheesemaker Nancy Gaffney fell in love with goats 20 years ago, when she met and cared for Fanny – a capricious, beguiling and extremely fertile Alpine goat.

Nancy's small, beautifully presented cheeses are gentle, moist and lemon-fresh. Soft and spreadable, with just a hint of goat, they are exquisitely garnished with nasturtiums, marigolds and other edible flowers. The range includes two chèvre tortas, one with layers of sun-dried tomatoes and basil and the other with layers of pistachio and dried apricots. Nancy's cheeses have won her first place at the American Cheese Society's conferences, and are now to be found in all the best places up and down America's West Coast.

BELOW: Sonoma Jack flavoured with hot peppers

SHELBURNE CHEDDAR

REGION: *Vermont*
TYPE: *Traditional, farmhouse, unpasteurized, vegetarian, hard cheese*
SOURCE: *Cow's milk (Brown Swiss)*
DESCRIPTION: *Block cheese without rind*
CULINARY USES: *Table cheese, also widely used in cooking*

Mariano Gonzales uses the traditional cheddaring process to make this prize-winning cheese for Shelburne Farms. The cheese has a firm, biteable texture, and the milk yielded by Brown Swiss cows gives the flavour a rich complexity. Shelburne Cheddar is matured for 18–24 months and has a fat content of 51 per cent. At the annual conference of the American Cheese Society in 1990, it was declared Best of Show. Four years later, it won the Best Farmhouse Cheese category.

SONOMA JACK

REGION: *California*
TYPE: *Traditional, farmhouse, semi-soft cheese*
SOURCE: *Cow's milk*
DESCRIPTION: *Block cheese in various sizes without rind*
CULINARY USES: *Table cheese, grilling*

This mild, white cheese has won the hearts of Americans since it was introduced by David Jacks in the late nineteenth century. Supple and moist, it was probably modelled on the Scottish cheese, Dunlop. The sweet and creamy taste is balanced by a citrus bite. Now made in a wide range of flavours, including hot pepper, it has become a cheese for all seasons and occasions.

In 1931, Celso Viviani and Tom Vella started the Sonoma Cheese Factory to make Jack, which was already popular in northern California. When the partnership dissolved, Tom formed the equally well-regarded Vella Cheese Company down the road. A new generation of Vivianis continues to maintain the traditional cheesemaking methods, despite the strong pressure of demand for this popular cheese. They also produce Teleme, Cheddar, Havarti, Dry Jack (the rind of which is coated with cocoa) and their own ricotta.

ABOVE: Shelburne Cheddar – a prize-winning cheese made in the traditional way

TELEME

REGION: *California*
TYPE: *Traditional, farmhouse, vegetarian, semi-soft cheese*
SOURCE: *Cow's milk*
DESCRIPTION: *5kg/11lb square, 30cm/12in across. The pale pinkish-orange rind is dusted with rice flour*
CULINARY USES: *Table cheese, baking, salads*

The Peluso family have been making Teleme for three generations. Delicious when young, it really comes into its own when ripened. The pale pinkish rind, mottled with moulds and yeasts, literally bursts at the seams, and the aroma is utterly compelling. The taste conjures up conflicting images – meadow flowers, wild game and sour cream – and the cheese has a yeasty finish.

Teleme was introduced to America by Greek immigrants over a century ago. It is based on Touloumotyri or Touloumi, a goat's milk cheese similar to feta but not as salty. The immigrants did not have access to goat's milk, so used cow's milk instead. Italian cheesemakers found the cheese to their liking, made a few adjustments, and Teleme was born.

Peluso Cheese is one of only two companies currently making Teleme. They also produce Monterey Jack, Dry Jack, Halloumi and Raw Milk Cheddar.

BELOW: Teleme develops a wonderful aroma when it is left to ripen

TILLAMOOK CHEDDAR

REGION: *Oregon*
TYPE: *Traditional, creamery, vegetarian, hard cheese*
SOURCE: *Cow's milk (90 per cent Holstein; 10 per cent Jersey)*
DESCRIPTION: *White and annatto-coloured block cheeses*
CULINARY USES: *Table cheese, grating, grilling, baking, sauces*

Tillamook Cheddar is made using milk that has been heat-treated rather than pasteurized, a process that allows some of the bacteria essential for producing top quality Cheddar to be retained. To comply with American health regulations, the Cheddar must be over 60 days old before being sold, although most is aged for longer, to allow the cheese to reach the level when it can be labelled "sharp" or "extra sharp".

The white, uncoloured Cheddar is made with animal rennet, as it was found that aged cheeses made using non-animal rennet failed to achieve the desired quality and taste. Its mouth-watering, fruity tang is hard to resist.

Tillamook County Creamery Association, a co-operative of 160 dairymen, also produce Monterey Jack, Jalapeno, Colby and Smoked Cheddar. The plant handles a third of all the milk produced in Oregon. To do this, it runs 24 hours a day, 365 days a year. To maintain its enviable reputation as producer of one of America's finest Cheddars, every batch of milk is tested, and farmers are paid according to the quality and butterfat content of their milk.

TOSCANA

REGION: *California*
TYPE: *Modern, farmhouse, vegetarian, hard cheese*
SOURCE: *Sheep's milk*
DESCRIPTION: *900g/2lb round with convex sides. The hard, yellowish-grey, waxy, natural rind has a criss-cross pattern on top and bottom*
CULINARY USES: *Table cheese, grating*

Like many of America's modern cheese-makers, Cindy Calahan and her son Liam arrived at that position by accident, rather than design. When they left the city, they planned to produce superb, farm-raised lamb for the chefs of California. They were successful, but the excess milk after lambing proved too much of a temptation for Cindy, who could not resist making it into cheese. After some coaching in Tuscany they returned to the wild pastures of Bellwether Farms and now produce a magnificent American-style Pecorino.

The texture is hard and flaky, with small eyes irregularly scattered throughout the cheese. At first, Toscana feels dry in the mouth, but it dissolves to reveal a symphony of flavours and aromas, reminiscent of a warm summer's day in the mountains. Floral, aromatic, nutty and earthy, with the underlying sweetness of caramelized onions, Toscana is a wonderful cheese with a character all its own.

VERMONT CHEDDAR

REGION: *Vermont*
TYPE: *Traditional, creamery, hard cheese*
Source: *Cow's milk (Friesian and Jersey)*
DESCRIPTION: *Cylinders and truckles in various sizes, with waxed rind*
CULINARY USES: *Table cheese, grating, cooking*

Despite the time, money and space it takes to make a good Cheddar, the Cabot Farmers Co-operative Creamery has never faltered. Founded in 1919, the creamery is now owned by over 500 farmers, and produces both hard and soft cheeses. Once tasted, the rich, robust flavour, smooth texture and mouth-watering, tart finish of the Extra Sharp or Private Stock Cheddars are unforgettable.

VERMONT SHEPHERD

REGION: *Vermont*

TYPE: *Modern, farmhouse, unpasteurized, hard cheese*

SOURCE: *Sheep's milk*

DESCRIPTION: *4.5kg/10lb wheel with convex sides. The natural rind is hard and rustic-looking*

CULINARY USES: *Table cheese, grating*

When David Major took over the family sheep farm in 1983, he realized they would have to diversify to survive. Since 1989, David and his wife Cynthia have been making Vermont Shepherd cheese.

It is a modern, artisan cheese based on traditional cheesemaking methods. Each cheese is turned and scrubbed every day during the three-month ageing process to ensure that the good moulds survive and the bad die young.

Firm and dense, rather than hard, Vermont Shepherd is deliciously nutty. The sweetness of cream caramel that is so typical of sheep's milk cheese is balanced by a green-grass tang, reminiscent of meadow flowers and lanolin.

WIENINGER'S GOAT CHEESE

REGION: *New York State*

TYPE: *Modern, farmhouse, unpasteurized, hard cheese*

SOURCE: *Goat's milk*

DESCRIPTION: *6kg/13lb Gouda-style wheel with smooth, pale lemon, polished, natural rind*

CULINARY USES: *Table cheese, grating over pasta, in salads and sauces*

Sally and Ted Weininger base their cheese on Dutch Gouda, but have adapted the recipe to create a cheese that belongs in a class of its own. Using minimal salt, they still achieve a real depth of flavour.

A well-rounded, buxom, pale yellow wheel, Wieninger's Goat Cheese is sold young (at four to eight months) or aged (eight to 13 months). When young, the texture is firm and dense, yet still creamy, and the cheese has a sweet, fruity, herbaceous flavour. With age, the texture becomes more like that of Pecorino. The cheese is best eaten in chunks so that the coarse, grainy texture can be enjoyed and the layers of complex flavours can be fully appreciated.

THE CHEESES OF CENTRAL AND SOUTHERN AMERICA

The Altiplano or High Andes, the backbone and natural border dividing Chile from Argentina and running north through Bolivia and into Peru, is the home of the indigenous llama, alpaca and vicuna. The native Indians domesticated these fascinating creatures, relying on them not only as beasts of burden but also as a source of meat, milk, wool and hides. Cheese, however, was unknown until the Spanish and Portuguese missionaries arrived in the sixteenth and seventeenth centuries.

Even then, there was no instant conversion to cheesemaking. The High Andes were a hostile territory to all but the native beasts, and the lowlands were too humid for cows or goats. Only in the cooler areas in between did cows thrive.

As cheesemaking became established, it was the mild, fresh *queso blanco* that proved most popular, partly because it suited the diet of the people and partly because the cooler temperatures made it less important to mature the cheese. In Peru, where a few hardy goats survive the rigorous climate, the locals suspended sacks or skins containing the curd over slow-burning wood fires to speed up the draining process. More recently, in Chile, there has been a move to imitate the sheep's milk cheese of the Pyrenees.

Argentina is famous the world over for the quality of its beef, but was never a great cheese producer. The greatest influence on the cheese industry, such as it is, was the immigration of large numbers of Italians in the middle of the nineteenth century. Unable to survive without their cheese – and too far away to rely totally on imports – they started making a Parmesan equivalent, Treboligiano, together with a mozzarella-type cheese called Moliterno.

In Brazil, too, cattle are regarded principally as a source of meat. The humid conditions make cheesemaking extremely difficult, so cheese has never really caught the imagination – or the palates – of the people. Most of the cheese that is consumed is imported, but some local cheese is made in the Minas Gerais region, north of Rio de Janeiro. Minas Frescal (fresh cheese) and Minas Prensado (a stretched curd cheese) are no doubt based on recipes introduced by the early missionaries.

YERBA SANTA SHEPHERD'S CHEESE

REGION: *California*

TYPE: *Modern, farmhouse, unpasteurized, hard cheese*

SOURCE: *Goat's milk (Alpine)*

DESCRIPTION: *1.6kg/3½lb oval. The thick, beige to yellow, natural rind is hard and slightly oily*

CULINARY USES: *Table cheese, cooking*

Easily as good as any of the hard, artisan, goat's milk cheeses of Spain, Yerba Santa Shepherd's Cheese is very hard, dry and flaky, with small holes. The intensity and diversity of flavour is magnificent: at first the cheese has an almost minty freshness that tingles on the palate, then its more powerful, aromatic character, suggesting toffee, herbs and almonds, kicks in.

A consistent winner in the hard aged section at the annual conference of the American Cheese Society, Yerba Santa Shepherds Cheese is made by Chris and Jan Twohy at their farm near Clear Lake. They take pride in the quality of their milk and use no pesticides, artificial feed supplements or stabilizers.

BELOW: Yerba Santa Shepherd's Cheese

MEXICAN CHEESES

Although Mexican civilization dates back to at least 2000BC, it wasn't until the Spanish conquest of 1521 that cheeses were first introduced to Mexico. The Spanish brought with them chickens, pigs, cattle, goats and a few sheep. They established huge estates for themselves. Trade with the Old World created considerable wealth, not only from precious metals, but also from the export of the hitherto unknown tomatoes, peppers, chillies, potatoes and cocoa beans. The intrepid monks who travelled with the conquerors introduced cheesemaking. Pecorino, Manchego, fresh cheeses and hard cow's milk cheeses were welcome reminders of home.

Maize (corn), the main crop of Mexico, played an integral part in the national cuisine, especially in the form of tortillas. In addition, the ubiquitous beans ensured the diet was rich in fibre. These staples, plus tomatoes, chillies and peppers, along with cheese, have created some of Mexico's most famous dishes.

Queso blanco – a crumbly, soft, white cheese – is famously used in enchiladas, when it is mixed with raw onion and wrapped in a hot tortilla, which is then covered with a tomato and chilli sauce. Queso anejo, a clothbound goat's or cow's milk cheese, is crumbled into numerous dishes, while the stretched-curd cheese Asadero is popular as a melting cheese.

In the last 20 years, travel and the influence of a growing multinational community have created new markets for cheese in Mexico. Local producers now make versions of Gruyère, Camembert and Port Salut. Cream cheese is also produced, often with a flavouring of jalapeños or other chillies.

ASADERO
REGION: *Various*
TYPE: *Traditional, creamery, stretched-curd cheese*
SOURCE: *Cow's milk*
DESCRIPTION: *Various shapes, ranging in weight from 225g–5kg/8oz–11lb. The rind is smooth and polished*
CULINARY USES: *Grilling or baking*

The name of this cheese means "fit for roasting". It melts superbly and is used in numerous dishes. Originally from Oaxaca – and sometimes referred to as queso Oaxaca – it is similar to Provolone. The curd is stretched, then shaped into balls, loaves or plaits (braids). White and supple, it ranges from bland to buttery and sweet.

QUESO ANEJO
REGION: *Various*
TYPE: *Traditional, farmhouse and creamery, hard cheese*
SOURCE: *Cow's and goat's milk*
DESCRIPTION: *5–10kg/11–22lb rounds or blocks, without rind*
CULINARY USES: *Grilling or baking*

Queso anejo (aged cheese) was originally made with goat's milk, but today cow's milk is often used. Crumbly and salty, it resembles feta when fresh. When dried, it acquires a texture not unlike that of Parmesan.

ABOVE: Queso anejo

QUESO BLANCO
REGION: *Various*
TYPE: *Traditional, creamery, fresh cheese*
SOURCE: *Cow's milk*
DESCRIPTION: *Various shapes and sizes, often in block form*
CULINARY USES: *Grilling, pan-frying, baking, salads*

The name simply means "white cheese". Queso blanco is made in most Latin American countries, and resembles a cross between mozzarella and salty cottage cheese. Traditionally, it is produced from skimmed milk or whey, coagulated with lemon juice, although recently some creameries have begun making it with full-cream milk coagulated with rennet. The curd is scalded and pressed to create an elastic texture which holds its shape when heated. Like Halloumi, it can be sliced and fried. The flavour is mild, creamy and lemon-fresh.

QUESO FRESCO
REGION: *Various*
TYPE: *Traditional, farmhouse and creamery, fresh cheese*
SOURCE: *Cow's or goat's milk*
DESCRIPTION: *Various sizes and shapes, often round*
CULINARY USES: *Grilling and baking, also used fresh in salads*

Based on the Spanish cheese Burgos, queso fresco (fresh cheese) is normally eaten within a few days of making. Soft and breakable, rather than crumbly, it has a grainy feel and very mild, fresh acidity. It holds its shape when heated.

LEFT: Asadero, which is also known as queso Oaxaca

AUSTRALIAN CHEESES

Australia's often inhospitable climate, extraordinary marsupials and abundant wildlife did not exactly inspire the nomadic Aborigines to set up homesteads, domesticate their animals and start cheesemaking, unlike their counterparts in the Northern Hemisphere. Instead, cheesemaking had to wait until the first European settlers arrived in the late 1700s, bringing with them cows, goats and sheep.

At first, cheese was made in kitchens on the isolated farms with tree stumps and boulders as presses, but gradually, as herds grew, the dairy farmers formed co-operatives.

Until the late 1960s, however, butter and Cheddar or variations on those themes were virtually the only dairy products being made, for it was largely the British and Irish who colonized Australia, and much of their production was exported back to the "home country".

The cheese revolution was fired by immigrants from Italy, Greece, Yugoslavia, Holland and Germany, who arrived in droves after the Second World War. Cheese was an integral part of their culture, and before long European cheesemakers were setting up factories. Most notable of these was Czech-born Milan Vyhnalek, who established Lactos in 1955 to make Brie, Camembert, Gouda

BELOW: Surprise Bay Cheddar

ABOVE: Gabriella Kervella, one of Australia's new breed of artisan cheesemakers with her herd of goats

and Edam. Kraft followed suit, developing a Pecorino-style cow's milk cheese and a Parmesan.

In the 1980s, when soft, smelly, flavoursome cheeses were first airfreighted in by Bill Studd, rather than being shipped, the large dairy companies and wholesalers watched in disbelief as chefs responded with almost indecent haste, snapping up the new arrivals as fast as they became available, despite the high prices and the availability of indigenous (if bland) copies.

It took about another 10 years before the number of modern, Australian, farmhouse cheeses could be

counted on more than one hand, but things were changing. A new breed of Australian cheesemaker was emerging.

Despite the revolution, farmhouse production remains small and industrial Cheddar dominates the market. However, as with wines, the best cheeses are made by individuals striving to perfect their craft. Unlike Europe, where land is scarce and cattle must often live in barns, having their fodder delivered on the back of a tractor, the majority of Australian cows graze on natural pastures – clean, pure and healthy. Regrettably, regulations in Australia ban the production of unpasteurized cheese, a ban shared by New Zealand and South Africa, so much of the character and flavour of the milk is lost.

Unlike their European counterparts, Australian cheeses tend to be made by one cheesemaker in an area, rather than several. This section therefore lists the makers to look out for, and highlights one or two examples of their cheeses. Also included is the occasional exception from a large creamery that has proved to be particularly good.

Other names to look out for are Elgaar Farm Cheddar from Tasmania, which also makes the herb- and spice-flavoured Meadow cheeses, and Faudel Farm in South Gippsland, whose goats yield fine fromage frais and curd cheese.

GIPPSLAND BLUE

REGION: *Victoria*
TYPE: *Modern, farmhouse, blue cheese*
SOURCE: *Cow's milk (Friesian)*
DESCRIPTION: *5kg/11lb round with natural, orange crust covered with a dusting of white and blue-grey moulds*
CULINARY USES: *Table cheese, grilling, salads*

Gippsland Blue is produced by the Tarago River Cheese Company, a joint venture begun in 1982 by Laurie Jensen, Richard Thomas and Robert Johnson, cheese lovers with a pioneering spirit that led them to make one of Australia's finest and best-known blue cheeses. Using milk from their own herd (and occasionally making their own starter cultures), they have adapted methods learnt in Europe to their own climatic and grazing conditions.

Gippsland Blue was probably the first genuine farmhouse cheese to be made in Australia. It resembles traditional Dolcelatte: sharp, yet sweet and buttery, with a spicy, lingering, blue-cheese tang.

ABOVE: Meredith Blue (left), Bass Straight Blue (right) and Gippsland Blue (front)

The chunky veins of blue mould spread unevenly through the dense, rich cheese, which ripens in eight to 10 weeks.

Learning from the marketplace and continuing to build on their own experience, the cheesemakers have created a variety of other blues as well as softer Camembert and Brie-style cheeses, using Jersey milk to obtain a deeper yellow colour and a more velvety, smooth texture. Committed to both good quality and consistency while acknowledging the seasonal nature of milk, they have successfully introduced numerous other cheeses, the more eclectic being Tarago Lavender, whose unusual additive has inspired local chefs to create some interesting dishes.

Shadows of Blue is milder than Gippsland Blue, with a Brie-like texture and taste, whereas Blue Orchid has a somewhat more vicious, intense nature

and should not be treated lightly. Thanks to the richness of the Jersey milk, Gippsland Brie is in the Double Brie category, with a buttery texture softened by the white moulds, which also help create the mild, milky flavour with its mushroomy overtones.

GRABETTO

REGION: *Victoria*
TYPE: *Modern, farmhouse, cheese (fresh and aged)*
SOURCE: *Goat's milk*
DESCRIPTION: *25g/1oz thimble-like cheese. The fine, crusty, natural rind has touches of white and grey*
CULINARY USE: *Table cheese*

When young, Grabetto has a taste not unlike crushed Brazil nut ice cream with a tingle of lemon sorbet. With age, the cheese becomes very hard and flaky in texture. It develops a sharp, mouthwatering flavour with more than just a hint of the goat's milk. Grabetto is produced by Yarra Valley Cheese. It ripens in three to six weeks.

ABOVE: *Two of the many different Kervella goat's cheeses – Affine (back) and Chèvre Frais log (front)*

HEIDI GRUYÈRE

REGION: *Tasmania*
TYPE: *Traditional, farmhouse, vegetarian, hard cheese*
SOURCE: *Cow's milk (Friesian)*
DESCRIPTION: *20–35kg/44–80lb wheel. The classic, crusty, Beaufort-type, natural rind looks almost polished*
CULINARY USES: *Table cheese, grilling, fondue*

Experienced in the traditional cheese-making techniques of his native country, Switzerland, Frank Marchand was brought out to Tasmania by Lactos in the 1970s. Like so many others, he fell in love with his adopted country. In 1985, with a small herd of 100 Friesians, he started Heidi Farm in order to make the cheeses of his childhood: Tilsit, Gruyère and Raclette.

Frank is fascinated by cheese and loves develop new varieties. Heidi Gruyère has a firm yet supple texture, similar to French Beaufort, with tiny, crunchy crystals and a profusion of flavours. The sweet, fruity taste initially suggests pineapple, then becomes nutty. The more mature the cheese, the better it tastes.

JINDI BRIE

REGION: *Victoria*
TYPE: *Modern, farmhouse, soft-white cheese*
SOURCE: *Cow's milk (Shorthorn/Jersey)*
DESCRIPTION: *2.75kg/6lb round with smooth, velvety, white penicillium rind*
CULINARY USES: *Table cheese, also used in salads*

George Ronalds has been farming in Gippsland since the early 1980s. He saw the opportunities for European-style cheeses in Australia and he and his team have concentrated on Camembert- and Brie-style cheeses.

Jindi Brie is semi-stabilized to give it a longer shelf life. The texture is rich and buttery and has slightly sweet tones. The flavour of the cheese resembles young mushrooms in melted butter. It ripens in four to five weeks.

Other cheeses made by George Ronalds include Jindi Camembert and a triple cream cheese.

LEFT: *Heidi Gruyère*

KANGAROO ISLAND BRIE

REGION: *Adelaide*
TYPE: *Traditional, farmhouse, soft-white cheese*
SOURCE: *Cow's milk*
DESCRIPTION: *20cm/8in wheel with a smooth, velvety, white penicillium rind*
CULINARY USE: *Table cheese*

Mos and Liz Howard have been making cheese at the family farm on Kangaroo Island for the past five years, using only milk from their own cows. Each cheese is made by hand, the curd being gently ladled into the moulds or hoops.

The young curd is drained and turned; after about 12 hours it will reduce to about half the original volume. Some four to six weeks later, each batch is tasted, tested and checked, then labelled and sent to the mainland.

Kangaroo Island Brie is smooth and voluptuous, with the sweet, creamy taste of fine mushroom soup. It melts like butter in the mouth, with just a hint of lush, green grass and a whisper of sea breezes. As the cheese is made all year round, and the curd is not stabilized, it is subject to subtle seasonal changes – the mark of a true hand-made cheese.

Like all cheeses, Kangaroo Island Brie is at its best when eaten at room temperature. It has a fat content of 55 per cent.

KERVELLA AFFINE

REGION: *Western Australia*
TYPE: *Modern, farmhouse, organic, soft-white cheese*
SOURCE: *Goat's milk*
DESCRIPTION: *100g/3³⁄₄oz round or log with soft, fine, white rind*
CULINARY USE: *Table cheese*

Named for the cheesemaker, Gabrielle Kervella of Fromage Fermier, this goat's milk cheese can be eaten at two weeks, when it has a mild, sweet taste. More often, though, it is allowed to mature to eight weeks, when the soft curd becomes hard and flaky and the aromatic character of the goat's milk intensifies. The distinct, lingering taste of this more mature cheese suggests crushed, salty macadamia nuts.

KERVELLA CHÈVRE FRAIS

REGION: *Western Australia*
TYPE: *Modern, farmhouse, organic, fresh cheese*
SOURCE: *Goat's milk*
DESCRIPTION: *Round or log-shaped cheese, made in various sizes*
CULINARY USES: *Table cheese, grilling, spreading, soufflés*

Gabrielle Kervella has become synonymous with Australian cheese, yet she only started making her traditional French-style goat's cheese in Gidgegannup around the mid-1980s. In the years that followed, she worked alongside French artisan cheesemakers, returning to Australia to adapt the recipes to prevailing conditions that were very different from those she encountered in Europe. Heat, dust and significant seasonal variations in the pastures were just some of the difficulties she had to contend with, but she has produced a range of delicious cheeses.

Kervella Chèvre Frais is a classic, French-style, fresh chèvre. It ripens in a few days, has no rind and has a light mousse-like texture. Smooth and lemon-fresh, it melts in the mouth with a hint of almonds and just a suggestion of goat's milk. The finish is slightly sweet. It is sometimes dusted with ash or herbs.

KING ISLAND CAPE WICKHAM BRIE

REGION: *Tasmania*
TYPE: *Modern, creamery, soft-white cheese*
SOURCE: *Cow's milk*
DESCRIPTION: *1kg/2¼lb wheel with thick, velvety, soft rind*
CULINARY USE: *Table cheese*

Small and exposed, King Island guards the western entrance to Bass Strait, which separates Tasmania from the Australian mainland. The winds that buffet the island are legendary, and flotsam and jetsam from wrecked ships have often fetched up on these shores.

Straw from shipwrecked sailors' mattresses is thought to have been responsible for the unusual and varied grasses on which the King Island cattle graze all year round, contributing to the unique character of the island cheeses.

Founded in 1902, King Island Dairy became a co-operative in 1939, but it was not until 1988 that the company started producing the cheeses that have made it a household name – rich, sweet-tasting cream cheeses, spicy, aromatic blue cheeses, the famous Cape Wickham Brie

BELOW: Cape Wickham Brie (front) and Jindi Brie (back)

and the rich, full-flavoured, hand-made Surprise Bay Cheddar.

King Island Cape Wickham Brie is a stabilized cheese, with cream added. It ripens in 20–45 days and is covered in a soft-white rind with a mushroomy aroma and taste. The creamy yellow interior melts like butter in the mouth and the flavour hints of sea breezes and sweet pastures.

KING RIVER GOLD

REGION: *Victoria*
TYPE: *Modern, farmhouse, semi-soft cheese*
SOURCE: *Cow's milk (Jersey/Friesian)*
DESCRIPTION: *600g/1¹/2lb round. The washed, natural rind is pinkish-orange, with a dusting of grey mould*
CULINARY USES: *Table cheese; also good if the rind is removed and the cheese sliced and melted over vegetables*

David and Anne Brown have come a long way since they stumbled across an old butter factory in Milawa, 200km/125 miles north of Melbourne. With the help of Richard Thomas for the first two years, they developed the Gorgonzola-style Milawa Blue. As David's expertise increased, they gradually widened their repertoire, and today they produce a wide range of excellent cheeses, including several made from sheep's and goat's milk.

A pilgrimage by one of their cheesemakers to France to work alongside the artisan makers of Reblochon, Chevrotin des Aravis, Cabicou and Beaufort has obviously influenced the quality and flavour of cheeses like Oxley Traditional Blue, Milawa White (a fresh, acid cheese) and their two washed-rind cheeses, King River Gold and Milawa Gold.

The rind of King River Gold is washed and rubbed to encourage the pinkish-orange bacteria to spread over the cheese, sealing in the flavour and creating a smooth, dense, voluptuous interior with random small holes. The flavour hints at warm cow's milk and the cheese has a slightly sharp, green-grass finish. Milawa Gold is a stronger, more piquant version of the same cheese. Inspired by the Trappist-style cheeses of Europe, it has a distinctive, red-gold rind and a supple, smooth texture.

MEREDITH BLUE

REGION: *Victoria*

TYPE: *Modern, farmhouse, blue, cheese*

SOURCE: *Cow's milk*

DESCRIPTION: *1.5–2kg/3–4¹/₂lb round. The crusty, natural rind is orange, covered with grey, white and blue moulds*

CULINARY USE: *Table cheese*

Now in her fifth year at Meredith Dairy, Julie Cameron, the cheesemaker, is producing a number of different types of cheeses using sheep's milk, including a version of the fresh French cheese, fromage blanc. She also makes a delicious, sweet, caramel-tasting yogurt that has just a hint of fresh rosemary and eucalyptus flavours. More recently, she has been experimenting with goat's milk and makes a lovely, fresh chèvre and a goat's milk fromage frais.

Although described as Roquefort-style, Meredith Blue is a mild and creamy blue cheese with its own unique character. The sweetness of the sheep's milk comes through the distinct and spicy, but not overly strong finish.

Meredith Blue ripens in two months and, because it is made using sheep's milk, is a seasonal cheese.

The dairy also produces Woodburne, which is a small moulded, white, sheep's milk cheese.

MILAWA BLUE

REGION: *Victoria*

TYPE: *Modern, farmhouse, blue cheese*

SOURCE: *Cow's milk*

DESCRIPTION: *6kg/13lb squat cylinder. The rugged, wrinkled, natural rind is grey or pink, with various shadings of mould*

CULINARY USE: *Table cheese*

Made by David and Anne Brown of the Milawa Cheese Company. The streaks of blue invade a rich, buttery interior that melts in the mouth. Milawa Blue has a lovely, vegetal taste, with undertones of bitter chocolate. Matured for eight to 12 weeks, it ranges from the sublime to the slightly disappointing.

POLKOLBIN

REGION: *New South Wales*

TYPE: *Modern, farmhouse, semi-soft cheese*

SOURCE: *Cow's milk*

DESCRIPTION: *250g/9oz square. The fine, slightly wrinkled, orange rind tends to be sticky*

CULINARY USES: *Table cheese; grilling*

At the Hunter Valley Cheese Company, set up in 1995 by David Brown of Milawa, cheesemaker Peter Curtis produces the popular Polkolbin. Similar to the French cheese Pont l'Evêque, it has the aroma of damp washing or a farmyard. Sharp and spicy, it has a lingering, piquant, almost meaty taste.

LEFT: Woodburne is a moulded, white sheep's milk cheese made by Meredith Dairy

PURRUMBETE MOZZARELLA

REGION: *Victoria*

TYPE: *Traditional, farmhouse, stretched-curd cheese*

SOURCE: *Water buffalo's milk*

DESCRIPTION: *200g/7oz ball*

CULINARY USES: *Melting, grilling, in salads*

The water buffalo grazing at the edge of beautiful Purrumbete Lake look as though they have been there for ever, yet it took a man with determination and a dream to make it happen. Roger Haldane's fascination with the animal kingdom began when he introduced alpacas into Australia, but it was the magnificent water buffalos of southern Italy that really captured his imagination and drove him through red tape to import 55 of the animals in 1996.

Roger's imposing blue-stone homestead overlooks the meadows running down to the lake. The milking parlour has been upgraded to house the buffalo (which demand more tranquil surroundings and more privacy than their bovine cousins) and, with the help of confirmed cheese addict Nick Haddow, Roger has developed Australia's first buffalo's milk mozzarella.

Purrumbete Mozzarella has the authentic perfume and nutty taste of Italian mozzarella and is a tribute to the months Nick spent in Italy learning the process from artisan producers. The porcelain-white colour is equally accurate, but most importantly, the texture – springy, stringy and wet – is entirely right.

The company also produces Dancing Brolgo, a washed-curd cheese named after a native bird famous for its weird dance.

ABOVE: Purrumbete Mozzarella – Australia's first true buffalo's milk cheese

PYENGANA CHEDDAR

REGION: *Tasmania*
TYPE: *Modern, farmhouse, hard cheese*
SOURCE: *Cow's milk*
DESCRIPTION: *8kg/18lb and 18kg/40lb truckles. The natural rind has the imprint of the cloth, with some moulding*
CULINARY USES: *Table cheese, grilling, grating*

Firm, but neither as hard nor as smooth as traditional Cheddar, this cheese has a slightly granular feel to it. After about 12 months, the natural bacteria in the milk produce a rich, nutty cheese with a real depth of flavour. The cheesemaker is John Healey, who took over the old Pyengana cheese factory in the mid 1990s. He uses pasteurized milk from his own farm and continues to follow the old Pyengana methods, which are often labour-intensive but produce wonderful results.

RACLETTE

REGION: *Tasmania*
TYPE: *Traditional, farmhouse, vegetarian, semi-soft cheese*
SOURCE: *Cow's milk (Friesian)*
DESCRIPTION: *5kg/11lb flat wheel. The brown, leathery rind is drier than that of traditional Raclette and can be somewhat sticky*
CULINARY USES: *Table cheese; also marvellous if sliced and grilled*

Frank Marchand's Raclette comes close to the original French cheese, and is elastic and supple, yet dense. Small holes, spread through the paste, give it a slightly open texture. There is a hint of sweetness, but the overriding taste is savoury, meaty and yeasty. Made by Heidi Farm, the cheese is produced only in spring and summer, and it matures in two months.

ROMNEY MATURE

REGION: *Victoria*
TYPE: *Traditional and modern, farmhouse, semi-soft cheese*
SOURCE: *Sheep's milk (Romney)*
DESCRIPTION: *1.5kg/3¼lb cylinder with natural rind imprinted with the marks of the cheesecloth, and some light grey mould*
CULINARY USES: *Table cheese; also used for cooking*

Robert Manifold's family have been in this area for so long that you expect to find mountains or rivers bearing the names of his ancestors. He bases his cheesemaking at the Mount Emu Creek Dairy in Camperdown and uses the milk from two or three local farms. Romney (named for the breed of sheep) is a washed-curd cheese and comes in two different forms. For the waxed version, the young curd is shaped and drained in a mould, then waxed while still moist. As a result, the finished cheese is fresh, moist and springy, with tiny holes and a mild, sweet flavour.

For Romney Mature, the curd is bound in cloth and allowed to mature for up to six months. The sweet, caramel taste of the sheep's milk intensifies and the cheese develops a more nutty flavour and a hard, flaky texture.

Mount Emu Creek Dairy also makes Romney Fresca, as well as its own feta.

BELOW: Pyengana Cheddar is not as hard as some traditional Cheddars

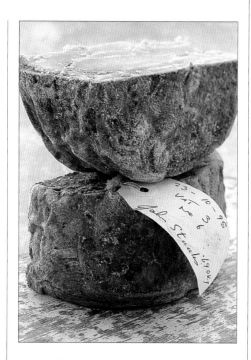

ABOVE: Romney Mature

ST CLAIRE

REGION: *Tasmania*
TYPE: *Traditional, creamery, hard cheese*
SOURCE: *Cow's milk*
DESCRIPTION: *9kg/20lb wheel with fine, leathery, waxed, yellow rind*
CULINARY USES: *Table cheese, grating, grilling*

Made in the style of a traditional Gruyère, the deep yellow St Claire is smooth and firm (and a little too rubbery for the author's taste). Sweeter and milder than traditional Gruyère, it has a fairly mellow, fruity finish.

It is made by one of Australia's oldest manufacturers of Continental-style cheeses, Lactos, which was founded by Milan Vyhnalek in 1955. Bongrain, the huge French cheese company, soon realized its potential and bought Lactos in 1981. Now highly successful, with plants in several locations, Lactos makes a range of cheeses and consistently wins prizes around the world for their quality. Although best known for its Brie- and Camembert-style cheeses, it also makes Edam, Gouda, Neufchâtel and several blues in addition to cream and processed cheeses. St Claire is its only Gruyère-style cheese.

TASMANIA HIGHLAND CHÈVRE LOG

REGION: *Tasmania*
TYPE: *Modern, farmhouse, fresh cheese*
SOURCE: *Goat's milk (Toggenberg/Saanen)*
DESCRIPTION: *150g/5oz log*
CULINARY USES: *Table cheese, grilling*

John Bignell's chèvre is fresh and lemony, with a moist, cheesecake texture. It has a distinct, but not overpowering, goat taste, redolent of thyme and white wine. Both plain and ash-covered versions are available. They mature in one to three weeks and have a fat content of 35 per cent.

John and Jill Bignell also make sheep's milk cheeses, both fresh and aged. Their semi-hard Sheep's cheese has a natural rind, a spongy, Havarti texture and a sweet, fruity finish. The author has yet to track this cheese down, but had it described to her by Bill Studd, joint owner of the Richmond Hill Cafe and Larder in Melbourne, who stocks a marvellous selection of Australian artisan cheeses.

The Bignells' newest venture, is a wickedly rich, triple cream cheese based on the French Brillat-Savarin.

TIMBOON BRIE

REGION: *Victoria*
TYPE: *Traditional and modern, soft white, organic cheese*
SOURCE: *Cow's milk*
DESCRIPTION: *1kg/2¼lb round with soft-white, velvety penicillium crust*
CULINARY USE: *Table cheese*

Herman Schultz and his family must have felt like pioneers when they started making cheese in 1984. Today there are more than 30 farmhouse dairies in Australia, but Herman is still an innovator. His cheeses are made using only bio-dynamic milk (a type of organic milk).

Timboon Brie ripens in 45–60 days. It is not stabilized, and therefore has a more tempestuous nature and a greater depth of flavour than many cheeses of the same type. Because the milk is pasteurized, the rind does not develop the wild yeasts and pigments that would give Timboon the authenticity of a traditional Brie, but it comes closer than most.

Other Timboon Farmhouse Cheeses include Buetten and Fleurie.

ABOVE: *Washed Rind (back) and Timboon Brie (front)*

TOMME DE CHÈVRE

REGION: *New South Wales*
TYPE: *Modern, farmhouse, semi-soft cheese*
SOURCE: *Goat's milk*
DESCRIPTION: *1kg/2¼lb cylinder with orange, natural rind patched with blue and white moulds*
CULINARY USES: *Table cheese, grilling, baking, salads*

Hunter Valley Cheese Company's Tomme is smooth and dense, with a slightly salty tang and the subtle background flavour of tarragon and white wine that is characteristic of goat's milk cheese. It is slightly firmer than an unpasteurized French Tomme, and does not have quite the same depth of flavour.

Cheesemaker Peter Curtis also produces Chèvre Brie, which is based on an old French recipe for Brie de Melun. The fresh curd is dusted with vine ash and salt.

WASHED RIND

REGION: *Victoria*
TYPE: *Modern, farmhouse, semi-soft cheese*
SOURCE: *Cow's milk (Red Shorthorn)*
DESCRIPTION: *3kg/6½lb flat wheel. The sticky, orange, washed rind is dusted with blue, grey and white moulds*
CULINARY USE: *Table cheese*

Fred Leppin entered the world of cheesemaking in the late 1980s. His English and French-style cheeses are not mere copies of the originals. Instead, he creates new world versions. His semi-soft, washed-rind cheese, while made in the Trappist style, has different qualities from the original. The cheese has a meaty, pungent aroma with a soft, springy texture, and the flavour seems to have absorbed the warm, minty aroma of the eucalyptus trees.

Fred Leppin's washed rind cheeses – Whitelaw, Bass River Red, Wine Washed Rind, Cronwell, Ranceby, Loch and Kardella – have been greeted with great enthusiasm in Australia.

WOODSIDE CABECOU
REGION: *Adelaide*
TYPE: *Traditional, farmhouse, fresh and aged cheeses*
SOURCE: *Goat's milk*
DESCRIPTION: *30g/1¼oz disc. The thin, natural crust is yellowish and wrinkled. It may develop rogue moulds, but these can easily be brushed off*
CULINARY USE: *Table cheese*

Paula Jenkins has a passion and an innate talent for cheesemaking. Much of her knowledge was acquired through working alongside artisan cheesemakers in France and Britain, and she is skilled at adapting their recipes and methods for the Australian climatic conditions and milk.

Along with chef Simon Burr, Paula has been running Woodside Cheese Wrights for just over two years. The cheesery is located in the old Farmers' Union factory at Heritage Park in Woodside, where Paula makes a variety of cheeses from both goat's and cow's milk.

Woodside Cabecou is ivory-white, soft and mousse-like when young, with a fresh acidity. After a few days, it develops a fine surface skin which blossoms into a delicate, white

mould. This helps to ripen the fresh curd. With age, the cheese hardens, the herbaceous, mushroomy flavour and aroma become more obvious and some furry, grey mould may appear.

The fresh chèvre curd makes an excellent alternative to cream cheese, adding an extra dimension to salads, grilled vegetable dishes and snacks.

Edith takes its name from an artisan cheesemaker with whom Paula worked in Burgundy. A soft cheese with a luxurious texture, it is encouraged to grow its velvet coat before being rolled in vine ash and aged for a few weeks. The texture is the result of the laborious task of hand-ladling the curd into the moulds. This, together with the lingering goaty flavour, is ensuring its success.

The company also produce Capricorn and Charleston, a cloth-matured Cheddar.

LEFT: Yarra Valley Feta

SOUTH AFRICAN CHEESES

Most cheeses sold in South Africa today are factory-made copies of Gouda and Cheddar, which is not surprising, given that the majority of European immigrants who first settled in this country came from Holland and Great Britain. Small amounts of feta, Edam and Brie are produced locally, and it is possible to obtain industrial imports of European cheeses, but cheeses that are uniquely South African are difficult to come by.

Cheesemakers like Christine Briscoe are doing their best to change the situation, however. Christine farms Ayrshires in Natal, some 3,000 miles from her main market, Cape Town. This does not prevent her from ensuring her cheeses are delivered in peak condition to the wine farms where they sell extremely well. She simply air freights them in from Durban. Her range, sold under the name Galtee Mare, consists mainly of English-style territorials like Sage Derby, Leicester and Cheddar, and she even makes two blues. All her cheeses are hand-made.

The Harris family also farm in Natal, but their herd consists of Jerseys, not Ayrshires. They make small volumes of several cheeses under the name Bellavigne. These include Saint-Paulin, Tilsit and a soft, creamy, sweet cheese that looks like Edam.

Fairview Estate, a wine farm near Paarl, in the Cape Province, has been producing a soft, Brie-style blue since the early 1980s. It can be found in supermarkets and speciality shops.

The booming tourist industry will undoubtedly lead to a demand for more locally produced cheeses, as has happened elsewhere in the world. When it does, South African cheesemakers – as determined and dedicated as any of their international colleagues – will come into their own.

YARRA VALLEY PYRAMID
REGION: *Victoria*
TYPE: *Modern, farmhouse, fresh cheese*
SOURCE: *Goat's milk*
DESCRIPTION: *Small pyramid, plain or ash-covered*
CULINARY USES: *Table cheese, grilling*

Firm, yet light in texture, Yarra Valley Pyramid resembles Sainte-Maure. Creamy, lemon-fresh and slightly salty, it melts in the mouth like ice cream. If left to age, the cheese becomes firmer and may develop some mould.

The cheese is produced by Richard Thomas, a man who is in danger of becoming a living legend in the Australian cheese world. His name first appeared when, in partnership with David Brown, he started the Milawa Cheese Company. Next, he helped to set up Meredith Dairy. Yarra Valley is his first venture with goat's milk cheese, but looks like becoming another Australian success story.

They also make Yarra Valley Feta. This cheese is sold packed into small cans. The little balls of refreshingly salty, moist cheese are immersed in olive oil and fresh herbs to give extra flavour to the cheese.

THE CHEESES OF NEW ZEALAND

It is thought that the Maoris, travelling in canoes from Polynesia, were the first to settle New Zealand, around the first century AD. Some historians say that the red-headed Morioris arrived first, but were wiped out by the Maoris. In any event, the early settlers found no indigenous mammals to provide milk or meat, and their diet consisted mainly of ferns, roots, birds, fish and shellfish.

The absence of indigenous mammals meant that when the first British settlers arrived in the late eighteenth century, they had to bring their cattle with them. To provide grazing for their Friesian, Jersey and Guernsey cows, they hacked and burned vast areas of primeval forest. The sheep were chosen for their meat and wool rather than for milking, and the few goats that survived the treacherous sea voyages were mainly for domestic use.

Co-operative dairies, owned by the farmers, were established throughout New Zealand to process milk from the many small and isolated farms. From the late 1840s Cheddar became a major export to

BELOW: A cheesemaker at Kapiti turning Aorangi cheeses to ensure the white mould coats the entire cheese

the home country. Blue cheese was also being made in small quantities by the middle of the nineteenthth century.

During the Second World War, Cheddar from New Zealand was welcomed in a Britain enduring rationing. Customer loyalty and consistency of quality have kept it on British tables, although the volume has been cut back considerably since Britain's entry into the Common Market.

New Zealand has been forced to look elsewhere for trading partners, and today large volumes of cheese and other dairy products are exported to North America, the Middle East, Russia and Japan.

Over the past 30 years or so, the small co-operatives have merged, and New Zealand now has some of the largest and most efficient milk-processing factories in the world. However, much of the cheese is being made to meet the requirements of large overseas customers. Consistency is important and regional characteristics are quashed so that a buyer can purchase cheese with an identical profile – good news for buyers looking for uniformity, but disappointing for those seeking subtle nuances of flavour.

In a country the size of Britain, but with a population of just over 3.5 million,

it is a challenge for the large co-operatives to produce a variety of cheeses and yet remain profitable. Blue cheese was introduced commercially in the 1950s by the New Zealand Rennet Company, now Ferndale Dairies, who are the country's largest producer of speciality cheeses, especially blue cheeses.

The redoubtable Ross McCallum saw the potential for more specialized cheeses, and started his own company – Kapiti Cheese – in 1985. His aim was to produce New Zealand cheeses rather than European imitations, and he set about developing a range of cheeses with Maori names. Equally important, he created an image that would encourage New Zealanders to buy the local cheese by choice and not just because there was nothing else. His strategy has worked, and Kapiti Cheese now produces over 50 different cheeses.

Several resourceful Dutch cheesemakers emigrated to New Zealand in the 1980s. Combining traditional methods with modern practices, they recreated the traditional cheeses of their homeland – Gouda, Leiden, Edam and Maasdam, many of which are delicious when aged.

Change was afoot. Large factories started to mass-produce Camembert and Brie, and a few took courage and introduced New Zealanders to chèvre, but it was not until Kapiti's small, feta-like, sheep's milk cheese, *hipi iti* (which means "little sheep" in Maori) hit the market in 1990 that New Zealand could boast a commercially produced sheep's milk cheese. Considering that at the time there were over 40 million sheep in New Zealand, this seems quite extraordinary.

Today there are around 14 factories and 19 independent or artisan cheesemakers, producing over 200 different cheeses. Many are uniquely New Zealand discoveries, bearing local names and exhibiting distinct characteristics and considerable charm. Because it would be impossible to list them all, they have been selected on the basis of their success at the New Zealand Cheese Awards.

AIREDALE

REGION: *Oamaru*

TYPE: *Modern, farmhouse, vegetarian, semi-hard cheese*

SOURCE: *Cow's milk*

DESCRIPTION: *2kg/4¹/₂lb straight-sided round. The thin, natural crust has a coating of red cheese "paint"*

CULINARY USES: *Table cheese, grating, grilling*

Made by Bob Berry for Whitestone Cheese, Airedale is compact, rather than elastic. Its texture is on the borderline between semi-soft and hard. Special red cheese "paint" conceals its deep sun-yellow centre and encourages the cheese to develop a real depth of flavour. Fruity when young, it becomes full-bodied, with an onion aroma and memorable savoury aftertaste.

BARRY'S BAY CHEDDAR

REGION: *Banks Peninsula*

TYPE: *Traditional, creamery, hard cheese*

SOURCE: *Cow's milk*

DESCRIPTION: *35kg/80lb cylinder, waxed and clothbound*

CULINARY USES: *Table cheese, grating, grilling*

Cheesemaking was first introduced to the Banks Peninsula around 1844 by English and Scottish settlers. By the late 1890s there were at least nine factories, producing butter, Cheddar and other cheeses; today Barry's Bay is the only one left. Here cheesemaker Don Walker and his team successfully combine modern technology and traditional cheesemaking methods to produce a range of European cheeses, which consistently win medals at the New Zealand Cheese Awards. Their rinded Cheddar is the only traditional, cloth-bound Cheddar in New Zealand. It is made in large cylinders, which are first waxed and then left to mature for six to 36 months. This results in a firmer texture than that of Cheddars that are made in blocks and matured in plastic. At around 18 months, the flavour intensifies and the cheese seems to develop a mind and style of its own. Barry's Bay Cheddar is a past gold medal winner at the New Zealand Cheese Awards.

BLEU DE MONTAGNE

REGION: *Various*

TYPE: *Modern, creamery, blue cheese*

SOURCE: *Cow's milk*

DESCRIPTION: *200g/7oz and 1.8kg/4lb tall cylinders. The fine, straw-coloured rind has a dusting of white, pale blue and sometimes red moulds*

CULINARY USE: *Table cheese*

Made by Ferndale Dairies, Bleu de Montagne is smooth and quite creamy, with a spicy, blue tang that becomes more pronounced with age. A few weeks after the cheese is made, the natural crust is rubbed with salt, then pierced with stainless-steel rods. This allows the blue mould already present in the cheese to breathe in the oxygen and weave the threads and patches of blue-grey mould through the open-textured, creamy interior. Bleu de Montagne ripens in 60 days. It won a gold medal at the 1997 New Zealand Cheese Awards.

BRICK

REGION: *Wellington*

TYPE: *Modern, small, creamery, semi-soft, vegetarian cheese*

SOURCE: *Cow's milk*

DESCRIPTION: *2kg/4¹/₂lb brick with sticky, burnt-orange, washed rind*

CULINARY USE: *Table cheese*

Brick was first made in America in the early nineteenth century, based upon the traditional, monastery-style cheeses of Europe. Kapiti Cheese began experimenting with Brick in the 1990s. Having tried it in America, they tested it in New Zealand by entering it for the 1994 Cheese Awards. It won a gold medal that year and the Cheese Lover's Cheese Award in 1995.

The rind has a marvellous, pungent aroma with overtones of yeast and roast lamb. The pale yellow interior is velvety-smooth and dense – typical of a washed-rind cheese. It has a sweet and savoury taste, with a spicy tang.

The sticky orange rind has, however, not responded well to being entombed in plastic film – a prerequisite in New Zealand supermarkets. This factor, combined with the pungent aroma, has caused retailers some concern. Sadly, Kapiti have either withdraw it or sold a younger, less exciting version. Fortunately the young chefs of New Zealand love Brick and it continues to find its way on to numerous cheeseboards. Hopefully, it is the first of many washed rind cheeses to be made in New Zealand.

BRIE

REGION: *Various*

TYPE: *Modern, creamery, soft-white cheese*

SOURCE: *Cow's milk*

DESCRIPTION: *Various sizes and shapes, with thick, white penicillium rind*

CULINARY USE: *Table cheese*

Numerous Brie- and Camembert-style cheeses are made in New Zealand. The quality is uniform and consistent. Because most of these soft-white cheeses are stabilized, there is little variation in taste. Stabilization means that once the curd has broken down and the cheese has a dense but creamy consistency, it will remain in that state rather than continuing to ripen.

It is becoming more usual for the locally produced cheeses to be given Maori names. Kapiti's Aorangi, for instance, is a Brie-style cheese whose Maori name means "white cloud".

BELOW: Brick

CHEDDAR

REGION: *Various*
TYPE: *Traditional, creamery, hard cheese*
SOURCE: *Cow's milk*
DESCRIPTION: *Sizes vary, but they are typically block-shaped and free of rind*
CULINARY USES: *Table cheese, grating, in salads and sauces, baking*

Block Cheddars are never as hard as those matured in cloth, but when aged for 18 months or more, they develop a firm, bite-able texture and a delicious cheese-and-onion tang that intensifies when the cheese is cooked. The natural carotene in the grass gives New Zealand Cheddar extra depth of colour and strict controls imposed by the dairy boards ensure that Cheddars of the same age will have a virtually identical profile, no matter where in New Zealand they are produced.

It is this predictable uniformity, regardless of season or place of origin, that has made New Zealand Cheddar the popular choice of buyers the world over. However, because the grazing and climate are so diverse, there is a move by smaller producers to produce Cheddar-style cheeses that celebrate these differences.

A recent development (presumably a marketing initiative) has seen the word Cheddar disappearing from the labelling on some pre-packed cheeses, leaving only the strength of flavour to identify the cheese. Degrees of strength are as follows: Mild, Medium, Mature, Tasty, Extra Mature and Vintage.

There are so many New Zealand Cheddars it would be impossible to name them all or say which were the best. However, in recent years Duke of Marlborough, Marlborough Tasty Cheddar and Tararua BONZ Cheddar and have each been declared to be Champion Cheddar at the New Zealand Cheese Awards. One of the "Best Cheddars up to 12 months" is Anchor Mild Cheddar, which is made by Anchor Products.

COLBY

REGION: *Various*
TYPE: *Traditional, creamery, semi-soft cheese*
SOURCE: *Cow's milk*
DESCRIPTION: *Sizes vary, but they are generally block-shaped and free of rind*
CULINARY USES: *Table cheese, grating, grilling, snacks and salads*

Colby was named after the town in Wisconsin, USA, where it was first made. It came to New Zealand in 1882 and is still one of the most popular cheeses.

It is a washed-curd cheese, which means that the curds are thoroughly rinsed in fresh water to remove all excess whey and any stray lactose. This prevents the acidity in the curd from rising, so the cheese remains soft and springy, with a sweet and mild flavour.

Colby has a higher moisture content than Cheddar and feels more elastic. It is also sweet, rather than savoury, thus lacking the depth of flavour acquired by a good Cheddar. For this reason, it is seldom cooked; if it is used in recipes, it is for reasons of texture rather than flavour.

Colby ripens in four months.

EVANSDALE FARMHOUSE BRIE

REGION: *South Island*
TYPE: *Modern, farmhouse, vegetarian, soft-white cheese*
SOURCE: *Cow's milk*
DESCRIPTION: *Thick rounds in various sizes, with soft, fine, white rind*
CULINARY USE: *Table cheese*

Colin Dennison seems to make the impossible look easy. A school teacher, he makes cheese in his "spare time", helped by members of his family. Self-taught, he has

BELOW: New Zealand Cheddar

a zealous desire for perfection and a strong dose of the New Zealand attitude that if you need something doing you do it yourself.

He had not planned to become a cheesemaker, but when Daffodil, their house cow, produced more milk than the family could consume, Colin entered the challenging cheese world. His first attempt, Monterey Jack, was not a great success, but Colin persevered. The result was Evansdale Farmhouse Brie, still his most popular cheese.

Deeper in hieght than traditional Brie, Evansdale Farmhouse has a soft-white rind and a smooth, creamy texture that melts in the mouth, gradually releasing its flavour of mushrooms, melted butter and green grass. The cheese ripens in six weeks. Seldom found outside Dunedin, it is available by mail order from Colin at Evansdale Cheese, who also make Caerphilly, Komene Kaas, Sage Derby, Wensleydale, ricotta and feta.

FOUR HERB GOUDA

REGION: *Christchurch*
TYPE: *Traditional, farmhouse, organic, vegetarian, hard cheese*
SOURCE: *Cow's milk*
DESCRIPTION: *5kg/11lb boulder-shaped cheese with waxed, natural rind*
CULINARY USES: *Table cheese*

Rients Rympa grew up in Holland, close to a cheese factory. When he and his wife Karen decided to emigrate to New Zealand, they first spent a year studying and learning about cheese in Holland. Nearly 15 years later, they have a thriving business and the Karikaas brand is familiar throughout South Island.

Their Four Herb Gouda is made from organic milk from a nearby farm's herd of Friesian/Holstein cows, the same breed that is used in Holland to make the traditional cheese. The creamy, rich and nutty taste of the cheese marries well with the flavour of the fresh, finely cut herbs that are distributed through it. Four Herb Gouda is matured for three to six months.

They also produce Leyden, Maasdam, plain Gouda and Kwark (Quark).

HIPI ITI

REGION: *Wellington*

TYPE: *Modern, creamery, vegetarian, fresh cheese*

SOURCE: *Sheep's milk*

DESCRIPTION: *90g/3¹/₂oz cylinder*

CULINARY USES: *Table cheese, grilling, baking, salads*

In a country where sheep vastly outnumber people, it is perhaps surprising that New Zealand had to wait until 1990 for its first sheep's milk cheese to appear. Using the milk from an experimental herd, Kapiti created a fresh cheese similar to feta. It is called Hipi Iti, from the Maori meaning "little sheep", and is packed with herbs in jars of oil.

Fresh and lemony, with the characteristic sweet, caramel taste of sheep's milk, Hipi Iti is crumbly like feta but is only slightly salty. It gradually absorbs the subtle taste of the herbs in the oil in which it is stored.

Hipi Iti ripens in two months and has a fat content of 52 per cent. It won silver medals at the New Zealand Cheese Awards of 1996 and 1997.

JUBILEE BLUE

REGION: *Various*

TYPE: *Modern, creamery, blue cheese*

SOURCE: *Cow's milk*

DESCRIPTION: *250g/9oz log with smooth, velvety-soft-white rind*

CULINARY USES: *Table cheese, salads*

The first New Zealand blue cheese, Blue Vein, was launched in 1951 by the NZ Rennet Company. Jubilee Blue was created to celebrate Blue Vein's 40th anniversary and the 75th anniversary of the founding of the company. Smooth, creamy and Brie-like, it has small blotches of blue mould scattered throughout the white paste. There is a delicate aroma of mushrooms, and the taste suggests melted butter with rather spicy, slightly bitter overtones, reminiscent of rocket (arugula) or radiccio. Jubilee Blue ripens in 40 days.

RIGHT: Hipi Iti (front) and Aorangi, a Brie-type cheese (back), are just two of the many excellent cheeses made by Kapiti Cheese in Wellington on the North Island

KIKORANGI

REGION: *Wellington*

TYPE: *Modern, creamery, vegetarian, blue cheese*

SOURCE: *Cow's milk*

DESCRIPTION: *2kg/4¹/₂lb cylinder. The slightly moist, natural rind is cream in colour, with grey and blue moulds*

CULINARY USE: *Table cheese*

Another fine cheese from Kapiti, Kikorangi is superbly creamy, almost buttery, with a slightly gritty texture. The distinct, blue veins give the cheese a very strong, piquant, blue taste. Vibrant rather than vicious, it makes the tastebuds hum.

MAHOE AGED GOUDA

REGION: *Kerikeri*

TYPE: *Traditional, farmhouse, vegetarian, speciality cheese*

SOURCE: *Cow's milk*

DESCRIPTION: *6kg/13lb millstone. The smooth, pale yellow, natural rind is coated in yellow wax*

CULINARY USES: *Table cheese, grilling, grating*

Mahoe Cheese began as an experiment in the kitchen. When Anne and Bob Roastrevear decided to make cheese, they originally made varieties from their native Holland – Edam and Gouda – but demand and the desire for experimentaition led to the production of other cheeses, including feta, ricotta and Mahoe Aged Gouda.

Mahoe Aged Gouda is a very firm, smooth cheese with a slightly pliable texture that is almost chewy. It has a fruity, fresh tang and is rich and buttery in the mouth. The finish suggests caramel. The cheese is matured for 15 months and is a consistent medal winner at the New Zealand Cheese Awards.

MERCER GOUDA

REGION: *Hamilton*

TYPE: *Traditional, farmhouse, hard cheese*

SOURCE: *Cow's milk*

DESCRIPTION: *10–12kg/22–26lb boulder-shape. The smooth, pale yellow, natural rind is waxed*

CULINARY USES: *Table cheese (enjoyed for breakfast), grilling, snacks*

Like many artisan cheesemakers, Albert Alfernick believes that the best cheeses are made with unpasteurized milk, which gives them a deeper, more complex flavour. Regulations in New Zealand do not permit either the production or the importation of cheeses made with raw milk, but this does not stop Albert from producing a range of wonderful cheeses.

Enter Albert and Enika's tiny shop in Mercer, just off the main Auckland to Hamilton road, and you will be faced with shelves groaning with golden orbs of cheese, just begging to be tasted: Goudas of all ages, some with cumin, cracked pepper, garlic or herbs; delicious aged Edam; and sweet, fruity Maasdam.

*LEFT: Sainte
Maure*

MEYER VINTAGE GOUDA

REGION: *Hamilton*
TYPE: *Traditional, farmhouse,
semi-hard cheese*
SOURCE: *Cow's milk*
DESCRIPTION: *10–12kg/22–26lb boulder-
shape with smooth, mellow yellow,
waxed rind*
CULINARY USE: *Table cheese*

Declared Supreme Champion at the New Zealand Cheese Awards of 1994, Meyer Vintage Gouda is firm, smooth, dense and creamy. The peach-coloured interior won the hearts and palates of the judges with its aroma of almonds and rich, nutty flavour. Phrases like "sweet and fruity"; "hard, granular and crunchy" and "wonderful depth of character" were bandied about. The pronounced tang and lingering, fruity finish were also lovingly described.

It is therefore not surprising that demand has grown steadily for Ben and Fieke Meyer's Vintage Gouda, which takes about 12 months to develop its full potential. The price reflects the time and labour involved in its production, but it is definitely value for money.

Ben and Fieke emigrated to New Zealand in 1994 and set up a small dairy near Hamilton. They brought with them a passion for cheese and a belief in the traditional methods of their native Holland. What they had not encountered before, however, was the way the composition of milk could alter with the seasons when animals had natural grazing. Their first cheese, made with rich, spring milk, was "very hard indeed", according to Fieke. With the help of Albert Alfernik, another Dutch cheesemaker, they tried again and this time met with success.

Their shelves are now filled with wonderful, round, yellow cheeses – over 3,000 at the last count – each one turned and brushed by hand as they slowly reach maturity. The Meyers produce Gouda at various stages of maturity, some plain, others flavoured with cumin, cloves or pepper.

PORT NICHOLSON

REGION: *Wellington*
TYPE: *Modern, creamery, vegetarian,
semi-soft cheese*
SOURCE: *Cow's milk*
DESCRIPTION: *1.8kg/4lb round with
smooth, bright orange, washed rind*
CULINARY USES: *Table cheese,
grilling, melting*

Port Nicholson has the characteristic, sweet-sour, slightly smoked aroma and taste of the Trappist-style cheese Port-Salut, upon which it is based, but is more supple and open textured. The producers, Kapiti, named the cheese after the magnificent harbour of New Zealand's capital city, Wellington.

*BELOW: Port
Nicholson*

SAINTE-MAURE

REGION: *Wellington*
TYPE: *Modern, creamery, vegetarian,
soft-white cheese*
SOURCE: *Goat's milk*
DESCRIPTION: *200g/7oz log with thick,
white penicillium rind*
CULINARY USES: *Table cheese,
grilling, salads*

Ross McCallum and his wife Glenys founded Kapiti Cheese in 1985 and rapidly made their mark on the gourmet world with an impressive range of quality speciality cheeses. Their meteoric rise is due to the passion Ross has for cheese, his vision and uncompromising attitude to quality and his desire to create cheeses with a unique New Zealand identity. Using names inspired by the Maori language, traditional cheesemaking methods and elegant and informative packaging, he set out to conquer the local market.

In the early 1990s, Kapiti began working alongside young chefs excited at the possibilities of their wonderful range of cheeses. Sainte-Maure, was Supreme Champion at the 1997 New Zealand Cheese Awards. It is firm yet velvety-smooth and melts in the mouth to release a medley of flavours – aromatic, distinctly nutty and deliciously sweet.

SARATOGA

REGION: *Masterton*
TYPE: *Modern, farmhouse, vegetarian, fresh cheese*
SOURCE: *Goat's milk*
DESCRIPTION: *100–150g/3¾–5oz rounds, waxed in various colours*
CULINARY USES: *Table cheese, grilling, salads and pastries*

Dee Lever is a woman of extraordinary courage. Before a serious car accident left her severely disabled, she had never made cheese. A few years ago her tiny, fresh, goat's milk cheese, Saratoga, won two of the top New Zealand Cheese Awards. Not only was it declared Best Fresh Cheese, but it also scooped the Cheese Lover's Cheese Award.

Saratoga has a moist, almost mousse-like texture. Lemon-fresh, it has just a hint of almonds, tarragon and white wine, characteristics of good goat's milk. Each cheese is carefully dipped in wax to protect it and prevent it from drying out.

Production at Saratoga Dairy Goats is small, but the cheeses improve from year to year. The latest additions – Piccolo, Encore, Sonata, Minuet and Opus – have a delicate, aromatic flavour, achieved not merely through careful handling of the curd, but also through good feeding and care of the goats and a commitment to consistent quality. Piccolo was declared Best New and Experimental Cheese at the 1997 New Zealand Cheese Awards.

WAIMATA FARMHOUSE BLUE

REGION: *Gisbourne*
TYPE: *Modern, farmhouse, vegetarian, blue cheese*
SOURCE: *Cow's milk*
DESCRIPTION: *2.5kg/5½lb cylinder with sticky, natural rind blotched with some grey and blue mould*
CULINARY USES: *Table cheese, salads and sauces*

Unanimously chosen Best Blue at the 1997 New Zealand Cheese Awards, where it was also declared to be Best Vegetarian Cheese, Waimata Farmhouse Blue is creamy without being rich, spicy without being vicious: in short, it is everything a blue should be.

Cheesemaker Carol Thorpe is a relative newcomer to the New Zealand cheese scene. She and her husband Rick first became interested in cheesemaking when they visited Wales in the late 1970s to further their knowledge and experience of self-sufficiency, but it was only in 1992, when the kiwifruit industry looked rather gloomy, that Carol examined the prospect of making cheese on a commercial basis.

By late 1994, Carol felt that her cheeses were ready for the market. Making blue and white moulded cheeses at the same location proved a challenge, but less than a year later, her success at the New Zealand Cheese Awards proved she was a master of the moulds.

Her company, Waimata Cheese, now makes various Brie-style blues, plus both a traditional Camembert and a version made with double cream. Also on the list are Port Gisborne, Vine Ash and feta.

WHITESTONE FARMHOUSE

REGION: *Oamaru*
TYPE: *Modern, farmhouse, vegetarian, soft-white cheese*
SOURCE: *Cow's milk*
DESCRIPTION: *800g/1¾lb or 1.5kg/3¼lb cylinder with a fine powdering of penicillium mould*
CULINARY USE: *Table cheese*

This is one of a handful of cheeses that are uniquely New Zealand. Produced from Friesian cows grazing the North Otago limestone country, it is made in an open vat. Covered in a fine, penicillium rind, it has the fragrance of grass and an elasticity, rather like a young Caerphilly. The curd remains moist and crumbly in the centre, becoming softer towards the rind, and there is a slight fruity tang, reminiscent of feijoa (pineapple guava), on the finish.

Unlike many New Zealand cheeses, which are stabilized to improve their shelf life, Whitestone Farmhouse is allowed to continue to ripen, developing more character as it does so. At the 1995 New Zealand Cheese Awards, it was declared Best Original New Zealand Cheese.

Whitestone Cheeses, owned by Bob Berry also produces Airedale, Mt Dasher, Monte Cristo and Windsor Blue.

THE NEW ZEALAND CHEESE AWARDS

In 1993 the New Zealand Cheese Awards were created. The aim was to raise the profile of New Zealand cheese both nationally and internationally and to provide a recognized symbol of excellence for those judged to be of a high standard. The judges, working in pairs, are assigned to a class of 15–20 cheeses. One judge will be an industry expert, the other a well-respected chef or food writer. Between them they must agree a final score based on texture, taste and general appearance.

Unlike most competitions, there are no guaranteed first, second or third prizes awarded. Only those reaching a high level of quality and flavour will receive a gold, silver or bronze medal. Some classes may have several gold, silver and bronze medal winners. Others may have none.

After the initial judging, the gold medal winners from the 10 main categories are grouped together, and one cheese is chosen as the "Best of Each" category: Best Blue cheese, Best Cheddar cheese and so on. From these the Supreme Champion for that year is selected – an accolade that is guaranteed to bring huge increases in sales and popularity.

The medals are printed on the wrappers or labels of the winning cheeses, making it easy for the consumer to identify the very best of New Zealand cheese.

ABOVE: *The New Zealand Cheese Awards "symbol of excellence", which medal winners are allowed to print on their cheese labels or wrappers*

THE RECIPES

Cheese is such a wonderful ingredient that there is little to beat it as a food on its own and
most cheeses are best eaten simply with bread or fruit. However, there are some excellent
cooking cheeses. A few, especially some fresh cheeses, are even better cooked than uncooked
as their flavor and texture act as a foil for other ingredients to shine. The recipes that follow
are mainly quick and simple, they include some wonderful, classic dishes that have stood the
test of time and other more up-tempo dishes, which are appropriate for modern life-styles.

SOUPS
AND SNACKS

———————◆———————

Place cheese between slices of fresh bread for sandwiches, crumble it on top of soup, stuff

cubes of it into hot baked potatoes—these are just a few ideas of how you can use a wonderful

food quickly and elegantly. These recipes are great for many simple meals such as

brunches and suppers, picnics and even easy entertaining.

2 tablespoons butter
1 onion, chopped
1 potato, peeled and chopped
2 heads of broccoli, chopped
4 cups water
4 ounces Maytag Blue cheese,
rind removed and cubed
freshly grated nutmeg
salt and ground black pepper
a little walnut oil, to serve

SERVES 4

VARIATION
Use Stilton or a milder blue cheese
such as Dolcelatte (Gorgonzola dolce)
or Bleu d'Causses.

1/4 cup butter
2 onions, sliced
2 teaspoons all-purpose flour
4 cups vegetable or chicken broth
1/4 cup dry white wine or
2 tablespoons dry sherry
4 slices crusty white bread
5 ounces Gruyère or Emmental
cheese, grated
salt and ground black pepper

SERVES 4

COOK'S TIPS
To give the soup a good color, make
sure the onions are lightly browned
before you add the broth.
Cheddar can be substituted for
Gruyère or Emmental, but the
soup will no longer be authentic.

BROCCOLI AND MAYTAG BLUE SOUP

—

*Broccoli is such a flavorful vegetable that it needs few additional
ingredients to make a tasty soup. However, the creamy tang of a blue
cheese makes it quite special.*

1 Heat the butter in a large saucepan
and stir in the onion and potato. Cover
and cook gently for 5 minutes, then
add the broccoli and cook for another
5 minutes. Add the water, bring to a
boil, season and simmer for 15 minutes.

2 Strain, reserving the liquid. Put the
cooked vegetables in a food processor
and moisten with a little of the cooking
liquid. Process until very silky and
smooth. With the motor running,
gradually add the remaining cooking
liquid through the feed tube.

3 Strain the soup back into the clean
saucepan. Reheat until nearly boiling,
then remove from the heat.

4 Stir in the cheese until melted. Add
nutmeg, salt and pepper to taste. Serve
in four warmed bowls with a trickle of
walnut oil in each.

FRENCH ONION SOUP

—

*Bread and cheese soups are popular in many countries. One of the great
classics is the soup made famous in Les Halles in Paris. It is sold there today,
although sadly the market itself has moved on. It is always served with a
lightly chewy topping of melted Gruyère.*

1 Melt the butter in a large saucepan.
Add the onions and cook for about
12 minutes, or until lightly browned.
Stir in the flour and continue to cook
until the flour turns a sandy color.

2 Pour in the broth and wine and bring
to a boil, stirring. Season, cover and
simmer for 15 minutes.

3 Meanwhile, preheat the broiler.
Lightly toast the bread. Cover the toast
with the cheese. Return to the broiler
and heat until the cheese is bubbling.
Place in four warmed bowls.

4 With a slotted spoon, divide the
onions among the bowls. Pour in the
soup, then serve immediately.

2 thick slices of bread
a little unsalted butter, for spreading
4 ounces Cheddar or similar
cheese, sliced
2 teaspoons spicy or mild mustard
or good pinch of paprika or
cayenne pepper
ground black pepper

SERVES 2

Cheddar is an excellent cheese
for melting.

4 1/2 ounces Cheddar or similar
cheese, grated
2 teaspoons all-purpose flour
2 teaspoons mild mustard
1/4 cup beer or milk
4 thick slices of country-
style bread
good pinch of paprika or
cayenne pepper
fresh basil leaves and tomato
wedges, to garnish

SERVES 4

VARIATIONS
For Buck Rarebit, top Traditional
Welsh Rarebit with a poached egg and
perhaps a strip or two of bacon. For a
more festive presentation, top plain
Welsh Rarebit with roasted bell
peppers or plum tomatoes, or
caramelized red onions. Serve with a
mixed herb and green leaf salad.

WELSH RAREBIT

———

Also called Welsh Rabbit, this has been a favorite snack in the British Isles for generations and is made in a wide variety of ways. Use a good melting cheese, such as Cheddar, Lancashire, Monterey Jack or Cheshire.

1 Preheat the broiler and lightly toast the bread on both sides. Spread sparingly with butter, then top with the cheese, leaving a narrow border around the edges. Heat under the broiler until the cheese melts and starts to brown.

2 Spread the cheese quickly with the mustard or sprinkle with a pinch of paprika or cayenne. Add a grinding of black pepper. Cut in half diagonally and serve immediately.

TRADITIONAL WELSH RAREBIT

———

Toasted bread can also be topped with a deliciously rich, creamy cheese sauce, which can be made with either beer or milk. Beer gives the sauce a mellow taste and a wonderful country flavor.

1 Preheat the broiler. Mix the cheese, flour and mustard in a small saucepan. Pour in the beer or milk and stir well.

2 Heat gently, stirring until thick and creamy. Do not allow it to boil. Toast the bread lightly under the broiler. Pour the melted cheese mixture onto the toast and spread to the edges. Return to the broiler and cook until the cheese is browned.

3 Sprinkle the grilled cheese with paprika or cayenne and serve at once, garnished with basil and tomatoes.

CROQUE MONSIEUR

A popular French snack that literally translated means "crunch (or munch) gentleman." This is an easy dish for children to prepare, especially when a sandwich toaster is used.

1 Preheat a sandwich toaster or the broiler. Lightly butter the bread and lay the ham and cheese on two of the slices (*left*). Top with the other slices of bread and press firmly together.

2 Cook in the sandwich toaster, following the manufacturer's instructions, or broil until browned on both sides. Serve hot, garnished with parsley.

a little butter, for spreading
4 thin slices of country-style bread
2 lean honey-roast ham slices
3 ounces Gruyère or Cheddar cheese, sliced
ground black pepper
flat-leaf parsley, to garnish

SERVES 2

BELOW: Traditional Welsh Rarebit (LEFT) and Croque Monsieur (RIGHT).

MEXICAN TACOS

Ready-made taco shells make perfect edible containers for shredded salad, meat fillings, grated cheese and sour cream. For an authentic touch, use Mexican queso blanco or queso anejado.

1 tablespoon olive oil
8 ounces lean ground beef or turkey
2 garlic cloves, crushed
1 teaspoon ground cumin
1–2 teaspoons mild chili powder
8 ready-made taco shells
1/2 small head iceberg lettuce, shredded
1 small onion, thinly sliced
2 tomatoes, chopped in chunks
1 avocado, halved, pitted and sliced
1/4 cup sour cream
1 cup crumbled queso blanco or anejado, or grated Cheddar or Monterey Jack cheese
salt and ground black pepper

SERVES 4

1 Heat the oil in a large frying pan. Add the meat, with the garlic and spices, and brown over medium heat, stirring frequently to break up any lumps. Season, cook for 5 minutes, then set aside to cool slightly.

2 Meanwhile, warm the taco shells according to the instructions on the package. Do not let them get too crisp. Spoon the lettuce, onion, tomatoes and avocado slices into the taco shells. Top with the sour cream followed by the ground beef or turkey mixture.

3 Sprinkle the crumbled or grated cheese into the tacos and serve immediately. Tacos are eaten with the fingers, so have plenty of napkins handy.

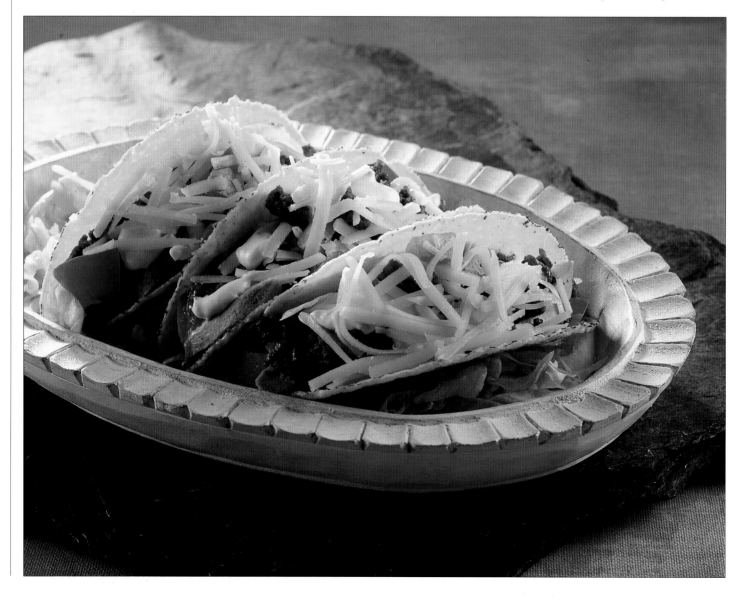

FONTINA PAN BAGNA

When the weather is hot, a crusty baguette filled with juicy tomatoes, crisp red onion, green bell pepper, thinly sliced Fontina and sliced black olives makes a refreshing snack.

1 small red onion, thinly sliced
1 fresh baguette
extra virgin olive oil, for brushing
3 ripe plum tomatoes, thinly sliced
1 small green bell pepper, cored,
halved and thinly sliced
7 ounces Fontina cheese,
thinly sliced
about 12 pitted black olives, sliced
a handful of flat-leaf parsley or
basil leaves
salt and ground black pepper

SERVES 2–4

VARIATIONS
Instead of Fontina, try Havarti or Taleggio. Use chopped canned anchovies instead of olives.

1 Soak the red onion in plenty of cold water for at least an hour, then drain well in a colander, drain on paper towels and pat dry.

2 Slice the baguette in half lengthwise and brush the cut sides well with olive oil. Lay the tomato slices down one side and season well.

3 Top with the pepper slices followed by the onion slices, then add the cheese and olives. Scatter over the parsley or basil leaves and season again.

4 Press the halves together, then wrap tightly in plastic wrap to compress. Chill for at least 1 hour. Unwrap and cut diagonally in thick slices to serve.

MOZZARELLA IN CAROZZA WITH FRESH TOMATO SALSA

7 ounces mozzarella cheese,
thinly sliced
8 thin slices of bread,
crusts removed
a little dried oregano
2 tablespoons freshly grated
Parmesan cheese
3 eggs, beaten
olive oil, for frying
salt and ground black pepper
fresh herbs, to garnish

FOR THE SALSA
4 ripe plum tomatoes, peeled, seeded
and finely chopped
1 tablespoon chopped fresh parsley
1 teaspoon balsamic vinegar
1 tablespoon extra virgin olive oil

SERVES 4

The name of this delectable Italian snack translates as cheese "in a carriage." The recipe is similar to Croque Monsieur except that it contains mozzarella and is dipped in beaten egg and fried like French toast.

1 Arrange the mozzarella on four slices of the bread. Season with salt and pepper and sprinkle with a little dried oregano and the Parmesan. Top with the remaining bread slices and press them firmly together.

2 Pour the beaten eggs into a large shallow dish and season with salt and pepper. Add the cheese sandwiches, two at a time, pressing them into the egg with a spatula until they are well coated. Remove to a plate. Repeat with the remaining sandwiches, then set them aside for 10 minutes.

3 To make the salsa, put the chopped tomatoes in a bowl and add the parsley. Stir in the vinegar and the extra virgin olive oil. Season well with salt and pepper and set aside.

4 Heat olive oil to a depth of 1/4 inch in a large frying pan until very hot. Carefully add the sandwiches in batches and cook for about 2 minutes on each side until golden and crisp. Drain well on paper towels. Cut in half and serve garnished with fresh herbs and accompanied by the salsa.

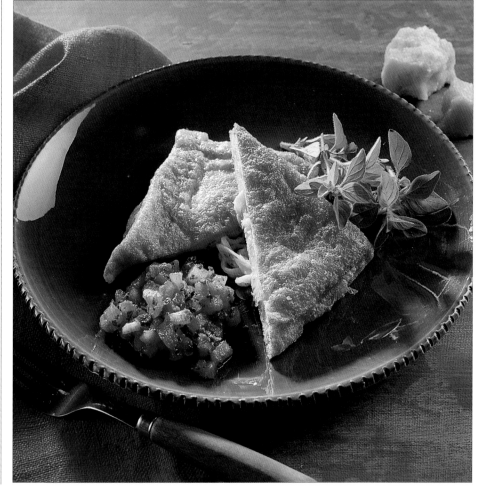

CHEESE AIGRETTES

These cheese puffs, flavored with mature Gruyère and dusted with grated Parmesan, are a bit tricky to make, but the dough can be prepared ahead and then deep fried to serve. They make a wonderful party snack.

scant 1 cup bread flour
1/2 teaspoon paprika
1/2 teaspoon salt
6 tablespoons cold butter, diced
scant 1 cup water
3 eggs, beaten
3/4 cup coarsely grated aged Gruyère cheese
corn or vegetable oil, for deep frying
ground black pepper
2 ounces Parmesan cheese, finely grated, to serve
sprigs of flat-leaf parsley, to garnish

MAKES 30

VARIATION
Make slightly larger aigrettes, slit them open and scoop out and discard any soft paste. Fill the centers with taramasalata or crumbled Roquefort mixed with a little fromage frais.

1 Sift the flour, paprika and salt onto a sheet of waxed paper. Add a generous grinding of black pepper.

2 Put the butter and water into a medium saucepan and heat gently. As soon as the butter has melted and the liquid starts to boil, pour in all the seasoned flour immediately and beat hard with a wooden spoon until the dough comes away from the sides of the pan.

3 Remove the saucepan from the heat and cool the choux paste for 5 minutes. This step is important if the puffs are to rise well. Gradually beat in enough of the beaten egg to create a stiff dropping consistency that still holds a shape on the spoon. Mix in the Gruyère.

4 Heat the oil for deep frying to 350°F. Take a teaspoonful of the choux paste and use a second spoon to slide it into the hot oil. Make more puffs in the same way. Fry a few at a time for 3–4 minutes until golden brown. Drain on paper towels and keep warm while cooking successive batches. To serve, pile the aigrettes on a warmed serving dish, sprinkle with Parmesan and garnish with sprigs of parsley.

2 red onions, sliced

1 teaspoon sugar

6 tablespoons red wine vinegar

1/2 teaspoon salt

generous pinch of dried dill

1 1/4 pounds new potatoes, halved if large, scrubbed

9 ounces raclette cheese, cut into slices

salt and ground black pepper

selection of salamis, garlic sausages or country-style ham, to serve

SERVES 4

COOK'S TIP
Raclette cheese is available at most large supermarkets and specialty cheese stores.

RACLETTE WITH NEW POTATOES

—

Made in both Switzerland and France, raclette melts to a velvety creaminess and warm golden color. Melted over hot new potatoes and served with cold meats and red onion pickles, it makes the ideal quick meal.

1 First, make the pickles. Spread out the onions in a dish, pour in boiling water to cover and let soak until cold. Meanwhile, mix the sugar, vinegar, salt and dill in a small saucepan. Heat gently, stirring until the sugar has dissolved, then cool. Drain the onions, pour the vinegar mixture over them, cover and set aside for at least 1 hour, preferably overnight.

2 Boil the potatoes in their skins, then drain and place in a roasting pan. Preheat the broiler. Season the potatoes and arrange the raclette on top. Place under the heat until the cheese melts. Serve hot with sliced cold meats. Drain the excess vinegar from the pickled red onions and serve the pickles with the potatoes.

---

1 can tuna (7 ounces), drained and flaked

1 scallion, chopped

1 small celery stalk, chopped

1 tablespoon chopped canned pimiento or 1 medium tomato, chopped

2 tablespoons mayonnaise

generous pinch of dried oregano or marjoram

2 whole-wheat English muffins, split

2 1/2 ounces aged Monterey Jack or Cheddar cheese, coarsely grated or sliced

8 pimiento- or anchovy-stuffed olives, sliced

salt and ground black pepper

SERVES 2

TUNA MELT MUFFINS

—

Try this delicious and nutritious snack consisting of whole-wheat English muffins topped with tuna and bubbling hot cheese. Use whole-wheat toast instead of the muffins, if desired.

1 Mix the tuna with the scallion, celery, pimiento or tomato, mayonnaise and oregano or marjoram. Stir in salt and pepper to taste, then set aside.

2 Preheat the broiler and toast the cut side of the muffins until golden.

3 Spoon a quarter of the tuna mixture onto each muffin half, then top with the cheese and stuffed olive slices. Broil until the cheese has melted and is bubbling. There is no need to brown the cheese. Serve hot, sprinkled with more black pepper.

SALADS AND VEGETABLE DISHES

Cheese has an affinity with vegetables. Many cheeses taste best uncooked and at room temperature, so they are ideal for using in salads and look sensational tossed into crisp green leaves and colorful salad vegetables. However, cheeses can also be turned into satisfying hot main dishes, stirred into simple sauces and used to coat lightly cooked vegetables.

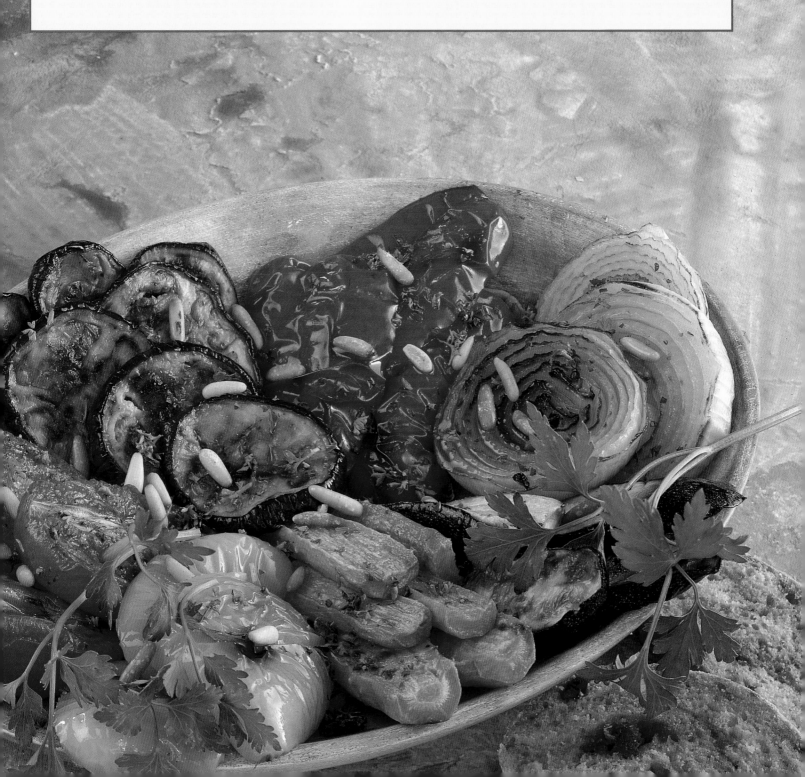

CAESAR SALAD

Not a classic dish of ancient Roman times, but a salad created in Mexico in the 1920s by a restaurateur called Caesar Cardini. Fresh Parmesan is an essential ingredient, as is cold Romaine lettuce.

2 large garlic cloves, halved
3 tablespoons extra virgin olive oil
4 slices of whole-wheat bread
2 small Romaine lettuces
2 ounces Parmesan cheese, shaved or coarsely grated

FOR THE DRESSING
1 egg
2 teaspoons Dijon mustard
1 teaspoon Worcestershire sauce
2 tablespoons fresh lemon juice
2 tablespoons extra virgin olive oil
salt and ground black pepper

SERVES 4

VARIATIONS

Anchovies can be added to the salad. Drain a 2-ounce can and cut the anchovies into long, thin strips. Pat dry using paper towels. Instead of adding a lightly cooked egg to the dressing, hard-cook 2 eggs, quarter them and use in the salad itself.

1 Preheat the oven to 375°F. Rub the inside of a salad bowl with one of the half cloves of garlic. Mix the oil with the remaining garlic in a frying pan and heat for 5 minutes, then remove and discard the garlic.

2 Remove the crusts from the bread and cut the slices into small cubes. Toss these in the garlic-flavored oil, making sure that they are well coated. Spread out the bread cubes on a baking sheet, bake for about 10 minutes until crisp, then set aside to cool.

3 Separate the lettuces leaves, wash and dry them with paper towels and arrange in a shallow salad bowl.

4 To make the dressing, boil the egg for 1 minute only. Crack it into a bowl, using a teaspoon to scoop out any softly set white. Using a whisk, beat in the mustard, Worcestershire sauce, lemon juice, olive oil and salt and pepper. Sprinkle the Parmesan onto the salad and drizzle the dressing on top. Scatter with the croutons. Take the salad to the table, toss lightly and serve immediately.

TRICOLOR SALAD

A popular salad, this dish depends for its success on the quality of its ingredients. Mozzarella di bufala is the best cheese to serve uncooked. Whole ripe plum tomatoes give up their juice to blend with extra virgin olive oil for a natural dressing.

1 Arrange the sliced cheese and tomatoes randomly on two salad plates. Sprinkle a few large pinches of sea salt on them. This will help to draw out some of the juices from the tomatoes. Set aside in a cool place to marinate for about 30 minutes.

2 Just before serving, cut the avocado in half using a large sharp knife and twist to separate. Lift out the pit and remove the peel.

3 Slice the avocado flesh horizontally into half moons, or cut it into large chunks if that is easier.

4 Place the avocado on the salad, then sprinkle with the basil or parsley. Drizzle on the olive oil, add a little more salt and some black pepper. Serve at room temperature, with chunks of crusty Italian ciabatta.

5 ounces mozzarella di bufala cheese, thinly sliced
4 large plum tomatoes, sliced
sea salt, to taste
1 large avocado
about 12 basil leaves
or a small handful of flat-leaf parsley leaves
3–4 tablespoons extra virgin olive oil
ground black pepper

SERVES 2

VARIATIONS
A light sprinkling of balsamic vinegar added just before serving gives the salad a refreshing tang, while a few thinly sliced red onion rings would add extra color and flavor.

ROQUEFORT AND CANNELLINI BEAN SALAD WITH HONEY DRESSING

—

scant 1 cup dried small cannellini beans, soaked overnight in water to cover
1 bay leaf
1 sprig of thyme
1 small onion, sliced
2 tablespoons chopped fresh parsley
2 tablespoons chopped walnuts
7 ounces Roquefort cheese, lightly crumbled
salt and ground black pepper
red and green lettuce leaves, to serve

FOR THE DRESSING
1/4 cup extra virgin olive oil
2 tablespoons rice wine vinegar or half wine vinegar and half water
1 teaspoon Dijon mustard
2 teaspoons honey

SERVES 4

Pungent and creamy, classic sheep's milk Roquefort from the Massif Central of France makes an excellent salad cheese. It goes particularly well with small cannellini beans and a light sweet-sour dressing.

1 Drain the beans and put them in a saucepan. Pour in cold water to cover. Bring to a boil. Cook over medium heat for 10 minutes, then reduce the heat. Add the bay leaf, thyme and onion and simmer for 45 minutes, or until the beans are tender.

2 Drain the beans, discarding the herbs but not the onion. Pour into a bowl, season and set aside until just warm.

3 Make the dressing. Mix the oil, vinegar or vinegar and water, mustard and honey in a small bowl. Add salt to taste and a generous grinding of pepper. Pour the dressing over the beans. Add the parsley and walnuts.

4 Gently mix the crumbled Roquefort into the salad. Serve the salad at room temperature accompanied by red and green lettuce leaves.

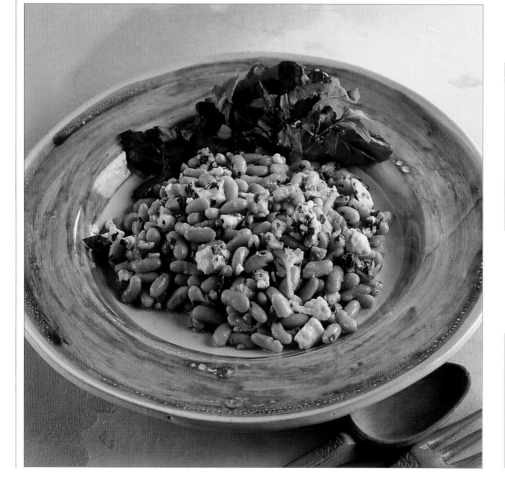

VARIATIONS
Any other sheep's milk blue cheese can be used instead of Roquefort. The salad is also delicious with either cooked green or Puy lentils instead of the beans.

TOASTED CROTTINS WITH BEET SALAD

Crottins grill to a delicious, nutty creaminess in a matter of minutes for serving on thinly sliced walnut bread toast. A salad of grated raw beets makes a colorful accompaniment.

*2 raw beets, about 7 ounces
total weight
1 celery stalk
2 scallions
¼ cup French dressing
generous pinch of ground cumin
4 small slices of walnut bread
4 crottins (small goat's milk cheeses),
about 2¼ ounces each
a little butter, for spreading
salt and ground black pepper
arugula or watercress leaves, to serve*

SERVES 4

1 Peel the beets and grate coarsely. Ideally, the beets should be served raw, but, if you prefer, blanch them in boiling water for 3 minutes, then drain, refresh under cold running water and drain again. Put the beets in a bowl.

2 Slice the celery and scallions finely and toss with the beets, dressing and cumin. Add salt and pepper to taste. Let marinate for an hour or so, if possible, then mound onto four salad plates.

3 Preheat the broiler. Toast the walnut bread lightly on each side. Keep warm. Place a sheet of foil on the rack, add the crottins and broil for 3–5 minutes, until they turn golden brown on top and just start to melt.

4 Meanwhile, butter the toast lightly. Place on the plates, then, using a spatula, transfer the crottins to the toast and serve immediately, accompanied by the arugula or watercress leaves.

Hot Halloumi with Roasted Bell Peppers

The best-known cheese from Cyprus is the salty, hard Halloumi. Delicious served simply sliced or cubed, it takes on a wonderful texture when broiled or fried. A tumble of roasted bell peppers makes a fine accompaniment.

selection of 6 bell peppers, red, green or yellow
olive oil
2 tablespoons balsamic or red wine vinegar
small handful of raisins (optional)
11 ounces Halloumi cheese, thickly sliced
salt and ground black pepper
flat-leaf parsley, to garnish
sesame seed bread, to serve (optional)

Serves 4

COOK'S TIPS
For a crisp coating on the Halloumi, toss the slices in flour before frying them. Plain Halloumi can be broiled instead of fried. Simply preheat a ridged broiler pan, add the cheese slices and cook until golden brown, turning once. They are good grilled on a barbecue, too.

1 Preheat the oven to 425°F. Cut the peppers in quarters, discard the cores and seeds, then place cut side down on a nonstick baking sheet. Roast for 15–20 minutes, until the skins start to blacken and blister. Remove and cover with several layers of paper towels. Set aside for 30 minutes, then peel off the skins. Slice the flesh into a bowl. Save any roasting juices and mix these with the peppers.

2 Pour a little olive oil over the peppers. Add the vinegar and raisins, if used, with salt and pepper to taste. Toss lightly and set aside to cool.

3 When ready to serve, divide the pepper salad among four plates. Heat olive oil to a depth of about 1/4 inch in a large heavy-bottomed frying pan. Fry the Halloumi slices over medium-high heat for 2–3 minutes, turning them halfway through cooking, until golden brown on both sides.

4 Drain the Halloumi thoroughly on paper towels and serve with the roasted peppers and a parsley garnish. Offer chunks of sesame seed bread, if desired.

LENTIL, TOMATO AND CHEESE SALAD

—

Lentils and cheese are a natural combination. The small dark Puy lentils from France are perfect for salads; red Egyptian lentils or yellow lentils are also good. Chunks of crumbly feta or a mild goat's milk cheese provide a color and flavor contrast, but cubes of hard cheese are also inviting.

1 Drain the lentils and place them in a large saucepan. Pour in plenty of fresh cold water and add the onion and bay leaf. Bring to a boil, boil hard for 10 minutes, then lower the heat and simmer for 20 minutes or according to the instructions on the package.

2 Drain the lentil mixture, discard the bay leaf and pour it into a bowl. Add salt and pepper to taste. Toss with the olive oil. Set aside to cool, then mix with the fresh parsley, oregano or marjoram and cherry tomatoes.

3 Add the cheese. Divide the endive or frisée leaves among six salad plates and spoon the salad on the side. Scatter on the pine nuts and garnish with herbs.

scant 1 cup lentils (preferably Puy lentils), soaked for about 3 hours in cold water to cover
1 red onion, chopped
1 bay leaf
1/4 cup extra virgin olive oil
3 tablespoons chopped fresh parsley
2 tablespoons chopped fresh oregano or marjoram
9 ounces cherry tomatoes, halved
9 ounces feta or chèvre (goat's milk cheese), crumbled
salt and ground black pepper
leaves of Belgian endive or frisée
2–3 tablespoons lightly toasted pine nuts, to serve
fresh herbs, to garnish

SERVES 6

3 celery stalks, thinly sliced
1 small onion, thinly sliced
1 carrot, coarsely grated
14 ounces green cabbage
1 tart apple
1/2 teaspoon caraway seeds
1/2 cup chopped walnuts
7 ounces Cheddar or other hard
cheese, cut into small cubes

FOR THE DRESSING
3 tablespoons olive oil
2 tablespoons sunflower oil
3 tablespoons cider vinegar or white
wine vinegar
generous pinch of sugar
generous pinch of dry mustard
generous pinch of dried tarragon
salt and ground black pepper

SERVES 6

WALDORF SALAD WITH CHEESE

A multipurpose salad that can serve as a side dish or a vegetarian main course. The salad is best made the night before, so that it can marinate and soften before serving.

2 Mix the dressing ingredients in a bowl and season well with salt and pepper. Stir the dressing into the vegetable mixture, cover and set aside for at least 1 hour, preferably overnight, to let the flavors blend. Mix in the cubes of cheese, then spoon into a dish and serve immediately.

1 Put the celery, onion and carrot in a bowl. Cut the cabbage in quarters, remove and discard the core, then shred each piece finely. Add the cabbage to the bowl. Grate the apple coarsely and add it to the bowl along with the caraway seeds and walnuts. Toss well.

VARIATIONS
For a color contrast, try making this salad with red cabbage or a mixture of red and green cabbage. Substitute toasted hazelnuts for the walnuts, if desired.

---

4 just-ripe pears
watercress, to garnish
2-ounce piece of Parmesan cheese
water crackers or rye bread,
to serve (optional)

FOR THE DRESSING
2 tablespoons extra virgin olive oil
1 tablespoon sunflower oil
2 tablespoons cider vinegar or white
wine vinegar
1/2 teaspoon light brown sugar
good pinch of dried thyme
1 tablespoon poppy seeds
salt and ground black pepper

SERVES 4

PEAR AND PARMESAN SALAD WITH POPPY SEED DRESSING

This is a good first course when pears are at their seasonal best. Try Bartletts or Comice when plentiful, drizzled with a poppy seed dressing and topped with shavings of Parmesan.

2 Make the dressing. Mix the oils, vinegar, sugar, thyme and seasoning in a bowl. Mix well, then pour in the poppy seeds. Drizzle the dressing over the pears. Garnish with watercress and shave Parmesan over the top. Serve with water crackers or thinly sliced rye bread, if desired.

1 Cut each pear lengthwise in quarters and remove the cores. Cut each pear quarter in half lengthwise and arrange them on four small serving plates. Peel the pears if desired, though they look more attractive unpeeled.

VARIATION
Blue cheeses and pears also have a natural affinity. Stilton, Gorgonzola dolce, Gorgonzola or Danish Blue (Danablu) are good substitutes. Allow about 7 ounces and cut into wedges or cubes.

POTATO GRATIN WITH MUENSTER CHEESE

Muenster melted in cream creates a superb topping for layered potatoes.

1¼ pounds potatoes
5 ounces Muenster cheese, rind removed, and diced
¼ cup heavy cream
⅔ cup milk
2 tablespoons snipped fresh chives or chopped fresh parsley
freshly grated nutmeg
salt and ground black pepper

SERVES 4

VARIATION
Any semi-soft or washed rinded French cheese can be used for this dish. Reblochon gives excellent results. For an extra-punchy flavor, try Langes or Epoisses.

1 Peel the potatoes and slice them thinly. Cook the slices in boiling, lightly salted water for about 10 minutes, until tender. Drain and place in a gratin dish. Preheat the broiler.

2 Mix the cheese, cream and milk in a small saucepan. Heat gently until the cheese has melted. Do not let boil. Remove from the heat, stir in the chives or parsley, add nutmeg to taste and season lightly. Pour the mixture onto the potatoes. Broil until the topping is golden brown and serve.

PARSNIP, CARROT AND GOAT'S MILK CHEESE FRICASSÉE

This excellent vegetarian main course also makes a fine accompaniment for roasted or broiled meats or fish. Serve it with roasted potatoes.

4 parsnips
4 carrots
1 red onion, sliced
2 tablespoons pine nuts or slivered almonds, lightly toasted
sprigs of tarragon, to garnish

FOR THE SAUCE
3 tablespoons butter
⅓ cup all-purpose flour
1¼ cups milk
4½ ounces chèvre (goat's milk cheese)
1 tablespoon chopped fresh or ½ teaspoon dried tarragon
salt and ground black pepper

SERVES 4–6

1 Cut the parsnips and carrots into sticks. Put them in a large saucepan and add the onion. Season, cover with cold water and bring to a boil. Lower the heat and simmer for 10 minutes, or until the vegetables are just tender. Drain, reserving scant 1 cup of the cooking water. Put the vegetables in a dish and keep hot.

2 Make the sauce. Melt the butter in a medium saucepan and stir in the flour. Cook for 1 minute, stirring, then gradually beat in the reserved vegetable water and the milk. Heat, beating, until the sauce boils and thickens. Simmer gently for 2 minutes.

3 Remove from the heat and stir in the chèvre, tarragon and salt and pepper. Pour the sauce on the vegetables and sprinkle with the pine nuts or almonds. Garnish with tarragon and serve.

Try other goat's milk cheeses such as Chevrotin.

ROASTED MEDITERRANEAN VEGETABLES WITH PECORINO

Eggplant, zucchini, bell peppers and tomatoes make a terrific medley when roasted and served drizzled with fragrant olive oil. Shavings of sheep's milk Pecorino add the perfect finishing touch.

1 eggplant, sliced
2 zucchini, sliced
2 bell peppers (red or yellow or one of each), cored and quartered
1 large onion, thickly sliced
2 large carrots, cut in sticks
4 firm plum tomatoes, halved
extra virgin olive oil
3 tablespoons chopped fresh parsley
3 tablespoons pine nuts, toasted
4-ounce piece of Pecorino cheese
salt and ground black pepper
crusty bread, to serve (optional)

SERVES 4–6

VARIATION
Any hard sheep's milk cheese can be used for the topping. Try Spanish Manchego or British Malvern.

1 Layer the eggplant slices in a colander, sprinkling each layer with a little salt. Let drain over a sink or plate for about 20 minutes, then rinse thoroughly, drain well and pat dry with paper towels. Preheat the oven to 425°F.

2 Spread out the vegetables in one or two large roasting pans. Brush the vegetables lightly with olive oil and roast them in the oven for about 20 minutes, or until they are lightly browned and the skins on the peppers have begun to blister.

3 Transfer the vegetables to a large serving platter. If desired, peel the peppers. Drizzle on any vegetable juices from the pan and season with salt and pepper. As the vegetables cool, sprinkle them with more oil. When they are at room temperature, sprinkle over the parsley and pine nuts.

4 Using a vegetable peeler, shave the Pecorino and scatter the shavings over the vegetables. Serve with crusty bread, if desired, as a first course or a side dish for a buffet or barbecue.

CAULIFLOWER AND BROCCOLI MORNAY

As we become more aware of the value of simple, honest flavors, this classic dish is enjoying a revival. The secret of a good cheese sauce is not to make it too thick and to stir in the cheese off the heat so that it melts gently.

1 medium cauliflower
2 heads of broccoli
1 onion, sliced
3 hard-cooked eggs, quartered
6 cherry tomatoes, halved (optional)
2–3 tablespoons dried plain bread crumbs

FOR THE SAUCE
3 tablespoons butter
1/3 cup all-purpose flour
2½ cups milk or a mixture of milk and vegetable cooking water
1¼ cups grated aged Cheddar cheese
freshly grated nutmeg
salt and ground black pepper

SERVES 4–6

VARIATIONS

The sauce can also be used for Macaroni and Cheese. Cook 1¾ cups dried macaroni or pasta shapes according to the package instructions. Add 1 sliced onion when boiling the macaroni, if desired. Drain and mix with the sauce, quartered hard-cooked eggs and tomato halves.

Use any aged hard cheese suitable for cooking. Red Leicester gives the sauce a deep golden color. For a more pungent flavor, try a Muenster.

To make a quick cheese sauce, melt 2¼ cups grated aged Cheddar into 2 cups scalded light cream. Season. Flavor with freshly grated nutmeg.

1 Trim the cauliflower and broccoli and cut them into even-size florets, slicing the thinner parts of the stalks if you prefer. Bring a large saucepan of lightly salted water to a boil and cook the cauliflower, broccoli and onion slices for 5–7 minutes, or until just tender. Do not overcook.

2 Drain, reserving some of the vegetable water if you intend using it for the sauce. Place the vegetables in a shallow heatproof dish and add the quartered eggs.

3 To make the sauce, melt the butter in a medium saucepan and stir in the flour. Cook for 1 minute, stirring.

4 Gradually add the milk, or milk and vegetable water, beating constantly until the mixture boils and thickens to a smooth sauce. Lower the heat and simmer for 2 minutes until glossy. Remove from the heat. Beat three-quarters of the cheese into the sauce and season with nutmeg, salt and pepper.

5 Preheat the broiler. Pour the sauce onto the vegetable mixture and dot with the tomato halves, if using. Mix the remaining cheese with the dried bread crumbs. Sprinkle the cheese and bread crumb mixture onto the vegetables, broil until the top is bubbling and golden brown, then serve immediately.

MAIN DISHES

———⟨⊃●⊂⟩———

There are meals in which cheese is a good complementary ingredient to meat or fish.

Generally, it is a good idea to use a cheese that does not overpower the rest of the ingredients,

but sometimes a strong cheese works very well; for instance, a piquant blue cheese

is delicious with veal, and a full-flavored Greek cheese with eggplant and meat sauce

makes a memorable moussaka.

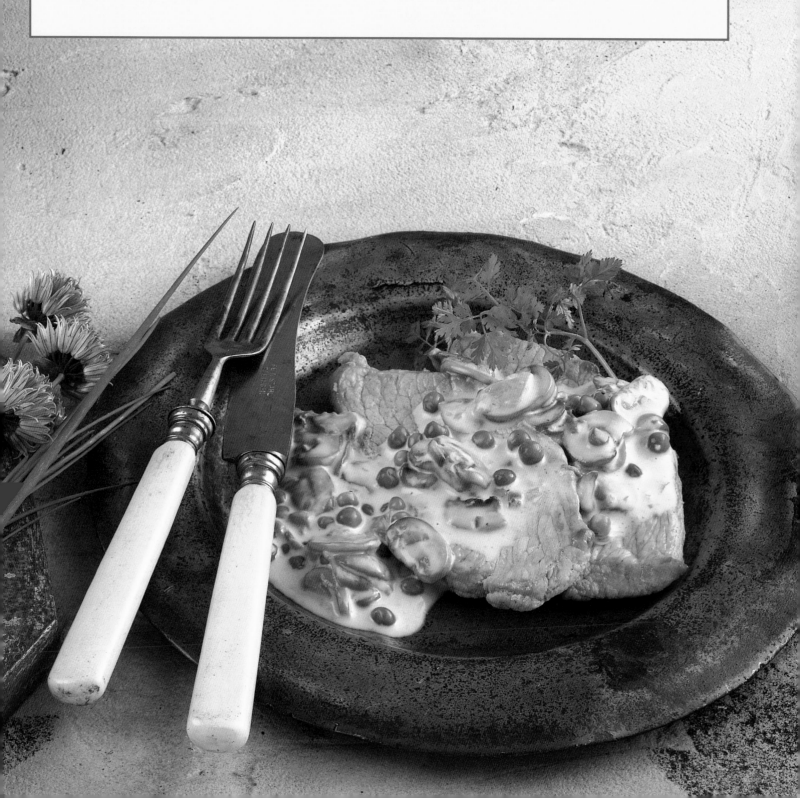

VEAL SCALOPPINE WITH SMOKED CHEESE SAUCE

2 tablespoons butter
*1 tablespoon extra virgin
olive oil*
8 small veal scaloppine
2 garlic cloves, crushed
2¼ cups button mushrooms, sliced
1 cup frozen peas, thawed
¼ cup brandy
1 cup heavy cream
*5 ounces Idiazabal (smoked sheep's
milk cheese) or
Manchego cheese, diced*
salt and ground black pepper
*sprigs of flat-leaf parsley,
to garnish*

SERVES 4

*Sheep's milk cheeses melted with cream make a simple and luxurious sauce
for serving with sautéed veal scaloppine or chops. The scaloppine are used as
purchased—there is no need to pound them thin.*

VARIATION
This dish would also work well with lean pork cutlets. However, because it is important that pork is cooked through, they will need a longer sautéing time.

1 Melt half the butter with the oil in a large heavy-bottomed frying pan. Season the scaloppine with plenty of pepper and brown them on each side in batches over high heat. Reduce the heat and cook for about 5 minutes on each side until just done. The scaloppine should feel firm to the touch, with a very light springiness.

2 With a slotted spatula, lift the scaloppine onto a serving dish and keep hot. Add the remaining butter to the pan. When it melts, stir-fry the garlic and mushrooms for about 3 minutes.

3 Add the peas, pour in the brandy and cook until all the pan juices have been absorbed. Season lightly.

4 Using a slotted spoon, remove the mushrooms and peas and place on top of the scaloppine. Pour the cream into the pan and stir in the diced cheese. Heat gently until the cheese has melted. Season with pepper only and pour the sauce over the scaloppine and vegetables. Serve immediately, garnished with sprigs of flat-leaf parsley.

MEATBALLS WITH FONTINA

Meatballs are easy to stuff with nuggets of creamy cheese that melt during cooking. In this Italian dish, the meatballs are filled with Fontina cubes and then rolled in crumbs and sautéed.

1¼ pounds lean ground beef
1¼ pounds lean ground pork
3 garlic cloves, crushed
grated rind and juice of 1 lemon
2 slices of day-old bread, crumbed
½ cup freshly grated Parmesan cheese
½ teaspoon ground cinnamon
1 teaspoon dried oregano
2 eggs, beaten
1 teaspoon salt
5 ounces Fontina cheese, cut into 16 cubes
1–1¼ cups dried plain bread crumbs
olive oil, for shallow frying
ground black pepper
fresh herbs and freshly grated Parmesan cheese, to garnish
cooked pasta, a mixed green salad and tomato sauce, to serve

SERVES 6–8

VARIATION
Use cubes of raclette, Gouda or Monterey Jack instead of Fontina.

1 Preheat the oven to 350°F. Put the ground beef and pork with the garlic, lemon rind and juice, fresh bread crumbs, Parmesan, cinnamon and oregano in a bowl. Stir in the beaten eggs and beat well. Add the salt and a generous grinding of black pepper.

2 Using clean hands occasionally dipped into cold water, knead the mixture to ensure that all the ingredients are well distributed, then shape it into 16 balls. Cup each ball in turn in your hand and press a cube of Fontina into the center. Reshape the ball, making sure the cheese is well covered.

3 Roll the meatballs in the dried crumbs. Heat the olive oil in a large frying pan. Add the meatballs in batches and cook them quickly all over until lightly browned and sealed. Transfer them to a roasting pan and bake for 20 minutes, or until cooked through. Garnish with fresh herbs and Parmesan and serve with pasta, salad and tomato sauce.

2 large eggplants, thinly sliced
3 tablespoons olive oil
1½ pounds lean ground beef
1 onion, chopped
2 garlic cloves, crushed
2 large fresh tomatoes, chopped, or
7 ounces canned chopped tomatoes
½ cup dry white wine
3 tablespoons chopped fresh parsley
3 tablespoons fresh bread crumbs
2 egg whites
salt and ground black pepper

FOR THE TOPPING
3 tablespoons butter
⅓ cup all-purpose flour
1⅔ cups milk
½ teaspoon freshly grated nutmeg
1¼ cups grated Kefalotiri cheese
2 egg yolks, plus 1 whole egg

SERVES 6

1 Layer the eggplant slices in a colander, sprinkling each layer with salt. Drain over a sink for 20 minutes, then rinse and pat dry with paper towels.

2 Preheat the oven to 375°F. Spread out the eggplant slices in a roasting pan. Brush them with a little of the olive oil, then bake for 10 minutes, until just softened. Remove and cool. Leave the oven on.

MOUSSAKA

Although feta is perhaps their best-known cheese, the Greeks have a number of others that can be used in cooking. Kefalotiri, a hard cheese made with sheep's or goat's milk, makes the perfect topping for a classic Moussaka.

3 Make the meat sauce. Heat the remaining olive oil in a large saucepan and brown the ground beef, stirring frequently. When the meat is no longer pink and looks crumbly, add the onion and garlic and cook for 5 minutes.

4 Add the chopped fresh or canned tomatoes to the pan and stir in the wine. Season with plenty of salt and pepper to taste.

5 Bring to a boil, then lower the heat, cover and simmer for 15 minutes. Remove the pan from the heat, let cool for about 10 minutes, then stir in the chopped parsley, fresh bread crumbs and egg whites.

VARIATION
Use sliced parboiled potatoes instead of the eggplant and substitute grated aged Cheddar or Gruyère for the Kefalotiri.

6 Lightly grease a large baking dish, then spread out half the sliced eggplant in an even layer on the bottom. Spoon over the meat sauce, spread it evenly, then top with the remaining eggplant.

7 To make the topping, put the butter, flour and milk in a saucepan. Bring to a boil over low heat, beating constantly until the mixture thickens to form a smooth, creamy sauce. Lower the heat and simmer for 2 minutes. Remove the pan from the heat, season, then stir in the nutmeg and half the cheese.

8 Cool for 5 minutes, then beat in the egg yolks and the whole egg. Pour the sauce over the eggplant and meat sauce and sprinkle with the remaining cheese. Bake for 30–40 minutes, or until golden brown. Let the dish stand for 10 minutes before serving.

VEAL SCALOPPINE WITH ANCHOVIES AND MOZZARELLA

—

1/4 cup unsalted butter

1 can (2 ounces) anchovies

4 fresh tomatoes, peeled and chopped

2 tablespoons chopped fresh flat-leaf parsley

6 veal scaloppine, about 3¾ ounces each

7 ounces mozzarella cheese, cut in thin slices

2 tablespoons olive oil

¾ cup Marsala or medium dry sherry

2–3 tablespoons heavy cream

salt and ground black pepper

fresh herbs, to garnish

cooked pasta, to serve

SERVES 6

VARIATIONS
Try smoked mozzarella, or Provolone or Bel Paese instead of regular mozzarella. If you prefer not to eat veal, substitute thinly sliced pork tenderloin or sliced turkey breast.

Scaloppine are thin slices of veal cut across the grain from the top round so that they hold their shape while cooking. For this Italian dish, they are rolled around a filling of anchovies, tomatoes and mozzarella before being pan sautéed and served with a rich Marsala sauce.

1 Melt half the butter in a small saucepan. Drain the anchovies and add them to the pan. Cook gently, stirring with a wooden spoon, until they break down to a pulp. Stir in the tomatoes and cook for about 5 minutes, until they have softened and reduced. Pour into a bowl, let cool, then stir in the parsley.

2 Place each veal scaloppine between two sheets of waxed paper and pound with a rolling pin or mallet until thin. Spread the scaloppine out on a board and sprinkle with ground black pepper. Divide the anchovy and tomato mixture among them, leaving the edges uncovered.

3 Top with the slices of cheese. Fold the long edges of each scaloppine toward the center, then bring up the sides to form a neat parcel. Secure with kitchen string or toothpicks.

4 Heat the remaining butter with the oil in a large frying pan. Brown the rolled scaloppine, then pour in the Marsala or sherry. Cook, uncovered, for 5 minutes, or until the Marsala or sherry has reduced and thickened. Transfer the rolls to a serving plate, stir the pan juices to incorporate any browned residue, then pour in the cream. Reheat without boiling, then strain over the rolls. Garnish with fresh herbs and serve with pasta.

CHICKEN CORDON BLEU

A classic that is perennially popular, this consists of chicken breasts stuffed with smoked ham and Gruyère, then coated in egg and bread crumbs and fried until golden.

4 skinless, boneless chicken breast halves, about 4 1/2 ounces each
4 very thin smoked ham slices, halved and rind removed
about 3 1/2 ounces Gruyère cheese, thinly sliced
all-purpose flour, for coating
2 eggs, beaten
3/4 cup dried plain bread crumbs
1 teaspoon dried thyme
3 tablespoons butter
2 tablespoons olive oil
salt and ground black pepper
mixed green salad, to serve

SERVES 4

VARIATION
Instead of Gruyère, try one of the herb-flavored hard cheeses, such as Double Gloucester with chives.

1 Slit each chicken breast half about three-quarters of the way through, then open them up and lay flat. Place a slice of ham on each cut side of the chicken, trimming to fit if necessary so that the ham does not hang over the edge.

4 To cook, heat the butter and oil in a frying pan. When the fat stops foaming, gently slide in the coated breasts, two at a time. Sauté over medium-low heat for about 5 minutes on each side, turning over carefully with a spatula. Drain on paper towels and keep hot while you cook the remaining breasts. Serve with a side salad.

2 Top with the Gruyère slices, making sure that they are smaller than the ham slices. Fold over the chicken and reshape, pressing well to seal and ensuring that no cheese is visible.

3 Spoon the flour for coating into a shallow bowl. Pour the beaten eggs into another shallow bowl and mix the bread crumbs with the thyme and seasoning in a third bowl. Toss each stuffed breast in the flour, then coat in egg and then bread crumbs, shaking off any excess. Lay the crumbed breasts flat on a plate, cover and chill for at least 1 hour in the refrigerator to set the coating.

FRENCH ROASTED CHICKEN WITH COMTÉ CHEESE

Comté is excellent for cooking because it melts easily to a creamy, glossy texture with a good flavor. To make this French dish, you will need a large flameproof casserole and a shallow ovenproof serving dish.

6 tablespoons butter
2 tablespoons sunflower oil
4–4½-pound roasting chicken
3 carrots, sliced in rings
2 leeks, sliced
2 celery stalks, sliced
4 cups chicken broth or water
1¼ cups dry white wine
4 sprigs of thyme
2¼ cups button mushrooms, halved
2 tablespoons all-purpose flour
⅔ cup crème fraîche or
heavy cream
1 egg yolk
2 tablespoons fresh lemon juice
freshly grated nutmeg
1 cup grated Comté cheese
or Gruyère
salt and ground black pepper

SERVES 6

1 Heat one-third of the butter with the oil in a large flameproof casserole. Add the chicken and brown it all over in the fat until it is golden. Remove and set aside.

2 Add the vegetables to the casserole. Sauté gently for 5 minutes, then place the bird on top. Pour in the broth or water and the wine, with 1 sprig of thyme. Season well, bring to a boil, then lower the heat and cover the casserole. Simmer very gently for about 1 hour, or until the chicken is cooked though.

3 Meanwhile, melt half the remaining butter in a small frying pan and stir-fry the mushrooms for 2–3 minutes. Do not let them soften or they will release their liquid. Lift them out with a slotted spoon and set them aside. Mix the last of the butter with the flour to make a paste. Set this aside too.

4 Preheat the oven to 425°F. Put the crème fraîche in a cup and stir in the egg yolk, lemon juice and nutmeg to taste.

5 Transfer the cooked chicken to a shallow heatproof dish and cover with tented foil. Remove the sprig of thyme from the casserole and discard it.

6 Return the casserole to the heat and boil rapidly until the liquid has reduced by half, then purée the liquid and vegetables together in a blender or food processor. Scrape the purée back into the casserole, return to a gentle simmer and gradually beat in knobs of the butter-and-flour paste until the sauce has thickened and is smooth. Remove from the heat again and slowly beat in the crème fraîche mixture.

7 Surround the chicken with the mushrooms. Press half the cheese onto the chicken breast, drizzle on the sauce and sprinkle on the rest of the cheese. Bake for about 15 minutes, or until the cheese is golden brown. Garnish with the remaining thyme sprigs and serve.

SALMON KEDGEREE, FRENCH-STYLE

This all-in-one supper dish is ideal for informal entertaining as it can be made ahead of time, then reheated for about half an hour before being served with a tossed salad.

1 Put the salmon in a wide, shallow pan. Add the bay leaf and parsley stalks, with salt and pepper. Pour in the water and poach the fish for about 12 minutes, until just tender. Lift out the fish, discard the herbs and pour the liquid into a saucepan. Let the fish cool, then remove any bones and flake the flesh.

2 Add the basmati rice to the saucepan containing the fish poaching liquid. Bring the liquid to a boil, then lower the heat, cover and simmer for 10 minutes without lifting the lid. Remove the pan from the heat and let the rice stand undisturbed for 5 minutes.

3 Meanwhile, make the sauce. Mix the milk, flour and butter in a saucepan. Bring to a boil over low heat, beating constantly until the sauce is smooth and thick. Stir in the curry paste or mustard, with salt and pepper to taste. Simmer for 2 minutes.

4 Preheat the broiler. Remove the sauce from the heat and stir in the chopped parsley and rice, with half the cheese. Using a large metal spoon, fold in the flaked fish and eggs. Spoon into a shallow gratin dish and sprinkle with the rest of the cheese. Heat under the broiler until the topping is golden brown and bubbling.

VARIATIONS
Shrimp can be substituted for the salmon and Lancashire or Mahon can be used instead of Cheddar. The dish also works well with pasta shapes instead of rice.

1 1/2 pounds fresh salmon fillet, skinned
1 bay leaf
a few parsley stalks
4 cups water
2 cups basmati rice
2–3 tablespoons chopped fresh parsley
1 1/2 cups grated Cheddar cheese
3 hard-cooked eggs, chopped
salt and ground black pepper

FOR THE SAUCE
4 cups milk
1/3 cup all-purpose flour
3 tablespoons butter
1 teaspoon mild curry paste or Dijon mustard

SERVES 6

SIRLOIN STEAK WITH ROQUEFORT AND WALNUT BUTTER

—

2 shallots, chopped

6 tablespoons butter, slightly softened

5 ounces Roquefort cheese

2 tablespoons finely chopped walnuts

1 tablespoon finely snipped fresh chives

1 tablespoon olive oil or sunflower oil

4 lean sirloin steaks, about 4 ounces each

1/2 cup dry white wine

2 tablespoons crème fraîche or heavy cream

salt and ground black pepper

fresh chives, to garnish

green beans, to serve

SERVES 4

Make a roll of savory blue cheese butter to keep in the refrigerator to melt on top of steaks. It is also good served on pork chops.

1 Sauté the shallots in one-third of the butter. Pour into a bowl and add half the remaining butter, the cheese, walnuts, snipped chives and pepper to taste. Chill lightly, roll in foil to a sausage shape and chill again until firm.

2 Heat the remaining butter with the oil in a heavy-bottomed frying pan and cook the steaks for about 3 minutes on each side, or until cooked to your liking. Season the steaks and remove them to four serving plates.

3 Pour the wine into the pan and stir to incorporate any browned pieces. Let bubble up for a minute or two, then stir in the crème fraîche or cream. Season and pour over the steaks. Cut pats of the Roquefort butter from the roll and put one on top of each steak. Garnish with chives. Lightly cooked green beans make the ideal accompaniment.

PAN-ROASTED COD WITH A VERMOUTH AND CHÈVRE SAUCE

—

Team chunky white cod with a quick pan sauce of vermouth and a light, creamy chèvre sauce. Broiled tomatoes sprinkled with herbs add color.

4 pieces of cod fillet, about 5 ounces each, skinned
2 tablespoons olive oil
4 scallions, chopped
2/3 cup dry vermouth, preferably Noilly Prat
1 1/4 cups fish stock
3 tablespoons crème fraîche or heavy cream
2 1/2 ounces chèvre (goat's milk cheese), rind removed, and chopped
2 tablespoons chopped fresh parsley
1 tablespoon chopped fresh chervil
salt and ground black pepper
flat-leaf parsley, to garnish
broiled plum tomatoes, to serve

SERVES 4

VARIATION
Instead of cod you can use salmon, haddock or pollock. The cooking time may change according to the thickness of the fish fillets.

1 Remove any stray bones from the cod fillets. Rinse the fish under cold running water and pat dry with paper towels. Place the pieces on a plate and season generously with salt and pepper.

2 Heat a nonstick frying pan, then add 1 tablespoon of the oil, swirling it around to coat the bottom. Add the pieces of cod and cook, without turning or moving them, for 4 minutes or until nicely caramelized. Carefully turn each piece over and cook the other side for a further 3 minutes or until just firm. Remove the fish to a serving plate and keep hot.

3 Heat the remaining oil and stir-fry the scallions for 1 minute. Add the vermouth and cook until reduced by half. Add the stock and cook again until reduced by half. Stir in the crème fraîche and chèvre and simmer for 3 minutes. Add salt and pepper, stir in the herbs and spoon onto the fish. Garnish with parsley and serve with broiled tomatoes.

VEGETARIAN DISHES

Since cheese is a fairly rich protein food, many classic cheese dishes are also vegetarian. Some of the best come from Italy: Eggplant Parmigiana, risotto flavored with Parmesan, crisp risotto fritters with nuggets of mozzarella inside, and polenta cooked with Gorgonzola. There are also classic recipes for a cheese soufflé, an omelette and a fabulous fondue, and twice-baked spinach and cheese roulade—a superb dinner-party dish.

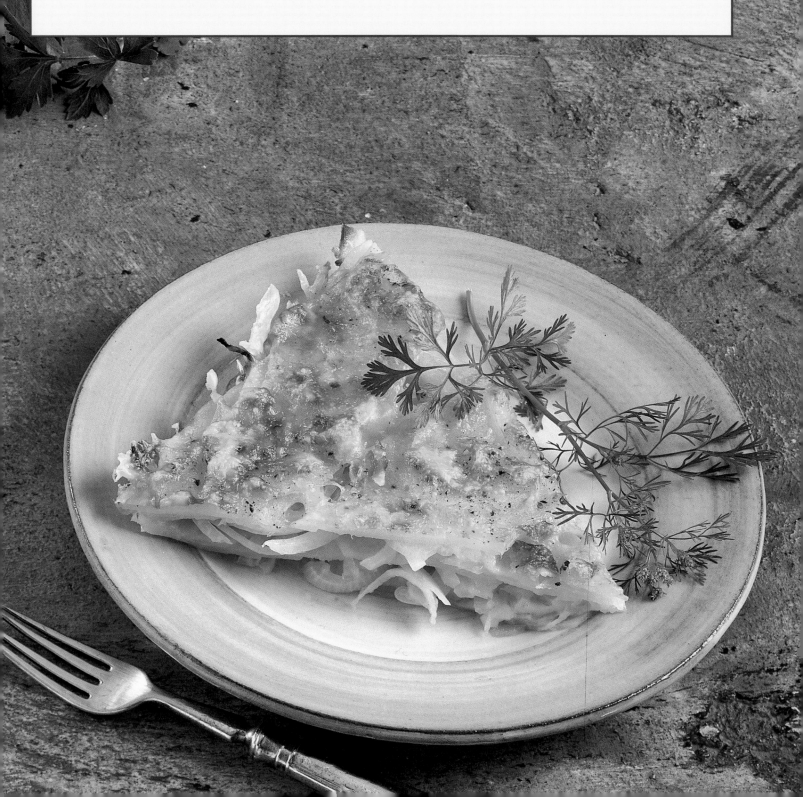

EGGPLANT PARMIGIANA

A classic Italian dish, in which tender sliced eggplant is layered with melting creamy mozzarella, fresh Parmesan and a good homemade tomato sauce.

3 medium eggplants, thinly sliced
olive oil, for brushing
11 ounces mozzarella cheese, sliced
1 1/3 cups freshly grated Parmesan cheese
2–3 tablespoons dried plain bread crumbs
basil sprigs, to garnish
salt and ground black pepper

FOR THE SAUCE
2 tablespoons olive oil
1 onion, finely chopped
2 garlic cloves, crushed
1 can (14 ounces) chopped tomatoes
1 teaspoon sugar
about 6 basil leaves

SERVES 4–6

1 Layer the eggplant slices in a colander, sprinkling each layer with a little salt. Drain over a sink for about 20 minutes, then rinse thoroughly under cold running water and pat dry with paper towels.

2 Preheat the oven to 400°F. Lay the eggplant slices on nonstick baking sheets, brush the tops with olive oil and bake for 10–15 minutes, until softened.

3 Meanwhile, make the sauce. Heat the oil in a saucepan and sauté the onion and garlic for 5 minutes. Add the canned tomatoes and sugar, with salt and pepper to taste. Bring to a boil, then lower the heat and simmer for about 10 minutes until reduced and thickened. Tear the basil leaves into small pieces and add them to the sauce.

4 Layer the eggplant slices in a greased shallow ovenproof dish with the sliced mozzarella, the tomato sauce and the grated Parmesan, ending with a layer of Parmesan mixed with the bread crumbs. Bake for 20–25 minutes, until golden brown and bubbling. Let stand for 5 minutes before cutting. Serve garnished with basil sprigs.

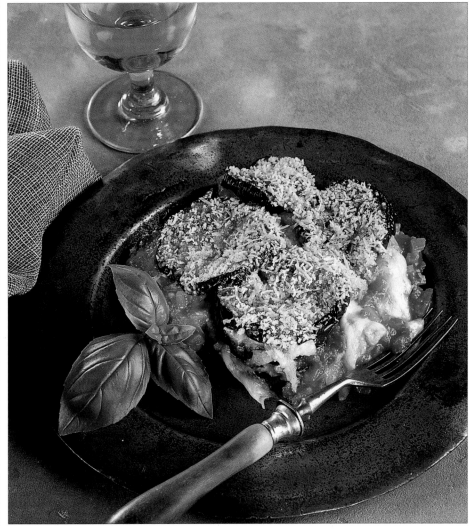

MALFATTI WITH ROASTED BELL PEPPER SAUCE

The Italians use their rich but light cream cheese—ricotta—in sweet and savory dishes. This recipe has it beaten into deliciously light spinach dumplings, called malfatti, served with a smoky pepper and tomato sauce.

1¼ pounds young leaf spinach
1 onion, finely chopped
1 garlic clove, crushed
1 tablespoon extra virgin olive oil
1½ cups ricotta cheese
3 eggs, beaten
½ cup dried plain bread crumbs
½ cup all-purpose flour
⅔ cup freshly grated Parmesan cheese
freshly grated nutmeg
2 tablespoons butter, melted
salt and ground black pepper

FOR THE SAUCE
2 red bell peppers, quartered and cored
2 tablespoons extra virgin olive oil
1 onion, chopped
14-ounce can chopped tomatoes
⅔ cup water

SERVES 4

1 Make the sauce. Preheat the broiler and broil the pepper quarters skin side up until they blister and blacken. Cool slightly, then peel and chop. Heat the oil in a saucepan and lightly sauté the onion and peppers for 5 minutes. Add the tomatoes and water, with salt and pepper to taste. Bring to a boil, lower the heat and simmer gently for 15 minutes. Purée in a food processor or blender, then return to the clean pan and set aside.

2 Trim any thick stalks from the spinach, wash the leaves well, then blanch in a pan of boiling water for about 1 minute. Drain, refresh under cold water and drain again. Squeeze dry, then chop finely.

3 Put the finely chopped onion, garlic, olive oil, ricotta, eggs and bread crumbs in a bowl. Add the spinach and mix well. Stir in the flour and 1 teaspoon salt with half the Parmesan, then season to taste with pepper and nutmeg.

4 Roll the mixture into 16 small logs and chill briefly.

5 Bring a large saucepan of water to a boil. Carefully drop in the malfatti in batches and cook for 5 minutes. Remove with a slotted spatula and toss with the melted butter. To serve, reheat the sauce and divide it among four plates. Arrange three or four malfatti on each and sprinkle on the remaining Parmesan. Serve immediately.

BELL PEPPERS WITH RICE, FETA AND PINE NUT STUFFING

A popular family supper dish, which can be prepared ahead and reheated.
Serve it with a cheese sauce for a delicious change.

4 large red, green or yellow bell peppers, or a mixture
2 cups vegetable broth
1 cup long grain rice (not converted)
2 tablespoons olive oil
1 onion, chopped
2 garlic cloves, crushed
1 cup button mushrooms, chopped
1 carrot, grated
4 tomatoes, chopped
1 tablespoon chopped fresh dill
3 1/2 ounces feta cheese, crumbled
1 cup pine nuts, lightly toasted
2 tablespoons currants
1/3 cup freshly grated Parmesan cheese
salt and ground black pepper
salad of mixed greens, to serve

SERVES 4

1 Cut each pepper in half lengthwise and remove the cores and seeds. Bring a large saucepan of water to a boil, add the peppers and blanch for 5 minutes. Remove from the pan using a slotted spoon. Set aside to drain upside down, then place, hollow up, in a lightly greased baking dish.

Any strong-flavored Cheddar (right) could be used in place of the feta. Or try fresh chèvre instead.

2 Put the broth in another saucepan. Add the rice and bring to a boil, then lower the heat. Cover the pan and simmer gently for 15 minutes. Remove the pan from the heat without lifting the lid and let stand in a warm place for 5 minutes. Preheat the oven to 375°F.

3 Meanwhile, heat the olive oil in a saucepan and sauté the onion and garlic for 5 minutes. Stir in the mushrooms, carrot and tomatoes and season to taste. Cover, cook for 5 minutes until softened, then mix in the rice, dill, feta, pine nuts and currants.

4 Divide the mixture among the pepper halves, sprinkle over the Parmesan and bake for 20 minutes or until the topping has browned. Serve with a mixed green salad.

SEMOLINA AND PESTO GNOCCHI

These gnocchi are cooked rounds of semolina dough, which are brushed with melted butter, topped with cheese and baked. When carefully cooked, they taste wonderful with a homemade tomato sauce.

3 cups milk
generous 1 cup semolina
3 tablespoons pesto sauce
1/4 cup finely chopped oil-packed sun-dried tomatoes, patted dry
4 tablespoons butter
1 cup freshly grated Pecorino cheese
2 eggs, beaten
freshly grated nutmeg
salt and ground black pepper
tomato sauce, to serve
basil, to garnish

SERVES 4–6

1 Heat the milk in a large nonstick saucepan. When it is at the point of boiling, sprinkle in the semolina, stirring constantly, until the mixture is smooth and very thick. Lower the heat and simmer for 2 minutes.

2 Remove from the heat and stir in the pesto and sun-dried tomatoes, with half the butter and half the Pecorino. Add the eggs, with nutmeg, salt and pepper to taste. Spoon into a shallow baking dish to a depth of 1/2 inch and level the surface. Set aside to cool, then chill until firm.

3 Preheat the oven to 375°F. Lightly grease a clean shallow baking dish. Using a 1½-inch round cutter, stamp out as many rounds as possible from the semolina dough.

4 Place the leftover semolina on the bottom of the greased dish and arrange the rounds on top in overlapping circles. Melt the remaining butter and brush it on the gnocchi. Sprinkle over the remaining Pecorino. Bake for 30–40 minutes, until golden. Serve with tomato sauce and garnish with basil.

VARIATIONS
Substitute any aged hard grating cheese for the Pecorino, such as the Spanish cheeses Manchego or Mahon. Instead of pesto, use a small package of chopped frozen spinach that has been thawed and squeezed of excess water or 6 tablespoons mixed chopped herbs.

PORCINI AND PARMESAN RISOTTO

2 tablespoons dried porcini
mushrooms
1¼ cups warm water
5 cups vegetable broth
generous pinch of saffron strands
2 tablespoons olive oil
1 onion, finely chopped
1 garlic clove, crushed
1¼ cups arborio rice
⅔ cup dry white wine or
3 tablespoons dry vermouth
2 tablespoons butter
⅔ cup freshly grated
Parmesan cheese
salt and ground black pepper

SERVES 4

VARIATIONS

There are endless variations on this
delectable dish. The proportion of
broth to rice, onion, garlic and butter
must remain constant but you can be
creative with the flavorings and
cheese. Try Pecorino with lightly
blanched baby vegetables for risotto
primavera. Chopped bacon and peas
make the famous risi e bisi.

1 Soak the dried mushrooms in the
warm water for 20 minutes. Lift out
with a slotted spoon. Filter the soaking
water through a layer of paper towels
in a sieve, then place it in a saucepan
with the broth. Bring the liquid to a
gentle simmer.

*The success of a good risotto depends on the quality of the rice used and the
technique. For this variation of the classic risotto alla milanese, saffron,
porcini mushrooms and Parmesan are stirred into the creamy cooked rice.*

2 Put about 3 tablespoons of the hot
broth in a cup and stir in the saffron
strands. Set aside.

3 Finely chop the mushrooms. Heat the
oil in a separate pan and lightly sauté
the onion, garlic and mushrooms for
5 minutes. Gradually add the rice,
stirring. Cook for 2 minutes, stirring.
Season with salt and pepper.

4 Pour in the wine or vermouth. Cook,
stirring, until it has been absorbed, then
ladle in a quarter of the simmering broth.
Bring to a boil, stirring. Cook until most
of the liquid has been absorbed.

5 Continue to add the simmering broth
a ladle at a time, stirring and cooking
after each addition. The secret of good
risotto is to add the broth gradually
and to stir frequently to encourage a
creamy texture from the starch grains.

6 After about 20 minutes, when all the
broth has been absorbed and the rice is
cooked but still has a "bite," stir in the
butter, saffron liquid and strands and
half the Parmesan. Serve hot, sprinkled
with the remaining Parmesan.

*Pecorino makes a good alternative to
Parmesan in this risotto.*

SUPPLI AL TELEFONO

3 tablespoons finely chopped
fresh parsley
1 quantity Porcini and Parmesan
Risotto (see page 202), made without
the saffron
7 ounces mozzarella cheese, cut into
20 cubes
2 eggs, beaten
1¼ cups dried plain bread crumbs
corn or vegetable oil, for
deep-frying
fresh herbs, to garnish

MAKES 20

VARIATION
For the filling, use cubes of Emmental,
Provolone or even Monterey Jack
instead of mozzarella.

These are risotto fritters with nuggets of mozzarella inside. When bitten into, the cheese is drawn out in thin strings, like telephone wires, hence the name.

1 Stir the parsley into the risotto, cool, then chill until firm. Divide into 20 portions and shape each into a ball. Press a cube of cheese into each ball of rice and reshape neatly. Coat the rice balls in the beaten egg, then the bread crumbs, and chill again for 30 minutes to set the coating.

2 Heat the oil for deep-frying to 350°F. Cook about five fritters at a time for 3–5 minutes, until golden brown and crisp. Drain the fritters on paper towels and keep warm on an uncovered plate in a warm oven so that the coating remains crisp. Serve immediately, garnished with fresh herbs.

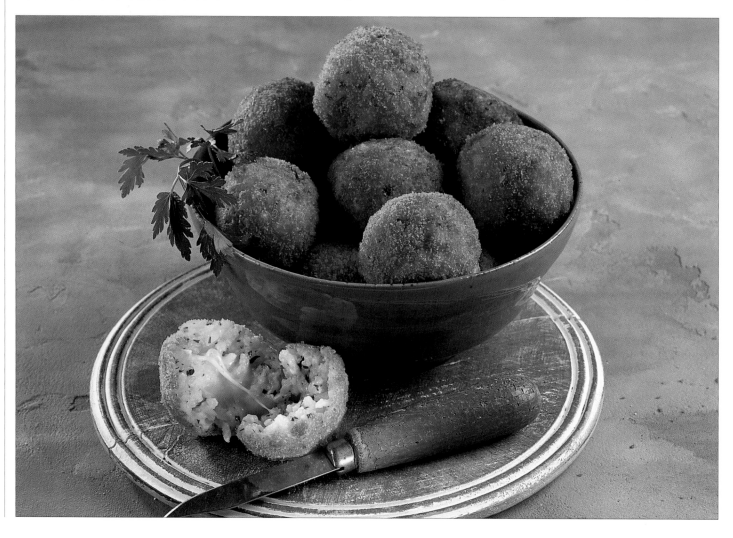

CHILI CHEESE TORTILLA WITH FRESH TOMATO SALSA

—

Good warm or cold, this dish is like a quiche without the pastry. Cheese and chilies are more than a match for each other.

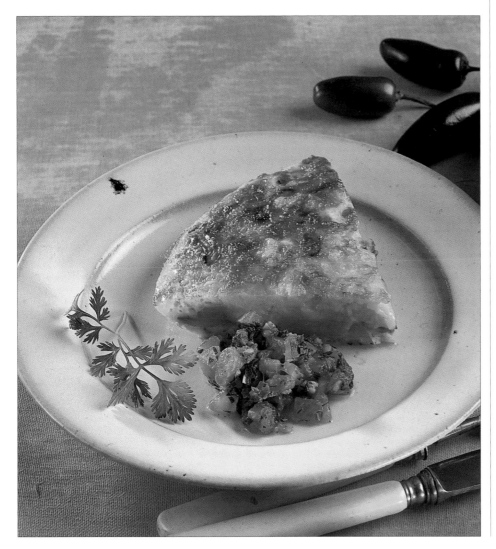

3 tablespoons sunflower or olive oil
1 small onion, thinly sliced
2–3 fresh green jalapeño chilies, sliced
7 ounces cold cooked potato, thinly sliced
generous 1 cup grated Manchego, Mexican queso blanco or Monterey Jack cheese
6 eggs, beaten
salt and ground black pepper
fresh herbs, to garnish

FOR THE SALSA
1¼ pounds fresh ripe tomatoes, peeled, seeded and finely chopped
1 fresh mild green chili, seeded and finely chopped
2 garlic cloves, crushed
3 tablespoons chopped fresh cilantro
juice of 1 lime
½ teaspoon salt

SERVES 4

COOK'S TIP
If desired, you can brown the top of the tortilla under a hot broiler, using a frying pan with a flameproof handle.

1 Make the salsa. Put the tomatoes in a bowl and add the chopped chili, garlic, cilantro, lime juice and salt and pepper. Mix well and set aside.

2 Heat half the oil in a large nonstick omelette pan and gently sauté the onion and jalapeños for 5 minutes, stirring once or twice, until softened. Add the potato and cook for another 5 minutes until lightly browned, taking care to keep the slices whole.

3 Using a slotted spoon, transfer the vegetables to a warm plate. Wipe the pan with a paper towel, then pour in the remaining oil. Heat well and return the vegetable mixture to the pan. Sprinkle the cheese on top.

4 Pour in the beaten eggs, making sure they seep under the vegetables. Cook the tortilla over low heat until set. Serve in wedges, garnished with fresh herbs, with the salsa on the side.

POLENTA WITH GORGONZOLA AND WILD MUSHROOM SAUCE

—

Like semolina gnocchi, polenta is made with a ground cereal—cornmeal. After it is cooked and thickened, creamy Gorgonzola is stirred in and the mixture is left to set before being cut into wedges and broiled.

3¾ cups milk
3¾ cups water
1 teaspoon salt
generous 2 cups polenta
¼ cup butter
4 ounces Gorgonzola cheese
sprigs of thyme, to garnish

FOR THE SAUCE
1½ ounces dried porcini mushrooms, soaked in ⅔ cup hot water for 15 minutes
2 tablespoons butter
1 cup button mushrooms, chopped
¼ cup dry white wine
generous pinch of dried thyme
¼ cup mascarpone cheese
salt and ground black pepper

SERVES 4–6

1 Pour the milk and water into a large heavy-bottomed saucepan. Add the salt and bring to a boil. Using a long-handled spoon, stir the liquid briskly with one hand while drizzling in the polenta with the other. When the mixture is thick and smooth, lower the heat to a gentle simmer and cook for about 20 minutes, stirring occasionally.

2 Remove from the heat and stir in the butter and Gorgonzola. Spoon the polenta into a shallow dish, level the surface and cool. Let the polenta set until solid, then cut into wedges.

3 Meanwhile, make the sauce. Drain the porcini, reserving the soaking liquid. Finely chop the porcini and strain the liquid through a sieve lined with a paper towel.

4 Melt half the butter in a small saucepan. Sauté the chopped fresh mushrooms for about 5 minutes. Add the wine, porcini and strained soaking liquid, with the dried thyme. Season to taste. Cook for 2 more minutes. Stir in the mascarpone and simmer for a few minutes, until reduced by a third. Set the sauce aside to cool.

5 Heat a ridged broiler pan and broil the polenta pieces until crisp. Melt the remaining butter and brush it onto the polenta. Serve hot, with the cooled sauce. Garnish with thyme.

Twice-baked Spinach and Goat's Milk Cheese Roulade

A roulade is really a soufflé in the shape of a jelly roll. Because it has air trapped inside, it magically rises again on reheating and becomes quite crisp on the outside. This is an impressive dinner-party dish.

1¼ cups milk
½ cup all-purpose flour
¼ cup plus 6 tablespoons butter
4 ounces chèvre (goat's milk cheese), chopped
½ cup freshly grated Parmesan cheese, plus extra for dusting
4 eggs, separated
2¼ cups fresh shiitake mushrooms, sliced
10 ounces young spinach leaves, washed
3 tablespoons crème fraîche or fromage frais
salt and ground black pepper

SERVES 4

1 Preheat the oven to 375°F. Line a 12 × 8-inch jelly roll pan with baking parchment, making sure that the paper rises well above the sides of the pan. Lightly grease the paper.

2 Combine the milk, flour and ¼ cup of the butter in a large saucepan. Bring to a boil over low heat, beating until thick and creamy. Lower the heat and simmer for 2 minutes, then mix in the chèvre and half the Parmesan. Cool for 5 minutes, then beat in the egg yolks and plenty of salt and pepper.

3 Beat the egg whites in a grease-free bowl until soft peaks form. Carefully fold the whites into the chèvre mixture, using a large metal spoon. Spoon the mixture into the prepared pan, spread gently to level, then bake for 15–17 minutes, until the top feels just firm.

4 Let the roulade cool for a few minutes, then invert it onto a sheet of baking parchment dusted with Parmesan. Carefully tear off the lining paper in strips. Roll the roulade up in the parchment and set aside to cool completely.

5 Make the filling. Melt the remaining butter and set aside 2 tablespoons. Add the mushrooms to the pan and stir-fry for 3 minutes. Stir in the spinach and drain well, then add the crème fraîche or fromage frais. Season, then cool.

6 Preheat the oven to the original temperature. Unroll the roulade and spread on the filling. Roll it up again and place, seam side down, in a baking dish. Brush with the reserved melted butter and sprinkle with the remaining Parmesan. Bake for 15 minutes, or until risen and golden. Serve immediately.

1/4 cup butter
2–3 tablespoons dried plain bread crumbs
scant 1 cup milk
3 tablespoons all-purpose flour
pinch of cayenne pepper
1/2 teaspoon curry paste or mustard or freshly grated nutmeg
1/2 cup grated aged Cheddar cheese
1/3 cup freshly grated Parmesan cheese
4 eggs, separated, plus 1 extra egg white
salt and ground black pepper

SERVES 2–3

1 Preheat the oven to 375°F. Melt 1 tablespoon of the butter and grease a 5-cup soufflé dish. Coat the inside of the dish evenly with the bread crumbs.

2 Put the milk in a large saucepan. Add the remaining butter, flour and cayenne, with the curry paste, mustard or nutmeg. Bring to a boil over low heat, beating steadily until the mixture thickens to a smooth sauce.

CLASSIC CHEESE SOUFFLÉ

At its simplest, a soufflé is merely a thick sauce with beaten egg whites folded in—not at all difficult to achieve, especially if the base is made ahead and the whites added just before baking. Timing is the only difficult part, as a soufflé waits for no one.

3 Simmer the sauce for a minute or two, then turn off the heat and beat in all the Cheddar and half the Parmesan. Cool a little, then beat in the egg yolks and check the seasoning. The mixture should be well seasoned.

4 Beat all the egg whites in a large grease-free bowl until they form soft, glossy peaks. Do not overbeat or the whites will become grainy and difficult to fold in.

VARIATIONS
Crumbled blue cheese, such as Stilton or Shropshire Blue or Fourme d'Ambert, makes a delicious flavoring. For a more substantial soufflé, put a chopped vegetable mixture, such as ratatouille or sautéed mushrooms, on the bottom of the dish before adding the cheese mixture and baking as above.

5 Spoon some of the beaten egg whites into the sauce to lighten it. Beat well, then scrape the rest of the whites into the pan and, using a figure-eight movement, carefully fold them into the mixture with a large metal spoon.

6 Pour the mixture into the prepared dish, level the top and place the dish on a baking sheet. Sprinkle on the remaining Parmesan. Bake for 20–25 minutes, until risen and golden. Serve.

Stilton is ideal for this soufflé.

CLASSIC CHEESE OMELET

Perhaps the ultimate fast food—a couple of eggs, some nicely flavored cheese, a pat of butter and a good pan and you have a full and satisfying meal within minutes. Technique is important with omelets. The center should be soft and the cheese just melted and creamy.

2 large eggs
1 tablespoon chopped fresh herbs,
such as chives, parsley or dill
a pat of unsalted butter
1/2 cup grated full-flavored cheese,
such as Gruyère, Gouda or Cheddar
salt and ground black pepper
tomato wedges, to serve
flat-leaf parsley, to garnish

SERVES 1

VARIATIONS
You can add ingredients to the cheese. Crunchy garlicky croutons are good, as are sautéed sliced mushrooms, flaked cooked smoked haddock and chopped tomatoes. As for the cheese, this is a good time to experiment.

1 Heat an 8-inch heavy-bottomed omelet pan or nonstick frying pan. Break the eggs into a bowl and beat in the herbs and seasoning. It is not necessary to add water or milk, which would only dilute the eggs.

2 Heat the butter in the pan. Pour in the beaten eggs, swirling the pan so the mixture coats the bottom. Using a fork or spatula, pull the cooked areas of egg away from the pan sides, letting the uncooked egg run in to fill the space. When the egg at the sides is firm, but the center still soft, sprinkle on the cheese.

3 Let cook undisturbed for about 30 seconds, then fold the edge of the omelet nearest the handle over a third. Roll the omelet over onto a warmed plate. Serve immediately, with tomato wedges and a garnish of flat-leaf parsley.

POTATO AND CHEESE CAKE

This dish appears in many guises, cheese and potatoes having a natural affinity. Choose a hard, well-flavored cheese—in France, where it is called Truffade, this cake would be made with a Tomme or Cantal. In England, Cheddar would be used, and the dish would be called Pan Haggarty.

a little sunflower oil or
melted butter
1 1/2 pounds potatoes, peeled and
very thinly sliced
1 large onion, thinly sliced
1 1/4 cups grated hard cheese, such as
aged Cheddar, Tomme or Cantal
freshly grated nutmeg
salt and ground black pepper
mixed salad greens,
to garnish

SERVES 4–6

VARIATION
In France, this is cooked with diced bacon (lardons) and the cheese is chopped, not sliced or grated. The ingredients are mixed and cooked slowly in a little lard in a pan on top of the stove.

1 Preheat the oven to 375°F. Lightly grease the bottom of a shallow baking dish with the oil or melted butter.

2 Layer the potatoes, onion and cheese in the dish, brushing the potatoes with oil or butter and seasoning with nutmeg, salt and pepper. Finish with a layer of cheese. Bake for 45 minutes, or until golden brown. Leave to stand for about 5 minutes, then serve in wedges, with a salad garnish.

Sweet Bell Pepper and Zucchini Frittata

Eggs, cheese and vegetables form the basis of this excellent supper dish.
Served cold in wedges, it makes tasty picnic fare, too.

3 tablespoons olive oil
1 red onion, thinly sliced
1 large red bell pepper, cored and
thinly sliced
1 large yellow bell pepper, cored and
thinly sliced
2 garlic cloves, crushed
1 medium zucchini, thinly sliced
6 eggs
5 ounces Italian cheese, such as
Fontina, Provolone or
Taleggio, grated
salt and ground black pepper
dressed mixed salad greens,
to garnish

SERVES 4

1 Heat 2 tablespoons of the oil in a heavy-bottomed frying pan. Fry the onion and pepper slices over low heat for about 10 minutes, until softened.

2 Pour the remaining oil into the pan. When it is hot, add the garlic and zucchini slices and sauté for 5 minutes, stirring constantly.

3 Beat the eggs with salt and pepper in a bowl. Mix in the cheese.

4 Pour the egg and cheese mixture over the vegetables, stirring lightly to mix. Make sure that the bottom of the pan is evenly covered with egg. Cook over low heat until the mixture is just set. Traditionally, a frittata is inverted onto a plate and slid back into the pan to cook the top, but it may be easier to brown the top lightly under a hot broiler for a few minutes (protect the pan handle, if necessary).

5 Let the frittata stand in the pan for about 5 minutes before cutting. This is delicious served hot or cold, with a salad garnish.

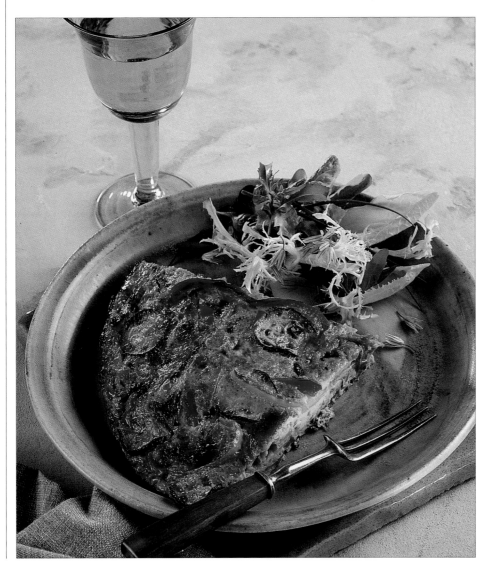

FONDUE

—

A fondue is simply a mixture of melted cheeses with wine to keep it liquid. Flavorless starch prevents the cheeses from separating, while garlic and Kirsch add extra flavor.

1 Rub the inside of a *caquelon* (traditional fondue pot) or deep flameproof pan with the cut sides of the garlic halves. If desired, you can then chop the garlic finely and place it in the pan.

2 Mix the arrowroot or potato starch with 2 tablespoons of the wine in a small bowl. Set aside. Pour the rest of the wine into the pan.

3 Heat the wine very slowly. Add about a third of the sliced or grated cheese, and continue heating the mixture, stirring until the cheese starts to melt and the liquid to bubble.

4 Gradually stir in the arrowroot or potato starch mixture, then the rest of the cheese, a little at a time. Add the Kirsch and pepper. Place the fondue over a candle warmer on the table, with cubes of bread for dipping.

1 fat garlic clove, halved
1 teaspoon arrowroot or potato starch
1¼ cups dry white wine
2¼ pounds mixed hard, melting cheeses (see Cook's Tip), thinly sliced or coarsely grated
3–4 tablespoons Kirsch
ground black pepper
cubes of country-style bread, for dipping

SERVES 6

COOK'S TIP
In Switzerland the cheese mixture would comprise Emmental, Gruyère and Appenzeller or raclette, while the French favor Comté or Beaufort.

PASTRIES, PIZZAS AND PASTA

Many of the world's great street foods rely on cheese. Because it melts so easily, either over direct heat or in the most rustic oven, it is ideal for slicing onto a pizza or wrapping between sheets of phyllo pastry. There are also dozens of cheesy pasta dishes, where the cheese is tossed into hot pasta or layered to make a mouthwatering lasagne. This sort of food is ideal for feeding a crowd with speed and without fuss.

BOREK

9 ounces feta cheese, crumbled
1/2 teaspoon freshly grated nutmeg
2 tablespoons each chopped fresh
parsley, dill and mint
10 phyllo pastry sheets, each about
12 × 7 inches
6 tablespoons melted butter or
olive oil
ground black pepper

MAKES 10

COOK'S TIPS
When using phyllo pastry, it is
important to keep unused sheets
covered so they don't dry out. The
quantities for phyllo pastry in the
recipe above are approximate, as the
size of phyllo sheets varies. Any unused
pastry will keep in the refrigerator for a
week or so if it is well wrapped.

Versions of these crisp, cheese-filled pastries are a common feature of street food throughout much of the Mediterranean. They are easy to make at home, but require a little time and patience.

1 Preheat the oven to 375°F. Mix the feta, nutmeg and herbs in a bowl. Add pepper to taste and mix to a creamy filling.

2 Brush a sheet of phyllo lightly with butter or oil, place another on top of it and brush that too.

3 Cut each buttered stack in half lengthwise to make 10 strips total, each 12 × 3½ inches. Place 1 teaspoon of the cheese filling at the bottom of a long strip, fold the corners in diagonally to enclose it, then roll the pastry up into a cigar shape.

4 Brush the end with a little butter or oil to seal, then place seam side down on a nonstick baking sheet. Repeat with the remaining pastry and filling. Brush the borek with more butter or oil and bake for 20 minutes, or until crisp and golden. Cool on a wire rack and serve at room temperature.

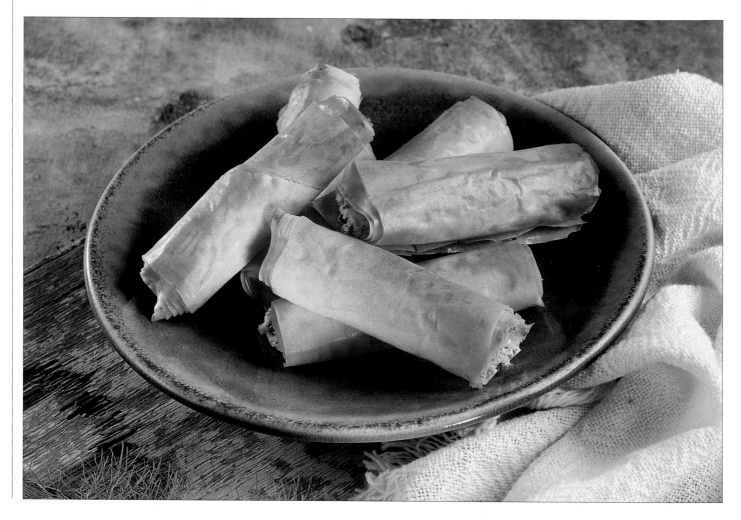

RATATOUILLE AND FONTINA STRUDEL

—

Mix a colorful jumble of ratatouille vegetables with chunks of creamy Fontina or Bel Paese, then wrap in sheets of phyllo and bake for a delicious, summery party pastry.

1 small eggplant, diced
3 tablespoons extra virgin olive oil
1 onion, sliced
2 garlic cloves, crushed
1 red bell pepper, cored and sliced
1 yellow bell pepper, cored and sliced
2 zucchini, cut into small chunks
generous pinch of dried mixed herbs
2 tablespoons pine nuts
2 tablespoons raisins
8 phyllo pastry sheets, each about 12 × 7 inches
1/4 cup butter, melted
generous 1 cup Fontina or Bel Paese cheese, cut into small cubes
salt and ground black pepper
dressed mixed greens, to serve

SERVES 6

VARIATION
Port-Salut, a soft French Tomme or a
Taleggio can be used instead of
Fontina or Bel Paese.

1 Layer the diced eggplant in a colander, sprinkling each layer with salt. Drain over a sink for 20 minutes, then rinse and pat dry.

2 Heat the oil in a large frying pan and gently sauté the onion, garlic, peppers and eggplant for about 10 minutes.

3 Add the zucchini, herbs and salt and pepper. Cook for 5 minutes, until softened. Cool to room temperature, then stir in the pine nuts and raisins.

4 Preheat the oven to 350°F. To assemble the strudel, brush two sheets of phyllo pastry lightly with a little of the melted butter. Lay the phyllo sheets side by side, overlapping them by about 2 inches, to make a large rectangle. Cover with the remaining phyllo, in the same way, brushing each layer with a little of the melted butter. Save some butter for the top. Spoon the vegetable mixture down one long side of the phyllo.

5 Sprinkle the cheese over, then roll up. Transfer the roll to a nonstick baking sheet, curling it around in a circle. Brush with the remaining melted butter and bake for 30 minutes, until golden. Cool for 10 minutes, before slicing. Serve with mixed greens.

CHEESE AND ONION QUICHE

1³/4 cups all-purpose flour
1/2 teaspoon salt
scant 1/2 cup butter or sunflower
margarine

FOR THE FILLING
2 tablespoons butter
1 large onion, thinly sliced
4 lean bacon strips,
chopped (optional)
3 eggs
1¹/4 cups crème fraîche, light cream
or milk
1/4 teaspoon freshly grated nutmeg
3¹/2 ounces hard cheese, such as
aged Cheddar, Gruyère or
Manchego, grated
salt and ground black pepper

SERVES 6–8

Perfect for picnics, parties or family suppers, this quiche celebrates a timeless combination: cheese and onion. Omit the bacon, if you prefer.

1 Make the pastry. Sift the flour and salt into a bowl. Rub in the fat until the mixture resembles fine crumbs. Trickle in enough water to make a firm dough, about 1/4 cup, tossing with a fork. Knead the dough lightly until smooth, wrap in plastic wrap and chill for 20 minutes.

2 Roll out the dough on a lightly floured surface and line a 9-inch tart pan with a removable base. Press the pastry well into the sides and let it rise above the rim by about 1/2 inch to allow for shrinkage. Prick the pastry shell a few times with a fork.

3 Line the tart pan with foil and baking beans, uncooked rice or pie weights and chill again for about 15 minutes. Preheat the oven to 400°F. Place a baking sheet in the oven. Stand the tart pan on the baking sheet and bake "blind" for 15 minutes. Remove the beans and foil and return the tart pan to the oven for 5 minutes more. Reduce the oven temperature to 350°F.

4 Make the filling. Melt the butter in a pan and sauté the onion and bacon, if using, for 10 minutes. In a bowl, beat the eggs and crème fraîche, cream or milk. Add the nutmeg and seasoning.

5 Spoon the onion mixture into the cooked pastry shell and sprinkle on the cheese. Pour the egg and cream liquid slowly over the filling, making sure none spills over the edge of the pastry shell. Place the quiche in the oven and cook for 35–40 minutes, or until the filling has just set. Remove from the oven, set aside to cool, then gently ease the quiche out of the pan and place it on a plate for serving.

CALZONE

—

Looking like a folded pizza, a calzone consists of bread dough wrapped around a cheese and vegetable filling. The traditional tomato and garlic can be enlivened with chunks of sweet melting cheese, olives, crumbled bacon, slices of pepperoni or chorizo or anchovy fillets.

2 tablespoons extra virgin olive oil
1 small red onion, thinly sliced
2 garlic cloves, crushed
1 can (14 ounces) chopped tomatoes
2 ounces chorizo sausage, sliced
1/2 cup pitted black olives
4 cups bread dough mix to make 1³/4 pounds bread dough
7 ounces mozzarella or other semi-soft cheese, diced
1 teaspoon dried oregano
salt and ground black pepper
oregano sprigs, to garnish

MAKES 4

VARIATION
Mozzarella is the classic pizza cheese, but you may wish to experiment with other semi-soft melting cheeses, such as Fontina or Provolone.

1 Heat the oil in a frying pan and sauté the onion and garlic for 5 minutes. Add the tomatoes and cook for 5 more minutes or until slightly reduced. Add the chorizo and olives. Season well.

2 Make up the dough mix according to the instructions on the package. Cover the bowl and leave the dough to rise until it has doubled in bulk.

3 Punch down the risen dough and divide it into four portions. Roll out each portion of dough into a circle measuring about 8 inches. Preheat the oven to 400°F. Lightly grease two baking sheets.

4 Spread the filling on half of each dough circle, leaving a border around the edge. Sprinkle on the cheese.

5 Sprinkle the filling with the dried oregano. Dampen the edges of the dough with cold water. Fold the dough in half and press well to seal.

6 Place two calzones on each baking sheet. Bake for 12–15 minutes, until risen and golden. Cool for 2 minutes, then loosen with a spatula and serve immediately, garnished with oregano.

CHICKEN, CHEESE AND LEEK JALOUSIE

3–3½-pound ready-roasted chicken
2 large leeks, thinly sliced
2 garlic cloves, crushed
3 tablespoons butter
1 cup button mushrooms, sliced
7 ounces low-fat cream cheese
grated rind of 1 small lemon
3 tablespoons chopped fresh parsley
2 sheets frozen puff pastry, thawed
1 egg, beaten
salt and ground black pepper
fresh herbs, to garnish

SERVES 6

A jalousie is a family-sized lattice pastry roll with a mild, creamy filling. Ready-made puff pastry and cooked chicken make this a good choice for informal entertaining.

3 Stack the sheets of pastry on top of each other and roll out on a lightly floured work surface into a large rectangle, about 14 × 10 inches. Drape the pastry over a rolling pin and lift it onto a nonstick baking sheet.

5 Brush the edges of the pastry with some of the beaten egg. Draw the pastry strips over each other in alternate crosses to "braid" the pastry. Seal the top and bottom edges.

1 Strip the meat from the chicken, discarding the skin and bones. Chop or shred the meat and set it aside.

4 Spoon the filling along the center of the pastry, leaving a generous border at the top and bottom, and 4 inches on each side. Cut the pastry sides diagonally up to the filling at ¾ inch intervals.

Try a creamy blue cheese, such as Gorgonzola Torta, for this jalousie.

6 Glaze the jalousie with the remaining beaten egg. Let it rest while you preheat the oven to 400°F. Bake for 15 minutes, then lower the oven temperature to 375°F and bake for another 15 minutes, or until the pastry is golden brown and crisp.

7 Let the jalousie stand for about 10 minutes before sliding it onto a board or platter to serve. Garnish with fresh herbs.

2 Sauté the leeks and garlic in the butter for 10 minutes. Stir in the mushrooms and cook for 5 minutes. Set aside to cool, then add the cream cheese, lemon rind, parsley and salt and pepper. When cold, stir in the chicken.

VARIATION
Chopped cooked ham can be used instead of chicken.

GOUGÈRE

Choux pastry is very easy to make. Add cubes of hard cheese, such as Gruyère or Cheddar, and bake it in a dish with a lightly spiced haddock and mushroom filling and you have an impressive supper dish.

scant 1 cup bread flour
¹/₄ teaspoon salt
6 tablespoons cold butter, diced
scant 1 cup water
3 eggs, beaten
5 ounces Emmental, aged Cheddar or Gruyère cheese, grated

FOR THE FILLING
9 ounces smoked haddock fillet
1 bay leaf
1 cup milk
3 tablespoons butter
1 small red onion, chopped
1¹/₄ cups button mushrooms, sliced
1 teaspoon mild curry paste (optional)
¹/₄ cup all-purpose flour
generous squeeze of fresh lemon juice
2 tablespoons chopped fresh parsley
salt and ground black pepper

SERVES 4

COOK'S TIP
Choose pale yellow, traditionally smoked haddock rather than vividly dyed, bright yellow fillets.

1 Lightly grease a shallow ovenproof dish. Sift the bread flour and salt onto a sheet of waxed paper. Place the butter and water in a medium saucepan and heat gently. As soon as the butter has melted, bring the water to a boil. Immediately pour in all the seasoned flour.

2 Beat the mixture hard until it comes away from the sides of the pan. (It will look alarmingly lumpy at first.) Remove the pan from the heat and cool for 5 minutes—this is important.

3 Gradually beat the beaten eggs into the dough until the mixture has a good dropping consistency and holds its shape. You may not need all the egg. Stir in two-thirds of the grated cheese.

4 Spoon the choux paste around the edge of the prepared dish, making sure it comes all the way up the sides. Set aside. Choux paste can be made in advance and kept chilled for 24 hours.

VARIATIONS
For an alternative filling, use cooked chicken or ratatouille. Both the choux paste and the filling can be flavored with blue cheese: Use slightly less than the quantity suggested in the main recipe.

5 Preheat the oven to 350°F. To make the filling, put the haddock in a baking dish with the bay leaf. Pour in the milk, cover and bake for 15 minutes, until just cooked. Lift out the fish. Discard the bay leaf but reserve the hot milk. Remove the skin from the haddock and flake the flesh. Keep the oven on.

6 In a saucepan, melt the butter and sauté the onion and mushrooms for 5 minutes. Mix in the curry paste, if using, then add the flour. Gradually stir in the hot milk. Heat, stirring, until the sauce is smooth. Simmer for about 2 minutes, then add the lemon juice, parsley and salt and pepper to taste.

7 Raise the oven temperature to 400°F. Spoon the filling into the center of the uncooked paste. Sprinkle with the rest of the cheese. Bake for 35–40 minutes, until the gougère has risen and is golden brown. Serve immediately.

FOUR-CHEESE CIABATTA PIZZA

Few dishes are as simple—or as satisfying—as this pizza made by topping a halved loaf of ciabatta.

1 loaf of ciabatta bread
1 garlic clove, halved
2–3 tablespoons olive oil
6 tablespoons tomato sauce
1 small red onion, thinly sliced
2 tablespoons chopped pitted olives
2 ounces each of four cheeses, one
aged (Parmesan or Cheddar), one
blue-veined (Gorgonzola or Stilton),
one mild (Fontina or Emmental)
and a chèvre (goat's milk cheese),
sliced, grated or crumbled
pine nuts or cumin seeds,
to sprinkle
salt and ground black pepper
sprigs of basil, to garnish

SERVES 2–3

1 Preheat the oven to 400°F. Split the ciabatta bread in half. Rub the cut sides with the garlic, then brush on the oil. Spread with the tomato sauce, then add the onion slices and olives. Season.

2 Divide the cheeses between the ciabatta halves and sprinkle on the pine nuts or cumin seeds. Bake for 10–12 minutes, until bubbling and golden brown. Cut into slices and serve immediately, garnished with basil.

CALIFORNIA ZUCCHINI AND CHÈVRE PIZZA

Chefs from the West Coast are adventurous when it comes to making pizzas. Their wood-burning ovens give crusts and cheese toppings a delicious smoky flavor. Cook this tasty pizza at a high temperature to char the vegetables lightly. Dot with goat's milk cheese for an interesting tang.

1 large ready-made, good-quality pizza crust
3 tablespoons drained oil-packed sun-dried tomatoes
3 tablespoons drained jarred oil-packed roasted bell peppers
1 zucchini, thinly sliced
1 red onion, thinly sliced
9 ounces young chèvre (goat's milk cheese), crumbled
1 tablespoon chopped fresh oregano or marjoram
a little extra virgin olive oil, to drizzle
salt and ground black pepper
fresh herbs, to garnish

SERVES 2

VARIATIONS
A creamy, crumbly blue cheese such as Bleu d'Auvergne makes a good alternative to chèvre. A smoked mozzarella would also work well.

For a Greek flavor, try lightly sautéed eggplant slices in place of the zucchini and use feta rather than chèvre.

1 Preheat the oven to 425°F. Place the pizza crust on a baking sheet. Chop the sun-dried tomatoes and peppers and spread them onto the pizza crust.

2 Scatter the slices of zucchini and onion on top, then dot with the crumbled chèvre. Sprinkle with oregano or marjoram, season well and drizzle a little olive oil on top.

3 Bake the pizza for 15–20 minutes, or until the cheese has melted and the vegetables have begun to char. Garnish with herbs and serve, cut into wedges.

Hard goat's milk cheese would be ideal—simply grate over the pizza.

LASAGNE AL FORNO

The classic lasagne is made with good homemade meat sauce (ragù) and a white sauce (salsa besciamella) layered with freshly grated Parmesan cheese. Keep the layers of sauces quite thin and don't make the lasagne too thick—the finished dish should hold its shape as you cut it.

about 8–10 lasagne noodles, green or white
1 cup freshly grated Parmesan cheese
salt and ground black pepper
sprigs of flat-leaf parsley, to garnish

For the Meat Sauce
3 tablespoons olive oil
1¼ pounds lean ground beef
3 ounces smoked bacon or pancetta, diced
4 ounces chicken livers, trimmed and chopped (optional)
1 onion, finely chopped
2 garlic cloves, crushed
⅔ cup dry white wine (optional)
2–3 tablespoons tomato paste
2 cans (14 ounces each) chopped tomatoes
3 tablespoons light cream (optional)

For the White Sauce
2½ cups milk
1 bay leaf
1 small onion, sliced
¼ cup butter
⅓ cup all-purpose flour
freshly grated nutmeg

Serves 6

1 Bring a large saucepan of water to a boil and blanch the noodles, a few at a time, for at least 2 minutes, taking care to keep them separate. Stir the pasta during cooking to prevent it from sticking. Drain the blanched noodles and set them aside in a bowl of cold water.

2 Make the meat sauce. Heat the oil in a large frying pan and brown the ground beef. Add the bacon or pancetta and chicken livers, if using, and cook for 3–4 minutes. Add the onion and garlic, and cook for 5 more minutes. Stir in the wine, if using. Cook until well reduced.

3 Stir in the tomato paste and the chopped tomatoes, with salt and pepper to taste. Bring to a boil, then lower the heat and simmer for 15–20 minutes, until thickened. Stir in the cream, if using, and set aside.

4 While the meat sauce is simmering, make the white sauce. Pour the milk into a saucepan and add the bay leaf and sliced onion. Heat gently until the milk is just below the boiling point, then remove the pan from the heat and set aside to infuse for 10 minutes. Strain the milk into a large glass measure and discard the bay leaf and onion.

5 Melt the butter in the clean saucepan and stir in the flour. Cook for 1 minute, stirring, then gradually stir in the strained milk until the mixture boils and thickens to a smooth sauce. Season and add nutmeg to taste. Drain the noodles and pat them dry with paper towels.

6 Spread some meat sauce in the bottom of a rectangular baking dish. Top with a single layer of pasta sheets. Drizzle on some white sauce and sprinkle with some Parmesan. Repeat the layers until all the ingredients have been used, finishing with a layer made by swirling the last of the two sauces together. Sprinkle with Parmesan.

7 Preheat the oven to 375°F and bake the lasagne for about 30 minutes until bubbling and golden brown. Let stand for 10 minutes before cutting. Serve garnished with flat-leaf parsley.

NEW YORK-STYLE LASAGNE

This more sophisticated lasagne is made by layering the meat sauce with ricotta cheese, spinach and sliced pepperoni or chorizo sausage. A mixture of ground beef and pork gives a good flavor.

about 8–10 lasagne noodles, white or green
14 ounces fresh spinach
2 1/2 cups ricotta cheese
4 ounces thinly sliced pepperoni or chorizo sausage
2/3 cup freshly grated Parmesan cheese
fresh herbs, to garnish

FOR THE MEAT SAUCE
2 tablespoons olive oil
9 ounces lean ground beef
9 ounces lean ground pork
1 onion, chopped
2 garlic cloves, crushed
2/3 cup dry white wine or
1/4 cup dry vermouth
1 can (14 ounces) chopped tomatoes
3 tablespoons tomato paste
2/3 cup beef broth or water
1/2 teaspoon dried oregano
salt and ground black pepper

SERVES 6

1 Bring a large saucepan of water to a boil and blanch the lasagne noodles, a few at a time, for at least 2 minutes, taking care to keep them separate. Stir the pasta during cooking to prevent it from sticking. Drain and set aside in a bowl of cold water.

2 Break off any thick stalks from the spinach, then blanch the leaves in a pan containing a small amount of boiling water for 2 minutes, until just wilted. Drain the spinach and refresh under cold water. Drain again, then squeeze dry and chop the leaves.

3 Put the ricotta on a plate and break or mash it up with a fork.

4 To make the meat sauce, heat the oil in a large frying pan, then add both ground meats and cook over high heat for about 5 minutes, until well browned, stirring to break up any lumps. Add the onion and garlic and cook for 5 more minutes.

COOK'S TIP

As an alternative, try low-fat ricotta cheese or ricotta salata. Ricotta salata can sometimes be difficult to find. However, it freezes well, so it is worth stocking up when you do locate a supply.

5 Pour the wine or vermouth into the frying pan and cook over high heat until well reduced. Stir in the chopped tomatoes, tomato paste, beef broth or water and dried oregano, then season to taste with salt and pepper. Bring to a boil, then lower the heat and simmer gently, uncovered, for about 15 minutes, until thickened.

6 Preheat the oven to 375°F. In a large baking dish, layer the meat sauce with the lasagne noodles, chopped spinach and sliced sausage. Dot each layer of spinach and sausage with some ricotta and sprinkle with some Parmesan. Finish with a generous topping of Parmesan.

7 Bake the lasagne for 35–40 minutes, until bubbling and golden brown. Set aside in a warm place for about 10 minutes before cutting and serving. Garnish with fresh herbs.

SPANAKOPITA

2¼ pounds fresh spinach
4 scallions, chopped
11 ounces feta or Kefalotiri cheese,
crumbled or coarsely grated
2 large eggs, beaten
2 tablespoons chopped fresh parsley
1 tablespoon chopped fresh dill
3 tablespoons currants (optional)
about 8 phyllo pastry sheets, each
about 12 × 7 inches
⅔ cup olive oil
ground black pepper

SERVES 6

VARIATION

Graviera or Kasseri can be used
instead of feta or Kefalotiri.
A crumbly English cheese, such as
Lancashire, also works well, even
though it is not authentic.

*This popular spinach and phyllo pastry pie comes from Greece. There are
several ways of making it, but feta or Kefalotiri is inevitably included.
No salt is needed in this recipe because these cheeses are salty.*

1 Preheat the oven to 375°F. Break off
any thick stalks from the spinach, then
blanch the leaves in a pan containing a
very small amount of boiling water for
1–2 minutes, until just wilted. Drain
and refresh under cold water. Drain
again, squeeze dry and chop roughly.

2 Place the spinach in a bowl with the
scallions and cheese, then pour in the
eggs. Mix in the herbs and currants, if
using. Season with pepper.

3 Brush a phyllo sheet with some oil
and fit it into a 9-inch pie pan, letting
it hang over the edges. Top with 3–4
more sheets; place these at different
angles and brush each one with more
oil, to make a roughly shaped pie crust.

4 Spoon in the filling, then top with all
but one of the remaining phyllo sheets.
Brush each phyllo sheet with oil. Fold
in the overhanging phyllo to seal in the
filling. Brush the reserved phyllo with
oil and scrunch it over the top of the pie.

5 Brush the pie with oil. Sprinkle with a
little water to prevent the phyllo edges
from curling, then place on a baking
sheet. Bake for about 40 minutes, until
golden and crisp. Cool the pie on a wire
rack for 15 minutes before serving.

PUMPKIN AND PARMESAN PASTA

The sweet flavor of pumpkin is nicely balanced by the flavor of aged Parmesan. Instead of being sprinkled on top of the pasta dish, this grated cheese is used in the sauce, and the crunch comes from garlic bread crumbs.

1 Bring a large saucepan of water to a boil. Add the pumpkin cubes. Cook for about 10 minutes, until just tender, then drain and set aside.

2 Melt two-thirds of the butter with the oil in a frying pan. Add the garlic and bread crumbs. Fry gently until the crumbs are golden brown and crisp. Drain on paper towels and keep warm.

3 Cook the tagliatelle according to the package instructions. Drain and set aside. Heat the remaining butter in a clean frying pan and sauté the bacon and onion for 5 minutes. Stir in the cream and bring to just below the boiling point. Add the pasta and reheat. Stir in the pumpkin, Parmesan, nutmeg, parsley, chives and seasoning. Serve sprinkled with garlic bread crumbs and garnished with parsley.

*2-pound baby pumpkin, peeled
and cut into small cubes
5 tablespoons butter
1 tablespoon olive oil
2 garlic cloves, crushed
1¹/₂ cups fresh white bread crumbs
11 ounces mixed green and white
tagliatelle
4 ounces bacon, diced
1 onion, sliced
²/₃ cup light cream
²/₃ cup freshly grated
Parmesan cheese
freshly grated nutmeg
2 tablespoons chopped fresh parsley
1 tablespoon snipped fresh chives
salt and ground black pepper
sprigs of flat-leaf parsley, to garnish*

SERVES 4

CHEESE SAUCES FOR PASTA

Here are three quick and easy sauces—all using cheese—to toss with cooked pasta. Each is sufficient for about 9 ounces of pasta.

MUSHROOM AND GORGONZOLA SAUCE

Gorgonzola melts easily with cream to make a delicious, quick sauce.

2 tablespoons olive oil
2¼ cups button mushrooms, sliced
1 garlic clove, crushed
1¼ cups light cream
6 ounces Gorgonzola cheese, rind removed, crumbled
salt and ground black pepper
1 tablespoon chopped fresh parsley and ½ cup chopped walnuts, to serve

1 Heat the olive oil in a pan and sauté the mushrooms for 5 minutes. Add the garlic and cook for 1–2 more minutes.

2 Stir in the cream, bring to a boil and cook for 1 minute. Stir in the Gorgonzola. Reheat gently to melt the cheese, but do not boil. Season and toss with cooked pasta. Serve immediately, sprinkled with the parsley and walnuts.

HOMEMADE PESTO

The ideal no-cook pasta sauce, this is best made by hand with a mortar and pestle, although a food processor can be used if time is short. Use a mixture of Parmesan and Pecorino cheeses. Pine nuts are a great addition and butter makes it enjoyably smooth.

1½ cups fresh basil leaves, stalks removed
2 tablespoons pine nuts
2–3 garlic cloves, roughly chopped
1⅓ cups mixed freshly grated Parmesan and Pecorino cheeses
½ cup olive oil
2 tablespoons butter, softened
salt

1 Put the basil, pine nuts and garlic into a mortar. Add ½ teaspoon salt and grind with a pestle until the mixture forms a chunky paste.

2 Work in the cheeses until smooth. Beat the paste with a wooden spoon, gradually trickling in the olive oil as when making mayonnaise. Finally, beat in the butter.

3 Store pesto in a screw-top jar in the refrigerator. When you toss it into cooked pasta, thin it slightly, if you wish, by adding a little of the hot water used for cooking the pasta.

FONDUTA

This Italian answer to fondue is also used as a sauce for pasta, rice and polenta. If you can't find Fontina cheese, Gruyère will do.

14 ounces Fontina cheese, cut into small cubes
1 cup half-and-half
¼ cup butter, cut into pieces
4 egg yolks
ground white pepper

1 Combine the cheese and half-and-half in a heavy-bottomed saucepan or the top of a double boiler over simmering water. Heat very gently, stirring frequently, until the cheese has completely melted. Stir in the butter. The cheese will form thin threads.

2 Beat the egg yolks in a large bowl with some pepper. Pour the cheese mixture onto them, beating as you pour. Return the mixture to the clean pan and reheat very, very gently. Do not let the mixture boil or it will curdle. Pour onto cooked pasta or rice or grilled polenta and eat quickly. The sauce is also good served by itself, with chunks of bread to scoop it up.

OPPOSITE (FROM LEFT): Fonduta, Homemade Pesto and Mushroom and Gorgonzola Sauce.

DESSERTS AND BAKED GOODS

Fresh young cheeses were created to be used in cooking or mixed with other ingredients, and their mild taste and slight astringency means that they are delicious sweetened with sugar or honey to make classic desserts such as Coeur à la Crème and Tiramisù, delectable cheesecakes and a cream cheese-frosted carrot cake. Full-flavored hard cheeses make delicious, moist breads and scones.

REFRIGERATOR CHEESECAKE

This dessert is so simple, anyone can make it. Serve the cheesecake with seasonal fruits. In late summer, poached plums or apricots cooked in a spiced syrup are particularly good, although soft red berries are also excellent. Make sure the cheese is at room temperature when you mix it.

3¹/2 cups graham cracker crumbs
7 tablespoons butter
1 tablespoon golden syrup or light corn syrup
seasonal fruit and raspberry coulis, to serve
strawberry leaves, to decorate

FOR THE FILLING
grated rind and juice of 1 lemon or 2 limes
1 package powdered unflavored gelatin
7 ounces low-fat cream cheese, at room temperature
scant 1 cup fromage frais
²/3 cup plain yogurt
¹/4 cup sugar
1 teaspoon pure vanilla extract

SERVES 4–6

COOK'S TIP
The gelatin can be dissolved in a suitable bowl in the microwave. Follow the instructions on the package.

1 Crush the graham crackers: Either place them in a plastic food bag and crush with a rolling pin or use a food processor fitted with a metal blade. Melt the butter and syrup in a saucepan, then mix with the crumbs.

2 Press the buttery crumbs into the base and up the sides of an 8-inch tart pan with a removable bottom. Chill for 1 hour.

3 Make the filling. Pour the lemon or lime juice into a small heatproof dish and sprinkle the gelatin on top. Let the mixture sit until the gelatin absorbs the liquid and looks spongy, then place the dish in a saucepan of barely simmering water and stir occasionally until the gelatin dissolves. Remove from the water.

4 Mix the cheese and fromage frais. Add the yogurt, citrus rind, sugar and vanilla. Beat until smooth, then beat some of the mixture into the dissolved gelatin. Add this to the cheesecake filling and beat well. Pour into the crumb crust and chill for 3 hours, until set. Remove the side of the pan. Serve with fruit and raspberry coulis. Decorate with strawberry leaves.

VELVETY CHEESECAKE

The secret of a perfect baked cheesecake is to take as much care over the cooling as you do with the cooking. If you do not overbake the mixture, it will stay beautifully moist and will firm as it cools.

10-inch round sponge cake
1¼ pounds cream cheese, softened
2½ cups sour cream
scant 1 cup granulated sugar
3 eggs, beaten
juice of 1 lemon
2 teaspoons pure vanilla extract
3–4 tablespoons crushed graham cracker crumbs
confectioners' sugar, for dusting
fresh fruit, to serve

SERVES 6–8

1 Preheat the oven to 325°F. Lightly grease a 9-inch springform cake pan. Using the bottom of the pan as a guide, cut out a round from the cake and fit this into the pan. It should fit snugly, without any gaps.

4 Sprinkle the crushed graham cracker crumbs evenly over the cheesecake and dust with a little sifted confectioners' sugar. Serve with fresh fruit.

VARIATIONS
Make the cheesecake without a base, if you prefer. If you like golden raisins in your cheesecake, add a generous handful.

2 Mix the cream cheese, sour cream and granulated sugar in a food processor. Process until smooth and creamy, then mix in the eggs, lemon juice and vanilla extract. Process briefly to blend.

3 Pour the filling on top of the sponge cake and level the surface. Bake for about 40 minutes, until the top is golden brown. Turn off the oven and leave the cake inside for another hour. Remove, let the cake cool on a wire rack to room temperature, then chill in the refrigerator overnight until firm. Run a table knife around the cheesecake and remove the sides of the pan. Slide a metal spatula under the cake and lift it onto a serving plate.

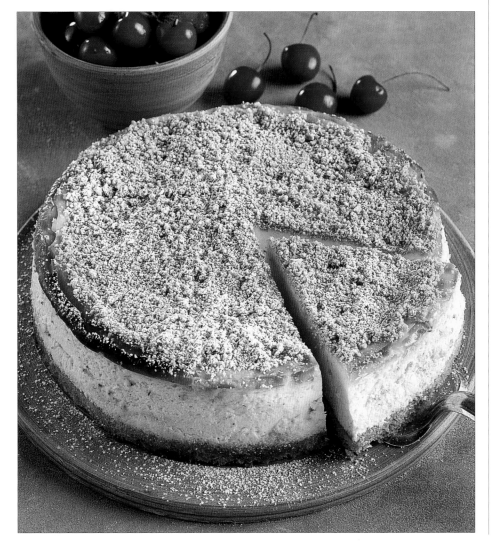

generous 1 cup cottage cheese
1¼ cups crème fraîche or
plain yogurt
2–3 tablespoons vanilla-flavored
granulated sugar
raspberry leaves, to decorate

FOR THE RASPBERRY COULIS
1½ cups fresh raspberries, hulled
confectioners' sugar, to sweeten

MAKES 8

COOK'S TIP
If using ramekins, spoon the cheese mixture into a cheesecloth-lined sieve set over a bowl. Let drain in the refrigerator for up to 2 days, then press into eight lightly greased ramekins. Remove the molded cheese immediately.

2 eggs, separated, plus
2 egg yolks
7 tablespoons sugar
1 teaspoon pure vanilla extract
1¼ pounds mascarpone cheese
1 cup freshly brewed strong
black coffee
4 tablespoons rum or brandy
about 24 Italian Savoiardi biscuits
or ladyfingers
¼ cup finely grated dark chocolate

SERVES 6–8

VARIATION
Dispense with the biscuit base, if you prefer, and serve the Tiramisù cream over a mixture of fresh prepared summer fruit.

COEUR À LA CRÈME

This dessert is sheer simplicity—cottage cheese blended with crème fraîche, then sweetened and drained. Traditionally, perforated heart-shaped molds are used (hence the name), but the mixture can be made in ramekins.

1 Beat the cottage cheese and crème fraîche or plain yogurt in a bowl. Add vanilla sugar to taste.

2 Set eight traditional perforated molds on a wire rack over a roasting pan. Spoon the cheese mixture into the molds, filling each one to the brim.

3 Transfer the roasting pan to the refrigerator and let the molds drain for up to 2 days.

4 To make the coulis, sieve the raspberries, then sweeten with confectioners' sugar. Remove the hearts and serve with the coulis, decorated with raspberry leaves.

TIRAMISÙ

The Italians consider this the ultimate "pick-me-up," which is what the name means. It makes great use of silky smooth mascarpone.

1 Beat all the egg yolks, sugar and vanilla in a heatproof bowl. Place over a pan of simmering water and beat until the mixture is pale and thick and the beater leaves a ribbon on the surface when lifted up. Remove the bowl from the pan and let cool, beating the mixture occasionally to prevent the formation of a skin.

2 When the mixture is cold, beat in the mascarpone. Beat the egg whites in a large grease-free bowl until they form soft peaks, then carefully fold them into the mixture.

3 Mix the coffee and rum or brandy in a bowl. Dip the Savoiardi biscuits or ladyfingers quickly in the liquid, then arrange them in a glass dish. Spoon the mascarpone mixture on top, then sprinkle with the grated chocolate. Chill for at least an hour before serving.

COOK'S TIP
If you prefer not to use uncooked egg whites, substitute powdered egg whites.

LEMON CHEESE MOUSSE WITH BRANDY SNAP BASKETS

—

1/4 cup butter
2 tablespoons light corn syrup
1/4 cup granulated sugar
grated rind and juice of 2 lemons
1/2 cup all-purpose flour
1 orange, for shaping the cookies
3 tablespoons water
2 teaspoons powdered
unflavored gelatin
generous 1 cup cottage cheese
2/3 cup plain yogurt
2 tablespoons honey, or to taste
1 tablespoon crystallized ginger
2 egg whites
mint sprigs, to decorate
selection of soft fruit, to serve

MAKES 6–8

COOK'S TIP
To save time, use purchased brandy
snaps to make the baskets. Just warm
them in a low oven until they uncurl,
then shape them over an orange.
If the brandy snaps harden before you
have a chance to shape them, then
simply pop them back in the oven
briefly to soften.

1 Make the baskets. Preheat the oven
to 375°F. Line a large baking sheet with
parchment paper. Melt the butter,
syrup and sugar in a saucepan, stirring,
then remove from the heat and stir in
half the lemon rind and all the flour.
Beat until smooth.

A delicious combination of a light cheesecake-style mousse with cookie cups.
Assemble the individual desserts at the last minute, so that they stay crisp.

2 Put about 2 tablespoons of the
mixture on the prepared baking sheet.
Using a small metal spatula, spread out
the mixture to a 5-inch circle. Add a
second circle, some distance from the
first to allow room for spreading. Bake
for 5–7 minutes, until the cookies have
spread out and are lacy and light
golden brown.

3 Let the cookies cool for about
1 minute to firm slightly, but not
harden, then lift each in turn off the
baking sheet using a metal spatula. One
at a time, gently press the cookies over
the orange, carefully fluting the edges,
and protecting your hands with a clean
dish towel, if necessary.

4 Remove the baskets when shaped
and let them cool on a wire rack.
Repeat the entire baking and shaping
process with the remaining mixture
until you have used it all.

5 Make the mousse. Pour the water
into a bowl and sprinkle the gelatin
over. Let sit until spongy, then dissolve
in a pan of simmering water.

6 Blend the cheese, yogurt, remaining
lemon rind, lemon juice, honey and
ginger in a food processor. Add the
gelatin, blend briefly and pour into a
bowl. Chill until just beginning to set.

7 Beat the egg whites to soft peaks and
fold into the mousse. Spoon into the
baskets and serve, decorated with mint
and accompanied by fruit.

SICILIAN CASSATA

2¹/2 cups ricotta cheese
³/4 cup confectioners' sugar, plus
extra for dusting
¹/2 teaspoon pure vanilla extract
grated rind and juice of
1 small orange
2 ounces bittersweet chocolate,
grated
1¹/2 cups mixed candied fruits,
including orange, pineapple, citron,
cherries and angelica
1 cup freshly brewed strong
black coffee
¹/2 cup rum
24 Italian Savoiardi biscuits or
ladyfingers
geranium leaves, to decorate

SERVES 8

Is this world-famous cheese dessert a chocolate-coated ice cream or a rum syrup-soaked cake? The answer is that it can be both, and a number of other variations, too. Try to track down authentic Savoiardi biscuits as they hold their shape better than ladyfingers.

1 Line the base and sides of an 8-inch round cake pan with plastic wrap. Put the ricotta in a bowl. Sift in the sugar, then add the vanilla extract with the orange rind and juice. Beat until smooth, then stir in the chocolate.

2 Cut the candied fruits into small pieces and stir into the ricotta mixture.

3 Mix the coffee and rum in a bowl. Line the bottom of the prepared pan with biscuits, dipping each biscuit in turn in the coffee mixture before fitting it in place. Cut the remaining biscuits in half, dip them in the liquid and arrange around the sides of the pan.

4 Spoon the cassata mixture into the center and level the top. Cover with more plastic wrap, then place a plate on top that exactly fits inside the rim of the pan. Weight this with a heavy weight, such as a bag of dried beans or sugar, then chill overnight, until firm.

5 Remove from the pan to serve, shaking the pan firmly if necessary and tugging the plastic wrap. Dust with a little sifted sugar and serve in wedges, decorated with geranium leaves.

PASHKA

This traditional Russian Easter dessert is made with cottage cheese and served with slices of kulich, a sweet yeast bread. The cheese mixture is pressed into a cheesecloth-lined wooden mold so that whey drains out to leave a rich and creamy mousse. In the absence of a pashka mold, use a clean flower pot.

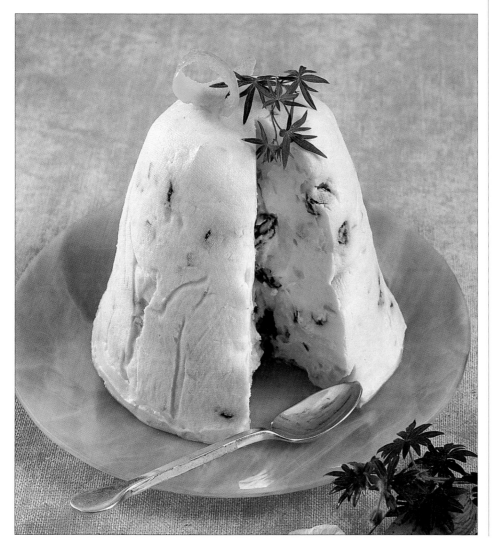

*2 1/2 cups cottage cheese, at room temperature
9 tablespoons butter, softened
2 large egg yolks, optional
1/2 cup sugar
1/2 cup candied fruit peel, chopped
1/3 cup raisins
1/2 cup chopped blanched almonds
grated rind of 1 lemon
1 teaspoon pure vanilla extract
pared lemon rind and geranium leaves, to decorate
sliced fresh kulich or fruited brioche, to serve*

SERVES 8

VARIATION
A mixture of ricotta and mascarpone can be used instead of the cottage cheese, and chopped pistachio nuts instead of the almonds.

3 Place the flower pot on a deep plate and let drain overnight at cool room temperature, or for a full day in the refrigerator.

4 Discard the whey, then uncover the flower pot and transfer it onto a pretty serving plate. Decorate with pared lemon rind and geranium leaves. To serve, slice horizontally from the top down or cut into thin wedges. Offer sliced fresh kulich or fruited brioche with the pashka.

1 Put the cottage cheese, softened butter, egg yolks, if using, and sugar in a bowl. Beat until smooth, then mix in the candied fruit peel, raisins, almonds, lemon rind and vanilla extract.

2 Line a clean, new 7-inch flower pot with wet cheesecloth. Pack in the cheese mixture. Cover with a plate that exactly fits the top and weigh down with heavy cans or weights.

CARROT CAKE WITH CREAM CHEESE ICING

This moist delicious cake has a rich cream cheese icing.
It makes a perfect grown-up birthday cake.

scant 1 cup whole-wheat flour
1 1/4 cups all-purpose flour
2 teaspoons baking powder
1 teaspoon baking soda
1 teaspoon ground cinnamon
1/2 teaspoon ground allspice
1 1/2 cups light brown sugar
3 carrots, coarsely grated
1 cup chopped walnuts
3 large eggs
juice of 1 orange
1/2 cup sunflower oil
shreds of pared orange rind,
to decorate

FOR THE ICING
1/4 cup butter, softened
7 ounces cream cheese, softened
grated rind of 1 orange
1 3/4 cups confectioners' sugar
1 teaspoon pure vanilla extract

SERVES 8

2 Sift all the dry ingredients except the brown sugar into a bowl, then add the bran from the sieve. Add the brown sugar, carrots and walnuts.

3 Beat the eggs and orange juice in a bowl. Make a well in the dry mixture and add the egg mixture and oil. Mix well. Spoon into the prepared pan and level the top. Bake for about 1 hour, until risen and springy to the touch.

4 Slide a knife between the cake and the pan to loosen, then transfer to a wire rack and remove the lining paper. Let cool.

5 To make the icing, beat the butter, cream cheese and grated orange rind in a large bowl. Sift the confectioners' sugar, then add to the bowl with the vanilla extract, beating well after each addition, until the mixture is creamy.

6 Split the cake horizontally in 2 layers using a large serrated knife. Fill the cake with about half the icing, then spread the rest of the icing on the top, swirling it attractively. Scatter the shreds of orange rind around the edge of the iced cake to decorate.

1 Preheat the oven to 350°F. Lightly grease a 9-inch round cake pan and line with baking parchment. Grease the paper.

VARIATION
Instead of using shreds of orange rind to decorate the cake, sprinkle the iced cake with a little ground cinnamon, finely chopped walnuts or coffee sugar crystals.

CHEESE AND ZUCCHINI CLUSTER BREAD

—

4 zucchini, coarsely grated
6 cups bread flour
2 packages rapid-rise active yeast
2/3 cup freshly grated
Parmesan cheese
2 tablespoons olive oil
milk, to glaze
poppy seeds or sesame seeds,
to sprinkle
salt and ground black pepper

SERVES 8

Home baking is enjoying renewed popularity, thanks to the convenience of rapid-rise yeast. This unusual bread owes its moistness to grated zucchini, and its depth of flavor to freshly grated Parmesan.

3 Gather the dough together with your hand, then transfer it to a lightly floured surface. Knead the dough for 5–10 minutes, or until it is smooth and elastic. Return to the bowl, cover with lightly oiled plastic wrap and let rise in a warm place until doubled in bulk.

5 Lightly grease a deep 9-inch round cake pan. Put the balls into the pan, placing one in the center and the remainder around the outside.

1 Put the grated zucchini into a colander and sprinkle with salt. Let stand in a sink for about 20 minutes to drain the juices, then rinse thoroughly. Drain and pat dry with paper towels.

4 Punch down the dough and knead again. Divide it into eight pieces and roll each piece into a smooth ball.

6 Glaze the loaf with a little milk and sprinkle on poppy seeds or sesame seeds. Cover the pan lightly with oiled plastic wrap and let rise in a warm place until the balls of dough have doubled in size.

7 Meanwhile, preheat the oven to 400°F. Bake the loaf for 35–45 minutes, until it is golden brown and sounds hollow when rapped on the base. Cool on a wire rack and eat as soon as possible.

2 In a large bowl, mix the flour with the yeast, Parmesan and ½ teaspoon salt. Add pepper to taste. Stir in the oil and zucchini, then add enough warm water to make a firm but still soft dough. How much water you need depends on how wet the zucchini are, but start with about 3 tablespoons.

Dry Jack (left) can be used instead of Parmesan in this bread. Or try an aged Gouda or Pecorino.

CHEESE AND MUSTARD SCONES

2 1/4 cups self-rising flour
1 teaspoon baking powder
1/2 teaspoon salt
3 tablespoons butter or sunflower
margarine
1 1/2 cups grated aged Cheddar
cheese, plus extra for sprinkling
2 teaspoons whole-grain mustard
about 2/3 cup milk, buttermilk or
plain yogurt
1 egg yolk beaten with
1 teaspoon water, to glaze (optional)
ground black pepper
garlic-flavored cream cheese,
snipped fresh chives and sliced
radishes, to serve (optional)

MAKES 12 MEDIUM SCONES

Depending on their size, these cheese scones can be served as little canapé bases, snack-time treats or even as a quick savory pie topping.

1 Preheat the oven to 425°F. Sift the flour, baking powder and salt into a bowl, then rub in the butter or margarine until the mixture resembles fine bread crumbs. Use a food processor if you prefer. Season with pepper and stir in the cheese.

2 Mix the mustard with the milk, buttermilk or yogurt. Add to the dry ingredients and mix quickly until the mixture just comes together. Do not overmix or the scones will be tough.

3 Knead the dough lightly on a lightly floured surface, then pat it out with your hands to a thickness of 3/4 inch. Cut into squares, or use a 2-inch cutter to stamp out rounds, re-rolling the dough as necessary.

4 Place the squares or rounds on a nonstick baking sheet. Brush with the egg glaze, if using, and sprinkle with extra grated cheese.

5 Bake for about 10 minutes, until risen and golden. You can test scones by pressing the sides, which should spring back. Remove to a wire rack to cool. Serve spread with garlic-flavored cream cheese, if desired. Top with chopped chives and sliced radish, if using.

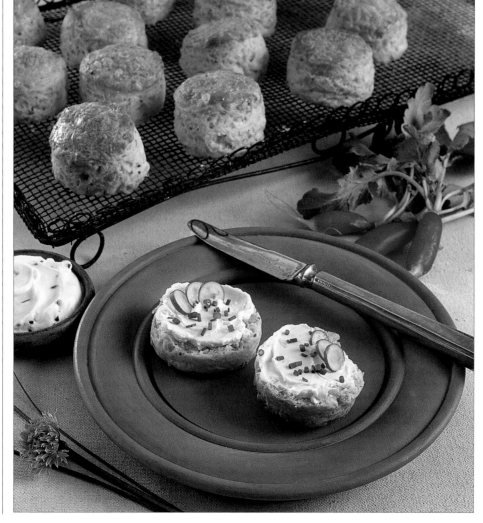

RICOTTA AND MARSALA TARTS

These sweet, melt-in-your mouth tarts have a crisp puff pastry base. The light cheese filling is flavored in the Italian way with Marsala.

13-ounce package frozen puff pastry, thawed
generous 1 cup ricotta cheese
1 egg, plus 2 egg yolks
3–4 tablespoons sugar
2 tablespoons Marsala
grated rind of 1 lemon
1/3 cup golden raisins

MAKES 12

VARIATIONS
Shortcrust pastry can be used instead of puff, but no other cheese will give the same texture as ricotta. Instead of Marsala you could add 1 teaspoon pure vanilla extract.

1 Roll out the pastry on a lightly floured surface. Cut out twelve 3½-inch rounds of pastry and line a 12-cup muffin pan. Let rest for 20 minutes.

2 Preheat the oven to 375°F. Put the ricotta in a bowl and add the egg, yolks, sugar, Marsala and lemon rind. Beat until smooth, then stir in the golden raisins.

3 Spoon the mixture into the lined cups. Bake for about 20 minutes, or until the filling has risen and the pastry is golden and crisp.

4 Cool the tarts slightly before easing each one out with a small spatula. Serve warm.

SHOPPING FOR CHEESE

For most of us, finding a good cheese means first finding a good cheese shop. The best shops are those that buy immature cheeses and nurture them until they are ready to reveal their true character and subtleties of flavor. Regrettably, most shops simply order cheese and sell it with little thought as to its ripeness.

Try to buy cheese as near to the time you want to eat it as possible. If there is a particular cheese that you want, order it well in advance to give the cheesemonger time to find it and ripen it, or ask his or her advice about what will be at its best on the day that you need it. Aging cheese is a time-consuming labor of love, so do not expect to pay the same for a cheese from a specialty shop as you would at a supermarket. Shop where you are allowed to taste before you buy, and where the assistant can suggest a choice of cheeses that provides a balance of mild and strong, hard and soft, with differing flavors, types of milk, shapes and characters.

If the cheese is strangled in plastic wrap it will become sweaty and develop bitter flavors. A good cheese shop will use plastic wrap sparingly on the cut surfaces so the cheese can breathe. They will know the name of the cheese, the name of the farm or creamery where it is made, and perhaps even how it was made.

In recent years, mail order has become a popular way for small producers and retailers to reach a wider audience. It is an extremely effective way of obtaining hard-to-find cheeses, and, in general, if the cheeses are well packed and sent overnight, they seem to suffer no ill-effects. Some companies will send the cheese by refrigerated transport, but this adds to the cost.

The following cheese shops are worth visiting.

AUSTRALIA

Ambrosia
Shop 44
Adelaide Central Market
Adelaide SA 5000
Tel (08) 8212 5810

Botega Ritolo
43 The Parade West
Kent Town SA 5067
Tel: (08) 8362 0455

Diamaru Food Hall
    Delicatessen
211 Latrobe Street
Melbourne VIC 3000
Tel: (03) 9660 6569

Simon Johnson, Purveyor of
    Quality Foods
181 Harris Street
Pyrmont, Sydney NSW 2009
Tel: (02) 9552 2522
and 12–14 Saint David Street
Fitzroy VIC 3065
Tel: (03) 9486 9456

David Jones Food Hall
Cnr. Market and Castlereagh
    Streets
Sydney NSW 2000
Tel: (02) 9266 6065

Myer Food Hall – Perth City
Forest Chase
200 Murray Street
Perth WA 6000
Tel: (09) 221 3444

Richmond Hill Cafe and Larder
48–50 Bridge Road
Richmond, Melbourne VIC
Tel: (03) 9421 2808

BELGIUM

La Baratte
rue de Tervaete, 55
1040 Etterbeek, Brussels

CANADA

Denninger's
284 King Street East
Hamilton, Ontario
Tel: 905 528 8468

ENGLAND

Blue Bird
350 Kings Road
Chelsea, London SW3 5UU
Tel: 0171 559 1173

Cambridge Cheese Company
4 All Saints Passage
Cambridge
Cambridgeshire CB2 3LS
Tel: 01223 328 672

Fortnum and Mason
181 Piccadilly
London W1A 1ER
Tel: 0171 734 8040

La Fromagerie (below)
30 Highbury Park
London N5 2AA
Tel: 0171 359 7440

Gastromania
The Market Place
Cirencester
Gloucestershire GL7 2PE
Tel: 01285 644 611

Harvey Nichols
109 Knightsbridge
London SW1X 7JR
Tel: 0171 235 5000

Jeroboams
96 Holland Park Avenue
London W11 3RB
Tel: 0171 727 9359

Neals Yard Dairy
17 Shorts Gardens
London WC2H 9AT
Tel: 0171 379 7646

Paxton and Whitfield
93 Jermyn Street
London SW1Y 6JE
Tel: 0171 930 0259
and 13 Wood Street
Stratford-upon-Avon
Warwickshire CV37 6JF
Tel: 01789 41544
and 1 John Street
Bath, Avon BA1 2JL
Tel: 01225 466 403

Ticklemore Cheese Shop
1 Ticklemore Street
Totnes, Devon TQ9 5EJ
Tel: 01803 865 926

Vivian's
2 Worple Way
Richmond
Surrey TW10 6DF
Tel: 0181 940 3600

Wensleydale Creamery
Gayles Lane
Hawes
North Yorkshire DL8 3RN
Tel: 01969 667 664

FRANCE

Barthelmy
51 rue de Grenelle
Paris

Roland Barthelmy
92 rue Grande
77300 Fontainebleu

Bon Marche – La Grande
Epicure de Paris
38 rue Sevres
75006 Paris

M. Daniel Boujon
7 rue Saint-Sebastien
74200 Thonon-les-Bains

Marie Cantin
12 rue du Champ de Mars
75006 Paris

La Ferme Savoyarde
22 rue Meynadier
06400 Cannes

Fromagerie Maréchal
Halle de Lyon
112 cours Lafayette
69300 Lyon

La Fromagerie de Phillippe
Olivier, Artisan-Affineur et
Marchand de Fromages
43–45 rue Thiers
62200 Boulogne-sur-Mer

Galleries Lafayette (Lafayette
Gourmet)
48 boulevard Haussmann
Paris

M. Jacques Ponnelle
12 rue St Vincent
71100 Chalon/Saone

M. Quatrehomme
Quatrehomme
62 rue Sevres
75006 Paris

IRELAND
Cavistons
59 Glasthule Road
Sandycove, Dun Laoghaire
Co Dublin
Tel: 003531 280 9120

SCOTLAND
I.J. Mellis Cheesemonger
492 Great Western Road
Glasgow G12 8EW
Tel: 0141 339 8998
and 30A Victoria Street
Edinburgh EH1 2JW
Tel: 0131 226 6215
and 205 Bruntsfield Place
Edinburgh EH10 4DH
Tel: 0131 447 8889

Valvona and Crolla
19 Elm Row
Edinburgh EH7 4AA
Tel: 0131 556 6066

NEW ZEALAND
Kapiti Cheeses
Lindale
Main Road North
Paraparaumu 6450
New Zealand
Tel: (04) 297 0450

SWITZERLAND
J.P. and J.A. Dufaux
4 rue Centrale
110 Morges
Canton de Vaud-Suisse

UNITED STATES
Balducci's
424 Avenue of the Americas
New York, New York 10011
Tel: (212) 673-2600

La Brea Bakery
624 South La Brea
Los Angeles, California 90036
Tel: (213) 939-6813

E.A.T.
1064 Madison Avenue
New York, New York 10028
(212) 772-0022

Grace's Marketplace
3rd Avenue and 71st Street
New York, New York 10021
(212) 737-0600

Sutton Place Gourmet
Bethesda Store
10323 Old Georgetown Road
Bethesda, Maryland 20814
Tel: (301) 564-3100

Wholefoods
4663 Mt Sinai Road
Durham, North Carolina 27706
Tel: (919) 419-7354

Zabar's
2245 Broadway (80th Street)
New York, New York 10024
(212) 787-2004

Zingerman's Delicatessen
422 Detroit Street
Ann Arbor, Michigan 48104
Tel: (313) 663-3354

WALES
Llangloffan Farm Shop
Castle Morris
Haverford West
Pembrokeshire SA62 5ET
Tel: 01348 891 241

BIBLIOGRAPHY

Androuet, Pierre, *Guide du Fromage* (Aidan Ellis, 1973)
Basan, Ghillie, *Classic Turkish Cookery* (Tauris Parke, 1997)
Bilson, Tony, *Cheeses – The Australian Kitchen (Buying, Preparing and Cooking)* (Barbara Beckett, 1995)
Boxer, Arabella, *Mediterranean Cookbook* (Penguin, 1983)
Burton, David, *The New Zealand Cheese Book – Cooking and Serving Dairy Produce* (Reed Methuen, 1988)
Carr, Sandy, *The Mitchell Beazley Pocket Guide to Cheese* (Mitchell Beazley, 1986)
Cheke, Val, *The Story of Cheese-Making in Britain* (Routledge & Kegan Paul, 1959)
Chenel, Laura and Siegfried, Linda, *American Country Cheese* (Aris, 1989)
Corato, Ricardo di, *Italian Cheeses – A Pocket Guide* (Idealibri, 1985)
Del Conte, Anna, *Secrets from an Italian Kitchen* (Corgi, 1993)
Halliday, James, *Australian Wine Guide* (Angus and Robertson, 1990)
Hickman, Trevor, *The History of Stilton Cheese* (Alan Sutton, 1995)
Jenkins, Steven, *Cheese Primer* (Workman, 1996)
Jones, Evan, *The Book of Cheese* (Macmillan, 1981)
Lambert, Gilles and Roche,
Narcisse, *La Cuisine au Fromage* (Stock, 1971)
Montagné, Prosper, *Larousse Gastronomique* (Crown, 1965)
Nichols, Lourdes, *Mexican Cookery* (Fontana, 1986)
Rance, Patrick (foreword), *Cheeses of the World* (Little, Brown, 1993)
Rance, Patrick, *The French Cheese Book* (Macmillan, 1989)
Rance, Patrick, *The Great British Cheese Book* (Macmillan, 1982)
Rewi, Adrienne and Nicholas, Juliet, *Fine Cheese – Gourmet Cheesemaking in New Zealand* (Hazard, 1995)
Robuchon, Joel, *French Cheese* (Dorling Kindersley, 1996)
Scott, R., *Cheesemaking Practice* (2nd edn, Elsevier Applied Science, 1986)
Simon, André, *Cheeses of the World* (Faber and Faber, 1961)
Smith, John, *Cheesemaking in Scotland – A History* (Scottish Dairy Association, 1995)
Stubbs, William, *Guide to the Cheese of France* (Apple Press, 1984)
United States Department of Agriculture, *Cheeses of the World* (Dover, 1969)
Whittle Fiona (ed), *Australian Farmhouse and Speciality Cheese Book* (Publicity, 1992)
UNALAT (ed), *DOC Cheese of Italy – A Great Heritage* (Angeli, Franco, 1992)

INDEX

ACKNOWLEDGMENTS

AUTHOR'S ACKNOWLEDGMENTS

The task of creating this book almost cured me of my desire to communicate the joy of cheese to others through the written word. Had it not been for the support of cheesemakers from around the world, and their wonderful letters of encouragement, I would not have completed it. I should also like to thank; all the friends who lent me books, brought back cheeses from strange places and tasted cheeses with me; Patrick Rance and Pierre Androuet, whose books first inspired in me a love of cheese; the owners and patrons of the Tite Inn in Chadington, whose *joie de vivre* and enthusiam to know more about cheese has given me much pleasure after the long nights at the word processor; the cheese team at Tesco, who helped me track down cheeses; and my staff, who put up with me and kept me on the straight and narrow.

Finally, the recipes, which include many of my favorites, have renewed my interest in cooking with cheese. Written by my friend, Roz Denny, they demonstrate her skills and her passion for cooking.

PUBLISHER'S ACKNOWLEDGMENTS

The publisher would like to thank Carol Tennant for tracking down all the cheeses for photography; William Lingwood and his assistant Louise Dare, who tirelessly photographed (and occasionally tasted) all the cheeses; Patricia Michelson at La Fromagerie in north London for all her help; and the following companies who generously supplied cheeses for photography:

Cambridge Cheese Company
All Saints Passage
Cambridge
Cambridgeshire CB2 3LS
Tel: 01223 328 672

La Fromagerie
30 Highbury Park
London N5 2AA
Tel: 0171 359 7440

Harvey Nichols
109 Knightsbridge
London SW1
Tel: 0171 235 5000

Iain Mellis
Cheesemonger
30A Victoria Street
Edinburgh EH1 2JW
Tel: 0131 226 6215

Kapiti Cheeses
Lindale
Main Road North
Paraparaumu 6450
Melbourne
Tel: (04) 297 0450

Jeroboams
96 Holland Park Avenue
London W11 3RB
Tel: 0171 727 9359

Neals Yard Dairy
17 Shorts Gardens
London WC2H 9AT
Tel: 0171 379 7646

Paxton and Whitfield
93 Jermyn Street
London SW1Y 6JE
Tel: 0171 930 0259

Richmond Hill Cafe and
    Larder
48–50 Bridge Road
Richmond
Melbourne
Tel: (03) 9421
    2808

PHOTOGRAPHY ACKNOWLEDGMENTS

Pictures in the recipe section (except cut-outs) are by John Heseltine, and those in the reference section are by William Lingwood, except for the following:
p6 Sopexa; p7 The Italian Trade Center; p9 Sopexa; p10 (top left) Cheeses from Switzerland, (top right) J.P. Quicke, (bottom) The Italian Trade Center; p11 (top left) Cheeses from Switzerland, (top right and bottom) Sopexa; p12 and 13 Sopexa; pp130 (bottom left), 131, 132, 133, 135, 136, 137, 138 (top and bottom left), 139, 140 and 141 Walt Chrynwski; p142 Gabriella Kervella; p150 Russ McCullum